Doctors and Demonstrators

Doctors and Demonstrators

How Political Institutions Shape Abortion Law in the United States, Britain, and Canada

DREW HALFMANN

The University of Chicago Press   Chicago and London

DREW HALFMANN is associate professor of sociology at the
University of California, Davis.

The University of Chicago Press, Chicago 60637
The University of Chicago Press, Ltd., London
© 2011 by The University of Chicago
All rights reserved. Published 2011.
Printed in the United States of America
20 19 18 17 16 15 14 13 12 11   1 2 3 4 5

ISBN-13: 978-0-226-31342-9 (cloth)
ISBN-13: 978-0-226-31343-6 (paper)
ISBN-10: 0-226-31342-5 (cloth)
ISBN-10: 0-226-31343-3 (paper)

Library of Congress Cataloging-in-Publication Data
Halfmann, Drew.
 Doctors and demonstrators : how political institutions shape abortion law in the United States, Britain, and Canada / Drew Halfmann.
  p. cm.
 Includes bibliographical references and index.
 ISBN-13: 978-0-226-31342-9 (cloth : alk. paper)
 ISBN-10: 0-226-31342-5 (cloth : alk. paper)
 ISBN-13: 978-0-226-31343-6 (pbk. : alk. paper)
 ISBN-10: 0-226-31343-3 (pbk. : alk. paper)   1. Abortion—Law and legislation—United States. 2. Abortion—Law and legislation—Great Britain. 3. Abortion—Law and legislation—Canada. 4. Abortion—Political aspects—United States. 5. Abortion—Political aspects—Great Britain. 6. Abortion—Political aspects—Canada.   I. Title.
 K5181.H35 2011
 342.08'4—dc22   2011003353

♾ The paper used in this publication meets the minimum requirements
of the American National Standard for Information Sciences—
Permanence of Paper for Printed Library Materials, ANSI Z39.48-1992.

Contents

List of Abbreviations vii
Acknowledgments ix

1   Introduction 1

PART ONE   Abortion Reforms of the Long 1960s   33

2   The Reforms and Their Roots 35
3   Medical Interests and Priorities 66

PART TWO   After Reform   99

4   Abortion Services 101
5   The Politicization of Abortion 125
6   Policy Change after Reform 166
7   Political Institutions and Abortion Policy 202

References 219
Appendix 1: Statements on Abortion in American Party Platforms,
    1972–2008 221
Appendix 2: U.S. Supreme Court Cases on Abortion 228
Appendix 3: Abortion Attitudes in the United States and Britain 231
Appendix 4: Abortion Funding and Provision in the United States, Britain,
    and Canada, 1970s–2000s 232
Appendix 5: Abortion Attitudes in the United States, Britain, and Canada,
    1975–2004 234
Notes 237
Index 341

Abbreviations

ACGME	Accreditation Council for Graduate Medical Education (United States)
ACLU	American Civil Liberties Union
ACOG	American College of Obstetricians and Gynecologists
ALI	American Law Institute
ALRA	Abortion Law Reform Association (Britain)
AMA	American Medical Association
AMCAL	Association for the Modernization of Canadian Abortion Laws
AMPAC	American Medical Political Action Committee
ASA	Association for the Study of Abortion (United States)
BMA	British Medical Association
BPAS	Birmingham Pregnancy Advisory Service (later, British Pregnancy Advisory Service)
CARAL	Canadian Association for the Repeal of Abortion Laws (1973–80)
CARAL	Canadian Abortion Rights Action League (1980–2002)
CBA	Canadian Bar Association
CCTA	California Committee on Therapeutic Abortion
CLSC	centre local de services communitaires
CMA	Canadian Medical Association
ERA	Equal Rights Amendment (United States)
FLQ	Front de libération du Québec
FPD	Family Planning Division (Canada)
G8	Group of Eight
GOP	Republican Party ("Grand Old Party")
GP	general practitioner
ICMCA	Illinois Citizens for the Medical Control of Abortion
LARC	Labour Abortion Rights Committee (Britain)
LPAS	London Pregnancy Advisory Service
NAC	National Abortion Campaign (Britain)

ABBREVIATIONS

NAF	National Abortion Federation (United States)
NARAL	National Association for the Repeal of Abortion Laws (United States, 1969–73)
NARAL	National Abortion Rights Action League (United States, 1973–present)
NCCB	National Conference of Catholic Bishops (United States)
NDP	New Democratic Party (Canada)
NHS	National Health Service (Britain)
NORC	National Opinion Research Center
NOW	National Organization for Women (United States)
NRLC	National Right to Life Committee (United States)
NWPC	National Women's Political Caucus (United States)
OB/GYN	obstetrician/gynecologist
OECD	Organisation for Economic Co-operation and Development
OMA	Ontario Medical Association
PCP	primary care practitioner
PLP	Parliamentary Labour Party (Britain)
PPFA	Planned Parenthood Federation of America
PQ	Parti Québécois
RCOG	Royal College of Obstetricians and Gynaecologists (Britain)
SPUC	Society for the Protection of Unborn Children (Britain)
ZPG	Zero Population Growth (United States)

Acknowledgments

I incurred many debts while I worked on this book, but by far the greatest is to Edwin Amenta. He first got me hooked on the question "How do movements matter?" and he was there for me every step of the way as I explored that question and others. I hope that I can be as wise, encouraging, and inspiring for my own students as he has been for me. I thank him heartily. I also thank Fred Block for his tremendous generosity, humor, and insight. Thank you also to all those who read the manuscript, and especially those who read the whole thing: Edwin Amenta, Jeb Barnes, Fred Block, Mark Brown, Craig Calhoun, Lori Freedman, Dorith Geva, Jeff Goodwin, John R. Hall, James Jasper, Carole Joffe, Matt Keller, Ellie Lee, Anulla Linders, Ming-Cheng Lo, Michael McQuarrie, Dina Okamoto, Adam Sheingate, Dan Slater, and Michael Young.

I would also like to thank my teachers, Dot Stegman and Chuck Hitt. I started thinking about abortion and politics as an undergraduate at the University of Wisconsin where I wrote my first college term paper for political scientist Leon Epstein on the Supreme Court's abortion funding decisions. I had no idea then that I would eventually write a book on abortion or that Professor Epstein's work on political parties would so influence me. I also learned a lot from R. Booth Fowler and Leon Lindberg. I thank my committee at New York University: Edwin Amenta (chair), Craig Calhoun, and Jeff Goodwin. I also benefited greatly from the guidance of Dalton Conley, Eliot Freidson, David Greenberg, Wolf Heydebrand, Ruth Horowitz, Robert Max Jackson, Ed Lehman, and Mildred Schwartz. Thanks also to the members of the

ACKNOWLEDGMENTS

NYU Power, Politics, and Protest Workshop and the East Coast All-Stars Dissertation Group, and especially Karen Albright, Vanessa Barker, Ellen Benoit, Chris Bonastia, Nancy Cauthen, Tina Fetner, Chad Goldberg, Ron Krabill, Jason Patch, and Michael Young. I also appreciate the input of my colleagues in the Robert Wood Johnson Foundation Scholars in Health Policy Research Program, especially Jeb Barnes, Pamela Herd, Ann Keller, Paula Lantz, Deborah Little, Steve Lopez, Mike Neblo, and Adam Sheingate. At the University of California, Davis, my colleagues have been unfailingly supportive and helpful. I would especially like to thank Bob Faris, Ryken Grattet, Laura Grindstaff, John R. Hall, Carole Joffe, David Kyle, Ming-Cheng Lo, Michael McQuarrie, Dina Okamoto, Vicki Smith, and Diane Wolf, as well as the members of the Power and Inequalities Workshop, and especially Lori Freedman, Cassie Hartzog, and Matt Keller. Several undergraduates helped me with the research and provided comments on the manuscript: Caitlin Hall, Andre Lee, Theo Roffe, and Negin Yazdani. Parts of chapter 2 previously appeared in *Social Problems*. I thank the anonymous reviewers and the editor, James Holstein. At the University of Chicago Press, I thank my incomparable editor Douglas Mitchell, his assistant Tim McGovern, and manuscript editors Lisa A. Wehrle and Renaldo Migaldi, as well as the outside readers of the manuscript: Ziad Munson, Monica Prasad, John Skrentny, and one anonymous reader.

Thanks also to the archivists and librarians, and their institutions. In the United States: Bobst Library at New York University; Shields Library at the University of California, Davis; the National Archives; the American Medical Association; the National Organization for Women; the National Religious Coalition for Abortion Rights; the Women's Collection at Northwestern University; the Free Library of Philadelphia; Planned Parenthood of California; the California History Library; and the State of California Archive. In Great Britain: the National Archives, the Royal College of Obstetricians and Gynaecologists, the British Library for Political and Economic Research, the Wellcome Institute for the History of Medicine, the Birth Control Trust, and the National Abortion Campaign. In Canada: the National Archives, the Canadian Abortion Rights Action League, the Canadian Medical Association, and Planned Parenthood of Canada. I would also like to thank members and staff of the American Medical Association and the British Pregnancy Advisory Service who shared their recollections of abortion politics during the late 1960s and 1970s. The research was supported by the National Science Foundation, the New York University Graduate School of Arts and Sciences, the Commonwealth Fund, the Robert Wood Johnson Foundation, the Institute for Governmental Affairs at the University of California, Davis, and the Committee on Research at the University of California, Davis. The views expressed here are my own and not necessarily those of the directors, officers, or staff of any of these organizations.

On a more personal note, thank you to my friends and family for their support, encouragement, and love. I thank Renée Skolaski; my parents, Thomas and Janet Halfmann; my sisters Pamela, Laura, and Stephanie Halfmann; my wife, Angela Meusel; and our son, Benjamin.

ONE

Introduction

Abortion is a complex and controversial terrain for most contemporary societies. Throughout the world, women's economic and social roles are changing as they increasingly enter the paid labor force, pursue education, and raise children on their own. As they take on these new roles, women seek greater control over their reproductive lives. Such control can help them protect their livelihoods, their health, their relationships, and their dreams—for themselves and for their loved ones. Moreover, because women bear children and still provide most of the care for them, many see reproductive control as a prerequisite for full and equal participation in society, in other words, for citizenship.[1] Contraception provides one avenue for reproductive control, but it is imperfect. The annual risk of pregnancy for women using contraceptives is quite low, but the lifetime risk is much higher. Women who use reversible methods of contraception during their entire reproductive lives will experience, on average, two contraceptive failures. Approximately half of American women who have abortions report using contraceptives during the month in which they became pregnant. Even with the best contraception, women cannot achieve full reproductive control without access to abortion.[2]

In response to women's changing roles and feminist demands for reproductive control, most rich democracies liberalized their abortion laws in the 1960s and 1970s. Other countries are doing so now. Almost all of these reforms produced intense conflict. Many religious traditions are deeply opposed to abortion. Some groups oppose changes in gender roles and see abortion as a key symbol of those changes. An additional source of conflict involves the question of who will perform abortions and in what circumstances they will do so. In many times and places, nonmedical actors provided abortions, but the modern medical profession has insisted on a monopoly over abortion provision. Moreover, in many countries, the state has delegated the regulation of abortion to medical professionals; they are charged with limiting abortions to particular circumstances such as the protection of the pregnant woman's health. But medical control often produces arbitrary and unequal care as doctors impose their personal beliefs on their patients and as abortion approvals vary by class and region. In other countries, the state has allowed women to access abortion without medical gatekeeping or legally defined grounds, but the medical profession often resists such arrangements because it does not want patients to make their own diagnoses and choose their own procedures. For all of these actors, the stakes of abortion policy are high and compromise is often difficult to find.[3]

During the late 1960s and early 1970s, Britain, Canada, and the United States, like other rich democracies, liberalized abortion laws dating from the nineteenth century. Although these countries have many political, economic, and cultural similarities (more about this later), they established very different abortion policies. Britain and Canada held onto a piece of the nineteenth century by allowing abortions only if doctors or hospital committees certified that pregnant women met requirements of medical or, in Britain, economic necessity. The United States abandoned such requirements. A pregnant woman could obtain an early abortion for her own reasons so long as a doctor agreed to provide it. The United States, with its history of Puritanism and backwards social and sexuality policies, had established the most liberal abortion reform in the West. The countries also differed in the way that abortions were provided and funded: In Canada, abortion services were located in public or nonprofit hospitals and paid for by the state; in the United States, the vast majority of abortions were provided in single-purpose clinics divorced from mainstream medicine where women paid for their own abortions; and in Britain, approximately half of abortions were provided in the Canadian style and half in the American style.

In all three countries, pro-life movements tried to roll back the reforms of the "Long 1960s" (the late 1950s to the early 1970s).[4] In Britain and Canada, they failed miserably. Prime ministers, members of Parliament (MPs), and political candidates ran away from the abortion issue. Pro-life movements in those countries not only failed to reduce the quality and availability of abortion services but also saw them expand through increased public funding and the loosening or elimination of medical gatekeeping requirements. In the United States, by contrast, the pro-life movement was more successful—moving abortion to the center of politics. Presidents, governors, state and federal legislators, judges, and political candidates spent thousands of hours debating the issue each year. The pro-life movement reduced the quality and availability of abortion services, mainly through reductions in public funding, requirements that minors obtain parental consent, and laws mandating that women of any age endure waiting periods and antiabortion propaganda. Brief vignettes from the end of the 1980s illustrate the differences in the abortion politics of the three countries.

United States

In 1989, the U.S. Supreme Court considered the constitutionality of Missouri's new restrictions on abortion.[5] Republican President Ronald Reagan asked the court to use the case to overturn the 1973 *Roe v. Wade* decision that had first established a limited right to abortion. Activists on both sides of the issue marched on Washington, and the pro-choice march was the largest protest in American history. The American Medical Association (AMA) filed a legal brief urging the court to retain *Roe* but did little else. The court did not overturn *Roe*; instead, it upheld the Missouri restrictions and said it would allow similar restrictions in the future. The author of *Roe*, Justice Harry Blackmun, complained that the court had cast "into darkness the hopes and visions of every woman in this country who had come to believe that the Constitution guaranteed her the right to exercise some control over her unique ability to bear children."[6]

Britain

In 1988, David Alton, an MP from Britain's Liberal Party, introduced a bill to reduce the upper time limit for abortions from twenty-eight to eighteen weeks. Activists on both sides of the issue lobbied Parliament and protested on the streets of London. The medical profession vigorously opposed the bill. Both the Conservative and the Labour parties remained officially neutral, though most Conservative MPs supported the proposal and most Labour MPs opposed it. Because the bill was introduced by an individual MP rather than by the Conservative Government, it was allotted only a short time for debate. When Alton asked for more time, the Government refused, and the bill died before coming to a final vote.[7]

CHAPTER ONE

Canada

In 1988, the Canadian Supreme Court struck down the country's 1969 abortion law, finding that strict medical gatekeeping arbitrarily denied abortions to eligible women. The court did not establish a right to abortion but instead left it to Parliament to design a new law. Progressive Conservative Prime Minister Brian Mulroney thought that abortion should be regulated in some way but, because his party was deeply divided over the issue, was reluctant to take it up. After some delay, he tried to find an approach that would not offend either side—his bill required medical gatekeeping, but gave doctors broad discretion. Typically, MPs from the ruling party were required to vote for Government bills, ensuring their passage, but Mulroney let most members of his party vote as they pleased. The bill barely passed the House of Commons and moved on to the Senate. Protestors from both sides squared off on Ottawa's Parliament Hill, and the medical profession threatened to stop performing abortions. Mulroney again let party members vote as they pleased, and the bill was narrowly defeated. Mulroney refused to offer new abortion legislation, and subsequent Governments refused as well—leaving Canada with no abortion law.[8] Said one pro-choice activist, "our government's decision to leave things alone was not based on a passionate belief in a woman's right to choose. It was simply based on distaste for having to deal with anything controversial. I guess we're lucky to have a do-nothing government on *our* side for a change."[9]

As these vignettes reveal, pro-choice and pro-life movements faced off in all three countries. But the involvement of other key actors—political parties and medical associations—varied across the countries. In the American case, political parties engaged heavily with the issue, while the medical profession stayed out of the fray. In the British and Canadian cases, political parties avoided the issue while medical associations defended abortion services.

Differences in the abortion policies and politics of the three countries provoke many questions:

- Why did three countries with strong social, cultural, and political commonalities establish different gatekeeping arrangements for abortion, and in particular, why did the United States establish the most liberal one?
- What accounts for differences in the public/private mix of abortion funding and provision?

- Why is abortion so much more controversial and politicized in the United States?
- What accounts for change in abortion policy over time?
- How and under what conditions do social movements affect policy?

This book attempts to answer these questions by filling a key gap in the abortion politics literature. Most books on abortion policy and politics explain differences between countries in terms of social movements or national values (and especially religious beliefs).[10] This book shows that *political institutions* go a long way toward explaining these differences. Moreover, of the studies that claim that institutions matter for abortion politics, few have convincingly demonstrated this through close historical analysis within and across cases. Finally, this study considers institutional factors that have previously received little attention, in particular, the construction of interest group priorities and the openness of political parties to social movements.[11]

Institutions and Abortion Policy

Roughly speaking, institutions are the "rules of the game." They are rules, norms, roles, and meanings that form the context for individual and group actions.[12] Some examples of *political institutions* include rules that establish multiple jurisdictions in a country and the relations between them (federalism), rules for electing presidents or members of legislatures (electoral institutions), and rules for determining whether laws are consistent with the constitution (judicial review). Many scholars, including myself, also consider existing government policies such as old-age pensions or medical care programs to be political institutions (policy legacies).

By focusing on political institutions, I offer a rereading of conventional accounts of abortion policy and politics. Students of abortion politics seldom highlight political institutions; instead, they take them for granted and treat them as almost natural occurrences. This book seeks to denaturalize institutions and expose the ways in which they bias politics and policy. As Alexis de Tocqueville demonstrated when he visited the United States in the early nineteenth century, a fruitful method for understanding the institutions of one country is to examine those of another. This book examines the institutions of three. And as historical sociologists such as Karl Marx, Max Weber, and Michel Foucault have shown, a useful method for interrogating the institutions of the present is to examine those of the past. This book compares numerous episodes of policy making over the last fifty years. During this time, some institutions

CHAPTER ONE

have changed—providing an opportunity to examine policy making before and after those changes.

The book focuses not just on institutions, but on interactions between actors in civil society and the political institutions that enable and constrain their actions. I analyze the effects of macro-level political institutions such as health-care policies, electoral and party systems, and policy venues on meso-level collective actors such as medical interest groups, political parties, and social movement organizations. I show that political institutions helped determine when, where, and how actors involved themselves in abortion policy making. Political institutions affected the interests and priorities that these actors constructed and shaped the meaning and salience that they attached to the abortion issue. Though political institutions powerfully shaped abortion policies, they did not determine them. Plenty of room remained for maneuver and choice by individual and collective actors as they faced strategic dilemmas and trade-offs. And chance played a role as well.[13]

In addition to explaining differences in the abortion policies and politics of three countries, I also use the case of abortion policy to assess and improve on existing theories of social policy development. In the last century, states, and especially richer ones, have established a wide range of social policies that attempt to protect citizens against various risks to their economic well-being such as unemployment, low skills, disability, poor health, and old age. Some social policies have also sought to promote greater equality among classes, genders, or racial and ethnic groups.[14] Reproductive policies can be considered social policies—first, because they insure women against unwanted pregnancies that threaten their economic, social, and physical well-being, second, because they promote the equal participation of women in society, and third, because many states fund or provide contraceptive and abortion services.[15]

The first generation of theories seeking to explain differences in health and welfare policies focused either on national values (political culture) or levels of industrialization.[16] A second generation focused on the differential strength of social classes—labor and capital—and the political parties that represented them.[17] A third generation emphasized institutional factors: decision points where minority interests could veto policy proposals, and policy legacies that shaped later political struggles.[18] In this study, I use the abortion case to demonstrate the centrality of three additional institutional factors. First, social groups do not have predetermined interests. Those interests are shaped by specific political-institutional environments—and sometimes in quite surprising ways. Second, the policy impacts of social movements are not just a function of members and money, but of the openness of political parties to pressure from newly organized groups. Third, the venues in which policies are made can have durable consequences for later policy making by increasing controversy and mobilizing opposition.

Although abortion policy is a form of social policy, it also involves social and moral regulation. At different times and in different places, abortion has been "about" population control, the value of life, the regulation of sexuality, the place of women in society, and parental authority, to name just a few dimensions.[19] By examining a relatively understudied case of social provision that is also a case of social and moral regulation, this book offers a unique opportunity to assess and advance theories of social policy. Institutional arguments about American social provision are always subject to dispute by those who emphasize the relative strength of social classes. They argue that American business is especially strong and American labor is especially weak, and perhaps that is all one needs to explain the relative tardiness and stinginess of American social policy. By examining a case with a different set of actors—medical professionals and abortion movements—I avoid such objections. And when we compare abortion reform struggles across countries, the importance of institutions becomes quite clear.

Explaining cross-national differences in abortion politics and policies is no easy task. Abortion politics involved thousands of actors with varying motivations and strategies, and these actors interacted with hundreds of organizations and institutions over a fifty-year period. Abortion policies resulted from interactions between pro-choice and pro-life activists, feminists, family planners, lawyers, doctors, religious leaders and their flocks, political party officials, judges, legislators, government bureaucrats, reporters, and voters. Many of these people pursued their own visions of the good and the right; others pursued wealth, status, power, peace and quiet, or all of the above. Many banded together in groups to pursue their goals collectively. Most of the time, these actors behaved in conventional ways and followed well-worn scripts; at other times, they acted in new, creative, and unpredictable ways. And sometimes these actors were surprised by the consequences of their own actions. As I will show, those actions were both enabled and constrained by institutions that shaped the very interests, identities, discourses, and practices of these actors.

My arguments combine political, historical, and sociological institutionalism. As Edwin Amenta points out, political institutionalism shares commonalities with historical institutionalism in political science.[20]

Both focus on institutions and both argue that institutions can affect the identities, interests, and organizational forms of individual and collective actors as well as the meso-level contexts in which they interact.[21] But the two approaches differ in three main respects. First, political institutionalists argue for the primacy of *political* institutions, such as party and electoral systems, processes of state and party building, federalism, and judicial review, while historical institutionalists often focus on economic or social institutions as well. Second, historical institutionalists see causation as multiple, conjunctural, and path dependent, and emphasize the contingencies of history. Political institutionalists recognize the complexity of historical causation, but focus on identifying broad patterns that can explain *most*, but probably not all, of a given phenomenon or set of events. Finally, historical institutionalists often emphasize that their causal arguments are limited to particular contexts, while political institutionalists are more likely to develop causal theories that they view as transportable to other cases and contexts. I also draw on the new institutionalism in the sociology of organizations—a broadly cultural approach to organizations that includes state organizations.[22] The new institutionalism argues that actors' choices depend heavily on interpretation of the situation rather than on pure calculation. Institutions and organizations shape action by providing templates, scripts, routines, and symbols that filter actors' interpretations of both themselves and the situations in which they find themselves. In addition, limits of time and information cause actors to rely on processing rules and logics of appropriateness that create bounded rationality.

My approach lies closest to political institutionalism but borrows elements of the other approaches as well. Like historical institutionalists, I pay close attention to the timing and sequence of historical events and leave plenty of room for contingency. Because actors are creative and the world is complex, it is often impossible to predict what will happen. I also embrace historical institutionalism's agnosticism about whether actions are driven mainly by rational calculation, or by the interpretation and enactment of cultural norms and scripts. Like political institutionalists, I try to develop parsimonious, transportable theories that explain *most* of a given phenomena, but I also try to develop more complete explanations of the policies and politics in the countries that I have chosen to study. As a result, some of the arguments in this book are transportable to other cases, but some are unique to the cases at hand. Finally, my approach borrows heavily from sociological institutionalism's focus on the ways that actors construct and interpret their interests in specific institutional and cultural contexts.

Many of the political institutions that I highlight have been the subject of previous political-institutionalist work, but I identify new effects of these institutions and new mechanisms by which they occur. Previous analysts have shown that "policy legacies" shape actors' understandings and interests but have not attended to the ways that such legacies shape actors' *priorities*.[23] Previous analysts have noted that some political systems are more "open" to social movements than others but have paid less attention to the openness of political *parties*.[24] And analysts who do attend to parties have focused on such factors as the number of parties, party discipline, whether electoral systems are proportional or majoritarian, and whether parties are programmatic or patronage oriented.[25] Political institutionalists have not paid close attention to the ways that campaign finance systems, intraparty democracy, and low-turnout elections affect the openness of parties to new movements. Finally, previous analysts have shown that policy-making venues shape policies in particular ways but have not systematically compared the unique properties of policies made through courts, state or provincial legislatures, and nonpartisan legislative processes.[26]

In the remainder of the chapter, I lay out my political institutional arguments. But before doing so, I situate the abortion policies and politics of the United States, Britain, and Canada among those of other rich democracies.

Abortion Policy and Politics in Rich Democracies

Comparing abortion policies across countries requires judgments about which aspects of abortion policy are most important. In my view, the key dimension of abortion policy is abortion gatekeeping—the degree to which state officials or deputized doctors, as opposed to women, control abortion decisions. I base this judgment on several feminist theories of reproductive freedom. Liberal feminist theories argue that abortion gatekeeping violates the right of property in one's own person. Biological/material theories argue that women should control pregnancy because it affects them physically—through pregnancy and birth, the capacity to enjoy sexuality, and the preservation of health. Theories based in the gendered division of labor argue that women should decide whether pregnancies continue because they are the primary caregivers for the children that result.[27] Finally, Ann Orloff argues that gender-specific threats to bodily integrity in the form of violence, sexual harassment, rape, and state control of reproduction hinder women's ability to exercise civil and political rights, and thus undermine their ability to participate in the polity as "independent individuals" and thus citizens.[28]

Table 1.1 locates twenty-eight rich democracies from the Organisation for Economic Co-operation and Development (OECD) among four policy types.[29] The types rest on three distinctions. First, I distinguish between countries in which women may obtain early abortions (before twelve to fourteen weeks' gestation) without gatekeeping (that is, "on request") and countries in which gatekeepers must approve abortions.[30] Second, among countries where women may obtain abortions on request, I distinguish between those in which they may do so for their "own reasons" and those in which they must first declare a state of "distress" or "emergency" and, in most cases, submit to mandatory counseling and/or reflection periods.[31] Proponents of the "distress" model argue that it expresses the moral gravity of abortion decisions even when it does not actually reduce the number of abortions.[32] The goals of such counseling vary across countries—from protecting fetal life to providing neutral information about the procedure and alternatives to it.[33] Third, among countries with abortion gatekeeping, I distinguish between those with liberal or strict gatekeeping (in practice rather than in law).[34] In countries with liberal gatekeeping, the legal reasons for which gatekeepers may approve abortions vary widely; some are broad and some are narrow, but in practice, gatekeepers approve more than 95 percent of early abortions.[35] The gatekeepers are typically doctors, though hospital abortion committees have played this role in the past.[36] Most countries with liberal gatekeeping started out with strict gatekeeping, and many countries of the "own reasons" type abandoned earlier gatekeeping policies after they became perfunctory.[37] This suggests that strict gatekeeping may not be sustainable over time. The British case, which I outline in chapter 4, bears this out.[38]

As the table shows, thirteen countries fit the *own reasons* type, seven fit the *distress* type, seven fit the *liberal gatekeeping* type, and three fit the *strict gatekeeping* type.[39] The types are "ideal types," so some countries may only approximate their type.[40] For example, the United States and Austria allow women to obtain abortions for their own reasons, but there are regional access disparities and the state refuses to fund most abortions. In addition, three-fifths of American states require counseling (often with mandated antiabortion messages) and half require waiting periods.[41] As such, these two countries fall somewhere between the own reasons and distress models.[42]

The typology of abortion policies helps to situate the policies of Britain, Canada, and the United States among the rich democracies and over

Table 1.1 Abortion Policy Types in OECD Countries

Gatekeeping	Reasons	
	Own	Legally specified
None (on request)	Own Reasons Austria (1937, 1945, 1974) Denmark (1937, 1973) Sweden (1938, 1946, 1974) Greece (1950, 1978, 1986) Czech Republic (1957, 1986) Slovakia (1957, 1986) United States (1967, 1971, 1973, 1988,* 1992*) Australia (1969, 1998, 2002, 2008) Canada (1969, 1988) Spain (1983, 1985,* 2010) Turkey (1983) Portugal (1984, 2007) Mexico Federal District (2007)	Distress Switzerland (1942, 2002) Norway (1964, 1975, 1978) Germany (1973, 1974, 1975,* 1992, 1993,* 1995) France (1974) Italy (1975, 1978) Netherlands (1981) Belgium (1990)
Liberal		Liberal Gatekeeping Japan (1948) Finland (1950, 1970) Hungary (1956, 1973, 1989, 1993) Korea (1962, 1973) Britain (1967) Australia (1969, 1971) New Zealand (1977)
Strict		Strict Gatekeeping Poland (1956, 1969, 1993,* 1997*) Ireland (1974,* 1983,* 1992) Mexico

Sources: R. Boland and L. Katzive, "Developments in Laws on Induced Abortion: 1998–2007," *International Family Planning Perspectives* 34 (2008): 110–20; H. P. David, "Abortion in Europe, 1920–91: A Public Health Perspective," *Studies in Family Planning* 23 (1992):1–22; A. Eser, "Abortion Law Reform in Germany in International Comparative Perspective," *European Journal of Health Law* 1 (1994):15; Albin Eser and H. G. Koch, *Abortion and the Law: From International Comparison to Legal Policy* (The Hague: Asser Press, 2005); A. Goto, C. Fujiyama-Koriyama, A. Fukao, and M. R. Reich, "Abortion Trends in Japan, 1975–95," *Studies in Family Planning* 31 (2000): 301–8; M. Minkenberg, "Religion and Public Policy: Institutional, Cultural, and Political Impact on the Shaping of Abortion Policies in Western Democracies," *Comparative Political Studies* 35 (2002): 221; A. Rahman, L. Katzive, and S. K. Henshaw, "A Global Review of Laws on Induced Abortion, 1985–1997," *International Family Planning Perspectives* 24 (1998): 56–64; Dorothy McBride Stetson, *Abortion Politics, Women's Movements, and the Democratic State: A Comparative Study of State Feminism* (Oxford: Oxford University Press, 2001); F. M. Tedesco, "Rites for the Unborn Dead: Abortion and Buddhism in Contemporary Korea," *Korea Journal* 36 (1996): 61–74; United Nations Population Division, *Abortion Policies: A Global Review* (New York: United Nations, 2002).

Notes: Iceland and Luxembourg are excluded. Dates indicate major abortion policy changes. All were liberalizations except those with asterisks. Where more than one date is listed, the earliest date was a gatekeeping reform (except for the own reasons reforms of East Germany and West Germany in 1973 and 1974, respectively). Abortion law or access varies by region in Australia, Austria, Canada, Germany, Italy, Mexico, Portugal, Spain, and the United States. Three Australian states have recently allowed women to obtain abortions for their own reasons—West Australia (1998), the Australian Capital Territory (2002), and Victoria (2008). In the other states, abortions are subject to liberal gatekeeping. Parental consent is required in the Czech Republic, Denmark, Greece, Italy, Norway, Slovakia, Turkey, and the United States (some states). Spousal consent is required in Japan and Turkey. Most abortions are funded privately in Austria, Germany, Greece, Ireland, Japan, Korea, Mexico, Poland, Spain, Turkey, and the United States.

time. The three countries began the 1960s with strict gatekeeping, but immediately after the abortion reforms of the Long 1960s, the United States moved to the own reasons type, Canada stuck with strict gatekeeping, and Britain combined strict gatekeeping in the public sector with liberal gatekeeping in the private sector. In the contemporary period, Britain has moved to liberal gatekeeping in both the public and private sectors, Canada fits the own reasons type, and the United States combines the own reasons type with elements of the distress type (mandatory counseling and waiting periods).

Gatekeeping is not the only criterion for distinguishing abortion policies. In chapter 4, I also attend to the organization, funding, and quality of abortion services.[43] Most OECD countries publicly fund almost all abortions. In twelve countries, however, the majority of abortions are paid out-of-pocket (see notes in table 1.1). Three main paths lead to this out-of-pocket funding. In the first, abortions are legal but government funding is restricted.[44] Another path is when private doctors interpret the law more liberally than public doctors or when doctors are reluctant to submit claims to public or private insurers because the abortions the doctors provide may not fully comply with the law.[45] A final path is when abortion laws are restrictive and most abortions are performed illegally or in other countries, and are thus paid out-of-pocket.[46]

The organization and funding of abortion services in Britain, Canada, and the United States has changed over time. Immediately after the reforms of the Long 1960s, most Canadian abortions were provided in hospitals (clinics were illegal) and funded by the state; however, many women obtained abortions in the United States and paid for them out-of-pocket. Although American abortions were available in both hospitals and freestanding, single-purpose clinics, most were provided in clinics. Furthermore, while some poor women could obtain publicly funded abortions, most women in the United States paid for abortions themselves. Britain combined the Canadian and American models: Half of abortions were provided for free and with relatively strict gatekeeping in the hospitals of the National Health Service (NHS), but the other half were provided in private clinics where gatekeeping was liberal and women paid for abortions themselves. Later, provision and funding in the three countries converged in some ways and diverged in others. All of the countries provided more abortions in clinics over time. Britain and Canada liberalized or eliminated medical gatekeeping—moving closer to the American model. In Britain, more abortions were provided in the private sector where gatekeeping was liberal, and gatekeeping liberalized in the public sector as well. In Canada, the Supreme Court struck down the 1969 abortion law and Parliament failed to replace it, leaving a legal vacuum with no gatekeeping requirements. But the countries moved apart on funding. The United States eliminated public funding for poor women's abortions in most states, while Britain expanded public funding to include abortions provided in private clinics. Canada had always provided public funding for legal abortions, but with the elimination of medical gatekeeping there were now more of these.

It is also useful to situate not only the abortion *policies* but the abortion *politics* of the three countries among the other rich democracies. As table 1.2 indicates, there are four main types of abortion politics—social democratic, negotiated, new democracy, and secular majoritarian.[47] The table assigns national abortion liberalizations to these types and also indicates the types of policies enacted—own reasons, distress, or gatekeeping (I do not distinguish between liberal and strict gatekeeping here because it is a matter of implementation rather than law). As with the policy typology, the types of abortion politics are "ideal"—some countries fit them better than others. The cases are assigned to their types based on the partisan alignments at the time that each reform was made.[48]

In the *social democratic* type, powerful left-wing parties controlled government and enacted abortion reforms of the "own reasons" variety (frequently after internal pressure from feminists). These countries were often the first to enact abortion liberalizations. Many Nordic countries fit this type. In most of these reforms, MPs were given a free vote, but most voted with their parties.[49] In the *negotiated* type, left parties (again after pressure from feminists) pushed for broad reforms, but Christian democratic parties opposed those reforms or tried to narrow them and liberal (free market) parties supported more moderate reforms than the social democrats. In these multiparty systems, coalition governments were common, and as a result reforms usually involved negotiation and compromise. The result was "distress" type reforms that allowed women to obtain abortions without gatekeeping but only for "serious" reasons and with counseling and waiting periods. These liberalizations tended to come later than those in the social democratic countries. Most of the Catholic countries of northern Europe fit this type. Most of these reforms were enacted by left-liberal or Christian democrat-liberal coalitions.[50] In the *new democracy* type, newly democratized Catholic countries with late feminist mobilization and women's suffrage produced late and narrow reforms. Many of these reforms were made by left-wing parties, but feminists were less powerful in these parties than in their counterparts in

Table 1.2 Abortion Liberalizations in Western Europe, North America, and Australasia after 1960

	Own reasons	Distress	Gatekeeping
Social Democratic	E. Germany (1973) Denmark (1973) Austria (1974) Sweden (1974) Greece (1986) Portugal (2007) Spain (2010)	Norway (1978)	Finland (1970) Norway (1975)
Negotiated	W. Germany (1974)	France (1974) Italy (1975,* 1978) Netherlands (1981) Belgium (1990) Germany (1992) Germany (1995) Switzerland (2002) United States (some states, 1988, 1992)	
New Democracy			Greece (1978) Spain (1983) Portugal (1984)
Secular Majoritarian	United States (1973)* Canada (1988)* West Australia (1998) Australian Capital Territory (2002) Victoria, Australia (2008)		United States (1967) Britain (1967) Canada (1969) South Australia (1969) Victoria, Australia (1969)* New South Wales, Australia (1971)* New Zealand (1977) Tasmania, Australia (2001) Northern Territory, Australia (2003)

Notes: Iceland and Luxembourg are excluded. Ireland, which never produced a substantial abortion liberalization and allows abortions only when pregnancy threatens the mother's life, is also excluded.

*Court decisions: All other liberalizations occurred through legislation.

other countries. The postdictatorship Mediterranean countries (Greece, Spain, and Portugal) fit this type.

The *secular majoritarian* type includes most English-speaking countries, including those that are the focus of this book. This suggests that the theoretical approach that I develop in this book will be most applicable to other countries in this type. Countries in this type have two major parties, weak or moderate labor movements, and no Christian democratic party.[51] Party polarization is moderate, and parties are more oriented to winning elections than to ideological programs.[52] In this type of politics, parties tried to keep abortion off the policy agenda and were reluctant to take strong positions on the issue. Because left-leaning parties were vote maximizers, they were less likely to take abortion positions than their policy-maximizing counterparts in other countries. Abortion also did not match the dominant left-right cleavage on which parties in the secular majoritarian type were based, so parties typically had supporters on both sides of the issue—center-left parties in particular often counted both feminists and working-class Catholics as supporters. Religiously affiliated parties, which often polarized debates on abortion policy in other countries, were not present to oppose abortion. Finally, parties also avoided strong abortion positions because most voters were located in the middle and not particularly concerned about the issue, and parties worried that action on abortion might mobilize intense minorities against them. If governments did act on abortion, they often used policy mechanisms that helped them avoid blame; where possible, they pawned off the abortion issue on the medical profession. As national parties avoided the issue, the policy vacuum was often filled by courts, states, or provinces. For example, courts produced own reasons reforms in the United States and Canada that were more liberal than those desired by the political parties.[53] I explain in chapters 2 and 6 how this happened. From the 1960s to the 1980s, countries of the secular majoritarian type typically produced gatekeeping policies that delegated responsibility for abortion to the medical profession. But later, these countries produced both gatekeeping and own reasons reforms. And many of these own reasons reforms were merely legal acknowledgments that gatekeeping had become pro forma.

Each of the four types also had distinctive *post-reform* politics. In the *social democratic* type, left dominance and low levels of Catholicism produced only modest pro-life mobilization and stable reforms. In the *negotiated* type, sizable pro-life movements tried to roll back initial reforms but were often disappointed by Christian democratic parties who had opposed or weakened initial reforms, but were often unwilling to reopen the issue. Some needed to govern in coalition with parties that supported abortion rights, and many were responsive to growing public support for abortion, including support among Catholics.[54] Pro-life groups tried to work around these parties by forcing referendums through petition drives, convincing individual legislators to introduce antiabortion bills or seeking rulings from constitutional courts.[55] In the *new democracy* type, some countries moved toward the social democratic or negotiated types as they consolidated their democracies, women's power increased, and the power of the Catholic Church declined; Spain, for example, moved to an own reasons model in 2010. Finally, parties in the *secular majoritarian* type continued to avoid the abortion issue and were mainly successful in doing so. The one exception was the United States, where abortion eventually became a partisan issue and American policy moved in the direction of the negotiated type. I explain this change in chapter 5.

Interactions between Political Institutions and Groups in Civil Society

In the remainder of this chapter, I lay out my institutional approach and discuss ways in which it builds on existing theories of policy making that focus on interest groups, political parties, social movements, and policy venues. (See table 1.3.)

Interest Groups Construct Preferences and Priorities

Interest group theories of policy making argue that powerful groups have special access to and influence over political officials, and, as a result, policies routinely reflect their preferences. Because the power of interest groups varies by time and country, policies should vary as well. For example, when and where business groups are strong, taxes should be low, and when and where they are weak, taxes should be high.[56] Following historical and political institutionalists, as well as new institutionalists in the sociology of organizations, I modify interest group theories by showing that the "interests" and identities of groups cannot be assumed a priori from their social positions.[57] Similar groups often perceive and articulate their "interests" differently. Business groups may oppose welfare state policies in some times or places, but support them in others.[58] Groups *construct* their perceived interests in specific historical and institutional contexts, and these constructions leave legacies for future political struggles.

I also modify interest group theories in a second way by focusing on the multitude of "interests" or goals held by social actors and the ways in which they *prioritize* among those goals in particular institutional and strategic contexts. As James Jasper puts it,

Every player will have many *goals* jostling for attention, each more or less explicitly recognized. . . . These cannot easily be compared or rank-ordered, in part because the salience of each changes according to circumstances. To make matters more complex,

Table 1.3 Political Institutional Modifications of Meso-level Actor Theories

Actor	Theory	Institutional Modification
Interest groups	Powerful interest groups have special access to and influence over political officials.	Groups construct "interests" and prioritize among them in specific historical and institutional contexts.
	Differences in policies result from differences in strength of interest groups.	Differences in policies can result from differences in constructed interests or priorities.
Political parties	Left-wing parties promote social spending and women's autonomy; right-wing parties oppose social spending; Christian democratic parties oppose women's autonomy; center parties sometimes promote modest social spending.	For issues that do not fit left-right, economic cleavages, party positions must be constructed.
		Party and electoral systems aid or hinder "new" movements (movements that want to join party coalitions).
Social movements (Amenta)	In negative political contexts, movements are most successful when they target hostile elected officials or state bureaucrats for assertive action.	Political officials are more likely to be supportive when political institutions help them avoid blame.
		In negative political contexts, evasive action (venue change) may be as useful as assertive action.
Social movements (framing and meaning construction)	Movements are more successful when they clearly articulate a problem and solution.	Political institutions help determine which actors participate in meaning construction.
	Struggles over meaning are more heated when they affect the status of social groups.	Political institutions, such as federalism, affect the scope, pace, and duration of policy making, and thus, the potential for policy learning and experimentation.
	Limiting frames are more successful.	
	Frames can promote some goals while hindering others.	

that salience depends partly on the strategic games meant to attain them: a goal may become more salient as the chance of attaining it seems to increase (or fade in adverse circumstances). The goals of [collective] actors are especially unstable, as individuals and factions battle to substitute their own favored goals (which may be either selfish or altruistic) for those of the team. Most actions are taken to address a number of non-comparable goals at the same time (contrary to game theory).

Most work on the construction of group interests asks: What did this group want, and why? I ask that question too, but I also ask: Of the many things that this group wants, which are most important, and why?[59] How does the group decide which things to pursue and which things to let go? What trade-offs is the group willing to make between its many desires? And how do institutions and strategic contexts affect these choices?

This modification of interest group theory helps explain abortion policy in Britain, Canada, and the United States. (See figure 1.1.) Medical associations powerfully influenced abortion policy in all three countries, but they did so in the pursuit of differing interests and priorities. Initially, medical associations in all three countries wanted to maximize clinical autonomy and medical paternalism by maintaining their roles as abortion gatekeepers. Though the medical professions were powerful in all three countries, scholars considered the American medical profession to be especially powerful given its success at warding off national health insurance. According to the interest group approach, if doctors managed to preserve abortion gatekeeping anywhere, they would do so in the United States. Instead, it was the American reform that abolished medical gatekeeping.

I show that political institutions—specifically, health-care policies that institutionalized relationships between the state and medicine—influenced the priority that different medical associations gave to their common interest in preserving abortion gatekeeping. Clinical autonomy over abortion decisions was a lower priority for American medical organizations because they were mainly concerned with preserving the private, fee-for-service medical system that had made American doctors the wealthiest and most powerful in the world. By contrast, British and Canadian medical organizations had already failed to prevent national health insurance but, in the process, received state guarantees of clinical autonomy, which they guarded jealously. As a result, they sought to preserve this autonomy in the context of abortion reform. Later, they continued to play a key role in abortion politics—defending abortion rights and advocating the expansion of abortion services. But in the United States, medical associations continued to avoid the issue.

Political Parties Embrace or Repel New Movements

Partisanship theories of welfare state development argue that left-wing parties tend to promote social spending and policies favoring women's autonomy and access to employment, right-wing parties tend to inhibit social spending, and Christian democratic parties tend to inhibit policies that promote women's autonomy.[60] Finally, some scholars argue that center parties, such as the American Democratic Party, can promote moderate expansions of the welfare state.[61]

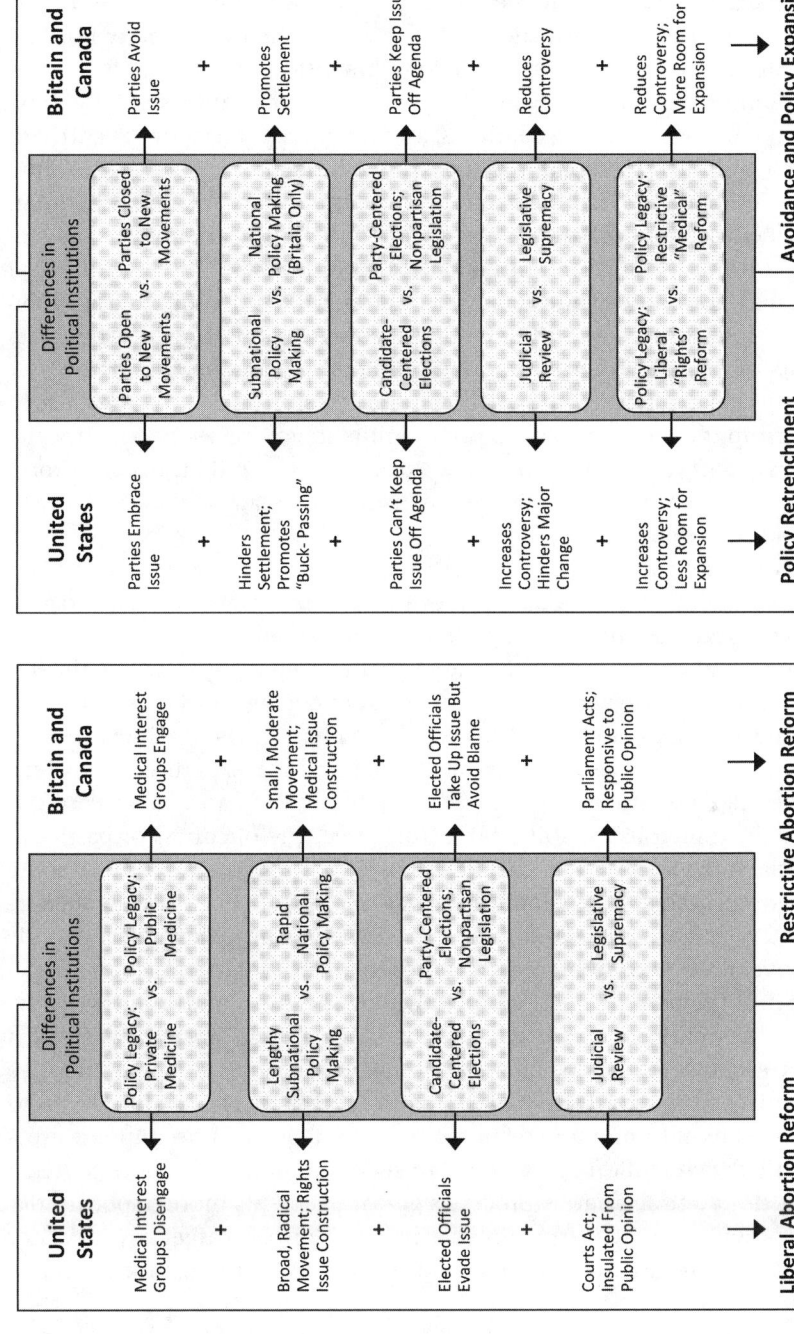

Figure 1.1 Institutional Effects on Abortion Politics and Policy Making in the United States, Britain, and Canada.

As with interest groups, there is danger in assuming the positions of parties from their similar social positions or constituencies. This is especially the case for issues such as abortion that have many possible meanings and have moral or religious dimensions that do not match the economic cleavages on which many party systems, and especially those in the English-speaking countries, are based. Proponents of the partisanship approach to explaining social policy usually focus on parties that are dominated by economic groups such as business or labor rather than parties that are a coalition of many different groups, and they usually focus on issues that clearly fit a left-right continuum. As a result, they treat movement-party alliances as givens. Left parties have supported abortion access in Nordic and central European countries, but they have been less supportive in southern Europe and in English-speaking countries. Party positions on abortion are not automatic but must be constructed. Partisanship theories typically do not examine the processes by which social movements persuade or pressure parties to take up their issues or form alliances, nor do they examine the institutional factors that facilitate or hinder that process.

I modify partisanship theories to focus on the degree to which party and electoral systems aid or hinder attempts by new movements to gain power and influence within parties. By "new movements," I mean movements that are not part of existing party coalitions but wish to join them.[62] Movements have various resources for influencing parties. They can appeal to sympathetic party leaders or try to replace them. They can offer money, campaign workers, publicity, policy ideas, expertise, and voters. They can also attempt to win spots on nomination and policy committees.[63] Numerous institutional factors affect the openness of parties to social movement influence. Decentralized parties give movements more points of access and potential influence. Parties with open and democratic systems of selecting candidates, party leaders and policy goals provide movements with more opportunities to affect the personnel and direction of the party. Open, but low-turnout, elections and meetings allow intense minorities to wield disproportionate power, since they are often better at turning out their members than other groups. Resource-intensive campaigns increase the reliance of parties and candidates on the labor and money of movements. And parties without mass memberships are especially dependent on movements for such resources. Candidate-centered elections and legislative processes give movements more opportunities to provide resources and influence policy. They can target any legislator rather than just the few that hold party leadership positions. Finally, coalitional parties increase the influence of movements because they respond to the needs of their multiple constituencies, rather than to one or two dominant interests such as business or labor, and movements can attempt to form or join new dominant coalitions.[64] I do not to mean suggest that all new movements will successfully infiltrate parties that are open to movements. This will depend on their numbers, resources, organization, strategies, and political contexts. My point instead is that movements will need less of these things to infiltrate open parties than closed ones.

As I show in chapter 5, American political parties are wide open to new movements while British and Canadian parties are largely closed, and this is reflected in the post-reform abortion politics of each country. All three countries developed sizable pro-choice and pro-life movements, but those movements made inroads only in American parties. In the late 1970s, pro-life activists, the New Right, and later the Christian Right gained power in the Republican Party while feminists did the same in the Democratic Party. The New Right and Christian Right gained control of key party positions and provided labor and money to electoral campaigns. They helped convince Republican Party leaders that abortion would be a winning wedge issue within the electorate.[65] The abortion issue eventually became a litmus test for the selection of candidates for both parties, and voters used it as an indicator of a candidate's positions on a host of other issues. In Britain and Canada, by contrast, abortion movements had little influence in parties. Parties sought to avoid the issue—refusing to introduce legislation or take an official position.

Social Movements Seek Venues and Define Issues

Social movement theories have paid more attention to the emergence and development of movements than to their impact on public policy.[66] But scholars who do study such impacts argue that they are determined by movements' levels of membership, resources, and protest activity; the degree to which they disrupt public order and threaten authorities; their persuasion of allies and bystanders; their organization and professionalization; and their participation in formal political processes.[67] Political opportunity theories argue that movement impacts are mainly determined by the political context of contention, including such factors as the openness of the political system, the stability of elite alignments, alliances with elites, and the repressive capacities of the state.[68]

In exciting new work, scholars have examined relationships between the internal characteristics of movements and their external environments. Kenneth Andrews argues that movements are most successful when they combine multiple tactics and strategies that provide flexibility in the face of changing political contexts. This is most likely when movements have multiple organizations, diverse leaders, extensive and cross-cutting informal networks, and labor and money from their own members rather than from outsiders. Edwin Amenta's political mediation theory argues that some movement tactics work better in some contexts than others; in particular, he finds an interaction effect (a conditional relationship) between the assertiveness of movement tactics and short-term political contexts.[69] When elected officials and state bureaucrats are supportive, minimally assertive tactics (such as public education) will do, but when both are hostile, highly assertive tactics (such as electoral challenges) are necessary. Moreover, if elected officials are supportive but bureaucrats are hostile or vice versa, movement organizations must assertively target the hostile parties rather than the favorable ones.[70]

Amenta's theory focuses on the conditional effect of assertive movement tactics and supportive political officials on movement impacts. I add to the theory in two ways. First, I argue that it is easier for political officials to offer support to movements when they can avoid blame for doing so—and political institutions can help with this. Second, I argue that when movements face hostile or evasive political officials, assertive action may well be useful, but venue change may be equally useful. Instead of fighting hostile officials, movements can move the fight to venues where political elites are more favorable. I show that, as Amenta would expect, the British abortion reform movement of the 1960s succeeded through minimally assertive actions because it faced a supportive Labour Government. But I argue that the Government had an easier time offering its support because nonpartisan parliamentary processes allowed it to avoid blame. I also show that American political officials were initially supportive of abortion reforms, but backed away once the issue became associated with the feminist movement and strong Catholic opposition.[71] Faced with political officials who wanted to avoid the issue, pro-choice activists succeeded not through assertive action but through *evasive* action. They changed policy venues and meanings—moving the issue from state legislatures to state and federal courts and developing constitutional definitions of the issue that found favor there.[72]

Some social movement theories have focused on the constructed meanings of issues (that is, issue definitions, policy images, frames). These meanings affect whether a social condition is viewed as a problem, who gets blamed, what solutions are offered, which actors become involved, the size of movements, and the policy venues in which the issue is addressed. Social movements strive to produce meanings that are to their advantage.[73] Most scholars of social movement framing have focused on the ways that framing facilitates mobilization, but a few have examined the ways that framing affects movement impacts. Daniel Cress and David Snow argue that movements will be more successful when they clearly identify and articulate a problem and a solution.[74] And several scholars argue that issue definitions played a key role in American abortion politics. Kristin Luker argues that the abortion issue is so heated in the United States because it is a debate about the social status of motherhood. Gene Burns argues that state-level abortion reforms succeeded when reformers used narrow "limiting" frames but failed when they invoked broader "moral worldviews" such as women's rights or fetal rights.[75] And journalist William Saletan argues that the libertarian, antistatist frames of the pro-choice movement contradicted its goals of obtaining welfare state guarantees for abortion access.[76]

I build on issue-meaning theories in two ways. First, I argue that political institutions mediate the construction of issue meanings by affecting which actors participate in such construction. I show that the failure of the AMA to participate in abortion policy making left a definitional vacuum that was filled by nonmedical meanings of abortion such as women's rights and fetal rights. I also show that the participation of feminists, the U.S. Supreme Court, and political parties in the abortion debate gave the issue new meanings—it became a symbol of judicial overreach, political liberalism, and changing gender roles.

Second, I argue that institutions affect the scope, pace, and duration of policy making, and this, in turn, affects possibilities for policy learning and experimentation, and thus issue definition. I argue that prolonged and dispersed state-level policy making aided the emergence of women's rights constructions of the abortion issue. First, early activists were radicalized by the disappointing results of early reforms, and second, prolonged policy making provided time for the emerging feminist movement and civil liberties lawyers to join the debate. After reform, the women's rights definition of abortion contributed to higher levels of controversy because it posed a direct threat to conservative Catholics and evangelicals. By contrast, British and Canadian medical associations participated heavily in abortion politics and supported medical gatekeeping. As a result, the reforms defined abortion as a medical necessity appropriately under the control of doctors, and did not assert the rights of women to privacy or bodily autonomy, and this reduced controversy.

Policy Venues

Institutionalist scholars have shown that every policy venue has its own roster of players, its own decision-making norms, and its own biases. As a result, policy venues shape the policies that emerge from them, often in quite durable ways.[77] I highlight three key venues—constitutional courts and state-level policy making in the United States, and nonpartisan parliamentary processes in Britain and Canada. (See table 1.4.) My arguments apply mainly to the specific venues that I examine, but some of these effects may be portable to similar venues. The broader point is that scholars of the policy making must pay close attention to the venues in which policies are made.

Constitutional Courts Make Controversial, "Undemocratic," Winner-Take-All Policies

Constitutional courts produce policies with several unique characteristics. Justices are usually appointed rather than elected, and often for life. As a result, policies made in courts are often less sensitive to public opinion and are often attacked by critics as undemocratic.[78] Court decisions are also powerful "focusing events" that draw public and media attention.[79] All of these factors increase the controversy of court decisions. In addition, the media often provide intensive coverage of court decisions, but not court deliberations. As a result, decisions seem to come "out of the blue"—creating shock or "suddenly imposed grievances" that contribute to public outrage and movement mobilization.[80]

Court decisions affect policy discourses too. Courts use limited, arcane, sometimes anachronistic language that makes it difficult for the public to understand their decisions and assess whether their reasoning is sound or fair.[81] Existing legal texts are often inadequate for the complex issues at stake, and courts often fail to deal with issues of practice and

Table 1.4 Effects of Policy Venues

Policy Venue	Effect
Constitutional courts	Make controversial, winner-take-all policies
Subnational venues	Provide access points, but hinder settlement and promote buck passing
Agenda control and non-partisan legislative processes	Help political parties avoid issues and blame

implementation. Courts also define issues as matters of rights. They must then rank, balance, and often completely trump rights claims. As a result, they do not allow the compromises that might result from bargaining in legislatures.[82] Finally, court decisions constrain elected officials by establishing requirements for the constitutionality of legislation, but they also provide opportunities for those officials to avoid issues by claiming that they are the proper domain of courts.[83]

Constitutional courts were stronger in the United States than in Britain and Canada. British courts do not have the power to strike down Acts of Parliament, though they can interpret them so that they are consistent with the courts' own views of constitutional rights.[84] The powers of Canadian courts were similar to those of British courts until 1982, when a new bill of rights gave the Canadian Supreme Court the power to strike down Acts of Parliament. American courts have had the power to strike down unconstitutional legislation since the Supreme Court's 1803 *Marbury v. Madison* decision. In fact, as Alexis de Tocqueville observed nearly three decades later, "there is almost no political question in the United States that is not resolved sooner or later into a judicial question."[85] This tendency became even more pronounced in the second half of the twentieth century; weak political parties and state bureaucracies, fragmented political institutions, and a minimal welfare state made it difficult for movements to achieve their aims through legislative and executive action, so many—beginning with the African American civil rights movement—turned to the courts instead.[86]

Political scientist Gerald Rosenberg argues that courts seldom produce significant social change because constitutional rights are limited, courts lack independence from other branches of government, and courts cannot implement their own rulings.[87] Other scholars, including myself, argue that courts are constrained, but hardly insignificant.[88] Still others accept Rosenberg's general point but argue that courts wield substantial autonomous power when they take on issues that elected officials wish to avoid.[89] As we will see, abortion is one such issue. Rosenberg argues that the impact of the *Roe v. Wade* decision has been overstated. In chapter 4, I argue that he is mistaken.

The venue of the American abortion reform gave it some unique characteristics. The insulation of the Supreme Court from voters allowed it to establish a more liberal policy than that supported by public opinion and most state legislatures. The court's decision also rested on shaky precedents and novel legal theories that subjected the decision to intense criticism for substituting its own policy preferences for those of legislatures. The *Roe* decision also strongly restricted the scope of federal and state policy making; pro-lifers were confined to arduous strategies of constitutional amendment, judicial nominations, and the gradual accumulation of court rulings that chipped away at abortion rights. The decision also increased the controversy of abortion: It stimulated an immediate and massive pro-life mobilization based on "shock"; it defined abortion as right of privacy, a less powerful and more contested right than that of a right to health in Britain and Canada; and finally, "rights talk" polarized abortion discourse, as compromises between the "right of privacy" and the "right to life" were unacceptable to both sides.[90]

Policy Making in States and Provinces: Easy Incrementalism, Unsettled Issues, and Buck Passing

Subnational (state or provincial) abortion policy making was more important in the United States than in Britain or Canada, and policies formed in this way have some unique properties. Many scholars argue that institutions that fragment political power hinder broad policy change because they provide multiple opportunities for narrow minorities to "veto" legislation.[91] But these scholars have not specified which types of fragmentation are most likely to have these effects and under what conditions; they do not distinguish, for example, between the separation of powers among legislative houses, presidents, and courts and the sharing of power between federal and subnational governments.

In the United States, federalism was a strong barrier to federal social policies before the South fully democratized in the 1960s.[92] In more recent times, it has posed difficulties for policies with a distinct geographic component such as farm or industrial policies. On other types of policy, however, federalism both aids and hinders policy change. It is often easier to enact policies in a few politically hospitable states or provinces than in the whole nation, and once enacted, these policies may be sources of demonstration and learning for activists and policy makers elsewhere. But state and provincial policy making is often slow and prolonged. After an innovator state enacts a new policy, other states may follow suit, but the time between the first and last state enactment might span decades. Frustrated by this slow pace, many movements try to move their issue to the federal level. But this is not always possible because some policy areas are historically or constitutionally reserved to states or provinces. The availability of multiple national and subnational venues can also hinder the settlement of issues. Instead of leaving the battlefield, losers simply seek new ones.[93] Finally, multiple levels of jurisdiction can promote buck passing as officials at all levels claim that they are not responsible for a given issue.

As I show in the next chapter, during the abortion reforms of the Long 1960s, prolonged state-level policy making in the United States provided opportunities for policy learning and interaction, and eventually alliance between abortion reformers from law and medicine and feminist and civil liberties groups. The lengthy policy-making process also meant that the national reform did not occur until 1973, when second-wave feminism, which swept all three countries at the end of the 1960s, was at its peak. As a result, feminist and rights-based definitions of the abortion issue played a stronger role in the United States than in the other countries. After the American reform, the abortion issue was kept alive and heated by the multiple venues for contesting abortion policy; the Supreme Court set the broad parameters of abortion law, but state and federal legislatures worked out the details. The court was forced to revisit the issue repeatedly as state enactments came into conflict with its rulings. Federalism also provided opportunities for buck passing in both the United States and Canada. In the United States, federal officials often avoided the abortion issue by reminding their constituents that it was a matter of state jurisdiction. In Canada, the federal government had jurisdiction over crime policy and the provinces had jurisdiction over health policy. Since abortion involved both, the two levels of government repeatedly blamed each other for problems with the abortion law.

Agenda Control and Nonpartisan Legislative Procedures Help Parliamentary Parties Avoid Issues and Blame

Agenda control and nonpartisan legislative procedures also affect the character of public policies. In the parliamentary systems of Britain and Canada, the vast majority of legislation is heavily partisan: Most bills are introduced by the Cabinet (party leadership) rather than by individual MPs, and MPs from the governing and opposition parties are required to vote as party leaders instruct (that is, votes are "whipped"). But some bills are handled in a less partisan fashion, usually in one or all of three ways: The Cabinet allows party members to vote as they please (a "free vote"), the Cabinet declares its "neutrality" on a bill, or an individual MP rather than the Cabinet introduces a bill (a "private member's bill").[94] These private member's bills may be introduced only by backbench MPs (MPs who are not party leaders) and typically involve free voting.[95] The bills are subject to severe time constraints for debate and voting, and, as a result, they typically fail before reaching a final vote if they are the least bit controversial.[96] In Britain and Canada, MPs secure the right to introduce a private member's bill through a lottery. Until recently, Canadian Governments could choose which private member's bills would be eligible to be considered by Parliament.[97]

In addition, some issues are labeled "issues of conscience," and these are typically handled through nonpartisan procedures such as private member's bills or free voting.[98] In Britain and Canada, such conscience issues have included abortion, contraception, stem-cell research, capital punishment, homosexuality, prostitution, censorship, divorce, fox hunting, Sunday commerce, disability rights, and seatbelt laws. There are no clear criteria for defining conscience issues, and in Britain, some issues, such as homosexuality, Sunday commerce, and divorce, have been unwhipped at some times and whipped at others. Even when the Government says that it is providing a free vote and remaining neutral, it may still pressure its members. As one Government spokesperson put it, "[there are] free votes and free votes."[99] The existence of "issues of conscience" allows Governments to avoid controversial issues, but it also allows them to use ostensibly nonpartisan processes to enact policies that they favor while avoiding blame for them. Even when votes are "free," most MPs vote with their party. Moreover, Governments can ensure that their favorite private member's bills come to a vote by providing extra time.[100] Thus the Government has it both ways; it is not responsible for a bill because it did not introduce it and declared neutrality, but the bill passed only because the Government gave it extra time and MPs from the governing party voted for it.[101] The MPs who take those free votes do not get blamed either. Because MPs in parliamentary systems have little power (given their obligation to toe the party line), voters tend to vote for parties rather than individual candidates at election time.[102] As one MP put it, "unless you were running a gynaecologist versus a priest, no by-election would be affected by a vote on abortion."[103] This creates a situation of democratic unaccountability on "issues of conscience."[104] A final notable feature of private member's bills and free voting is that once an issue is addressed through these processes, and especially if it is deemed an "issue of conscience," it tends to be addressed in the same way thereafter. As a result, policies made through private member's bills or free votes are difficult to change; they cannot be changed without extra time from the Government, yet the Government is not considered responsible for them.

Abortion has been treated as an "issue of conscience" in Britain and Canada, and, as a result, private member's bills and free voting have been central to abortion policy making. The British Parliament enacted the 1967 abortion reform through a private member's bill and free voting. The Labour Government allowed extra time for debate, and its MPs were the main supporters of the bill. After this reform, successive Governments, Conservative and Labour, claimed that abortion was a "issue of conscience" and refused to introduce abortion bills or allow extra time for private member's bills—ensuring their failure. Over thirty years, Parliament considered more than a dozen private member's bills on abortion, and all failed for lack of time. Only twice, in 1990 and 2008, did Conservative and Labour Governments, respectively, provide time (as part of Government embryology bills) for free votes on the narrow question of reducing the upper time limit for abortion. In both instances, the Government supported the status quo and it prevailed. In Canada, Parliament enacted the 1969 reform as part of an omnibus bill that decriminalized victimless crimes. Under pressure from its own MPs, the Government allowed a free vote on the abortion section of the bill. For the next twenty years, Canadian Governments did not initiate a single abortion bill, and private member's bills on abortion were declared ineligible for consideration ("unvotable"). Only after the Supreme Court created a legal vacuum in abortion law did the Conservative Government introduce a new bill. After it failed, successive Governments returned to avoiding the issue.

Some readers might wonder how private member's bills and free voting differ from normal legislative processes in the U.S. Congress. After all, most congressional bills are introduced by individual legislators rather than by the White House, and, because party discipline is weak, legislators are free to vote as they please. But there are a couple of key differences between the American system and the parliamentary systems of Britain and Canada. First, while parliamentary leaders remain neutral on private member's bills, congressional leaders often take formal positions on bills and try, however unsuccessfully, to whip the votes of their members. Second, MPs are less accountable to the electorate for their free votes than are members of Congress. In contrast to MPs, who are elected mainly on the basis of their party's platform, members of Congress are held accountable for their issue positions, at least to some degree, by the voters.

Looking Ahead

This chapter has outlined some of the main differences in the abortion policies and politics of the United States, Britain, and Canada; situated those differences among the rich democracies; and introduced an institutional approach to explaining them. I finish the chapter with a few words about my research strategies and a preview of the chapters to come. This study is an example of "comparative historical analysis," in which I select a small number of cases and move "back and forth between theory and history in an effort to identify the causes of a clearly defined outcome" (or several).[105] But I have goals that extend beyond causal analysis. I use interpretive methods to analyze the ways in which social actors have constructed and understood their identities, interests, and issues.[106] I also seek to draw the attention of comparative analysts of the welfare state to reproductive policies and politics. A great deal of work on gender and the welfare state has emerged in the last two decades. Most of that work has acknowledged the significant involvement of the state in its citizens' reproductive lives, and yet comparative work on the development of state policies relating to reproduction has been surprisingly sparse.[107]

A key challenge of research on a small number of cases is that the analyst usually hypothesizes more causal factors than there are outcomes on which to evaluate them. An analyst might wonder whether the main cause of high welfare spending is high union density, left-wing control of government, supportive capitalists, or a multiparty system. If the analyst tests these hypotheses by examining spending outcomes in only two countries—high-spending Sweden and low-spending United States, he or she cannot evaluate which of the four factors is most important because Sweden beats the United States on all of them. I try to address this problem in three main ways. First, I select my cases based on a "most similar systems" research design.[108] I have purposely chosen cases that have as much in common as possible to reduce the number of potential causal factors. The three countries in this study are all members of what Francis Castles has called the "English-speaking family of nations."[109] They cluster together on a wide range of socioeconomic, political institutional, and policy indicators.[110] They share a common language (except for Quebec), historical and geographic ties, and similar legal, political, cultural, and religious traditions. The United States and Canada are former British colonies, the three countries remain close allies, and their elites are in close communication and often imitate each other. The countries also share traditions of classical liberalism (individualism, voluntarism, anti-statism) and legal systems based on the common law (though Quebec has a civil law system). All are majority Protestant countries with significant Catholic minorities but no strong religious party. All have weak or moderate labor movements and majoritarian party systems that tend toward two major parties. Canada and the United States are both federal polities.

Canada and Britain both have parliamentary systems in which the upper house is subordinate to the lower house. Finally, as I discuss earlier in the chapter, the three countries have all experienced the "secular majoritarian" type of abortion politics—though the United States moved toward the negotiated type in the 1980s.

However, the countries also have important differences, some of which play a role in my analysis. Pro-life and pro-choice movements are largest as a percentage of the population in the United States, followed by Canada, and then Britain. Judicial review is strong in the United States, weak in Britain, and was weak in Canada until the Supreme Court gained new powers in 1982. American parties are factional while British and Canadian parties are cohesive and disciplined. Britain has a national health service, Canada has national health insurance, and the United States has national health insurance only for the poor and elderly—though the government will soon provide subsidies to help middle-class Americans buy private insurance.[111]

Another way of dealing with the problem of a small number of cases is through within-case analysis. Theories of policy making not only predict particular outcomes *across* cases but also have implications *within* those cases.[112] To evaluate the theory that welfare state generosity varies with public support for "big government," the analyst does not merely measure public opinion and welfare spending across several cases. The analyst also determines *within* each case whether the individuals and groups that support big government are the same ones who support generous welfare state policies, whether opponents of big government oppose welfare spending, whether supporters and opponents of welfare state programs justify their actions publicly and privately in terms of the role of government, and whether opponents of big government also oppose non-welfare policies that expand the role of government. Moreover, the analyst can determine these things for a variety of different policies, during numerous episodes of policy making, and at different stages of the policy-making process.[113] Thus, although there are only a few cases, there are a large number of potential observations within each case that can be used to evaluate theories.

A final strategy for dealing with a small number of cases is longitudinal analysis or "process tracing," which analyzes "a case into a sequence . . . of events and show[s] how those events are plausibly linked given the interests and situations faced by groups or individual actors."[114] In addition to providing leverage for testing theories, process tracing allows the analyst to identify causal mechanisms that link explanatory factors with outcomes—a key component of persuasive causal arguments.[115] Michael

Coppedge argues that longitudinal analysis is the ultimate "most similar systems" design because "every case is always far more similar to itself at a different time than it is to any other case."[116]

The book relies on data from records and reports of social movement organizations, interest groups, political parties, and government officials; from press accounts and government statistics; and from the accounts of movement activists. I also conducted several interviews with former officials of the AMA and the British Pregnancy Advisory Service (BPAS). The study draws too on the extensive secondary historiography of abortion politics. Most of these works are case studies of single countries. I reinterpret the data contained in these studies in light of cross-national patterns, correcting under- or overemphasis on particular factors, and presenting data from disparate sources in a new theoretical context.[117] I have triangulated these sources, attending to discrepancies among them, noting the sources that they use, and referring to primary materials to resolve disputes.

The remainder of the book is divided into two parts. The first part (chapters 2 and 3) describes and explains the abortion reforms of the Long 1960s. The second part (chapters 4 to 6) describes and explains abortion policies and politics in the years after those reforms. Chapter 2 looks at political struggles over the initial reforms and shows that differences among them are best explained by the differing participation of feminists, judges, political parties, and medical interest groups—all mediated by political institutions. Chapter 3 examines the ways in which medical organizations constructed their interests and priorities on abortion. Chapter 4 describes and explains the organization, funding, and quality of abortion services. Chapter 5 examines the differing degrees to which abortion has been politicized and partisanized in the three countries—a key factor in post-reform policy change. Chapter 6 explains policy change after the reforms of the Long 1960s. The concluding chapter summarizes the main ways in which my account challenges conventional understandings of American abortion policy and discusses the utility of my institutional approach for understanding policy making more generally.

The attentive reader will notice that the order in which I discuss the three countries changes throughout the book. I do this intentionally to heighten contrasts and present my arguments in the most accessible way. It is easier to describe a factor in the country where it is present before discussing the consequences of its absence in another country, and it is clearer to discuss the two poles of a comparison before discussing the case that falls in the middle.

PART ONE

Abortion Reforms of the Long 1960s

TWO

The Reforms and Their Roots

Immediately after World War II, the United States, Britain, and Canada had quite similar abortion policies. In each country, a doctor could provide a legal "therapeutic" abortion when it would preserve the "life" or "health" of a pregnant woman.[1] These terms were poorly defined and variably interpreted, giving doctors wide discretion. Still, legal abortions were difficult to obtain, especially for poor and working-class women, and the vast majority of abortions were "criminal" and unsafe. Most of these were self-abortions; the remainder were provided by nurses, midwives, beauticians, unlicensed "doctors," or licensed doctors acting outside the letter or spirit of the law.[2]

During the Long 1960s, the three countries enacted reforms that made legal abortions more readily available and virtually eliminated "criminal" abortions. But these reforms differed markedly. The main difference was how they handled medical gatekeeping. Such gatekeeping had three main dimensions—who, why, and where? Who authorized abortions—hospital committees, multiple doctors, elite specialists, a single doctor, or patients themselves? Why were abortions authorized—for grounds (or "indications") of life endangerment, physical or mental health, rape or incest, fetal abnormality, social reasons, or women's own reasons? (The specific meaning of "social reasons" varied, but it generally included such conditions as being poor, single, young, old, or caring for a large family.) And where were abortions provided—in hospitals or clinics? And were these facilities public or private, licensed or unlicensed, accredited or not? The location of abortion provision was relevant to medical gatekeeping because it was easier for mainstream doctors to supervise and regulate their colleagues in accredited hospitals than in unlicensed and unaccredited freestanding clinics.

The three countries answered these gatekeeping questions differently. The United States largely abandoned medical gatekeeping—allowing early abortion for a woman's own reasons and in any setting as long as a single doctor agreed to provide it. The other two countries maintained medical gatekeeping. Britain widened the grounds for legal abortions, adding "social" grounds and fetal abnormality to existing health grounds, but required approval by two doctors.[3] Britain also allowed abortions outside hospitals. The Canadian reform was the most restrictive. It allowed abortions only for grounds of "health" and required that they be provided in hospitals after approval by a committee. In this chapter, I describe these reforms in more detail and explain the differences between them by showing how social actors—social movements and political parties—interacted with political institutions such as state-level policy making, nonpartisan parliamentary processes, and constitutional courts. In the next chapter, I examine the institutionally mediated positions of another key actor: medical associations.

Britain: Medical Gatekeeping, Broad Grounds, and Clinics

Abortion was criminalized in England and Wales at the turn of the nineteenth century. At that time, British women (and Canadian and American ones too) had knowledge of a variety of abortion drugs and techniques through folk traditions, home medical guides, and thinly veiled advertisements for abortion medications. They could also obtain abortions, performed either with drugs or instruments, from "regular" or "irregular" medical practitioners. Regulars were middle- or upper-class men trained in universities. Irregulars were women or working-class men with little or no formal training. Despite their university training, regulars were no more medically effective than their competitors. Both groups used many of the same treatments for illnesses, and the regulars sometimes used more harmful ones such as laxatives and bloodletting. As they took the Hippocratic oath, regulars pledged: "I will not give a woman a pessary to produce abortion." But many still did so for profit, to preserve their patients' health, or because of diagnostic uncertainty.[4] Unable to distinguish themselves clinically from their competitors, the leaders of the regulars sought to do so by banning abortions except under certain conditions and assuming the power to determine when those conditions had been met. Regulars distinguished themselves from irregulars through their scientific expertise about when life began; most people thought it began at quickening (the first time that the pregnant woman feels the fetus move), but regulars claimed that it began at conception. Regulars also claimed ethical and moral superiority over irregulars through their purported observance of the Hippocratic oath and their defense of traditional gender roles.[5]

The British Parliament accepted the claims of the regulars about abortion. In 1803, and again in 1837, it enacted legislation subjecting abortion providers to a variety of penalties including whipping, banishment to the colonies, prison, and death.[6] Initially, these penalties applied only to providers, but in 1861, Parliament extended them to patients as well. At the same time, regulars successfully argued that "therapeutic" abortions, performed by a regular doctor for the purpose of preserving the life or health of a pregnant woman, were exempt from these statutes. This gave the regulars an effective monopoly on legal abortions. In 1929, the Infant Life Preservation Act codified this therapeutic exception, permitting abortions to preserve the "life" of a pregnant woman. In 1936, three veterans of the feminist, birth control, and eugenics movements, Janet Chance, Stella Browne, and Alice Jenkins, founded the Abortion Law Reform Association (ALRA). The association quickly prompted sympathetic reports on abortion from the British Medical Association (BMA) and an interministerial committee, but neither led to legislation. In 1938, ALRA member Dr. Aleck Bourne initiated a test case of abortion law that extended the therapeutic exception to "physical and mental health" in *Rex v. Bourne*.[7]

The English statutes and the *Bourne* decision did not apply in Scotland where abortion was regulated by the common law and doctors were free to provide abortions when they considered them in the best interests of their patients. Beginning in the late 1930s, abortions were available in Aberdeen for social reasons under the leadership of Professor Dugald Baird of the University of Aberdeen, but abortion practice was more conservative in the rest of Scotland, and especially in Glasgow.[8]

Between 1952 and 1966, the ALRA persuaded MPs to introduce six bills that sought to clarify and ease abortion restrictions.[9] All ran out of parliamentary time before a final vote, as private member's bills typically do, but Lord Silkin's 1965 bill went farther than most and set the stage for reform.[10]

In June 1967, Parliament enacted Scottish Liberal MP David Steel's private member's bill by a wide margin and mainly with Labour votes. The act allowed abortions up to the twentieth-eighth week of pregnancy, but required that signatures from two doctors be submitted to the ministry of health certifying that the abortion was necessary to preserve the life or the physical or mental health of the pregnant woman, to preserve the health of existing children in the family, or to avoid the birth of a child with a serious physical disability. The act allowed doctors to consider "the pregnant woman's actual or reasonably forseeable environment" when they evaluated health risks (an implicit social ground). The House of Lords also added a provision stating that abortion would be legal only if the risk posed by continuing the pregnancy exceeded the risk of the abortion. Proponents of this amendment thought it would restrict abortion because they believed that abortions were usually more dangerous than childbirth. But later it would become clear that early abortions were usually safer than childbirth, and some would argue that the clause made it impossible to prosecute doctors for providing them.[11]

The act allowed abortions in NHS hospitals but also in other places approved by the minister of health. Legislators expected that almost all abortions would be provided in the NHS, but in fact, large numbers would actually be provided in private clinics. At the behest of the medical associations, the act allowed doctors with a conscientious objection to refrain from providing abortions. The act did not apply to Northern Ireland.[12]

Canada: Medical Gatekeeping, Narrow Grounds, and No Clinics

As a colony, Canada's abortion law was identical to Britain's and remained quite similar even after Canada obtained internal autonomy in 1867. In 1892, Canada enacted its first criminal code, and its abortion provision was almost identical to the earlier British statute: It allowed doctors to perform abortions to save the life of a pregnant woman. Because of the similarity of these statutes, the 1938 English *Bourne* decision, which allowed abortions to preserve a pregnant woman's physical or mental health, was considered applicable to Canada.[13] In the early 1960s, provincial medical associations and eventually the Canadian Medical Association (CMA) began advocating for the clarification of abortion law, and in particular for the statutory codification of the *Bourne* decision and the extension of the therapeutic exception to fetal abnormalities. In 1966 and 1967, three private member's bills on abortion were introduced, referred to standing committees, and then folded into an omnibus Government bill that revised the criminal code, dealing with such issues as lotteries, passports, firearms, bail, homosexuality, divorce, and contraception.[14] In 1969, the Liberal Government allowed a free vote on an amendment to remove abortion from the omnibus bill, but that amendment failed 107 to 36; for the final bill, MPs were required to vote with their party, and it passed by a wide margin.[15]

Canada's new abortion statute allowed abortions only when pregnancy "would or would be likely to endanger the health of the woman,"[16] but it did not define "health." Minister of Justice John Turner testified that "health" did not include eugenic, social, or criminal offense (rape or incest) grounds.[17] But the Government had also rejected a proposal that the threat to health be "serious" and "direct."[18] In the end, although the Government claimed that the statute was tailored and narrow, it was actually quite vague, and doctors could interpret it in many ways. The statute required that abortions be certified by hospital committees made up of three doctors, not including the one who would provide the abortion. It also required that abortions be performed in an accredited hospital or a hospital approved by a province. Canada's new abortion law was more restrictive than Britain's. It required the approval of a three-doctor hospital committee rather than the two doctors in Britain. And unlike Britain, it did not include social or fetal abnormality grounds or allow abortions outside of hospitals.

The United States: Abortion on Request for Own Reasons and in Clinics

In early America, abortion was legal before quickening, but a misdemeanor afterward. Beginning in the late 1850s, the AMA, representing regulars, waged a successful state-level campaign against abortion. As in Britain, this was part of a professionalization project aimed at establishing medical licensing and driving irregulars out of business, but it also resonated with concerns that native-born Protestants were not reproducing as vigorously as Catholic immigrants. By the turn of the century, every American state had a new abortion law. All but six included a therapeutic exception that allowed doctors to perform abortions when they believed it was necessary to preserve the life of a pregnant woman. "Life" was often interpreted broadly to include health.[19] Around the same time, moral reformer Anthony Comstock persuaded Congress to outlaw "articles of immoral use" including abortion medications not prescribed by a doctor.[20]

The American reform of the Long 1960s was more lengthy and incremental, and was fought in many more venues, than those in the other countries. For most of the twentieth century, both strict and liberal abortion gatekeepers believed that they formed the majority. But in the 1950s, this false consensus began to break down; as medical advances made pregnancy safer, abortions for reasons other than physical health made up a larger share of all abortions; abortion decisions also became more public as medical care moved from home to hospital; and as birth control became more visible, the Catholic Church and Catholic doctors began to more forcefully oppose both birth control and abortion. In response to disputes among doctors, many hospitals established abortion committees, but these gradually lost legitimacy as they made class-biased decisions, imposed quotas, and acted with extreme caution.[21]

In the late 1950s, abortion reform started to reach the elite agenda. In 1955, the Planned Parenthood Federation of America (PPFA) held a well-attended conference on abortion at which Dr. Alan Guttmacher, a prominent New York obstetrician/gynecologist (ob/gyn), began calling for the liberalization of abortion laws. In 1956, Cambridge University law professor Glanville Williams, the president of Britain's ALRA, delivered a lecture on abortion reform at Columbia University;[22] and in 1958, Dorothy Kenyon, an American Civil Liberties Union (ACLU) board member, tried unsuccessfully to convince her colleagues that "a woman should have the right to determine whether or not she should bear a child."[23]

But 1959 was the year that abortion truly reached the public agenda; the American Law Institute (ALI), a respected association of judges and lawyers that sought codification of the common law, drafted a new model penal code with the assistance of the ALRA's Williams. It declared that physicians were justified in performing abortions if there was "a substantial risk that continuance of the pregnancy would gravely impair the physical or mental health of the mother or that the child would be born with grave physical or mental defect, or that the pregnancy resulted from rape, incest or other felonious intercourse."[24] The code also required that abortions be approved by two doctors and performed in a licensed hospital. The ALI summarily rejected proposals that abortions be allowed in cases of "illegitimacy" or "at-will."[25] In that same year, Stanford law professors Ralph Gampell and Herbert Packer published an influential article showing that large numbers of hospital abortions were provided for grounds that went beyond existing law, and Guttmacher published a book-length statement of his views that was excerpted in the *Reader's Digest* and *Redbook*, and covered by the *New York Times*.

Between 1959 and 1966, five states, including California and New York, considered and rejected ALI-style reforms.[26] In 1962, the case of Sherri Finkbine, the Phoenix host of the children's show *Romper Room*, drew national attention. Her doctor and hospital agreed to provide an abortion after she took thalidomide a drug that caused fetal deformities, but once her case drew public attention, the hospital balked, and she had to fly to Sweden for the abortion. In 1965, the *New York Times* endorsed ALI-style reforms, and a one-sided CBS documentary virtually did the same. In the spring of that year, a rubella epidemic brought public attention to abortions for reasons of fetal abnormality once again.[27] In 1966, Mississippi reformed its abortion laws to include grounds for rape. In 1967, California, Colorado, and North Carolina enacted the first ALI-style reforms, but twenty-seven other states rejected them. In 1968, Georgia and Maryland enacted ALI-style reforms, but two states rejected them. In 1969, Arkansas, Delaware, Kansas, New Mexico, and Oregon enacted ALI-style reforms, but seventeen states rejected them. That same year, four states rejected proposals for a new, more radical change, the complete repeal of abortion laws—making abortion available on request for women's own reasons. In 1970, Alaska, Hawaii, New York, and Washington enacted such repeals, while five states rejected them. That same year, South Carolina and Virginia enacted ALI-style reforms, but four states rejected them.

As the 1970 repeals in four states drew national attention and as the pro-choice and pro-life movements expanded, legislators shied away from the abortion issue, and legislative change came to a grinding halt. In 1971, an ALI-style reform bill was rejected in one state, and repeal bills were rejected in nine. In 1972, the New York legislature voted to repeal its 1970 repeal, but Republican governor Nelson Rockefeller vetoed the measure. After Connecticut's nineteenth-century abortion law was struck down by a federal court, the state legislature reenacted it in a more conservative form. Michigan and North Dakota voters rejected repeal referendums. The Florida legislature enacted an ALI-style reform, but only because the state supreme court had forced its hand by striking down the existing law.[28] In other words, no state voluntarily liberalized its abortion law after 1970. In Congress, Senator Robert Packwood (R-OR) and Representative Bella Abzug (D-NY) introduced abortion reform bills in 1970 and 1972 respectively, but neither made it out of committee.[29]

Of the fourteen ALI-style reforms (rather than repeals), all included grounds of life endangerment and rape, all included health grounds except Mississippi, and all included fetal abnormality grounds except

California and Mississippi. Oregon was the only state to include social grounds.[30] In addition, all required that abortions be approved by more than one doctor or by a hospital board or committee. And all except Kansas and Mississippi required that abortions be provided in a hospital. Half of the states had residency requirements. Thus, most state reforms were more restrictive than the British reform. They did not include social grounds and did not allow abortions outside hospitals or for nonresidents. The four states that completely repealed nineteenth-century abortion laws—New York, Washington, Hawaii, and Alaska—were more liberal than Britain. They all allowed abortions for women's own reasons, though all but New York had hospital and residency requirements.[31]

As abortion liberalization languished in statehouses after 1970, it progressed in the courts. In September 1969, the California Supreme Court struck down the state's nineteenth-century abortion law, raising questions about the constitutionality of its earlier ALI-style reform. A federal court also struck down the abortion law in the District of Columbia.[32] Over the next three years, state and federal courts struck down abortion laws (both from the nineteenth century and the 1960s) in eighteen states and upheld them in fifteen. These cases soon percolated up to the Supreme Court. In April 1971, the court upheld the District of Columbia's abortion law in *United States v. Vuitch*.[33] By December of that year, it heard oral arguments in cases from Texas and Georgia. These cases were reargued in October 1972, and in January 1973, the Supreme Court delivered its decisions in those cases in *Roe v. Wade* and *Doe v. Bolton*.[34]

The Texas statute dated from the nineteenth century and allowed abortions only for grounds of life endangerment. The Georgia statute dated from 1968 and included grounds of life endangerment, rape, health, and fetal abnormality, but the last two grounds were narrowly defined; the pregnancy had to "seriously and permanently injure" the woman's health, and the child had to be in danger of a "grave, permanent and irremediable mental or physical defect." The Georgia law also required that three doctors each examine the pregnant woman and that the abortion then be approved by a hospital abortion committee.[35]

In *Roe*, the lead opinion, the court found that during the first trimester of pregnancy the abortion decision was between a woman and her doctor. In the period between the end of the first trimester and viability, the state could regulate abortion to protect maternal health.[36] After viability, the state could regulate and even prohibit abortion to protect "the potentiality of human life," but such regulation must make an exception for the life or health of the pregnant woman.[37] In *Doe*, the court defined "health" broadly to include "all factors—physical, emotional, psychological, familial, and the woman's age—relevant to the wellbeing of the patient."[38] The court also struck down Georgia's hospital requirement and its requirement that abortions have the approval of multiple doctors and an abortion committee.

The American national reform was the most liberal of the three countries under study here. Unlike both the British and Canadian reforms, it allowed early abortion on request for women's own reasons and with the assistance of a single doctor, and unlike the Canadian reform, it allowed abortions outside of hospitals.

Explaining the Reforms

How did the three countries end up with such different abortion reforms? And how did the United States end up with the most liberal one? In the remainder of the chapter, I attempt to answer that question. Given their many similarities, the three countries had very similar political struggles over abortion. Reforms throughout the Western democracies were prompted by similar social and demographic factors: the sexual and contraceptive revolutions, the greater numbers of women entering higher education and the labor force, declining fertility and marriage rates, and changing attitudes about the place of women in society.[39] All three countries were also influenced by epidemics of fetal abnormalities caused by rubella (German measles) and the sedative thalidomide, a drug that was commonly prescribed to pregnant women to alleviate symptoms of morning sickness before its dangerous effects on fetal development were discovered. The Finkbine case was an international cause célèbre in 1962. In all three countries, professional elites strongly influenced the reforms. The legal profession sought to decriminalize private sexual behavior and ensure that unenforceable statutes did not reduce the public's respect for the law. Family planning, medical, and public health professionals sought to reduce deaths from illegal abortions (though Britain's family planning association stayed out of the abortion debate until after the 1967 reform). Ecologists worried about overpopulation. Doctors sought legal clarification for their existing practices, and especially for their provision of abortions in cases of fetal abnormality. In all three countries, the Catholic Church opposed reforms, but Protestants, both mainline and evangelical, were supportive, neutral, or ambivalent.[40] In all three countries, the public was broadly supportive of reform. Finally, Britain and its former colonies imitated one another, borrowing ideas, discourses, and strategies.[41]

Despite these many similarities, the reform struggles also differed in important ways. In particular, four types of actors—social movements, government officials, courts, and medical associations—played different roles in the three countries, and, in some cases, behaved differently than theories pertaining to those actors would predict. The resources, goals, and strategies of these actors were strongly mediated by political institutions such as federalism, nonpartisan legislative processes, judicial review, and medical-care systems. In the remainder of the chapter, I detail the institutionally mediated actions of these actors. But before I do so, let us consider the most common alternative explanation for differences among the abortion reforms of the three countries—national values.

Differences in "national values" are frequently offered as explanations for the tardiness and stinginess of American social policy. One prominent "national values" approach argues that *classical liberalism* (values such as individualism, voluntarism, and antistatism) has retarded the development of social protections in Britain, Canada, and especially the United States.[42] Legal scholar Mary Ann Glendon applies this argument to abortion. She argues that Anglo-American common law is individualistic and morally neutral, while continental European civil law is communitarian and pedagogical. As a result, European reforms allowed abortions only for specified grounds that did not necessarily restrict abortion in practice but taught compromise and respect for life. By contrast, the American reform was morally neutral and allowed "abortion on demand" for any reason.[43]

Glendon's argument has several shortcomings. First, it ignores the fact that the American ALI-style reforms of the late 1960s and the European reforms were quite similar—both restricted abortions to certain specified circumstances. American legal culture changed little between the ALI-style reforms of 1967–70, the abortion law repeals of 1970, and the *Roe* decision of 1973, and thus it cannot explain all three. Glendon also seems to suggest that American legal culture required the Supreme Court to decide the abortion cases in the way that it did. But, as I show in this chapter and the next, the court could have decided the cases in many different ways and almost did so. Most contemporary observers were shocked that it went as far as it did. Finally, Glendon's argument does not explain differences in abortion policy between the most-similar cases of Britain, Canada, and the United States—all three countries have strong traditions of classical liberalism.[44]

National values approaches often use public opinion data to bolster their claims. But public opinion does not explain differences in abortion policy very well either.[45] While polling on abortion is notorious for its sensitivity to question wording and should be treated with caution, I am mainly interested in broad patterns here. In each country, majorities supported legal abortion for health grounds and for fetal abnormalities but opposed abortions for soft grounds such as economic hardship, out-of-wedlock pregnancy, family limitation, or "own reasons." A 1966 Gallup poll (see appendix 3, table 1) showed that Americans and Britons both supported abortion for health reasons (77 and 79 percent respectively) and fetal abnormality (54 and 71 percent). But neither supported abortion for economic reasons (18 and 33 percent).[46] National Opinion Research Center (NORC) polls (see appendix 3, table 2) showed that American support for abortion increased from 1965 to 1972 across all grounds, but there was still not majority support for many of the "soft" grounds such as being poor, unmarried, or married but not wanting more children. Support for health grounds increased from 73 to 87 percent, support for economic grounds increased from 22 percent to 49 percent, support for abortions because the woman did not want to marry the father rose from 18 percent to 44 percent, and support for married women who did not want more children rose from 16 percent to 40 percent.[47] Similarly, a question commissioned for the 1972 Gallup poll found that only 40 percent agreed that there should be "no legal restraint on abortion."[48] In Canada, a 1970 poll showed that only 43 percent supported abortion for a woman's "own reasons" during the first three months of pregnancy.[49]

In addition to their inability to explain differences in the abortion reforms of the United States, Britain, and Canada, national values approaches have some more general shortcomings. They typically focus on values established hundreds of years ago but do not explain how or why these values have persisted over time—often the answer is institutions. They cannot explain the enactment of policies, such as the American New Deal, that appear to fly in the face of liberal values. National values approaches also tend to treat countries as monocultural when they actually include a wide variety of cultures. The "American Creed" contains multiple and often contradictory elements that include laissez-faire capitalism, constitutionalism, individualism, libertarianism, civic republicanism, populism, democracy, egalitarianism, sexism, racism, and nativism.[50] Lastly, national values approaches understate the multivocality of values and symbols. As theorists of social movement framing have noted, political actors work hard, and often successfully, to mobilize values and symbols for their own purposes. Broad national values do not determine the content of policies but instead provide a set of cultural resources for political actors. The challenge is to understand how those actors deploy values, symbols, and meanings and how institutions, events, and policies facilitate or hinder that deployment.[51]

CHAPTER TWO

Still, I do not mean to suggest that the American Creed was irrelevant to American abortion policy. Instead, its main contribution was the institutions that the founders left behind. Political institutions such as private health care, judicial review, federalism, and weak political parties reflect, at least in part, American traditions of antistatism, individualism, and suspicion of authority.[52] In the remainder of the chapter, and in the next, I examine how institutions affected abortion policies in the three countries, paying particular attention to the ways in which institutions mediated the actions of social movements, government officials, courts, and in the next chapter, medical associations.

Small, Moderate Movements in Britain and Canada; Large, Radical Movements in the United States

A number of social movement theories suggest possible explanations for differences in the abortion reforms of the three countries. Resource mobilization theory suggests that abortion reforms will be more liberal where pro-choice movements are larger and richer. Amenta suggests that movements will have greater impact when they match their tactics to the contexts in which they contend. Mildly assertive action might be enough when government officials are supportive, but more is required when they are hostile or neutral. Finally, issue meaning theories suggest that movements will be most successful when they develop discourses that resonate with potential supporters.[53] Each of these theories helps to explain the policy differences among the three countries. The American "abortion movement" was larger and more assertive than its counterparts in the other countries, and it used a "women's rights" frame that was not present elsewhere. But to fully understand this difference, we must attend to the ways that political institutions shaped the size, assertiveness, and issue framings of abortion movements in the three countries.

To begin, the duration, dispersion, and timing of abortion reforms strongly affected their content. As the result of state-level policy making, the American reform took longer, occurred in more venues, and came later than the reforms in the other countries. The length of time between the appearance of abortion on the governmental agenda and the enactment of a national reform was a mere two years in Britain and three in Canada, but twelve years in the United States. Abortion was debated only in the national parliaments of Britain and Canada but was debated in the courts and/or legislatures of almost every American state. Finally, the national reform came later in the United States (1973) than in Britain (1967) or Canada (1969). And after the national enactments, policy making halted for many years in Britain and Canada, but had just begun in the United States.

Table 2.1 provides a timeline of the abortion reforms in the three countries. In Britain, the ALRA put abortion on the public agenda shortly before World War II, but after the war, the association was moribund until a new generation of activists revived it in the early 1960s. Private member's bills were introduced in 1953, 1954, and 1961, but the sponsors of these bills drew such low places in the private member's lottery that their bills had no chance of enactment and were introduced merely for the purpose of publicizing the issue rather than changing the law.[54] Joseph Reeves's 1953 bill was debated for less than two minutes. Lord Amulree withdrew his 1954 bill before it could be debated after a dispute with the ALRA. Kenneth Robinson's 1961 bill was debated for a day but ran out of time before a vote could be taken. Renee Short's 1965 bill was debated for ten minutes. Abortion did not truly reach the governmental agenda until Lord Silkin's 1965 bill: It passed the House of Lords in 1966, but did not make it to the Commons because Parliament was dissolved for a general election. The next year, Parliament enacted David Steel's bill, and there were no further enactments until 1990.[55]

In Canada, the women's magazine *Chatelaine* first put abortion on the public agenda in 1959, and the call for abortion liberalization was soon taken up by the *Globe and Mail*. Provincial medical associations and eventually the CMA also called for reform. The issue did not reach the Parliamentary agenda until 1966 when Ian Wahn introduced a private member's bill. The national reform was enacted three years later, and there were no further enactments until 1988.[56]

In the United States, abortion reached the public agenda in 1959 with the ALI resolution on abortion and reached the government agenda in 1961 with the introduction of an ALI-style abortion reform in the California legislature.[57] For the next twelve years, state legislatures and courts debated the abortion issue until the Supreme Court established the national reform in 1973.[58] Abortion was addressed by legislatures or courts in every single state except for Wyoming and West Virginia. Not only was this debate longer than in the other countries, but it took place in more venues, involved more people, and offered more opportunities for policy learning than those in Britain and Canada. After the national reform, states continued to enact abortion policies within (and sometimes outside) of the constraints imposed by the court, and this continues today.

The duration, timing, and dispersion of the abortion debates in the three countries affected the size, character, and demands of the abortion

Table 2.1 Abortion on the Governmental Agenda in Britain, Canada, and the United States

Britain	Canada		United States
		1959	New York bill dies in committee
		1960	
		1961	New Hampshire bill passes legislature, governor vetoes; California bill dies in committee
		1962	
		1963	California bill dies in committee
		1964	
Silkin bill		1965	California, New Mexico, New York bills introduced
Silkin bill passes Lords; Steel bill	Wahn bill dies	1966	Mississippi enacts bill with rape grounds
Steel bill enacted	MacInnis, Herridge bills added to Government bill	1967	California, Colorado, North Carolina enact ALI reforms; 27 states reject ALI bills[1]
		1968	Georgia and Maryland enact ALI reforms; 2 states reject ALI bills[2]
	Government bill enacted	1969	Arkansas, Delaware, Kansas, New Mexico, Oregon enact ALI reforms; 17 states reject ALI bills;[3] 4 states reject repeal bills;[4] courts strike down California and District of Columbia laws
		1970	Alaska, Hawaii, New York, Washington enact repeals; South Carolina, Virginia enact ALI reforms; 4 states reject ALI bills;[5] 5 states reject repeal bills;[6] courts strike down 6 state laws,[7] uphold 7 state laws;[8] Supreme Court rejects California case
		1971	Iowa rejects ALI bill; 9 states reject repeal bills;[9] courts strike down 5 state laws,[10] uphold 4 state laws;[11] Supreme Court refuses cases from 5 states,[12] upholds District of Columbia law, hears arguments in Texas and Georgia cases
		1972	Florida enacts ALI reform after court decision; New York governor vetoes restrictive bill; Connecticut enacts restrictive law; voters defeat repeal referendums in Michigan, North Dakota; courts strike down 5 state laws,[13] uphold 4 state laws;[14] Supreme Court hears arguments again in Texas and Georgia cases
		1973	Supreme Court strikes down Texas and Georgia laws

movements in each country. All three countries started out with small, elite movements making modest demands. But the longer, more dispersed American debate aided the development of new tactics, alliances and claims.

The pro-choice movements in Britain and Canada were small and did not articulate claims for abortion on request. Britain's ALRA was a small organization of about one thousand elite and professional women with extensive contacts in the House of Commons and the government ministries at Whitehall. The ALRA's president, Vera Houghton, was married to Douglas Houghton, the leader of the Parliamentary Labour Party (PLP), and the association had many other Labour allies. During debate on the Steel bill, the association focused on deaths from back-alley abortions rather than claiming that abortion was a women's right or that it should be available on request. Before World War II, Stella Browne advocated "abortion on demand," but the other founders of the ALRA did not. During the war and after, the association's membership and activity declined markedly, but after the thalidomide crisis of 1961, the association was reborn with a new generation of leaders, Diane Munday, Madeleine Simms, and Vera Houghton, and new funding from the Hopkins Foundation of

---

[1] Alabama, Arizona, Connecticut, Delaware, Florida, Georgia, Hawaii, Illinois, Indiana, Iowa, Maine, Maryland, Michigan, Minnesota, Missouri, Nebraska, Nevada, New Jersey, New Mexico, New York, North Dakota, Ohio, Oklahoma, Pennsylvania, Rhode Island, Texas, Wisconsin
[2] Florida, Hawaii
[3] Arizona, Connecticut, Hawaii, Iowa, Maine, Massachusetts, Michigan, Minnesota, Nevada, New Hampshire, New Jersey, New York, Rhode Island, Tennessee, Texas, Utah, Virginia
[4] Illinois, Michigan, New York, Washington
[5] Idaho, Massachusetts, Michigan, Vermont
[6] Arizona, Georgia, Iowa, Maryland, Michigan
[7] Georgia, Michigan, Pennsylvania, South Dakota, Texas, Wisconsin
[8] Iowa, Louisiana, Maryland, Minnesota, Missouri, North Carolina, Ohio
[9] Colorado, Georgia, Iowa, Maryland, Massachusetts, Minnesota, Montana, New Mexico, Texas
[10] California, Connecticut, Florida, Illinois, Michigan
[11] Kansas, Louisiana, Utah, Virginia
[12] Georgia, Iowa, Maryland, Minnesota, Wisconsin
[13] California, Connecticut, Kansas, New Jersey, Vermont
[14] Indiana, Kentucky, Mississippi, South Dakota

Sources: Chicago Tribune, June 22, 1967, p. B6; The Day (New London, CT), July 3, 1967, 22; Alphonse de Valk, Morality and Law in Canadian Politics: The Abortion Controversy (Montreal: Palm, 1974); David J. Garrow, Liberty and Sexuality: The Right to Privacy and the Making of Roe v. Wade (New York: Macmillan, 1994); Keith Hindell and Madeline Simms, Abortion Law Reformed (London: Peter Owen, 1971); New York Times, April 30, 1967, 194; Associated Press, Prescott (AZ) Evening Courier, February 7, 1969, 3; Heather Sigworth, "Abortion Laws in the Federal Courts: The Supreme Court as Supreme Platonic Guardian," Indiana Legal Forum 5 (1971): 130–42; St. Petersburg (FL) Times, April 1, 1967, 9; Roe v. Wade, 410 U.S. 113 (1973); Spokesman-Review (Spokane, WA), March 21, 1970, 6; Raymond Tatalovich and Byron W. Daynes. The Politics of Abortion: A Study of Community Conflict in Public Policy Making (New York: Praeger, 1981); Pat Vergata, Charlyn Buss, Barbara Schain, and Donna Greenfield, "Abortion Cases in the United States," Women's Rights Law Reporter 1 (1972): 50–55.

California. The new leadership was more energetic and assertive than its predecessors, but also more pragmatic. In 1963, the association's president, Cambridge law professor Glanville Williams, advocated abortion on request before the thirteenth week of pregnancy, and in February 1964, the association's executive committee passed a resolution to that effect, but four days later, the association backtracked from this position after Vera Houghton discussed it with MPs and found that none would support such a bill.[59]

In Canada, abortion reform was put on the public agenda by the media and medical associations rather than by movement organizations. Abortion reform had the support of the National Council of Women, the largest women's group of the time, but the group did not support abortion on request. Neither did the Association for the Modernization of Canadian Abortion Laws (AMCAL). The Toronto Women's Liberation Group and the Humanists of Canada called for abortion on request, but these groups were small and their arguments carried little weight with Parliament.[60]

In the United States, the early reformers were mainly doctors, lawyers, and family planning professionals seeking reforms that maintained medical gatekeeping. Initially, there was a division between those who advocated ALI-style reforms and those who advocated the complete repeal of abortion laws. Much of this dispute was strategic rather than ideological, as many of the reform proponents had a long-term goal of eliminating abortion laws but believed that they could get there only incrementally. On the repeal side were Pat Maginnis and Lana Phelan, who established California's Society for Humane Abortion in 1962, and Garrett Hardin, an ecology professor and population control advocate, who, in 1963, called for "abortion on demand" and said that "any woman at any time should be able to procure a legal abortion for herself without even giving a reason. The fact that she wants it should be enough." Hardin argued that "the emancipation of women is not complete until women are free to avoid the pregnancies they do not want."[61] Later, the repeal side also included Lonny Myers who founded the badly misnamed Illinois Citizens for the Medical Control of Abortion in 1966. That same year, Dr. William Ober, of New York's Knickerbocker Hospital, argued for "abortion on request" in the *Saturday Evening Post*. Many of the repeal advocates saw ALI-style reforms as counterproductive. Hardin argued in 1964 that "a trifling improvement of this sort might well delay for generations the much larger step."[62] The Society for Humane Abortion's Lana Phelan agreed, calling the reform measures "'a lie and a cruel farce.'"[63]

On the gradualist side was the Association for the Study of Abortion

(ASA), the first national abortion reform organization, founded in 1964 by Dr. Alan Guttmacher, the president of the PPFA, and Dr. Robert Hall of Columbia University, along with about twenty other professional elites.[64] Guttmacher agreed that repeal was a worthy long-term goal but argued that "social progress should be made by evolution, not revolution."[65] Others on the gradualist side included the sponsors of state reforms who acknowledged that their narrow reforms would not solve the problem of illegal abortions but viewed such reforms as a first step.[66]

Eventually, the two sides converged around repeal. Soon after the reforms of 1967 some of the initial reformers started to publicly advocate repeal and newspapers began to highlight the shortcomings of the initial reforms. In Colorado and North Carolina, 95 percent of women seeking abortions still had their requests rejected after reform. A reporter for *Time* magazine said that "the key question is whether limited legislation is any solution. . . . [T]he new laws merely codify what hospitals are already doing." When Britain enacted its reform in October 1967, many newspapers noted that it was more liberal than the state-level reforms in the United States.[67]

In January 1968, ICMCA's Lonny Myers urged the ASA to acknowledge publicly that repeal was plausible. After Hall refused, Myers and the ASA's Lawrence Lader began planning a national repeal group. Guttmacher, who had recently been appointed to a commission to study New York's abortion laws, also refused to endorse repeal—"such an attempt would be impractical and the people are not ready for it," he said. Instead, he suggested broadening the ALI grounds to include women with three or more children, women over forty, unmarried girls under eighteen, and families who would provide "an adverse environment for the child."[68]

But by November 1968, at an ASA-sponsored conference in Hot Springs, Virginia, many activists were surprised to find that almost all their fellow attendees now supported repeal. According to the *New York Times*, "The consensus at the end of the meeting . . . was nearly unanimous: abolish all existing abortion laws."[69] The ASA's Bob Hall soon told a magazine, "abortion must be the right of every woman."[70] And in February 1969, Guttmacher announced that he too was joining the repeal side. He even argued that reform hindered repeal. Hall would not go quite that far. He and his ASA colleague, John Lassoe, argued that "reform, by demonstrating how few people it does help" can "provide the impetus for repeal." In February 1969, Myers and Lader launched the National Association for the Repeal of Abortion Laws (NARAL).

Just as the American abortion movement was coming to a consensus on repeal, second-wave feminism was emerging and taking up the abortion

CHAPTER TWO

issue. The feminist movement was divided into an older and a younger branch (both in the dates that organizations were founded and in the median age of members). The older branch included groups such as the National Organization for Women (NOW), Human Rights of Women, and the Women's Equity Action League, and the younger branch included local groups such as New York Radical Women, Redstockings, and the Chicago Women's Liberation Union. NOW was founded in June 1966 while the first organizations of the younger branch emerged independently in late 1967 and early 1968 in several cities—Chicago, Toronto, Detroit, Seattle, Gainesville, and New York. Many members of the younger branch were involved in other movements of the 1960s such as the civil rights and antiwar movements and the New Left. The younger branch tended toward more radical and disruptive tactics than the older branch. The emergence of these groups and their attention to abortion increased the grassroots reach of the pro-choice movement. In 1970, NARAL had only about 1,000 individual members and 23 organizational members. NOW had very few members until the media discovered feminism in 1969, but by 1973 it had 8,000. And the younger branch of second-wave feminism eventually included approximately 150 local groups nationwide.[71]

NOW members were initially divided over the abortion issue. The organization had been formed to work on issues of employment and educational equality. In 1967, it adopted a "Bill of Rights" that included "the right of women to control their reproductive lives," but this was the last item on the list.[72] Members argued about what priority to give to abortion and, in 1968, some left to form the Women's Equity Action League where they could focus on other issues. In 1969, NOW's president, Betty Friedan, helped found NARAL and joined its board, announcing "your movement is now mine." She said, "my only claim to be here, is our belated recognition, if you will, that there is no freedom, no equality, no full human dignity and personhood possible for women until we assert and demand the control over our own bodies."[73] Some NOW chapters (e.g., New York) embraced the abortion issue while others (e.g., Chicago) were only minimally involved. Among feminists of the younger branch, however, abortion was a central issue from the beginning.[74]

As second-wave feminism gained strength and began to address the abortion issue, abortion rights protests and speak-outs became more common. In New York, feminist activists protested at the trial of an abortion provider, at a city council hearing on abortion, and at the 1969 AMA convention. In February 1969, New York's Redstockings, a radical feminist group, disrupted a legislative hearing on a repeal bill. In Los Angeles, feminists protested at the district attorney's office. In August 1970, twenty thousand protestors marked the fiftieth anniversary of women's suffrage with a march down New York's Fifth Avenue and called for "abortion on demand."[75] In that same year, feminists held a funeral march remembering women who died from back-alley abortions in Detroit and disrupted the AMA convention in Chicago. Also in 1970, the Boston Women's Health Collective wrote the book *Women and Their Bodies* (later called *Our Bodies, Our Selves*), which became the basis for a course offered by women's liberation groups nationwide. Reproductive health was an important part of these courses. The Women's National Abortion Action Coalition (WONAAC) organized a Washington demonstration in November 1971 and a well-attended national conference in 1972, but dissolved the following year as many feminist groups rejected the coalition because of its ties to the Socialist Worker's Party.

Many of the young feminist organizations set up abortion counseling and referral services such as Chicago's Women's Liberation Abortion Counseling Service ("Jane"). These were joined by the Clergy Consultation Service, which mobilized thousands of ministers and rabbis nationwide. Finally, Zero Population Growth (ZPG), founded by Paul Erlich, author of the 1968 best seller *The Population Bomb*, took up the cause. In 1971, it had 35,000 members and 400 chapters, mainly on college campuses.[76]

In addition to the division over repeal versus reform-then-repeal, there was also a division, or at least a division of labor, between those who focused on legislative change and those who thought the courts were the best venue. ASA member and PPFA lawyer Harriet Pilpel, who helped develop the 1965 *Griswold v. Connecticut* case (in which the U.S. Supreme Court found a marital privacy right of contraception), argued that the case could be extended to abortion, and that litigation would be the best way to reform abortion laws.[77]

The ASA's Guttmacher, Hall, and Lader tried to launch a test case but could not find a hospital willing to test the law. In 1966, the SHA also advertised for lawyers who might be willing to launch a test case. In the same year, the New York and southern California affiliates of the ACLU tried unsuccessfully to convince their national organization that the fundamental right of privacy applied to abortion. In April 1967, NYU law student, Roy Lucas, wrote an essay exploring the possibilities for a judicial challenge. It so impressed Pilpel and Lader that the ASA commissioned Lucas to prepare a model brief for a judicial challenge. In the summer of 1967, Lucas's essay appeared in the *North Carolina Law Review* and was quickly influential.[78]

In July 1968, Lucas presented his model brief to the ASA and ACLU, and the organizations agreed to prepare a test of New York's abortion laws with Lucas taking the lead. Lucas's approach sought a declaratory judgment in behalf of physician plaintiffs. A 1934 federal statute allowed federal courts to issue declaratory judgments so that plaintiffs could test the constitutionality of laws without actually breaking them.[79] As Lucas explained in a cover memo, his approach would raise the constitutional issues "without the risk of a physician's license, without embarrassment to patients, and without the emotion-charged clamor too often brought on by opposition to legislative reform."[80] Another advantage of this strategy was that the case would be heard by a special three-judge district court and then go directly to the Supreme Court, as opposed to the usual path of a district court, then a federal circuit court of appeals, and finally the Supreme Court. This abbreviated process would allow a decision by the Supreme Court within two years of filing. Lucas's substantive approach claimed that "life" and "health" were vague, that the physician-patient relationship was protected by the freedom of association, and that *Griswold*'s marital right of privacy applied to abortion.[81]

The California Committee on Therapeutic Abortion (CCTA) had also become heavily involved in litigation. In January 1967, Dr. Leon Belous, a CCTA member, was convicted of referring a patient to an abortion provider in Mexico. The CCTA's Zad Leavy handled Belous's first appeal in August 1968, arguing unsuccessfully that *Griswold* applied to abortion. For the appeal to the state supreme court, Leavy was joined by two prominent attorneys affiliated with the ACLU. The ACLU and the CCTA, using the networks and money of prominent attorney and CCTA funder Charles Munger and his investment partner Warren Buffett, engineered impressive amicus briefs by prominent attorneys and physicians. In September 1969, the California Supreme Court, in *People v. Belous*, struck down the state's nineteenth-century abortion law (which was by then moot because of the 1967 reform) and found that women had a fundamental right to choose whether to bear children under both the California and federal constitutions.[82] Then, in November of that year, a federal district court struck down the District of Columbia's abortion law because its life endangerment and health grounds were too vague.

These two cases prompted a flood of others over the next three years. Some were brought by state ACLU organizations or lawyers affiliated with them (California, Georgia, Iowa, New Jersey, North Carolina), some were brought by abortion reform or repeal organizations (Georgia, Washington, Wisconsin), some were brought by legislative sponsors of previous reforms or repeals (Colorado, Oregon), and some were brought by feminist groups (Connecticut, Florida, Massachusetts, New York, Rhode Island, Texas). One case was initiated by Minnesota's Dr. Jane Hodgson, and another was initiated by the Vermont chapter of ZPG.[83] Though these cases were brought by a variety of local actors, they were assisted by a variety of national organizations such as the ACLU, NARAL, ASA, and Lucas's James Madison Constitutional Law Institute. Many of the cases brought by feminist groups were assisted by Nancy Stearns of the Center for Constitutional Rights. Most of the attorneys and organizations filing these cases communicated with one another and read one another's briefs.[84]

As feminists and pro-choice lawyers increasingly framed the abortion issue as one of women's rights, their opponents also spoke in constitutional terms, claiming that "the unborn have a right to life." This raised both the stakes and the controversy of the conflict.[85] Pro-life groups started to mobilize. In New York, 50 right-to-life groups tried to repeal the state's abortion law and drew 10,000 protesters to an April 1972 rally; the pro-choice movement drew a mere 700 people to their rally a month later.[86] After Connecticut passed its restrictive abortion bill in 1972, House majority leader Carl R. Ajello marveled at the strength of the right-to-life movement; "There's no question what I would have had to contend with if I had voted against the abortion bill. There are five Catholic churches in my area, and they told their worshipers in no uncertain terms what my position should be. I never received so many postcards, letters, petitions and phone calls."[87] By mid-1972, there were approximately 250 state and local organizations affiliated with the National Right to Life Committee.[88]

As the discussion above shows, the American pro-choice movement initially resembled those in Canada and Britain. It was small, dominated by elites, and made narrow demands. But by early 1969, the American movement was larger, more feminist, more radical in its demands, and more assertive in pursuing them than similar movements in the other countries. This development was aided by prolonged and dispersed state-level policy making. Although some activists articulated a women's right to "abortion on demand" as early as 1962, most made much narrower claims until late 1968. The demands of many reformers radicalized over time as the initial reforms proved unsatisfactory. This was not because the initial reformers had expected the initial reforms to solve the problem of illegal abortions. Most realized from the outset that the vast majority of women sought abortions for reasons other than those contained in the ALI model penal code, and, as a result, those ALI-style statutes would legalize only about 5 percent of all abortions.[89] But many of the reformers believed that the public was not yet ready for more radical demands. The initial reforms drew the attention of the public and professional elites to the problem of abortion, while at the same time demonstrating that those reforms could not solve the problem. After the "failed reforms" of 1967, the reformers were surprised to find that popular opinion, and especially elite opinion, had liberalized much more quickly than they expected. Once this became clear, reformers started to advocate repeal in the fall of 1968—not just privately, but publicly. At the same time, the litigation campaign that began in the summer of 1967 and was in full swing by the summer of 1968, framed abortion as a constitutional right. This framing was pushed still further by NOW's full embrace of the issue in early 1969, and the first protests by the younger branch of the feminist movement that same year.

The duration and dispersion of state-level abortion policy making allowed for "social learning" by the public and elites who discovered that ALI-style reforms were not sufficient. It allowed for "strategic learning" by abortion activists who discovered in the fall of 1968 that the public was now ready for repeal, and who learned from Lucas that *Griswold* could be extended to abortion and that declaratory judgments made it possible to pursue abortion litigation without risking the prosecution of doctors or hospitals.

It also allowed "policy learning" by the medical profession and the Supreme Court. As I show in the next chapter, medical associations were convinced by the experiences of California, the District of Columbia, and New York that large numbers of abortions could be safely provided in freestanding clinics with limited disruption to mainstream ob/gyn practices. The Supreme Court could also refer to the wording and practical implementations of a wide variety of state-level abortion laws, including total repeals. It could also refer to, and gain legitimacy from, state-level case law—for example, the influential 1969 *Belous* case that struck down California's abortion law on the basis of privacy rights. The state reforms also defined the debate for the court. In *Roe*, it attempted to walk a middle path between reform and repeal, right and medical necessity. The court also could take comfort in the fact that the AMA and American Bar Association (ABA) had eventually come out in favor of repeal. Finally, the length and dispersion of American policy making allowed for the intersection and eventual alliance of the abortion reform movement with the feminist, civil liberties, and population control movements.

Subnational policy making also meant that activists were able to shop for venues, filing court cases in New York and Texas because they believed they would draw favorable three-judge panels there, and choosing New York for repeal efforts because of a sympathetic legislature and governor.[90] Subnational policy making also provided multiple bites at the apple—legislative reforms and repeals as well as court cases failed in some jurisdictions only to succeed later in others.

Contrary to some accounts, I do not believe that the success of the American movement relative to those in other countries resulted mainly from its protests and disruptive tactics. Instead, it resulted mainly from the successful development of strategies and arguments for pursuing liberalization through the courts—though mass protest helped disseminate and build support for those arguments.[91] Moreover, the courts were especially receptive to constitutional claims about abortion because elites, and especially professional elites, were increasingly supportive of abortion liberalization. Between 1967 and 1972, approximately seventy-five national organizations announced their support for abortion reform or repeal, including the American Jewish Congress, the American Baptist Convention, the Lutheran Church of America, the Presbyterian Church of America, the ABA, Planned Parenthood, the American Public Health Association, the American Psychiatric Association, the American College of Obstetricians and Gynecologists (ACOG), and the YWCA.[92] The failure of the AMA to defend medical gatekeeping, in marked contrast to its counterparts in the other countries, aided the development of this elite consensus. As I argue in the next chapter, the AMA, because of Justice Blackmun's deep respect for medical opinion, probably could have vetoed the emerging elite consensus, but chose not to do so. Gene Burns persuasively argues that state legislators were supportive of abortion reform as long as it was framed as a technical, medical-humanitarian issue, but after 1970, legislators shied away because pro-choice and pro-life activists began articulating broad "moral worldviews" such as "women's rights" and "fetal rights."[93] In the face of such controversy and such broad claims, elected officials became hostile or evasive. According to Amenta, such a situation calls for assertive tactics.[94] But the pro-choice movement, despite its size and assertive tactics, lost all twelve of its thirteen legislative battles in 1971 and 1972, and was saved in New York only by the governor's veto. Assertive tactics did not work in the face of a growing countermovement and jumpy legislators. Instead, the movement succeeded because some of its members pursued the fight in a new venue—constitutional courts—where the emerging elite consensus could prevail.

Of course, as activists developed judicial strategies in 1967 and 1968, they did not know that legislative and referenda strategies would hit a wall after 1970, but at least some of them suspected that nationwide reform would take many years and ample resources. Many activists, such as Lawrence Lader, took a shotgun approach to choosing tactics—trying everything and seeing what did the most damage. Others, such as Roy

Lucas and Harriet Pilpel, were convinced that their tactics were the most promising. Because the reform movement contained advocates of many different tactics, most were tried, and the movement involved legislative reforms and repeals, referenda, civil disobedience (through abortion referrals to illegal providers), disruptive protests, and court cases.

In Britain and Canada, far fewer venues were available—national parliaments rather than fifty state legislatures and state and federal courts. Quick and early reforms codified the narrow demands of small, elite movements—foreclosing possibilities for social, strategic, or policy learning and locking in narrow reforms before the emergence of second-wave feminism. Medical definitions of the issue remained dominant both because the medical profession worked to maintain them and because such definitions were not countered by constitutional, feminist, or "failed reform" discourses.

Government Officials: Quietly Supportive of Reform in Britain and Canada, Evasive in the United States

Partisanship theories of social policy making suggest that governments controlled by left parties will enact the most liberal abortion policies, and in particular, policies that allow abortion on request for women's own reasons, as was the case in many Nordic countries (though this usually occurred after internal pressure from feminists). But partisanship theories do not offer clear predictions about the content of the abortion reforms in the three countries here because the governments of all three countries were broadly centrist and none had strong relationships with the feminist movement. The British Labour Party is sometimes considered a left party, but its leaders at the time were centrists. The Canadian Liberal and American Democratic parties are typically considered center-left or coalition parties. Moreover, at the time of the national abortion reform, the American federal government was divided between a Republican president and a Democratic Congress.

Although all three governments were centrist, they did indeed differ in their attitudes toward abortion reform, and political institutions help to explain why. The British and Canadian Governments were quietly supportive of abortion reform, while American state and federal governments, by 1970, wanted nothing to do with the issue. This difference was mainly the result of the gradual radicalization, discussed in the last section, of American movement demands and claims on both sides of the issue. The British and Canadian Governments did not have to contend with movements demanding abortion on request provided as a right (or opposing such demands). Instead, they faced narrow demands for abortion reforms that included medical gatekeeping. These governments supported abortion reform, but only of this type. They did not support abortion on request, especially because the medical associations opposed it. The support of the British and Canadian Governments for reform was also facilitated by nonpartisan parliamentary processes that helped them avoid blame for their actions.

The British reform had the support of key members of the Labour Government and was enacted mainly with Labour votes. The head of the PLP, Douglas Houghton, was married to the ALRA's Vera Houghton. The minister of health, Kenneth Robinson, had offered an abortion private member's bill in 1961. The chief whip, John Silkin, was the son of Lord Lewis Silkin, who had sponsored an abortion bill that passed the House of Lords in 1966. The home secretary, Roy Jenkins, and his deputy, Dick Taverne, as well as the leader of the House, Richard Crossman, were also sympathetic.[95] Jenkins, in particular, was crucial: He was a libertarian and, in his 1959 book *The Labour Case*, had asked whether Britain could be considered civilized with its "archaic" laws on divorce, suicide, homosexuality, and abortion. When he was appointed home secretary in December 1965, he began work on the reform of those laws, and when Steel drew a high place in the private member's lottery in 1966, Jenkins encouraged him to introduce a bill on either abortion or homosexuality. Steel chose the former because it was less objectionable to his constituents. Meanwhile, Jenkins and Crossman tried to build support in the Cabinet. Prime Minister Harold Wilson was indifferent about abortion reform, and this empowered the rest of the Cabinet—though Wilson worried that the reform might jeopardize Labour seats in the Catholic areas of northwest England and Scotland. Other Cabinet members expressed concerns that Labour would get a "permissive" reputation for supporting legislation on abortion, contraception, homosexuality, capital punishment, and Sunday observance. Jenkins and Crossman argued that the abortion legislation was well drafted, had strong support among backbenchers, and would build the morale of young left-wing MPs who were upset about Labour's support for the war in Vietnam.[96] The support of the party for the bill was also demonstrated by the strong turnout on the Labour benches (due in part to ALRA lobbying) during two all-night abortion debates.

Initially, Crossman suggested that the Cabinet develop a new practice in which the Government would formally support (but not whip) some private member's bills, but other members of the Cabinet argued that taking an official position on moral issues would lead ministers to resign,

CHAPTER TWO

and the Government should merely provide extra time.[97] In his memoirs, Jenkins said that it was impossible to convince the Cabinet to officially support reforms of homosexuality and abortion laws because "a substantial majority of ministers were in favor of both, but three or four were opposed, and another larger group wished the issues would go away." Instead, the Government "gave the bills a virtual guarantee of passage" by allowing "the House to sit for as long as was necessary to get the bills through." In addition, "while members of the cabinet would be free to vote against them," wrote Jenkins, "I would be free to speak (and vote, of course) in their favor from my ministerial place and with all the briefing and such authority as I could command as home secretary."[98] Not only did the Government give extra time to the abortion bill, but it also provided unusual drafting assistance and moved the bill to a new committee when long discussions on another bill threatened its progress.[99]

In Canada, the Liberal Government was also central to reform but shielded itself from blame by including the abortion reform in an omnibus criminal code reform and by allowing a free vote to remove abortion from the bill. In previous years, private member's bills on divorce and contraception had been handled in the typical manner—they had been filibustered or let die without debate. But Lester Pearson's Liberal Government referred the private member abortion bills of 1966 and 1967 to a standing committee and then included abortion reform in its own omnibus bill revising the criminal code.[100] Abortion reform was now part of a Government bill on which Liberal MPs would be obliged to vote with their party. The bill itself was broadly motivated by the desire to decriminalize victimless crimes.[101] Justice minister, and future prime minister, Pierre Trudeau famously remarked that "the state has no business in the bedrooms of the nation." He was referring to homosexuality, but later applied the principle to abortion as well.[102] Similarly, John Turner, Trudeau's successor as justice minister, told the House of Commons, "Public order, in this situation of a pluralistic society, cannot substitute for private conduct. We believe that morality is a matter for private conscience. Criminal law should reflect the public order only."[103] The Canadian Bar Association (CBA) agreed and advocated abortion reform under this rationale.[104]

Canadian Governments have even stronger party discipline than British ones. Almost all votes are considered "confidence votes" (a vote where a Government defeat would require a new election), and Governments are harsh with backbench dissenters. Free voting is rare: During the period of this study, the only major issues on which it was allowed were the adoption of a new Canadian flag, capital punishment, same-sex marriage, and abortion.[105] During the Pearson Government, the prime minister and his justice minister Pierre Trudeau wanted a party vote on abortion, but Health Minister Alan MacEachen, along with Quebec's Liberal caucus, argued for a free vote. When Trudeau succeeded Pearson as prime minister, he again resisted a free vote and MacEachen pushed for it. Others suggested removing abortion and homosexuality to their own bills.[106] Eventually, Trudeau agreed to a free vote on the question of removing abortion from the bill. This removal was rejected 107 to 36, with only two Liberals voting to remove abortion from the bill. The antiabortion votes came from the Progressive Conservatives (Tories) and Quebec's Social Credit Party.[107]

In the United States, the state-level reforms and repeals were largely nonpartisan. Pro-reform majorities did not divide along party or liberal-conservative lines.[108] About half of the reforms occurred in the Democratic, but conservative, South.[109] Gene Burns convincingly debunks claims that southern states liberalized abortion laws to suppress black birthrates or allow abortions for white women allegedly raped by black men. Instead, he argues that abortion reform was successful in the South because the region was hospitable to medical elites and lacked strong Catholic groups that might have challenged the prevailing, and uncontroversial, medical frame of the early reforms.[110] Once the abortion battle became a heated contest between the rights of women and the rights of fetuses, and there was strong movement mobilization on both sides, most state legislators shied away, and legislative reforms came to an abrupt halt. The issue was still considered a matter of state jurisdiction, and federal policy makers had no desire to take over. As Republican Senator Bob Packwood (R-OR) put it in 1970: "Most of the legislators in the nation I have met and certainly many members of Congress would prefer the Supreme Court to legalize abortion, thereby taking them off the hook and relieving them of the responsibility for decision-making."[111] This reluctance by state and federal legislators to deal with the issue, along with numerous contradictory rulings in the state and federal courts, likely encouraged the Supreme Court to become involved.

The national reform occurred under a Republican president and a Democratic Congress, but neither played much of a role. The abortion issue was not yet part of partisan politics. Though President Nixon began to oppose abortion in 1970 as part of a strategy to lure Catholic voters, the Republican Party itself had not yet embraced the pro-life cause.[112] Nixon made four appointments to the Supreme Court in the years before *Roe*, but he chose justices for their views on issues such as law and order, not abortion. The *Roe* majority included five justices appointed by

CHAPTER TWO

Republican presidents and two appointed by Democratic presidents, and there was one dissenter from each party.[113] None of these justices were appointed for their views on abortion.

Reform through the U.S. Supreme Court

The policy venues of abortion reforms were also crucial. The British and Canadian reforms occurred through Parliament while the American reforms occurred first in state legislatures and then through courts. Earlier in the chapter, I argued that prolonged and dispersed state-level reforms in the United States allowed social learning by the public and elites and strategic learning by abortion reformers who eventually called for abortion on request as a woman's right. In Britain and Canada, nonpartisan parliamentary processes helped Governments to avoid some blame for abortion reforms, but these Governments were still concerned to some degree about potential electoral repercussions. By contrast, the life tenure of American Supreme Court justices insulated them from electoral pressure and allowed them to take a more liberal position on abortion than that of the public and most state legislatures. Reform through the court also amplified the voices of professional elites from law, medicine, and academia who had largely come to a consensus in favor of repeal by the time of the court's decisions.[114] These professional elites came from the same class and educational background as the justices, often had social and professional contacts with them, and assisted them in the regulation and administration of society.

The court probably had no choice but to take up the abortion cases. By 1970, abortion law reforms and repeals had become so controversial that they came to a complete halt in the states. Although there is no clear constitutional principle for dividing state and federal powers, abortion had historically been a state-level domain, and federal legislation seemed out of the question.[115] Reformers looked instead to state and federal district courts, and they responded with a slew of contradictory rulings. The Supreme Court likely felt compelled to resolve these discrepancies and motivated to fill the policy vacuum. The power and legitimacy of the judiciary were also at issue. A federal district court had struck down the Texas abortion law in 1970, but in 1971, a state court ignored this ruling. This may have reminded the Supreme Court of earlier southern resistance to its civil rights rulings.[116]

Thus, few were surprised that the court took up the abortion cases, but many were shocked by its rulings.[117] The court could have taken a narrow approach and simply overturned the nineteenth-century laws that allowed abortions only for life endangerment. Instead, it struck down not only those laws, but also the ALI-style reforms, and thus the laws of every state, allowing early abortion on request for women's own reasons. Harriet Pilpel, who wrote Planned Parenthood's amicus brief in the cases, was among those surprised: The decision "scaled the whole mountain. We expected to get there, but not on the first trip."[118]

The court's relative insulation from democratic mechanisms helps to explain the expansiveness of *Roe*. Justices are not unconstrained by public opinion; they usually avoid straying too far from it to preserve the court's institutional legitimacy and avoid attacks from other branches of government. But justices are certainly less constrained than elected officials. They can act against public preferences without losing office. They can attempt to anticipate changing public opinion. And without frequent contact with constituents, they are probably less aware of the daily state of public attitudes than most legislators. It appears that most members of the court did not anticipate the eventual extent or duration of the abortion controversy. According to historian David Garrow, "the *Roe* Justices, to a man, did not believe that the pair of cases before them entailed social and political implications at all comparable to *Brown* [v. *Board of Education*]."[119] According to his biographer, Justice Powell expected the public to eventually support the decision:

He predicted—or rather assumed—that misgivings about the origin of the constitutional right would be lost in the widespread satisfaction with the result. . . . To Powell, abortion looked like *Griswold* [the court's contraceptive privacy rights decision]. There too, the origin of the right was obscure. There too theoreticians had complained about the Justices injecting their personal preferences into the Constitution. There too, the Catholic hierarchy had objected. But there had been no widespread public outcry.[120]

Powell was correct that public opinion was becoming more supportive of abortion rights. From 1965 to 1972, support for health grounds had risen from 73 to 87 percent, and support for economic grounds had risen from 22 to 49 percent.[121] But he and the other justices may not have realized that the majority of Americans still supported abortion rights only for hard grounds (health, rape, and incest). And he was incorrect in assuming that public support would eventually extend as far as abortion on request for women's own reasons.[122]

In *Roe*, Justice Blackmun wrote that the court was aware of the "sensitive and emotional nature of the abortion controversy, of the vigorous opposing views, even among physicians, and of the deep and seemingly absolute convictions that the subject inspires."[123] But he also seemed to underestimate the eventual scale of the controversy. Before the cases were argued, he served on a screening committee that decided which difficult or important cases should be set aside until the court filled its two vacancies. *Roe* did not make the list. In an interview twenty years later, Blackmun said, "I don't know why we didn't set it aside. I think probably the implication, the obvious implication, is that we didn't think it was that important at that time."[124] Blackmun's files show that he read a *Washington Post* article reporting on a June 1972 Gallup poll that said that 64 percent of Americans agreed that the abortion decision should be between a woman and her doctor.[125] This poll likely overestimated support for abortion on request because of the inclusion of the word "doctor" in the question. Other polls from the same year showed that support was more limited. Only 27 percent (NORC) and 38 percent (Gallup) approved of abortions for married women who did not want more children.[126] Blackmun's notes predicted that the court would be "excoriated" for its decision, but when he considered the potential impact on state legislatures, he predicted only that "it will be an unsettled period for awhile."[127] His opinion also noted "a trend toward liberalization" of state abortion laws, but this trend had in fact come to a halt a few years before.[128]

Blackmun noted, correctly, however, that elite opinion favored reform. In his "hand-down" announcing the decisions, he said, "We cannot escape noting too the change in attitudes—in recent years—of professional bodies such as the American Medical Association, the American Public Health Association, and the American Bar Association, and, indeed the changing attitudes of the courts of this country."[129] Blackmun's files contained articles from the *American Journal of Public Health* that made abortion reform seem almost inevitable, as well as an article from the *Atlanta Journal-Constitution* in which a Georgia doctor argued that the state's abortion reform law was too restrictive and thus unworkable. Greenhouse and Siegel suggest that Blackmun and the other justices may have also taken the support of Powell, the former president of the ABA, as yet another indicator of establishment support for reform.[130]

Conclusion

In this chapter, I showed that the British and Canadian reforms preserved medical gatekeeping while the American reform abandoned it, and Canadian gatekeeping requirements were stricter than those in Britain. I explained these differences by showing how political institutions (state-level policy making, nonpartisan legislative processes, and judicial review) mediated the actions of social movements, governments, and courts. I showed that the American pro-choice movement eventually became larger and more radical than its counterparts in Britain and Canada. I also argued that prolonged and dispersed state-level policy making in the United States facilitated social learning by the public and elites and strategic learning by abortion reformers. It also facilitated alliances among the abortion reform movement and the feminist, civil liberties, and population control movements. In the other countries, abortion reforms occurred quickly and early—locking in the narrow demands of elite reformers. The British and Canadian governments quietly supported abortion reform while American politicians shied away from the abortion issue after 1970. The British and Canadian reforms were also facilitated by nonpartisan parliamentary processes that helped governments avoid blame. The American reform was enabled by a policy venue, the Supreme Court, that insulated decision makers from mass opinion and amplified the influence of professional elites.

In the next chapter, I examine the construction of medical interests and priorities on abortion. Medical interest groups in all three countries initially tried to preserve their gatekeeping power over abortions, but, as we shall see, the AMA eventually yielded to abortion on request. The next chapter explains why this was so.

THREE

Medical Interests and Priorities

Few scholars have noticed the relative disengagement of the American medical profession from abortion politics and policy making.[1] It is particularly surprising, given the highly medicalized language of the *Roe* and *Doe* decisions. This disengagement is especially glaring when American medical associations are compared with their counterparts in Britain and Canada, and it is crucial for understanding differences in abortion politics and policies among the three countries. First, the differing positions and priorities of the medical associations affected the reforms of the Long 1960s—one reason that the American reform was more liberal than the others was because American doctors did not push as hard as British and Canadian doctors to maintain their status as gatekeepers, eventually accepting abortion on request, with important implications for Supreme Court decision making. Second, the positions of medical associations during the reforms of the Long 1960s affected their orientations during later political struggles.[2] British and Canadian medical associations, unlike the AMA, have remained involved in the abortion issue—opposing most antiabortion legislation and sometimes pushing for the expansion of abortion services. Third, the decline of medical issue definitions and medical responsibility for the issue in the United States increased controversy and made abortion rights more vulnerable to attack. In Britain and Canada, abortion discourse focused on a widely accepted "right to health," while in the United States the discourse focused on more contested and controversial rights of "privacy" and "bodily integrity."[3] The British and Canadian reforms delegated responsibility for abortion to the medical profession, removing the issue from public decision making and confining it to a realm in which decisions were made "neutrally" on the basis of "knowledge." By contrast, the American reform made abortion a public issue decided on the basis of "values."[4] Finally, the minimal involvement of American mainstream medicine in abortion provision reduced the availability of abortions by concentrating provision in single-purpose clinics in large cities and served by doctors that were often stigmatized by their mainstream peers. British abortion services were better distributed and better integrated into mainstream medicine, though Canadian ones were not.[5] In this chapter, I explain the differing engagement of the medical associations with abortion politics by focusing on the ways in which they constructed their "interests" and priorities in the context of national medical-care systems.

Professional Dominance and Medical Gatekeeping

Many scholars, most famously Eliot Freidson, have argued that doctors held the dominant position in the health-care division of labor during the Long 1960s. A key facet of this "professional dominance" was "clinical autonomy"—doctors' control over the substance of their work, autonomy from supervision, and power over patients and other health workers. Clinical autonomy was a source of considerable power as doctors argued from expertise that could be challenged only by other doctors. Doctors maintained and strengthened this special status by claiming to be trustworthy, knowledgeable, and ethical and by institutionalizing their control over licensure, services, and facilities.[6]

The professional dominance perspective, a form of interest group theory, suggests that medical organizations faced with the abortion issue will seek protection from prosecution while maximizing their clinical autonomy. And indeed, this is how medical associations in all three countries initially approached abortion reform. When policy makers began to consider reform proposals in the 1960s, medical associations worried aloud that legal regulation of abortion might intrude on clinical autonomy by too closely specifying when abortions could be provided. They also worried that abortions for "nonmedical" reasons might reduce clinical autonomy by creating categories of patients who were automatically eligible for abortions. These patients might "expect" abortions—removing the necessity of diagnoses and turning doctors into "mere technicians." For these and other reasons, medical organizations also opposed "abortion on demand."[7] The associations also sought to guard against abortion "profiteers" who might provide large numbers of abortions "on demand" and for exorbitant fees and thus bring the profession into disrepute. To prevent this, the associations advocated gatekeeping by either hospital abortion committees, multiple doctors, or elite specialists. They also thought that abortions should be confined to hospitals. Only mainstream doctors could practice in hospitals, and there they could supervise each other. Although requirements that more than one doctor approve abortions or that they be performed in hospitals reduced the clinical autonomy of individual doctors, they maintained doctors' collective autonomy by preserving their shared reputation for ethicality and trustworthiness.

Interest group theories of policy making argue that policy differences across countries are mainly the result of differences in the relative power of interest groups. Though the medical profession was quite powerful in all three of the countries, American doctors were usually viewed as the strongest given their success in preserving a highly lucrative, private fee-for-service medical system. Thus, interest group theories would predict that the American medical profession would be the most likely to succeed in preserving the medical gatekeeping of abortion. Instead, it was British and Canadian doctors who did so. In this chapter, I argue that, contrary to the assumptions of interest group theories, the preferences, and especially the priorities, of medical organizations varied across the three countries, and as a result, so did their engagement with abortion policy. British and Canadian medical associations were deeply involved in abortion policy making, while American medical associations were much less so. In other words, it was not the differing strength of the associations that mattered, but their differing preferences and priorities.

As I mention in the last chapter, medical gatekeeping had three main dimensions—why, who, and where? Why were abortions approved—for reasons of life endangerment, health, fetal abnormality, rape, incest, social reasons, or patients' own reasons? Who approved them—hospital committees, elite specialists, multiple doctors, a single doctor, or patients themselves? And where were they provided—in accredited hospitals, unaccredited hospitals, or private clinics? Table 3.1 summarizes the positions of the medical associations on each of these dimensions. Initially, all of the medical associations supported abortions for grounds of life endangerment, health (including mental health), and fetal abnormality but opposed abortions for social grounds and for patients' own reasons. But while the Canadian and American associations supported grounds

Table 3.1 Positions of Medical Associations on Abortion Gatekeeping[1]

	BMA-RCOG 1966	CMA 1967	AMA 1967	AMA 1970
Why are abortions approved?				
Life endangerment and health (including mental health)	+	+	+	
Fetal abnormality	+	+	+	
Social grounds[2]	(−)	(−)	(−)	
Patient's own reasons ("abortion on demand")	(−)	(−)	(−)	+[4]
Rape (including statutory rape) or incest	(−)[3]	+	+	
Mental disability of pregnant woman	(−)[3]			
Who approves abortions?				
Multiple doctors	+	+	+	+
Elite specialists	+			
Hospital committees		+		
Patient	(−)	(−)	(−)	(−)
Where are abortions provided?				
Public or accredited hospitals	+	+	+	+
Private nursing homes (by NHS consultants)	+			

[1] The British Medical Association (BMA), the Royal College of Obstetricians and Gynaecologists (RCOG), the Canadian Medical Association (CMA), and the American Medical Association (AMA). Support (+), Opposition (−). Blank cells indicate that the associations did not express a view on the issue.
[2] The specific meaning of "social grounds" varied, but it generally included such conditions as being poor, single, young, old, or caring for a large family.
[3] The BMA and RCOG opposed explicit grounds for these situations and argued that they should be incorporated under health grounds.
[4] The AMA's 1970 resolution did not specify abortion grounds but said that abortions should be provided only when they were in "the best interests of the patient" and not in "mere acquiescence to the patient's demand."

for rape (including statutory rape) and incest, the British associations opposed such grounds, as well as grounds for the mental disability of the pregnant woman, because they thought such situations should be covered under health grounds. And although the AMA initially supported abortion only for specified grounds, it abandoned such specification in 1970, requiring only that abortions be provided when they were "in the best interests of the patient," but not in "mere acquiescence to the patient's demand." On the issue of who would approve abortions, the British associations and the AMA thought that abortions should be approved by multiple doctors (two for the BMA and three for the AMA), and the British associations thought that one of these should be a consultant (an elite specialist in the NHS). The CMA thought that abortions should be approved by a three-person hospital abortion committee. All of the associations opposed letting a single doctor or the patient herself decide. On the issue of abortion facilities, all of the medical associations supported the restriction of abortions to mainstream medical settings—public hospitals in Britain and accredited hospitals in Canada and the United States.[8] The BMA also supported the provision of abortions in private nursing homes if they were performed by NHS consultants.

The degree to which medical associations participated in reform efforts also varied. As table 3.2 shows, the British and Canadian medical associations were much more active than the AMA. The BMA and the CMA took both internal and external actions on abortion—lobbying and sending reports to policy makers, testifying before Parliament, and making their case in the press. The AMA merely enacted internal resolutions on abortion and avoided taking actions outside the association.

As the professional dominance perspective would expect, British medical associations worked hard, and successfully, to preserve medical gatekeeping over abortion. The BMA and the Royal College of Obstetricians and Gynaecologists (RCOG) did not initially see a need for abortion reform; they thought that the existing law, with the health grounds supplied by the *Bourne* decision, was sufficient, but once reform became likely, the associations worked to ensure that it would preserve medical gatekeeping. The RCOG was the leader of the BMA-RCOG partnership on abortion and was also the association more hostile to reform. Steel claimed that the BMA influenced him more than the RCOG, but this was not quite accurate since the BMA often adopted the more conservative positions of the RCOG as its own.[9] In 1964, the BMA suspected that the new Labour Government might introduce abortion legislation because it had appointed Kenneth Robinson, the sponsor of an earlier abortion reform bill, as minister of health.[10] The BMA asked Parliament to delay legislation until a BMA committee could complete a report, and then released an interim report when Lord Lewis Silkin went ahead anyway.[11] The RCOG suggested that the Government establish its own committee to study abortion before proceeding with legislation, but the Government declined to do so.[12] In 1966, the BMA and RCOG issued a joint report on abortion.

Liberal MP David Steel consulted extensively with the medical associations during the drafting and subsequent amendment of his 1967 bill, and accepted many of their suggestions.[13] Over the objections of the ALRA, which had persuaded him to introduce the bill in the first place, he withdrew grounds for economic hardship, rape, underage pregnancy,

Table 3.2 Actions of Medical Associations on Abortion Reform

	Internal Actions	External Actions
British Medical Association and Royal College of Obstetricians and Gynaecologists		
1965	BMA Representative Body directs BMA Council to prepare report.[1]	BMA Representative Body directs BMA Council to ask government for delay.[1] BMA leaders ask bill sponsor to delay until release of BMA report.[2] RCOG calls for Interdepartmental Committee on abortion.[3]
1966	BMA Council approves interim report.[4] RCOG issues report, mentions potential for noncooperation.[7] BMA Council approves final report.[8] BMA and RCOG issue joint report.[9]	BMA Council sends interim report to bill sponsor. [4,5,6] BMA and RCOG meet with minister of health, home secretary, and bill sponsors.[2,10,11] BMA leaders send letter to bill sponsor welcoming amendments.[2]
1967		BMA Council sends copies of BMA-RCOG report to House of Commons standing committee.[10] BMA Council encourages BMA division secretaries to write to local MPs that are members of House of Commons standing committee.[10] BMA and RCOG leaders visit bill sponsors seeking amendments.[2,12,13,14] BMA and RCOG publish letter in *Times* opposing bill as written[2,12,13]
Canadian Medical Association		
1963	CMA discusses abortion reform at annual meeting.[15,16]	CMA asks justice minister for interpretation of abortion law.[17,18]
1965	Council adopts resolution to collect data on abortions in each province.[19]	Council adopts resolution to discuss issue with Canadian Bar Association[19]
1966	CMA adopts resolution with health grounds.[20]	CMA sends resolution to minister of justice and suggests that government reform abortion laws.[20]
1967	CMA adopts second resolution.[21]	CMA testifies before parliamentary committee.[22]
American Medical Association		
1964	Board of Trustees establishes Committee on Human Reproduction.[23]	
1965	Committee on Human Reproduction issues report urging states to enact ALI reforms; House of Delegates rejects.[24]	
1967	Committee on Human Reproduction issues report supporting ALI reforms, but not urging state action; House of Delegates approves.[25]	
1969	Section on Preventive Medicine offers resolution urging states to repeal abortion laws; House of Delegates rejects.[26]	
1970	Board of Trustees offers resolution stating abortion between woman and her doctor; House of Delegates approves compromise measure.[27]	
1971	Abortion rights attorneys ask AMA to submit amicus brief in *Roe v. Wade*; AMA declines.[28]	

Table 3.2 (*continued*)

[1] BMA, "Annual Representative Meeting: Abortion," *British Medical Journal Supplement*, July 17, 1965, 54.
[2] Keith Hindell and Madeline Simms, *Abortion Law Reformed* (London: Peter Owen, 1971).
[3] Hector MacLennan, "Draft of President's Letter to the *Times* for Comment by Members of the Finance and Executive Committee, Royal College of Obstetricians and Gynaecologists" (1965).
[4] BMA, "Proceedings of Council: Therapeutic Abortion," *British Medical Journal Supplement*, January 22, 1966, 19-20.
[5] British Medical Journal, "Leading Articles: Therapeutic Abortion," *British Medical Journal*, January 29, 1966, 248-49.
[6] British Medical Journal, "Leading Articles: Legislation on Abortion," *British Medical Journal*, March 5, 1966, 559-60.
[7] RCOG, "Legalized Abortion: Report by the Council of the Royal College of Obstetricians and Gynaecologists," *British Medical Journal* 1 (1966): 850-52.
[8] BMA, "Proceedings of Council: Therapeutic Abortion," *British Medical Journal Supplement*, July 9, 1966, 10-11.
[9] BMA and the RCOG, "Medical Termination of Pregnancy Bill: Views of the British Medical Association and the Royal College of Obstetricians and Gynaecologists," *British Medical Journal*, December 31, 1966, 1649-50.
[10] BMA, "Annual Report of Council: Therapeutic Abortion," *British Medical Journal Supplement*, May 6, 1967, 66.
[11] BMA, "Abortion Law Reform," *British Medical Journal Supplement*, November 12, 1966, 191.
[12] British Medical Journal, "Leading Articles: Abortion Law," *British Medical Journal*, December 31, 1966, 1607.
[13] Malcolm Potts, Peter Diggory, and John Peel, *Abortion* (Cambridge: Cambridge University Press, 1977).
[14] David Gullick, Under Secretary, BMA, to Sir John Peel, President, RCOG, Medical Termination of Pregnancy Bill, Meeting at House of Commons 4th May, 1967, May 4, 1967.
[15] Alphonse de Valk, *Morality and Law in Canadian Politics: The Abortion Controversy* (Montreal: Palm, 1974).
[16] Frederick Lee Morton, *Pro-Choice vs. Pro-Life: Abortion and the Courts in Canada* (Norman: University of Oklahoma Press, 1992).
[17] Jane Jenson, "Getting to Morgentaler: From One Representation to Another," in *The Politics of Abortion*, ed. Janine Shelly Brodie, S. A. M. Gavigan, and J. Jenson (Toronto: Oxford University Press, 1992).
[18] Marilyn J. Field, "The Determinants of Abortion Policy in Developed Nations," *Policy Studies Journal* 7 (1979): 771-81.
[19] CMA, *Transactions of the Ninety-eighth Annual Meeting of the Canadian Medical Association* (Ottawa: CMA Archives, 1965).
[20] CMA, *Transactions of the Ninety-ninth Annual Meeting of the Canadian Medical Association* (Ottawa: CMA Archives, 1966).
[21] CMA, *Transactions of the General Council at the One Hundredth Annual Meeting of the Canadian Medical Association* (Ottawa: CMA Archives, 1967).
[22] Canada House of Commons, "Minutes and Proceedings and Evidence of the Standing Committee on Health Welfare and Social Affairs," October 31, 1967, 97-116.
[23] Interview with AMA official no. 3, November 2002.
[24] AMA, *House of Delegate Proceedings, Clinical Convention* (Chicago: AMA, 1965).
[25] AMA, *House of Delegate Proceedings, Annual Convention* (Chicago: AMA, 1967).
[26] AMA, *House of Delegate Proceedings, Clinical Convention* (Chicago: AMA, 1969).
[27] AMA, *House of Delegate Proceedings, Annual Convention* (Chicago: AMA, 1970).
[28] David J. Garrow, *Liberty and Sexuality: The Right to Privacy and the Making of* Roe v. Wade (New York: Macmillan, 1994).

and mental disability of the pregnant woman. At the same time, he broadened health grounds to include the "future well-being" of the pregnant woman and included some implicit social grounds: the health of "existing children" in the family and a clause that allowed doctors to take account of the the pregnant woman's "actual or reasonably forseeable environment" while assessing "health." This medicalization of the social clauses was based on suggestions by Anglican church leaders and the Scottish abortion reformer Dr. Dugald Baird.[14] Steel later removed "future well-being" from the health clause in response to the BMA and RCOG's objection that it might lead to abortion "for convenience," but he did not agree to their request for a consultant requirement because he felt the small number of available consultants would serious restrict abortion access in the country.[15] As the House of Commons deliberated over the bill, the BMA and RCOG sent their joint report to the standing committee and published a joint letter in the *Times* opposing any bill without a consultant requirement.

In Canada, the reform also fit the professional dominance perspective. Canadian medical associations were deeply engaged with abortion reform and successfully preserved medical gatekeeping. In Canada, unlike the other countries, the profession was largely responsible for putting the issue on the public agenda and faced little movement opposition to its preferences. The profession first took up the issue in 1959, in a symposium on abortion law published in the *University of Toronto Medical Journal*. Doctors complained that the existing abortion law, resting on the English *Bourne* decision, was too vague and exposed them to possible prosecution. In 1961, leaders of the British Columbia Medical Association and the Ontario Medical Association (OMA) called for statutory codification of the *Bourne* decision.[16] The CMA also asked the federal justice minister to provide an interpretation of abortion law, but he declined, claiming that this was the responsibility of the provinces and the courts.[17] In 1966, and again in 1967, the CMA General Council called for a new abortion law;[18] the 1967 proposal allowed abortions for grounds of life, health (including mental health), rape, incest, or fetal abnormality, but it did not include social grounds or allow abortion on request.[19] Canada's 1969 abortion reform largely followed the CMA's recommendations.

The American case, however, ran contrary to the professional dominance perspective. American medical associations were only minimally involved in abortion policy making, did not fight very hard to preserve medical gatekeeping, and eventually lost it. Doctors played a central role in abortion reform, but they did so largely outside of mainstream professional associations. Many state-level reforms took place without state medical societies taking positions, let alone leadership. By the end of 1967, thirty states had considered abortion bills, but less than half of the medical societies in those states had adopted positions on those bills,[20] and of the ten state reforms enacted between 1967 and 1969, state medical societies took an official position in only five (California, Delaware, Georgia, Maryland, and Oregon).[21] Even in states where medical societies supported reforms, they often did not put them on the agenda.[22] In the four states that completely repealed their nineteenth-century abortion laws, state medical societies were early supporters of the Alaska repeal, late supporters of the Washington and Hawaii repeals, and opponents of the New York repeal.[23] The national AMA only endorsed the ALI model in June 1967, after three states had already enacted ALI reforms and twenty others were considering them. A proposal to allow abortion on request failed miserably at the AMA's 1969 annual meeting.[24] But at the 1970 annual meeting, the association passed a resolution that accommodated recent abortion law repeals; it suggested that three doctors should approve abortions but, unlike earlier resolutions, did not specify the grounds on which they should approve them. Abortions could be performed when they were "in the best interests of the patient," though not in "mere acquiescence to the patient's demand."[25] The AMA had yielded on medical gatekeeping—abortions could be provided for any reason.[26]

What accounts for these differences in the involvement of the medical associations in the abortion reforms and in their ability and willingness to preserve medical gatekeeping? Below, I argue that policy legacies—and in particular, systems of medical care—shaped the ways in which the associations constructed their "interests" and priorities. In all three countries, medical associations initially wished to retain their roles as abortion gatekeepers, but the AMA eventually ceded this role. The AMA's first priority was preserving private fee-for-service medicine, and this priority became particularly salient in 1970, as the AMA faced a growing movement for national health insurance. British medical organizations had already lost their battle against national health insurance two decades before and were thus free to focus on preserving clinical autonomy in the context of abortion gatekeeping. Canadian medical associations were fighting provincial health insurance battles, but because they put abortion reform on the agenda in the first place and faced little movement opposition to their preferences, they easily achieved them.

The medical-care system shaped the preferences of the medical associations in other ways as well. British and Canadian patients typically needed a referral from a primary care practitioner (PCP) before they could access the specialists that provided abortions. As a result, a larger number of doctors, both PCPs and ob/gyns, were involved in abortion provision, and abortions for mental health grounds brought psychiatrists into the mix as well. By contrast, American patients could access specialist abortion providers directly and abortion provision thus involved mainly ob/gyns. The creation of single-purpose clinics staffed by doctors specializing in abortion further narrowed the impact of abortion provision on the American medical profession.

The medical associations also had differing relations with the state—hostile in the United States and Canada, but cooperative in Britain. As a result, British doctors were more concerned about losing clinical autonomy to women patients, while American doctors were more concerned about losing it to the state. The Canadian medical profession was not particularly worried about either, mainly because it put abortion reform on the agenda, faced little opposition to its preferences from a tiny reform movement, and got most of what it wanted. In what follows, I examine the priorities of the medical associations, beginning with Britain where gatekeeping was a high priority, following with the United States where it was a low priority, and finishing with Canada—a mixed case.

Britain: Gatekeeping Is a High Priority; Patients Are More Threatening than the State

The BMA and the RCOG were the main medical associations involved in abortion reform—though others were active, none had the clout of these two.[27] The BMA represented both general practitioners (GPs) and consultants, but the majority of its members were GPs. The RCOG represented consultant ob/gyns, and especially the leaders of those specialties.[28] The executive councils of the two associations made most decisions on abortion policy; legislative bodies participated minimally.[29] The medical associations constructed their interests and priorities in the context of the NHS. Established in 1948, it was a classic example of a "state hierarchical" health-care system, in which a centralized organization controlled most aspects of medical care. The state owned and ran hospitals, and consultants were state employees. GPs were independent contractors, but almost all of their income came from the state.[30] British policy making often occurs through negotiation between insider interest groups and state bureaucrats, and health policy was no different. The health ministry and the medical associations were interdependent and closely linked; the NHS could not operate without medical labor, and British medical leaders were extensively involved in NHS administration.[31]

CHAPTER THREE

The British health-care system affected the engagement and positions of the medical associations on abortion reform in a number of ways. To begin, it determined the number of doctors affected by the reform. By the 1960s, virtually all doctors participated in the NHS—though approximately half of consultants and a third of GPs also maintained private practices on the side. Doctors and policy makers expected that the vast majority of abortions would be provided within the NHS, and by NHS rules and medical ethics, patients seeking specialist services (including abortion services) could access them only with a referral from their GP.[32] As such, abortion reform had everyday implications for the majority of the medical profession. It affected not only ob/gyns but psychiatrists and GPs as well.

The health-care system also shaped the priority that medical associations gave to clinical autonomy and affected the number of issues on which medical associations contended. At the founding of the NHS in 1948, individual doctors suffered a loss of economic and organizational power, but they were compensated for this loss by an "underlying agreement" that guaranteed them clinical autonomy.[33] In comparison with the United States and Canada, British doctors had great clinical freedom; the British health ministry had no formal control over GPs aside from restricting them to certain geographic areas; it had little control over salaried consultants; and GPs and consultants were not subject to any formal system of peer review or utilization review as in the United States.[34] The "underlying agreement" elevated the priority of clinical autonomy for British doctors: British medical associations viewed clinical autonomy as a core issue, even *the* core issue, and they rebelled against any infringement on it.[35]

Clinical autonomy gained further priority from the short list of issues on which British doctors contended. Moran and Wood write that:

The high water mark of UK medicine was probably in the late 1960s. In that era of what has often been labeled "consensus politics" the prevailing wisdom was that experts knew best. Hence health care should be left to doctors. . . . While the costs of the NHS, the pay of doctors, and the role and status of general practitioners had all at one time been extremely contentious political issues, by 1965 negotiated agreements between the BMA and the government had been reached on each of these three.[36]

Large questions of national health insurance and the relationship of doctors to the state had largely been settled by the time of the abortion reforms. With such a short agenda, British doctors were free to devote their resources to protecting clinical autonomy.

Given the large number of doctors affected by reform and the fact that the medical associations viewed clinical autonomy as a central issue, they prioritized *abortion* clinical autonomy and the preservation of medical gatekeeping. As I showed earlier, the BMA and RCOG were actively involved in the abortion debate from beginning to end. The positions of the British medical associations on abortion reform were fairly similar to those of the AMA and CMA, all approved of abortions for grounds of health and fetal abnormality, and all opposed social grounds and abortions for women's own reasons, but, unlike the AMA, the British medical associations explicitly and repeatedly expressed concerns about clinical autonomy. The associations argued that doctors should make the decisions about the necessity of abortions and should base those decisions solely on medical criteria. They argued that "nonmedical" criteria would prevent doctors from assessing each case "on its own merits," compromise the "freedom of action" of doctors, lead to doctors being "coerced" or "pressured," and lead patients to believe that abortions would be carried out "automatically."[37]

The RCOG's statement opposing grounds for underage pregnancy is telling:

Gynaecologists and other doctors concerned must retain their freedom of action and never be put in the position of being coerced by the terms of the Bill and the conditions of their employment into terminating a pregnancy if they have any ethical objections, and unless *they themselves* are convinced that it is in the best interests of a particular woman and her potential child.[38]

The medical-care system not only led the medical associations to prioritize clinical autonomy, but affected the balance that they sought between state and patient infringements on that autonomy. Given the close relationship between doctors and the state, contacts among the BMA, the RCOG, and policy makers on abortion had more the character of consultation than lobbying. The abortion bill's sponsor, Liberal MP David Steel, was very responsive to BMA and RCOG suggestions and visited the BMA's offices for some meetings.[39] Steel's main cosponsor in the House of Commons, Michael Winstanley, was a BMA local official. According to ALRA Executive Director Vera Houghton, "It was obvious to us ... that Mr. Steel [and] Dr. Winstanley ... were going to feel much happier if the bill had the support of the BMA and that they considered this support would greatly facilitate its passage."[40] A confidential exchange between Sir John Peel, president of the RCOG, and Steel illustrates Steel's desire to keep the medical associations on board. Steel asked the BMA and RCOG to offer more "positive encouragement" in the press for his attempts to translate "what we are agreed should be the intention of the law into actual words" rather than "dwelling on the negative attitudes of the profession to defects in the existing bill" and complained that the press had given "the unfortunate impression" that the associations "are opposed to the bill as such and this lends weight to the view of those who would argue that no weight should be attached to any views expressed by the B.M.A. and the R.C.O.G." Peel replied that the association's views had been "misrepresented in the newspapers," perhaps deliberately, and told Steel that "I very much take your point that we should try to be constructive and not deconstructive."[41] The BMA and RCOG also met with the Government's health and justice ministers, who in turn negotiated with Steel. Steel was not a member of the governing Labour Party and needed both Labour votes and extra time from the Government to pass his bill.[42] Because the NHS was dependent on medical labor, the RCOG threateningly declared that Parliament should assure that doctors would cooperate with the new law before changing it.[43]

Abortion reform threatened doctors' clinical autonomy by specifying the circumstances under which doctors could provide abortions. At the same time, *nonmedical* grounds allowed women patients to "demand" abortions. In their various reports, the BMA and RCOG expressed far more concern about patient infringements on clinical autonomy than state ones. The joint BMA-RCOG report argued that the law should not restrict doctors' discretion unduly by defining abortion grounds too narrowly. The associations opposed clauses in Steel's bill that required that risks to health be "serious" or "grave."[44] But these concerns about state infringements took a clear back seat to concerns about infringements by women patients. Repeatedly, the medical associations expressed misgivings about "demands" from women patients. The British medical associations opposed specific grounds for rape. By contrast, the AMA and CMA supported such grounds. The BMA argued that the legislation should not contain "nonmedical" grounds such as economic hardship, rape, or underage pregnancy because such circumstances would be adequately covered under health grounds. It argued that a ground for underage pregnancies "might lead to pressure being placed on the girl herself, or on the doctors in charge of the case, to terminate pregnancy in cases where the attending doctors believe in all the circumstances that there are insufficient grounds for terminating pregnancy."[45]

Likewise, the BMA-RCOG joint report argued that the so-called social clauses would lead women to believe that they were entitled to an "automatic" abortion.

These [clauses] are objectionable in specifying indications which are not medical. . . . They might well lead to an excessive demand for terminations on social grounds, and this would be unacceptable to medical professionals. Each case has to be assessed on its own merits, and express reference to [these grounds], though only permissive, would inevitably lead the public to believe that termination would automatically be carried out in the instances mentioned.[46]

The medical system affected the interests and power of medical associations in a few other ways as well. Because British doctors were employed by the state, their gatekeeping role seemed more legitimate than that of self-employed American doctors. And because preventive and curative medicine were not as divided in Britain as in the United States and Canada, British doctors may have felt greater responsibility for the injuries and deaths caused by illegal abortions.[47] Elite culture probably played a role too. "Red toryism," an ideology that emphasizes the social responsibilities of elites and encourages them to collaborate with the state on redistributive policies, may have increased British doctors' sense of responsibility for ensuring abortion access for the poor.[48] Furthermore, some scholars have argued that the British public is more willing to defer to technical elites than the American public.[49]

The BMA and RCOG treated abortion policy as a high priority: They expended considerable effort opposing "nonmedical" grounds for abortion and strongly influenced the reform. Still, they did not get everything they wanted. The reform included implicit social grounds—the health of "existing children in the family" and a clause that allowed doctors to take into account "the pregnant woman's actual or reasonably foreseeable environment" as they evaluated risks to health. The reform also did not include a consultant requirement as the doctors had asked; abortions could be performed by any doctor. Finally, as I show in the next chapter, although the doctors had no objection to the provision of abortions outside hospitals, they expected those abortions to be provided by NHS consultants—they did not envision the rapid emergence of single-purpose abortion clinics run by abortion rights activists.

United States: Gatekeeping Is a Low Priority; the State Is More Threatening than Patients

In the United States, the AMA, along with its affiliated state medical societies, was the central medical interest organization—no other had its influence.[50] Its membership included both family practitioners and specialists, but also a disproportionate number of older, conservative, family practitioners from rural areas.[51] The AMA's legislature, the House of Delegates, was quite democratic, but elections to that body were not. The presidents of state and county medical societies appointed the committees charged with nominating delegates, and because campaigning was prohibited, their nominees were rarely defeated, and a small group of influential incumbents and their hand-chosen successors dominated the organization.[52]

The interests and priorities of the AMA on abortion were constructed in the context of a fee-for-service health-care system that combined private and public elements. Most citizens had private insurance provided by their employer, but the Medicare and Medicaid programs (established despite the opposition of the AMA in 1965) provided health insurance for the elderly and some of the poor, and a little more than 10 percent of the population remained uninsured. Doctors billed patients or insurers directly for each service provided.[53] During the first half of the twentieth-century, the AMA opposed, usually successfully and often in the name of anticommunism, government involvement in the economics or organization of health care. It opposed national health insurance in the Progressive era, the New Deal, and Truman's Fair Deal; federal funding of medical schools until the 1960s; and Medicaid and Medicare during the Johnson administration.[54]

The medical-care system shaped the AMA's interests and priorities on abortion reform. To start, it determined the number of doctors affected by reform. In the private, fee-for-service system, patients could access specialists directly without a referral from a PCP; this limited the role of PCPs in abortion. Ob/gyns would be the main group affected, and they were initially quite concerned about this; a delegate to the AMA's 1967 convention worried that "the office hours of the obstetrician are going to be longer and longer, although he will spend less and less time in the delivery room."[55] But by the time the AMA changed position in 1970 to allow abortions whenever they were "in the best interests" of patients, ob/gyns were less concerned about the impact of abortion reform on their practices. By 1970, abortion law repeals had been enacted in New York and Hawaii, and de facto abortion on request had been established in California and the District of Columbia. The AMA's Board of Trustees referred specifically to these repeals when it proposed that the association liberalize its abortion position. The experiences of California and the District of Columbia suggested both that there would be less demand for abortions than predicted, and that this demand could be accommodated by a small number of hospitals or clinics doing large numbers of abortions. Such abortions had been deemed safe in a study by Johns Hopkins University and the University of California, San Francisco School of Medicine.[56] In essence, abortion could be organized as its own specialty rather than as a normal part of ob/gyn practice, and ob/gyns could avoid providing abortions if they so chose. Moreover, in a medical system in which doctors were private actors, they would not face pressure from state employers to provide abortions, as would their publicly employed counterparts in Britain. Reform would affect only a small number of AMA members. Its main effect would be on ob/gyns, and then only on those who chose to perform abortions. Ob/gyns would have ample opportunity to "exit" abortion provision, and they would eventually do so in large numbers; by 1980, a mere seven years after *Roe*, 75 percent of abortions were provided in single-purpose clinics.[57]

The medical-care system also affected the orientations of AMA leaders to clinical autonomy and the number of core issues on which they contended. Numerous analysts have suggested that the American medical profession has traded aspects of its clinical autonomy for power over the economics and organization of health care.[58] Many of the most burdensome controls on clinical autonomy occurred only after 1970, but even before then, the AMA accepted systems of peer review and utilization review that would have been unthinkable in Britain and Canada (e.g., the Joint Commission on Accreditation of Hospitals and utilization review under Medicare).[59] This does not mean that AMA leaders did not care about clinical autonomy. In fact, they often argued that economic power and organizational power were necessary for its preservation.[60] The point is that clinical issues had lower priority than economic and organizational ones. In contrast to Britain, American medical associations continued to battle over national health insurance and the role of government in medicine. Until these issues were settled, the AMA had to make decisions about how to allocate its political resources. Issues of clinical autonomy often got short shrift.

The AMA leadership initially avoided the abortion debate. In 1960, a Los Angeles psychiatry professor and a deputy district attorney urged the AMA convention to reform abortion laws, but received no response.[61] Four years later, the AMA Board of Trustees established a Committee on Human Reproduction,[62] which, a year later, submitted a report to the Board of Trustees recommending that the House of Delegates urge the states to enact ALI-style abortion legislation.[63] The board sent the report to the House of Delegates without endorsing it, and the reference committee charged with considering the report opposed AMA involvement in the abortion debate, arguing that it was the responsibility of state

CHAPTER THREE

legislatures.[64] The committee also suggested that a more liberal AMA abortion stance might jeopardize the legitimacy of state medical examining boards,[65] which had the power to grant and revoke licenses for medical practice and were usually controlled by the AMA's state affiliates. These boards gave the AMA control over the supply and regulation of doctors—central economic and organizational issues for the association.[66] The committee argued that the association should not involve itself in this matter of clinical autonomy, lest it jeopardize its economic and organizational power, and the House of Delegates agreed.[67]

In June 1967, the AMA finally took a position on abortion reform, but only after California, Colorado, and North Carolina had become the first states to institute ALI-style reforms and twenty other states were considering them. The AMA's Committee on Human Reproduction offered a new report suggesting that "rather than recommending changes in state laws, the American Medical Association should adopt its own statement of position which can be used as a guide for component and constituent societies in states contemplating legislative reform."[68] The board approved the committee's report and forwarded it to the House of Delegates, where the reference committee lauded this new approach because it merely altered the AMA's internal position, but did not urge the states to take any particular action. The resolution resembled the position of the BMA; it allowed abortions for grounds of physical and mental health, fetal abnormality, and rape or incest, but did not allow abortion for social grounds or on request. It also required that abortions have the approval of three doctors and that they be performed in an accredited hospital. The AMA, unlike the British medical associations, did not make explicit statements about threats to clinical autonomy nor contact policy makers to reiterate their concerns.[69]

In December 1969, the AMA's Section on Preventive Medicine, composed of liberal-minded mostly publicly employed doctors, proposed a resolution urging states to repeal, not just reform, their abortion laws. The House of Delegates reference committee labeled the proposal "extreme," reporting that testimony was 12 to 1 against it,[70] and noting that polls of doctors showed that "an overwhelming majority" opposed "abortion on demand." The House of Delegates rejected the proposal despite picketing by feminist groups.[71]

But a mere six months later, the AMA changed its position, adopting a new resolution that no longer specified grounds for the approval of abortions. It is unlikely that the policy preferences of AMA leaders changed in such a short time; instead, abortion gatekeeping, already a low priority for AMA leaders, became lower still. In 1970, the AMA faced several crises that threatened its power over the economics and organization of medical care. Most important, enactment of national health insurance appeared imminent as the AMA battled a temporary coalition of government officials, business leaders, the insurance industry, traditional liberal reformers, and consumers' movements. Even President Nixon and the National Governor's Association expressed support for national health insurance.[72] The AMA was also losing members to new medical specialty organizations and confronting critiques from young and left-wing doctors who disrupted the AMA annual meetings of 1968 to 1970.[73] This was in marked contrast to the relative peace of British health politics.

With core issues at stake, the AMA had to prioritize. Abortion had previously been a low priority, but given these threats to the economic and organizational power of doctors, it was now an even lower one. When asked if abortion was a high priority at the time, an AMA board member replied, "Not at all. There are so many other things. Frankly, most doctors don't want anything to do with abortion."[74] A staff member in the AMA's Washington office agreed: "Abortion was not a top priority, in fact, it was not even in the top ten."[75] According to the staff member, higher priority issues included health maintenance organizations (HMOs), national health insurance, appropriations bills for the Department of Health, Education, and Welfare, and grants from the National Institutes of Health. "We had so many other things nationally that the AMA was interested in. We just couldn't afford to spend that much time on the abortion issue."[76] According to another AMA staff member, "When you talk about the 1970 annual meeting of the AMA House of Delegates, abortion certainly wasn't the most controversial issue before the House."[77] According to this staffer, higher priority issues included "socialized medicine," Medicare, the establishment of new specialty organizations, and malpractice insurance.

Not only was the AMA facing crises, but it was also under new pragmatic leadership that was willing to prioritize among AMA policy desires to focus on core issues. After the AMA's failure to prevent Medicare in 1965, members associated with the American Medical Political Action Committee (AMPAC) gained control of the board, fired the executive director, F. J. L. Blassingame, and devoted more resources to public affairs. The old leadership had dug in its heels to fight government initiatives of all kinds, but the new leadership was pragmatic and eager to polish the AMA's image through various concessions and expressions of concern about social issues.[78]

In a January 1970 speech, Executive Vice President Ernest B. Howard acknowledged that the AMA had failed in some respects—it was late to recognize doctor shortages, it failed to moderate medical costs, and it was

CHAPTER THREE

late to support federal funding of medical schools. But now the AMA was "with it" on the issues confronting the nation's health-care system:

> Today the nation faces a crucial decision: Whether to change radically the entire system of health care as we know it or to identify the gaps and deficiencies that do exist and take responsible action to correct them. We share the concern widely expressed regarding health care costs, inaccessible services, the needs of the poor, the pollution of the environment and all of the other difficult problems that I have mentioned in this talk.[79]

Among these problems was abortion. Howard pointed to the AMA's 1967 resolution on the issue as evidence of its concern.

In early 1970, New York and Hawaii repealed their abortion laws. In mid-May, the AMA Board of Trustees proposed a House of Delegates resolution that stated that abortion should be between a woman and her doctor.[80] The Board of Trustees noted that several states now allowed abortions for "reasons other than therapeutic" and predicted that other states would soon follow. "As a result, many physicians find themselves unable to perform a legalized medical procedure without violating the policy of their professional association."[81]

In June, the House of Delegates considered the Board of Trustees proposal along with five others. The South Carolina delegation and the Section on Preventive Medicine called for the repeal of all abortion laws. The Michigan delegation called for a reaffirmation of the 1967 resolution. Oregon and California called for a compromise between the two. A New Jersey delegate criticized the board's rationale for the new resolution: "It will mean that the ethics of the AMA will follow the election returns. If it's legal, it's ethical."[82] Testimony before the reference committee was divided between the board's proposal and retaining the 1967 position. Members of the National Federation of Catholic Physicians' Guilds and the New Jersey delegation led the opposition. The reference committee rejected the board's resolution and substituted it with a vaguer, more restrictive one that was eventually approved by the House of Delegates. The House also approved an amendment requiring doctors to consult with two others. The new resolution implicitly allowed abortion for any reason (if a doctor agreed to provide it in a state that had repealed its abortion laws) because, for the first time, it did not spell out specific grounds for abortions.[83] The resolution read:

> Whereas, Abortion, like any other medical procedure, should not be performed when contrary to the best interests of the patient since good medical practice requires due

consideration for the patient's welfare and not mere acquiescence to the patient's demand; and

Whereas, The standards of sound clinical judgment, which, together with informed patient consent should be determinative according to the merits of each individual case; therefore be it

RESOLVED, That abortion is a medical procedure and should be performed only by a duly licensed physician and surgeon in an accredited hospital acting only after consultation with two other physicians chosen because of their professional competency and in conformance with standards of good medical practice and the Medical Practice Act of his State; and be it further

RESOLVED, That no physician or other professional personnel shall be compelled to perform any act which violates his good medical judgment. Neither physician, hospital, nor hospital personnel shall be required to perform any act violative of personally-held moral principles. In these circumstances good medical practice requires only that the physician or other professional personnel withdraw from the case so long as the withdrawal is consistent with good medical practice.[84]

Some newspapers portrayed this resolution simply as a liberalization.[85] But others saw it as either a minor change or a vague compromise.[86] The *Washington Post*, quoting the chair of the reference committee, Wendell G. Scott, claimed that the AMA had rejected abortion on demand but allowed abortion for social reasons such as teenage pregnancy or desertion by one's husband.[87] AMA president-elect Dr. Wesley Hall admitted that the measure contained "a lot of ambiguous language" and was "pretty elastic."[88]

Accounts that saw the new resolution solely as a liberalization missed the fact that it only slightly reduced the autonomy of doctors in relation to women patients and, more important, that AMA leaders believed that it increased the clinical autonomy of doctors in relation to the state. Because of the AMA's historic mistrust of the state and its desire to preserve private medicine, it was more threatened by the latter than the former.

Unlike the British medical associations, the AMA did not make explicit statements about clinical autonomy in relation to women patients. The AMA's 1967 resolution allowed abortions for grounds of rape or incest and did not claim, as had the British associations, that such grounds might cause women to "demand" abortions or seek "automatic" abortions, and that this would infringe on doctors' clinical autonomy. Still, most doctors were opposed to abortion on request.[89] Some expressed discomfort with the way that it would diminish doctors' clinical autonomy

CHAPTER THREE

in relation to women patients;[90] a member of the AMA House of Delegates complained that "legal abortion makes the patient truly the physician: she makes the diagnosis and establishes therapy."[91] Even within the ASA, Guttmacher had reservations about acting as a "rubber stamp," and Hall noted that "when it comes to the doctor, I think he is eventually going to be no more than a technician. This may be humiliating to him."[92]

The 1970 resolution reduced doctors' clinical autonomy in relation to women patients because it no longer specified grounds for approving abortions, but the resolution also said that abortion should be approved by three doctors and should not be provided in "mere acquiescence to the patient's demand." As a matter of policy and practice, doctors retained the power to refuse abortions. They would later use that power extensively.

Moreover, AMA leaders believed that the resolution increased the clinical autonomy of doctors from the state. According to a top AMA executive at the time, the resolution preserved clinical autonomy, both in relation to patients and state authorities, through its lack of specificity:

If you simply say it's between the patient and the physician, then the physician has a lot of latitude and those who don't want to do abortions have absolutely no need to. And those that do want to do them don't have to explain, to authorities and such, why they do them. So this goes along a lot with, the doctor should decide, the doctor is the authority figure.[93]

When asked if the liberalization constituted "abortion on request," the executive replied:

No, because you're looking at it from the point of view of the woman and the AMA is looking at it from the point of view of the doctor. I would hope, given they were being reasonable, they considered both, but your principle job if you run the AMA is to protect your membership—the doctors. So how do you protect them from this tangle? Well you say that the whole business is up to the doctor—then he or she is protected—from the patient either way, or from the other people in the community. If the doctor's Catholic, they don't have to go along with *Roe v. Wade*. And if they do believe in abortion, then they can do it for other grounds than those listed previously.[94]

Not only did the American medical system affect the orientation of the AMA to clinical autonomy, the state and patients, but it shaped the interests and power of the AMA in other ways as well. Because American doctors were not deeply involved in the administration of a national health service, they had a less systemic outlook than British doctors. Most simply wanted to be left alone to practice private medicine. American doctors also had more difficulty legitimating their medical gatekeeping. In Britain, the location of doctors within the state and the less rampant face of capital in medicine promoted favorable public attitudes toward doctors and legitimated their role as agents of social control. By contrast, gatekeeping by American doctors could be painted as an illegitimate use of private power, and doctors could be portrayed as untrustworthy profiteers. To make matters worse, American doctors were at that moment suffering from public disrepute because of their success in molding previous health-care policies to their own interests and their well-publicized abuses of the Medicare reimbursement system.[95] Finally, preventive and curative medicine were more segregated in the United States than in the other countries, so the public health consequences of illegal abortions fell outside of the traditional domain of the medical profession.[96]

The Influence of the AMA on the Supreme Court

Though the AMA was only minimally engaged with the abortion issue, it had a disproportionate impact on the 1973 reform. Justice Harry Blackmun, the author and swing voter in the *Roe* decision, was both ambivalent about abortion rights and deeply respectful of medical opinion—a position reflected in both the *Roe* and *Doe* opinions as well as his later statements about them. In fact, Blackmun's ambivalent abortion jurisprudence echoes the vague and contradictory position of the AMA at the time; if the AMA had defended abortion gatekeeping more strongly, it seems likely that Blackmun would have done the same. It was precisely the AMA's failure to defend abortion gatekeeping that enabled Blackmun's liberal *Roe* opinion.

Here I briefly venture into the realm of biography rather than political sociology, but that is an unavoidable consequence of a policy venue that gives tremendous power to a mere nine individuals. Justice Blackmun had great respect for the medical profession. He had planned to become a doctor when he was young and before joining the federal bench served as counsel for Minnesota's Mayo Clinic; he called his years there the "happiest of his life" and instructed that a portion of his ashes be scattered there; and as he prepared the *Roe* and *Doe* opinions, he researched the Hippocratic oath in the clinic's law library. His files contained an article from the clinic's alumni magazine about alumnus Jane Hodgson's prosecution for providing an abortion for grounds of fetal abnormality. In his pre-*Roe* jurisprudence, Blackmun was often protective of doctors.[97] During the *Roe* and *Doe* oral arguments, he asked the attorneys to comment on the

Hippocratic oath, and when Roe's attorney Sarah Weddington replied that the oath was irrelevant to constitutional rights, Blackmun testily insisted that it was "the only definitive statement of ethics of the medical profession."[98] In the *Roe* and *Doe* opinions themselves, he discussed the oath at length, praised doctors with purple prose, and quoted the AMA position on abortion. His files contained heavily marked manuscript copies of both the 1967 and 1970 AMA resolutions on abortion.[99]

Table 3.3 shows the justices' positions on privacy rights in key contraception and abortion cases. The 1965 *Griswold v. Connecticut* decision was the key precedent for *Roe* and *Doe*. In *Griswold*, six justices voted to strike down an 1879 Connecticut statute banning the use of contraceptives on the grounds that it violated a right of marital privacy.[100] By the time the court decided whether to accept the *Roe* and *Doe* cases, it had gained three new members, the liberal Johnson appointee Thurgood Marshall and two Nixon appointees, the "Minnesota Twins" Harry Blackmun and Chief Justice Warren Burger, and another two seats were vacant. In their December 1971 conference on the abortion cases, all of the justices except Burger and White agreed that the nineteenth-century Texas statute, with its grounds of life endangerment, should be overturned. But there was no clear majority on the ALI-based Georgia statute: Brennan, Stewart, and Marshall wanted to overturn it while Burger and White wanted to uphold it, and Douglas and Blackmun appeared undecided and suggested remanding the case to the lower court so that it could assemble a more detailed record.[101] In his notes on the conference, Blackmun wrote that his "general impression" was that the Georgia law was "pretty good and strikes a good balance of the asserted interests."[102] And according to Douglas's notes, Blackmun told the conference that "Georgia has a fine statute."[103]

Typically, when the chief justice is in the minority, he lets the senior justice in the majority assign the case. But this time, Burger, though in the minority, assigned the cases himself, and assigned them to Blackmun, mostly likely in hopes that the ambivalent Blackmun would write a narrow opinion. Douglas, the senior justice in the majority, protested that the cases were his to assign, but Burger argued that there had been no clear majority in either case,[104] and said that both cases were strong candidates for reargument once Nixon's new appointees, William Rehnquist and Lewis Powell, joined the court.

On the same day that the *Roe* and *Doe* cases were argued, Brennan circulated a draft opinion in *Eisenstadt v. Baird* that extended contraceptive privacy rights to unmarried persons, and implicitly extended them to abortion. Roy Lucas argues that Brennan circulated the draft on that

MEDICAL INTERESTS AND PRIORITIES

Table 3.3 Positions of Supreme Court Justices on Privacy and Abortion, 1965–73[1]

Case	Griswold	Roe 1st conf	Doe 1st conf	Baird	Roe & Doe reargue	Roe 2nd conf	Doe 2nd conf	Roe & Doe
Year	1965	1971	1971	1972	1972	1972	1972	1973
Margin	(6–3)[2]	(5–2)	(3–2)	(4–3)[4]	(5–4)[5]	(7–1)	(6–2)	(7–2)
Clark	+							
Goldberg	+							
Warren	+							
Harlan	+							
Black	(–)							
Douglas	+	+	n/a[3]	+	+	+	+	+
Brennan	+	+	+	+	+	+	+	+
White	(–)	(–)	(–)	(–)	(–)	n/a[6]	(–)	(–)
Stewart	(–)	+	+	+	+	+	+	+
Marshall		+	+	+	+	+	+	+
Blackmun		+	n/a[3]	(–)	(–)	+	+	+
Burger		(–)	(–)	(–)	(–)	+	n/a[7]	+
Powell					(–)	+	+	+
Rehnquist					(–)	(–)	(–)	(–)

[1] Support or opposition to privacy rights or the extension of those rights to abortion.
[2] The official margin was 7 to 2. White concurred in *Griswold* but refused to recognize a right of privacy.
[3] Douglas and Blackmun favored remanding the case to the lower court so that a more detailed record of the workings of the statute could be assembled.
[4] The official margin was 6 to 1. Blackmun and White concurred in *Baird*, but for substantive rather than constitutional reasons.
[5] A vote in favor of rearguing the cases was a vote against the extension of privacy rights to abortion because the two new members of the court were expected to vote against such an extension.
[6] White passed on *Roe*.
[7] Burger did not take a position on *Doe*.

day to influence his colleagues' votes in the abortion cases.[105] The draft included the most famous sentence of the eventual *Eisenstadt* opinion: "If the right of privacy means anything, it is the right of the individual, married or single, to be free from unwarranted governmental intrusion into matters so fundamentally affecting a person as the decision whether to bear or beget a child."[106] When *Eisenstadt* was handed down in March 1972, Burger dissented and Blackmun joined White's concurrence, agreeing with the substantive outcome of the case but not its extension of privacy rights to unmarried persons.[107] Burger and Blackmun hardly seemed like potential supporters of a broad extension of privacy rights to abortion.

When Blackmun circulated his first *Roe* draft in May 1972, it overturned the Texas statute for a narrow reason—the vagueness of the life endangerment ground. Douglas and Brennan were dissatisfied with the draft and urged Blackmun to address the core issues of the case. Several days later, he circulated a *Doe* draft that recognized women's privacy rights but sought to balance them with the rights of the fetus and the interests of the state.[108] Douglas and Brennan liked that draft better, but were dismayed when Blackmun also moved that the cases be reargued once the new appointees joined the court. Along with Burger, White, and the two new appointees, Rehnquist and Powell, he formed a majority for reargument. Douglas angrily accused Burger of trying to both change the outcome of the case and delay the decision until after Nixon's reelection.[109] The outcome of *Roe* was now in doubt; Blackmun would be the swing voter, with Douglas, Brennan, Stewart, and Marshall on one side, and Burger, White, and presumably Rehnquist and Powell on the other.

The court heard the cases again in October 1972. In conference, all but Burger maintained their original positions. Burger now voted to strike down the Texas statute but appeared undecided on the Georgia one.[110] Powell voted to overturn both statutes, and Rehnquist voted to uphold them. Burger assigned the cases to Blackmun once again. Blackmun's new *Roe* draft allowed states to regulate abortion at the end of the first trimester, but Brennan, Marshall, and Powell pushed him to change this to viability. Blackmun offered a compromise—regulations to protect women's health were permissible after the first trimester, but regulations to protect fetal life were not permissible until after viability.[111]

Most of the voting in *Roe* and *Doe* could be predicted by the earlier political and judicial careers of the justices. But pro-choice lawyers, and probably Burger, were surprised by Blackmun's position.[112] Blackmun's *Roe* opinion reflected both his ambivalence about abortion and his deference to the medical profession. His first reference to the abortion decision leaves it in the hands of the woman: "This right of privacy . . . is broad enough to encompass a woman's decision whether or not to terminate her pregnancy."[113] But his second reference to the decision, later in the same paragraph, treats it as a joint decision of the woman and her doctor: "All these are factors the woman and her responsible physician necessarily will consider in consultation."[114] All subsequent references, including Blackmun's final summation of the holding, refer only to the doctor:

The decision vindicates the right of the physician to administer medical treatment according to his professional judgment up to the points where important state interests provide compelling justifications for intervention. Up to those points, the abortion decision in all its aspects is inherently, and primarily, a medical decision, and basic responsibility for it must rest with the physician.[115]

In fact, it wasn't until *Thornburgh v. American College of Obstetricians & Gynecologists* in 1986 that Blackmun put women at the center of his abortion jurisprudence.[116]

Blackmun's "hand-down" announcement of *Roe* and *Doe* to the press contained a final paragraph that he crossed out and did not deliver. Its first three sentences also reflected his ambivalence: "In closing, I emphasize what the Court does not do by these decisions. The Court does not hold that the Constitution compels abortion on demand. It does not pronounce that a pregnant woman has an absolute right to an abortion."[117] In his dissent, White disagreed, claiming that the decision allowed abortion for any reason "or for no reason at all."[118] But in his concurrence, Burger agreed with Blackmun:

> I do not read the Court's holdings today as having the sweeping consequences attributed to them by the dissenting Justices; the dissenting views discount the reality that the vast majority of physicians observe the standards of their profession, and act only on the basis of carefully deliberated medical judgments relating to life and health. Plainly, the Court today rejects any claim that the Constitution requires abortions on demand.[119]

Burger said that doctors "observed the standards of their profession" and acted only on the basis of "medical judgments related to life and health." But the standards of the profession, at least according to the AMA, now appeared to be broader than "life and health." Blackmun's opinion and the 1970 AMA resolution were actually a good match. The AMA resolution required approval by three doctors and prohibited "mere acquiescence to the patient's demand" but did not specify reasons for approving abortions; Blackmun's opinion did the same. It said that the abortion decision was "primarily, a medical decision" and warned practitioners not to abuse "the privilege of exercising proper medical judgment" but struck down any legally defined specifications as to when doctors could approve abortions.

Blackmun and Burger apparently wanted to leave the medical profession unregulated in the abortion realm, while expecting or hoping that it would regulate itself in a way that would not allow abortions "on demand." In some ways, this faith was not misplaced—most ob/gyns refused to provide abortions. But as the justices soon found out, relying on medical gatekeeping without providing grounds for that gatekeeping meant that many doctors would provide abortions for women's own reasons— especially as new clinics motivated by profit or feminism emerged. And despite Burger's protestation that the decisions did not provide "abortion on demand," this is what many headlines proclaimed.[120] We are left to wonder how *Roe* might have read if it had been decided a few years earlier or if the AMA had stuck to its 1967 position favoring specific grounds for abortion gatekeeping.

Canada: Gatekeeping Is a High Priority; Little Threat from Patients or the State

The CMA is a mixed case. Like the AMA, it had a history of antagonistic relations with the state and was busy fighting over national health insurance at the time of abortion reforms, but like the BMA, it strongly valued clinical autonomy. The Canadian constitution reserved health policy to the provinces but reserved criminal law, which included abortion law, to the federal government. As a result, provincial medical associations were the main actors in health policy, but recognized the CMA as their voice at the federal level and on the issue of abortion. The CMA included both GPs and specialists.[121] Its abortion policies were drafted by its Committee on Maternal Welfare, approved by the CMA's legislature and implemented by the Board of Directors.[122] The Canadian medical-care system combined private, fee-for-service provision with a universal public health insurance program, Medicare, established by a Liberal Government in 1966 over the objections of the medical profession.[123] The Medicare Act established provinces as medical-care payers, but left all other aspects of the previously private medical system intact.[124] Most services were provided in private or nonprofit hospitals and doctors' offices, and doctors were free to use any procedures they wished. Provinces merely negotiated annual increases in fee schedules with provincial medical associations.[125]

The medical-care system affected the interests and priorities of the medical associations on abortion in several ways. In Canada, as in Britain, patients are discouraged from seeing specialists without a referral from a GP. As a result, both ob/gyns and GPs would be involved with abortion; abortion reform would affect more doctors in Canada than in the United States; but the number of requests for abortion was expected to be fewer since the Canadian reform did not include social grounds as in Britain, or abortion on request as in the United States. As a result, most observers did not expect the reform to markedly increase the number of abortions.[126]

As in Britain, the enactment of national health insurance in Canada elevated the priority of clinical autonomy for the medical associations.

Medicare centralized the funding of medical care in each province, but left untouched the decentralized delivery system and doctors' clinical autonomy; while Canadian doctors lost much of their individual power over the economics of medical care, they maintained organizational and clinical power, and this elevated the priority of clinical autonomy. As Carolyn Tuohy writes:

> Physicians retained their status as independent professionals, trading off a degree of entrepreneurial discretion (particularly over price, but not, as in Britain, over location and practice inputs) in order to retain substantial collective and individual autonomy in clinical matters.[127]

The enactment of national health insurance did not, however, shorten the list of important issues for Canadian medical associations, as it did in Britain. In the decades after World War II, the medical profession thoroughly dominated health policy and had a cooperative relationship with the state, but a period of intense conflict began in the 1960s. In 1962, doctors in Saskatchewan went on strike in response to the province's universal public health insurance program, and in 1966, the medical profession opposed Medicare.[128] After losing that battle, the CMA and provincial medical associations turned their attention to influencing provincial Medicare plans seeking, and in most cases obtaining, "extra-billing" privileges that allowed them to set fees higher than the government's reimbursement rate and require patients to pay the difference.[129] The CMA's efforts to influence provincial Medicare plans were contemporary with abortion reform. The CMA also worried about efforts by the federal government to control health-care costs during this time: In 1969, a Government task force began examining ways to limit the cost of health services and eventually made the incendiary proposal that the provinces limit the annual increase in health expenditures to a percentage of gross national product.[130]

Unlike their British and American counterparts, Canadian medical associations were the first to put abortion reform on the agenda and, along with the CBA, were the main proponents of abortion reform. As a result, they never faced a significant challenge to their preferences. The only actors that suggested social grounds or abortion on request were the Humanist Fellowship of Canada (represented by Dr. Henry Morgentaler) and the Toronto Women's Liberation Group, but neither group was particularly influential. The National Council of Women, Canada's largest and most influential women's organization, did not support abortion on request. Nor did AMCAL.[131] Had the CMA faced a stronger challenge to medical gatekeeping, it is not clear what priority it might have assigned to abortion reform. The CMA's crowded agenda suggests a low priority, but the large number of doctors potentially affected by reform and the commitment of the profession to clinical autonomy suggest a high one. At any rate, the CMA did not need to expend much capital to achieve its desires. Probably as a result of this, the Canadian medical associations were less explicit in their defense of clinical autonomy—from the state and from women patients—than were the medical associations in Britain and the United States.

The CMA did not express concerns about state interference with clinical practice, as did the AMA. Nor did it attempt to keep abortion grounds as vague as possible to maximize doctors' discretion, as did the BMA. By advocating an expansion of abortion grounds to include fetal abnormality, it certainly sought greater freedom of operation, but it did not justify this in terms of clinical autonomy or the "doctor-patient relationship." This lack of concern about state interference may seem odd given the acrimonious relationship of the medical profession with the state at this time, but much of this conflict concerned economic issues such as "extra-billing" and cost control—not clinical practice. Based on their accommodation with the state, Canadian doctors were quite secure in their clinical autonomy.

As I mentioned earlier, the BMA and RCOG had argued against grounds for rape and incest because they would require doctors to approve abortions on nonmedical grounds and cause doctors to face women who felt that their requests for abortion should be granted automatically. The CMA had a similar concern, but handled it differently: It suggested that abortions for grounds of rape or incest should be allowed without medical approval. "You will note that the section (b) which has to do with sexual offence is separated from the others," said Dr. Aitken in his testimony to the parliamentary standing committee considering abortion reform. "This is done because, except for this area, we feel the decision to produce a therapeutic abortion should be a medical decision. We do not feel that doctors would be comfortable or competent to judge in all cases of sexual offence."[132]

When asked whether the social grounds enacted in Britain should also be considered in Canada, the CMA representatives said that they could give only their personal opinions. Aitken said, "This is a sociological condition and we are attempting to stick with the medical grounds which we feel we are competent to discuss. We are no more competent than anyone else to discuss the sociological and economic factors involved."[133] The CMA representatives were also asked if medical opinion supported abortion on request. Aitken replied, "I am simply unable to answer your question. Certainly there may be many doctors who privately hold that view. No such view is held by any recognized body of doctors as an official statement."[134]

Thus, the Canadian case was a mix between the British and American ones. As in the United States, the CMA had contentious relations with the state, cherished fee-for-service payment, and was busy fighting over national health insurance, but like the British associations, it strongly valued clinical autonomy and had reached an accord with the state on that score. As in Britain, the abortion reform would affect many doctors, but because the reform was not expected to dramatically increase the number of abortions, it would do so only modestly.

With the CMA's position somewhere between that of the BMA and AMA, how did Canada end up with the most restrictive abortion reform— one that included only health grounds and required that abortions be provided in hospitals? The key is that Canadian medical associations set the agenda for reform and were essentially its lone voice. They faced little opposition to their preferences and achieved them with ease. Had the British reform fully incorporated the position of the BMA and RCOG, it would have resembled the Canadian reform: eschewing social grounds and restricting abortion provision to a small number of NHS consultants. But David Steel, though responsive to the concerns of the medical associations, also answered to the ALRA. The British medical associations, unlike their Canadian counterparts, did not get everything they wanted.

Alternative Explanations

In this chapter, I argued that the medical associations in the three countries constructed differing interests and priorities on abortion mainly because they were located in differing medical-care systems, but there are two alternative explanations for these differences—feminist demands for abortion on request and changes in medical opinion. As the last chapter explained, feminist demands for abortion on request were an important part of the American reform debate, but not the British or Canadian one. Perhaps this explains why the AMA eventually adopted a position that implicitly allowed abortion on request, while the BMA and CMA did not. Such demands probably had some impact on the AMA: There were voices in the AMA supporting abortion on request, such as the Section on Preventive Medicine and the South Carolina delegation. But this was a distinctly minority position: In 1970, women made up only 7 percent of doctors and only one woman sat among the 250 members of the 1970 AMA House of Delegates, so there was little internal pressure from feminists,[135] and because AMA elections were so undemocratic, insurgent movements had little success. The AMA experienced some external pressure on abortion from feminist groups, which protested at the 1969 and 1970 AMA annual meetings, but these protests were smaller and less disruptive than others focusing on health care for the poor.[136] Feminist activism played a key role in the passage of the repeal bill in New York and in legal challenges to abortion laws—helping to legitimate abortion on request.[137] Still, it is doubtful that feminist demands would have been enough to move the AMA leadership if abortion were not already a low priority for the association. On numerous other issues, AMA leaders faced stronger movement pressure but did not yield.

An alternative explanation for the AMA's 1970 change of position is that its members were swept up in a broader societal change in abortion attitudes. Polls of medical opinion provide some support for this: An unscientific 1967 survey by *Modern Medicine* magazine found that only 27 percent of doctors supported abortions for social reasons, and 14 percent supported abortion "at the request of the pregnant woman for any reason." A survey of psychiatrists, usually more liberal than other doctors, found that only 24 percent supported abortion "whenever the woman requests it." But by 1969, *Modern Medicine* found that 51 percent of doctors supported abortion on request. Similarly, a 1970 survey of Georgia doctors found that almost half supported abortion "at the request of the patient without other qualifications." But these were hardly overwhelming majorities, and the results of the *Modern Medicine* survey varied by specialty, with the main constituencies of the AMA continuing to oppose abortion on request; only 39 percent of general practitioners and 41 percent of ob/gyns supported abortion on request, while 72 percent of psychiatrists did so. More important, because AMA elections were so undemocratic, general medical opinion and AMA policy were only loosely coupled.[138]

Conclusion

In this chapter, I argued that institutional contexts mediated the interest and priorities of medical associations, producing different positions in each country. In all three countries, medical associations began the 1960s with the same position: They opposed abortion on request and abortion for social grounds. But this changed over the course of the decade: The

British and Canadian medical associations engaged with the abortion issue and successfully preserved medical gatekeeping, while the AMA was barely engaged and eventually accepted de facto abortion on request. As the results of their earlier experiences with the founding of the NHS, British medical associations strongly valued clinical autonomy and faced a short list of competing issues. They were also more concerned about threats to clinical autonomy by women patients than threats by the state. The AMA, in the context of private fee-for-service medicine and hostile relations with the state, gave clinical autonomy a lower priority; it was often willing to trade it away for economic and organizational power. It also faced a long list of competing issues and was more concerned about threats to clinical autonomy by the state than by women patients. Abortion became an even lower priority once national health insurance seemed likely. The CMA, in the context of a new single-payer health insurance plan, prized clinical autonomy, but was also busy fighting for favorable provincial implementations of that plan. Had push come to shove, it is not clear how high abortion gatekeeping might have ranked among its priorities. But push never came to shove. Canadian medical associations put abortion on the agenda, were the main drivers of abortion reform, and easily obtained their preferences.

In the remainder of the book, I examine contention over abortion policy after the reforms of the Long 1960s. In all three countries, large pro-life movements tried to roll back the abortion reforms but only the American pro-life movement achieved real success—reducing abortion funding and provision and moving abortion to the center of American politics. In the next chapter, I describe major changes in the abortion policies of the three countries after reform.

PART TWO

After Reform

FOUR

Abortion Services

The previous chapters focused on abortion gatekeeping. In this chapter, I examine the organization, funding, and quality of abortion services in each country in the years following their respective reforms. By quality, I mean factors such as safety, waiting times, cost, proximity, physical and emotional comfort, dignity, and privacy. I divide the discussion into two periods, implementation—the establishment of the main outlines of abortion provision during the first several years after reforms—and post-implementation—the forty years of policy making after that. The reforms themselves were silent about many aspects of abortion provision, and many developments were both unintended and unforeseen. During the implementation period, the key difference between the countries was the development of single-purpose abortion clinics in the United States and Britain, but not in Canada. Such clinics allowed women to bypass reluctant and sometimes obstructionist doctors and hospitals. The absence of clinics in Canada meant that abortions were least available there. Only about a third of Canadian hospitals established abortion committees, and those that did varied widely in their interpretations of abortion law. A small number of hospitals in the major cities interpreted "health" liberally and provided the vast majority of abortions. Most other hospitals interpreted the law conservatively, and about a fifth of Canadian women's abortions were provided in American clinics. Abortions were more available in the United States and Britain, where clinics provided prompt abortions on request or nearly so. About a third of American abortions (for some of the poor) and half of British ones (in

NHS hospitals) were publicly funded. In Canada, all in-country abortions were publicly funded, though women often made high copayments and incurred travel costs to the large cities. Canadian women who obtained abortions in the United States paid out of pocket.

In the period after implementation, abortion provision changed dramatically in all three countries. In the United States, Congress banned federal funding of abortions in 1976, though some states continued to fund them with their own money, clinics became ever more prominent, and states restricted abortion services through parental and husband consent requirements, waiting periods, and mandatory antiabortion counseling. In Britain, NHS doctors gradually loosened their interpretations of mental health grounds, clinic abortions increased, and the NHS began funding abortions in private clinics—strongly expanding public funding. But the biggest post-reform change occurred in Canada. In 1988, the Supreme Court struck down the 1969 reform, and Parliament failed to replace it. Abortions became available on request for women's own reasons, and private single-purpose clinics eventually provided half of all abortions.

Implementation: Hospitals, Clinics, and Funding

After the reforms of the Long 1960s, various actors—movement activists, doctors, hospitals, and government officials—worked to shape the implementations of the reforms. Table 4.1 shows differences across the three countries in the provision and funding of abortions during the implementation period. During implementation, abortions were provided mainly in single-purpose clinics in the United States, mainly in hospitals in Canada and Scotland, and in both settings equally in England and Wales.[1] Government funding was strongest in Canada, followed by Britain, and then the United States. In Canada, the government paid for 80 percent of abortions and patients paid for the other 20 percent (clinic abortions in the United States), but for a quarter of publicly funded abortions, patients were required to pay an additional fee averaging $74—almost half the cost of a clinic abortion in the United States. These copays resulted from the practice of extra-billing in Canada's Medicare system. In two provinces, Alberta and Nova Scotia, doctors were allowed to bill over and above the amount that they were reimbursed by the provincial health insurance system. In other provinces, extra-billing was prohibited except where patients self-referred to specialists, the treatment was not medically necessary, or it was unusual or time-consuming—all situations

Table 4.1 Provision and Funding of Abortions in the United States, England and Wales, and Canada, 1970s

	United States (1976)	England and Wales (1970)	Scotland (1970)	Canada (1976)
Percent in clinics	61	45	12[2]	20[1]
Percent publicly funded	26	50	88	80[3]
Percent out-of-pocket	64	50	12[2]	20[1]
Percent private insurance	10	n/a	n/a	n/a
Percent private financial assistance[4]	6	unknown	unknown	2

Sources: Robin F. Badgley, Denyse Fortin Caron, and Marion G. Powell, *Report of the Committee on the Operation of the Abortion Law* (Ottawa: Minister of Supply and Services Canada, 1977); Elizabeth Kathleen Lane, *Report of the Committee on the Working of the Abortion Act* (London: Her Majesty's Stationery Office, 1974); Barbara L. Lindheim, "Services, Policies and Costs in U.S. Abortion Facilities," *Family Planning Perspectives* 11 (1979): 283–89.

[1] Canadian women's abortions in the United States.
[2] Scottish women's abortions in England.
[3] Roughly one-quarter of these abortions required a copayment that was approximately half the cost of a clinic abortion.
[4] In all countries, abortions were sometimes provided for reduced fees. U.S. clinics reported reducing fees for about 9 percent of their patients (i.e., 6 percent of all abortions). No figure was available for Britain. The Canadian figure is for abortions provided in U.S. clinics.

that doctors could argue, either to themselves or to others, applied to abortion. In addition, doctors who did not "opt in" to the health insurance system were free to charge whatever they wanted.[2] Young women, immigrants and the least-educated were more likely to be extra-billed. According to the chief ob/gyn at one hospital, "if a woman is physically attractive, well educated, and can otherwise relate, then the fee is sometimes reduced."[3]

In Britain, abortion funding and provision varied by region. In England and Wales, the government paid for abortions provided in NHS hospitals and patients paid for those provided in private clinics, and about half of abortions were provided in each setting. In Scotland, the vast majority of abortions were provided in NHS hospitals, as private providers were scarce, but many women, and especially those in Glasgow, traveled to England for private abortions.[4] In the United States, patients paid for two-thirds of abortions, federal and state governments paid for a quarter (though this percentage declined after the federal government stopped funding abortions in 1976), and private insurance paid for 10 percent. In all three countries, some patients with financial need paid reduced fees. The prices of abortions also differed across countries (see appendix 4, table 1). British clinic abortions were three times as expensive as American ones (as a percentage of median income). And Canadian women who obtained abortions in the United States paid not only the cost of the abortions but also travel costs and sometimes fees to Canadian referral agencies.

There were several other differences among the three countries, related to the geographical distribution of abortion services, waiting times, length of stay, and consent requirements (see table 4.2). In the United States and Canada, less than a third of hospitals provided abortions, while in Britain, most hospitals provided at least some abortions, but there were strong regional disparities in NHS provision. In all of the countries, abortions were concentrated in major cities, but this was especially pronounced in Canada and the United States. In the United States, abortions were provided with less delay, took place at earlier stages of pregnancy, and were more likely to be provided on an outpatient basis than in the other countries. With their gatekeeping systems, delays were longer in the Britain's NHS and especially in Canadian hospitals, where the waiting time between the first consultation and the abortion averaged eight weeks. These delays produced large numbers of more risky second-trimester abortions and forced some women to forgo abortions entirely because their pregnancies became so advanced that hospitals would not provide them.[5] Twice as many Canadian abortions and three times as many British ones occurred in the second trimester as did American ones. These delays strongly affected the safety of abortions as the death-to-case ratio increased by 50 percent for each week after eight weeks' gestation.[6] The mortality rate per 100,000 abortions was 3.2 in the United States and 19.2 in Britain. No good figures are available for Canada, but the mortality rate likely exceeded the British one given long waiting times. The countries also differed in lengths of stay. In the United States, most abortions were provided on an outpatient basis, whereas in Britain and Canada the vast majority required an overnight stay. In Britain, NHS abortions typically required a two-night stay, and clinic abortions required a one-night stay. Finally, the consent of husbands and parents was usually required in Canada, less so in the United States, and not at all in Britain. In Canada, 68 percent of hospitals required that married women have their husband's consent, and 18 percent required the father of the fetus to give consent, even when the woman was separated, divorced, or never married.[7]

To summarize this somewhat complex picture, in the first years after reform, abortions were least available in Canada. There, hospital abortion committees interpreted health grounds narrowly, and many hospitals refused to establish committees at all. Clinics outside hospitals were illegal, so women could only evade obstructionist hospitals by traveling to less restrictive hospitals in major Canadian cities or to American clinics.

Table 4.2 Abortion Services in the United States, England and Wales, and Canada, 1970s

	United States	England and Wales	Canada
Percent of hospitals providing abortions	31% (1977)[1]	Most	30% (1974)
Waiting time	Hospitals: 1 week or less Clinics: 3 days or less (1976)	NHS: 3 weeks Clinics: 1 week or less (1971)	8 weeks (1976)
Second-trimester abortions	10% (1976)	29% (1971)	19% (1975)
Outpatient abortions	60% (1976)	5% (1972)	20% (1974)
Providers requiring parent consent	Most hospitals and 30% of clinics (1976)	None	Almost all (1976)
Providers requiring husband consent	18% of hospitals, but no clinics (1976)	None	68% (1976)
Abortion rate per 1,000 women ages 15–44	34.2 (1979)	10.6 (1976)[2]	11.3 (1978)

Sources: Robin F. Badgley, Denyse Fortin Caron, and Marion G. Powell, Report of the Committee on the Operation of the Abortion Law (Ottawa: Minister of Supply and Services Canada, 1977); Stanley K. Henshaw, "Induced Abortion: A World Review, 1990," Family Planning Perspectives 22 (1990):76–89; Elizabeth Kathleen Lane, Report of the Committee on the Working of the Abortion Act (London: Her Majesty's Stationery Office, 1974); Barbara L. Lindheim, "Services, Policies and Costs in U.S. Abortion Facilities," Family Planning Perspectives 11 (1979): 283–89; Statistics Canada, Some Facts about Therapeutic Abortions in Canada (Ottawa: Minister of Supply and Services Canada, 1984).

[1] The figure is for private hospitals. In public hospitals, the figure was 21% (1977).
[2] Includes residents only.

Though most abortions were funded by public health insurance, access to abortions was still stratified by class because better-off women could more easily travel to less restrictive providers. Many women also faced large copays. For women who managed to obtain legal abortions within their own country, there were long delays that increased the trauma and decreased the safety of abortions. Finally, most hospitals required consent from husbands and parents, even though the law did not require this.

Abortion access was much better in the United States and Britain—though both had their strengths and weaknesses. In both countries, women had access to clinic abortions available on request, or nearly so, and with little delay, but usually paid out-of-pocket. However, American clinics were less expensive and better distributed geographically than British ones, and provided publicly funded abortions for some women. As for hospital abortions, they were better distributed and cheaper (free) in Britain, though they were sometimes slower and more difficult to obtain. In both countries, access to abortions was stratified by class. The United States funded abortions for only some of the poor—leaving many poor and working-class women to scrape together funds to pay for their own. Better-off women had an easier time paying for abortions and traveling to clinics. In Britain, many women paid for clinic abortions to avoid the delays and humiliations of the NHS approval process. Below, I explain the origins of these post-reform provision and funding arrangements in each country, paying particular attention to the presence or absence of clinics. I begin with the United States and Britain, where clinics provided large numbers of abortions, and end with Canada, where clinics were prohibited.

The United States: Reluctant Hospitals, Willing Clinics

Even before *Roe*, single-purpose clinics had begun to play a central role in American abortion provision. The introduction of the vacuum suction machine in 1968 and new methods of anesthesia made abortions outside hospitals more feasible.[8] After California's 1967 abortion reform and subsequent court decisions, a 1969 court ruling in the District of Columbia, and the 1970 legislative repeal in New York, abortion became available on request, or nearly so, in these states, and they provided almost 90 percent of all American abortions. The 1967 California reform required that abortions be provided in accredited hospitals, but entrepreneurs found that they could convert small hospitals into abortion clinics either by making them dependent on abortion revenues or by buying them outright.[9] From 1967 to 1972, about 5 percent of hospitals provided 90 percent of the abortions in Los Angeles County.[10]

The largest number of clinic abortions were provided in New York. In the months before the 1970 repeal took effect, experts predicted that the number of abortions in the state would increase from about a thousand per year to 500,000 and that this would be far more than the state's hospitals could handle.[11] Clinics and doctor's offices could help meet the demand, but some experts argued that they were not capable of providing abortions safely. As a result, Dr. Robert Hall of ASA, though a longtime advocate of abortion liberalization, supported hospital and residency requirements:

> There isn't one doctor in the state of New York who has ever done an abortion under those three conditions—out-patient, local anesthesia, and suction. To do 50,000 with these strange new techniques will be trouble enough in a hospital. But let the floodgates open, let in 500,000, and you will have independent clinics to accommodate them. Then you will have deaths, profiteering, gruesome stories on the front pages of the newspapers. Next January, the Legislature will meet again and say, "See what a

mess they've made of the abortion law," and rescind it. The other 49 states, looking at the New York experience, will see us screwing it up and will stay away from abortion repeal. I'm even naïve enough to believe that Supreme Court Justices read the newspapers, and they'll wonder why they should legalize abortion repeal for the whole country if this is the way we behave in New York.[12]

NARAL disagreed with Hall. For years, it and other organizations had referred thousands of women for medically competent but illegal non-hospital abortions. "A qualified person can safely perform an abortion anywhere," said NARAL's Dr. Bernard Nathanson. NARAL and others argued that a hospital requirement was unnecessary and would create shortages and increase costs. After a great deal of controversy, New York City eventually allowed abortions in clinics without a residency requirement but did not allow abortions in doctors' offices.[13] By early 1973, twenty-one clinics had opened. Eighty percent were for-profit enterprises. Planned Parenthood ran two clinics—including one of the largest, which was funded by several major foundations. Like California, New York City also had several for-profit hospitals devoted solely to abortion.[14] Many women's organizations had provided abortion referrals for several years before the New York repeal, and afterward, they used their power over referrals to pressure abortion providers into lowering prices and providing more sensitive services. When New York's repeal first took effect, early hospital abortions cost $400 to $600, but by the end of the law's first year, for-profit hospitals charged around $250, municipal and nonprofit hospitals charged around $150, and clinics charged between $50 and $200.[15]

Although clinics helped New York City deal with the increased demand for abortions, this was not the only reason they were created. Many pro-choice activists and doctors believed that they were a better place for abortions because they were less expensive and provided more sensitive care. Said one Brooklyn obstetrician, "hospitals are no place for abortions, at least not for the simple, early ones. The entire hospital setup—with its involved bureaucracy, administrative delays, high overhead, and brusque efficiency—only serves to make abortions more costly, more complicated, and more traumatic for the patient."[16] Clinics often offered counseling and emotional support for abortion patients, while in hospitals, women often faced the disapproval of doctors and other hospital staff who opposed abortion.[17]

Clinics also emerged because mainstream doctors and hospitals resisted providing abortions. Some doctors were hostile to the abortion repeal because they believed that it reduced their clinical autonomy.

Others feared that they would be stigmatized if they provided abortions. Dr. Hall noted that

> on the obstetrical service of every hospital, no matter how large the staff, there seem to be two or three doctors who do more than half of the abortions. And the rest of the staff regards these doctors with esteem not markedly higher than that previously reserved for the back-street abortionist. . . . Their colleagues, who do only an occasional abortion on previous patients and the daughters of friends, still cling to the belief, perhaps defensible 50 years ago, that they, not pregnant women, should decide who should have an abortion.[18]

Dr. Leon Zussman, a Manhattan ob/gyn, summed up the attitude of many doctors: "We've all been frustrated all these years by having to refuse so many [abortions], so no one will say no now. But I would not want to be known as an abortionist. Maybe the next generation wouldn't consider that a stigma, but with me it will persist until I die."[19]

Hospitals avoided providing abortions through the development of restrictive policies relating to residency, spousal and parental consent, stage of gestation, overnight stays, general anesthesia, and various unnecessary tests. As Hall wrote, "some hospitals make it as difficult as they can for a woman to get an abortion. They make the entire process so expensive that women cannot afford it, so time-consuming that the pregnancy becomes too far advanced, or so restricted that women cannot qualify at all."[20] One hospital administrator expressly advocated this approach: "If it's too easy, she'll be back here in three months for another abortion."[21]

The pre-*Roe* clinic experiences of California, the District of Columbia, and New York aided the spread of clinics after *Roe*. The Supreme Court looked to the experience of these states when it considered Georgia's hospital requirement in the *Doe* decision. And the pre-*Roe* clinics also provided models for later ones. Planned Parenthood, after its experience operating abortion clinics in New York, sought to establish them across the country. In *Doe,* the appellants' argued that Georgia's requirement that abortions be provided in accredited hospitals was "irrational" given New York's experience with clinics and argued that the requirement manipulated plaintiff's rights "out of existence."[22] The amicus brief for the ACOG also opposed the hospital requirement—arguing that the experiences of California, the District of Columbia, and New York did not justify it, and that abortion should be treated the same as any other medical procedure.[23] In oral arguments, the court asked the appellant's counsel,

Margie Hames, whether she thought an accredited hospital requirement was constitutional. She replied, "I think that abortions should be performed in specialized facilities, regulated by the state. . . . [C]linics are fully capable, by virtue of the New York experience statistics that I was citing, to afford effective and safe abortion services."[24]

The court accepted these arguments, noting that "appellants and various *amici* have presented us with a mass of data purporting to demonstrate that some facilities other than hospitals are entirely adequate to perform abortions if they possess [appropriate staffing and services]."[25] In *Doe*, Blackmun rejected the hospital requirement mainly because it applied to all stages of pregnancy. He suggested that such a requirement might be appropriate after the first trimester of pregnancy, but the state would have to show, as it had not in *Doe*, that the requirement was legitimately related to the protection of maternal health.

Feminist and family planning organizations also promoted the spread of clinics. They opened their own clinics but also promoted clinics through their control of referrals and by contracting for services.[26] As they had done in New York, they pressured for-profit providers on quality and on price—pushing them to seek specialization and economies of scale. Outpatient clinics eventually offered much better prices than hospitals. And the abortion sector was quite price sensitive. It was self-pay, the procedure was fairly simple (reducing competition on quality), and the nonprofit referral services provided ample information for patients.

As in New York several years before, many mainstream hospitals and doctors resisted providing abortions after *Roe*. By 1976, abortion had become the most common surgical procedure in the United States, but the vast majority of American hospitals and doctors had never provided abortions and never would.[27] In the first year after *Roe*, clinics were responsible for 90 percent of the total increase in abortions.[28] From the first quarter of 1973 to the first quarter of 1976, the number of clinic abortions more than doubled while the number of hospital abortions remained roughly constant.[29] Hospital abortion provision peaked in 1977, and the number of hospitals providing abortions has declined ever since. Those doctors that did provide abortions were often subject to stigma from other members of the medical profession. Said one provider, "You can suddenly make something legal, but not moral. Everyone wanted to punish us. Other doctors, the law, the public." Another doctor said, "I hated the cold shoulder you got from everyone when they found out you were an abortionist."[30] As prices fell, abortion provision also became less profitable. In 1973, physicians typically received $50 per case; by 1992 that amount had not increased, though other prices certainly had. Said one doctor, "I can generate as much income seeing office patients with vaginitis as I can by doing abortion . . . and without the hassle."[31]

Gerald Rosenberg argues that the *Roe* decision is "far less responsible" for increased abortion access "than most people think" because the largest increase in legal abortions occurred prior to *Roe* (with abortion law repeals in California and New York). He concedes that the Supreme Court was "at least partially effective in easing access to safe and legal abortion." But he argues that this was mainly because pro-choice activists "got very lucky" when the court allowed abortions outside of hospitals.[32] Rosenberg is certainly correct that *Roe* was not the first important American abortion reform, but he understates its impact. His measure of that impact—the number of abortions—misses much of what was important about *Roe*. As Rosenberg notes, about 70 percent of post-*Roe* legal abortions replaced abortions that previously would have been obtained illegally. As such, the sheer number of abortions is not the best measure of social change. A better measure is the quality of abortion services. Legal abortions were not only much safer than illegal ones, they were far less stigmatic, demeaning, and emotionally taxing.[33] They no longer broke the law—indeed, they had been declared legitimate by the highest court in the land. They also did not carry the same risks of sexual harassment and victimization and were far less costly: First-trimester abortion prices declined from $500 before *Roe* to $150 after. This had significant implications for poor women's access to abortion.[34] Finally, legal abortions were much better distributed after *Roe* than before (though this distribution still left much to be desired). In 1972, California and New York provided 72 percent of all legal abortions, though only 20 percent of Americans lived there. By 1976, the two states provided only 25 percent of abortions.[35]

Britain: Hospitals and Clinics Share Provision

Clinics were at the center of the British implementation as well. Women were eligible for free abortions through the NHS, but within a few years of the reform, most abortions were provided in private clinics. In the first two years after the Abortion Act of 1967, the NHS provided more than 60 percent of abortions in England and Wales. But this fell to 40 percent by 1971 and stayed below that level for the remainder of the 1970s. In Scotland, however, most abortions were provided within the NHS. The private sector included charitable (nonprofit) and commercial (for-profit) clinics as well as NHS consultants who provided private abortions in NHS hospitals. Most of these private providers interpreted the law liberally.

Charitable providers had lower fees, sometimes waived them entirely, and provided grants and loans to women with financial need. The two main charitable providers were the Birmingham Pregnancy Advisory Service (BPAS) and London Pregnancy Advisory Service (LPAS), both founded by members of the ALRA in 1968. In 1970, BPAS and LPAS provided 15 percent of abortions, while commercial clinics provided 30 percent. Foreign women were not eligible for NHS services and were usually turned away from charitable clinics, so commercial clinics provided almost all of their abortions. But as abortions became more widely available in other countries, especially the Netherlands, commercial providers went out of business as they lost their foreign clients and could not match the low prices that the charitable providers offered their domestic clients.[36]

Britain's heavy private provision is a puzzle, given the popularity of the twenty-year-old NHS and the Labour Government's general desire to expand the NHS and limit private practice. Most participants in the abortion debate did not foresee or intend that so many abortions would be provided outside the NHS. During the debate over reforms, the BMA and RCOG recommended that abortions be provided either in NHS hospitals or in private nursing homes. But the medical associations imagined that abortions in nursing homes would be provided mainly by NHS consultants who had private practices on the side. Such abortions, though private, would be firmly under the supervision and control of mainstream medicine. The consultant requirement sought by the medical associations would have ensured this. But when David Steel eliminated it at the behest of the ALRA, he cleared the way for private abortions not only by NHS consultants but also by nonconsultants and doctors with no NHS affiliation at all.[37] The medical associations clearly saw the implications. The RCOG's John Peel worried about foreign doctors setting up practices solely devoted to abortion: "I wonder whether anybody has given any thought to the effects of entry into the Common Market with the consequent entry of a considerable number of European gentleman who are rather expert at this particular operation and who are not by any means Gynaecologists in our sense of the word."[38]

Many women sought private abortions because they were unable to obtain them in the NHS. In the first few years after the reform, the medical associations were quite hostile to social grounds for abortion. In 1969, the BMA denounced the "social" clauses of the Abortion Act, expressing "repugnance at this departure from traditional medical ethics."[39] In 1970, the BMA and RCOG supported unsuccessful private member's bills that added a consultant requirement to the act. An RCOG survey found that almost 60 percent of consultants wanted to see the abortion law, and especially its social grounds, made more restrictive. Ninety percent opposed "abortion on demand," and 80 percent thought that abortions should be provided only under the supervision of a consultant. The RCOG complained that the public and the press misunderstood the abortion law.

When the Abortion Bill was under discussion its advocates repeatedly assured the Houses of Parliament that abortion on demand was not their object. Had they done otherwise it is unlikely that the Bill would have become law. Once the Bill was passed, however, there has been a persistent and intense campaign which has had the effect of making the public believe that any woman has a right to have a pregnancy terminated if she so wishes, and that gynaecologists have a duty to apply their surgical skills when told and irrespective of their expert judgement.[40]

Despite the protestations of the RCOG, there was hardly a medical consensus on the interpretation of the abortion law. Approval rates were 70 percent or more in Newcastle, London, East Anglia, Southwest England, and Oxford, but only 51 percent in Birmingham and Liverpool. In Birmingham, pro-life consultant Hugh McLaren, sat on all consultant appointment committees and excluded consultants who provided abortions. These differences in approvals were reflected in regional ratios of NHS to private provision. The NHS provided more than 90 percent of the abortions in Newcastle and Scotland, 45 percent of those in London and only 23 percent of those in Birmingham. The NHS provided less than 60 percent of abortions in most other regions. The regions also varied in the degree to which women had to travel outside their home region for abortions—usually to private clinics in London or Birmingham. In London, Newcastle, and Scotland, less than 10 percent of patients traveled outside their region for abortions. In East Anglia, Southwest England, and Birmingham (home of a large private clinic) between 10 and 20 percent did so. But in Leeds, Sheffield, and Oxford, 40 percent or more of patients traveled to other regions.[41] As women sought NHS abortions in more liberal areas, NHS hospitals in some of those areas established residency requirements, and, as a result, most women who sought abortions outside of their local areas ended up turning to the private sector.

More liberal interpretations of the abortion law were also aided by the "statistical argument." The House of Lords had amended the 1967 reform to allow doctors to weigh the risk of childbirth against the supposedly greater risk of abortion. This was intended as an antiabortion amendment, but some doctors later argued that the abortion mortality rate was actually lower than the maternal mortality rate and, consequently, that the amendment allowed unlimited abortion. Pro-life activists complained that the amendment had created a de facto policy of "abortion on demand."[42] Liberal interpretations were also aided by the fact that the police and medical authorities showed little interest in investigating the reasons that doctors listed on abortion certificates.[43]

Women also sought private abortions because the NHS was overtaxed by the reform. During debate over the 1967 reform, Health Minister Kenneth Robinson suggested that hospitals would have enough resources to meet the increased demand for abortions because they would no longer be treating complications from illegal abortions. This calculation was off the mark, and a lack of facilities led to delays and rationing. As a result, general practitioners often approved abortion requests for their NHS patients, but then referred them to private clinics rather than NHS hospitals.[44] The RCOG complained that the Government's promise "that the necessary additional staff and beds would be provided to cater for any resulting increase in work load has never been honored."[45] Pro-choice activists argued that some of the claims about facility shortages were merely an excuse for antiabortion doctors to deny abortions. They also pointed out that hospitals could dramatically increase their abortion capacity if they provided outpatient abortions.[46]

In 1971, most Conservative and some Labour MPs voted to establish a committee to investigate the Abortion Act.[47] When the Lane Committee reported in April 1974, it recommended against major changes in the act, instead suggesting educational, administrative, and professional remedies.[48] The committee criticized high levels of private provision and even argued that the act establishing the NHS obligated it to provide a "reasonable level of service." To that end, it advocated expansion of NHS gynecological departments, earlier abortions, shorter hospital stays, and referral mechanisms that bypassed GPs who had conscientious objections to providing abortions.

The committee opposed two other options—that the NHS contract with private providers for its abortion services and that the NHS create its own segregated abortion clinics. The committee argued that contracting with private providers would promote "abortion on demand, paid for by the N.H.S.," divorce abortion from mainstream gynecology, and hinder the development of abortion services within the NHS. It acknowledged the potential advantages of segregated NHS abortion clinics—specialization, economies of scale, opportunities for counseling and follow-up, and the separation of abortion and obstetric patients—but in a set of arguments that foreshadowed contemporary American criticisms of stand-alone abortion clinics, the committee argued that there is the probability of stigma attaching to such a unit, both to the patients and the staff looking after them. There is a possibility that the patient's confidentiality would to some extent be lost. It seems likely that many doctors and nurses would be reluctant to devote themselves largely to this type of work. . . . There would be a lack of variety in the work and a limit to its potentiality for development that might result in the lowering of standards of staff recruited for the work. . . . The establishment of a large number of units would be likely to result in a move nearer to abortion on demand. The development of a separate sub-specialty could be detrimental to the careers of those working in it as well as removing from the specialty of obstetrics and gynaecology much of the work which has been an important part of it for many years, and this at a time when there are developments in experience and techniques which require the attention and understanding of the specialty.[49]

Despite its concern about high levels of private provision, the committee spoke highly of the charitable abortion services (LPAS and BPAS) and opposed calls for restricting abortions to the NHS. But it criticized commercial providers—"a very small number, of perhaps about 20 or 30 members, of the medical profession [that] have brought considerable reproach upon this country, both at home and abroad." According to the committee, these providers had advertised in other countries, charged exorbitant fees, provided poor and insensitive services, and failed in their duties as legal gatekeepers. To rein in these providers, the committee called for the licensing of for-profit private referral agencies.[50]

The committee rejected calls for abortion on request in ways that must have been music to the ears of the medical associations:

To expect doctors to operate under orders without reference to their judgment would be contrary to good medical practice and would also be to the disadvantage of their patients especially having regard to the complexities and uncertainties of the outcome of the operation. . . . Furthermore, the already high number of abortions would almost certainly be inflated and we consider it probable that many obstetricians and gynaecologists would be unwilling to operate under such a system.[51]

The committee also chided doctors who approved all abortions because aggregate statistics showed that the risk of early abortion was lower than that of childbirth (the "statistical argument"), and urged doctors to consider the risks facing each patient on an individual basis.

The Lane Committee's report was a turning point. Its recommendations were mild. The committee had also given the reform some breathing room. Because Parliament does not typically consider legislation on any issue that is still being investigated by a committee, abortion opponents could not introduce restrictive amendments to the Abortion Act until the committee had completed its three years of deliberation. And during that time, both the public and the medical associations became more accepting of the reform. In testimony to the committee, the medical associations had expressed support for the act as written, and they generally supported the committee's conclusions. In 1975, the medical associations opposed James White's bill to restrict the grounds for abortion.[52] Several factors led to the changing position of the medical associations: The Department of Health had reduced "abuses" by private providers by increasing its requirements for the licensing of private abortion providers, conducting random inspections, prohibiting foreign advertising, and establishing record-keeping requirements relating to admission, discharge, and fees. Abortions for foreign women also declined as European countries liberalized their abortion laws, reducing demand for abortions in the commercial sector.[53] And doctor's attitudes were changing as well. Said Dr. David Paintin of the ALRA:

At first, gynaecologists were not sure how permissive they could be, and there was establishment pressure against those who did a large number of abortions—they were regarded as outsiders and risked losing the respect of their colleagues. But attitudes changed as it became apparent that women could now have terminations legally when social factors threatened their mental health, and that this interpretation of the law has at least the tacit support of the Department of Health.[54]

Canada: Many Reluctant Hospitals, Some Willing Hospitals, Forbidden Clinics

Canadian women had much more difficulty obtaining abortions than British or American ones. Hospital boards were not required to establish abortion committees, and only 30 percent did so. Abortions outside hospitals were forbidden—though as I detail later in the chapter, this was contested in Quebec.[55] Of hospitals that did not establish committees, about half were unable to do so by law because they were unaccredited or did not meet provincial requirements that they have a certain number of beds, medical staff, operating rooms, or specialists. The other half claimed either that doctors, nurses, or community members opposed abortion or that there was no demand for abortion services in their area. In addition, many hospitals were religiously owned or affiliated.[56] Hospital administrators offered a variety of excuses to the Badgley Committee charged with investigating abortion law in 1975:

CHAPTER FOUR

The medical staff do not encourage abortion as a contraceptive measure as it is not consistent with good medical practice.

This small hospital, while it could perform this service, has been effectively stopped by the undercurrent of disapproval by many of the older nurses on the staff.

Why start a fight when by doing nothing we can keep the lid on?

In this small community of less than 25,000 people, the Right to Life group is very vocal. It intimidated local physicians with phone calls in the middle of the night. Hence, so few physicians are willing to perform the operation, that patients are referred to larger metropolitan centres.[57]

Provinces were authorized by the act to approve nonaccredited hospitals or nonhospital facilities to provide abortions, but most refused to do so. In 1979, only eleven facilities had been approved in this way.[58] In most provinces, less than a quarter of general hospitals established abortion committees. The main exceptions were Ontario and British Columbia, where half of hospitals established committees. Even when hospitals did establish committees, they often provided only a few abortions per year. About a third of hospitals with committees imposed either residency requirements or annual quotas. The overwhelming majority of abortions were provided by a small number of hospitals in the major cities of each province. In 1974, a mere 33 hospitals, 4 percent of all general hospitals, provided 70 percent of abortions.[59] As one observer noted, most abortion committee decisions were foreordained by the attitude of the hospital in which they were located: "A therapeutic abortion committee rarely carries out its intended function. Where there is a committee that is known for its reluctance to approve abortions, it receives almost no applications. Other committees serve only as a rubber stamp: they receive many applications and approve virtually all of them."[60]

To add to the access problems, many Canadians did not know that abortions were legal. About half of Canadians believed that abortions were illegal under any circumstances, and another 15 percent were unsure. The difficulty, or perceived illegality, of obtaining abortions led many women to seek them in the United States. In Quebec and the Maritimes (New Brunswick, Nova Scotia, and Prince Edward Island), 43 percent and 24 percent of abortions respectively were provided in the United States.[61]

Personal accounts submitted to the Badgley Committee demonstrate many of the problems discussed above, but also reveal inadequacies in the quality and professionalism of abortion services. Many women described care that was competent, respectful, and kind, but others wrote of cold, insensitive, rude, or judgmental treatment. One received a thirty-minute antiabortion lecture while "undressed and on the examining table." Another said the doctor "made me feel like an insignificant piece of dirt." Many women resented the need to exaggerate their distress and desperation to concoct a "good story" for the abortion committee. Others complained that doctors asked intrusive and voyeuristic questions and sometimes made sexual advances because they viewed abortion patients as "easy lays."[62]

Public Funding: Strong in Canada, Mixed in Britain, Weak in the United States

As I mentioned earlier, public funding of abortions was strongest in Canada, followed by Britain and then the United States. Much of this difference can be credited to differing health-care systems and differing discourses about the abortion issue. Britain had a national health service while Canada had national health insurance, and both countries provided universal coverage. The United States had only a minimal public health-care system. About 70 percent of Americans were covered by employer-provided health insurance, 20 percent were covered by public insurance (for the poor and some of the elderly) and about 10 percent had no health insurance at all.

In Britain and Canada, medical gatekeepers approved abortions based on legal grounds relating to health.[63] Abortion was viewed as a "medical need" that merited public funding.[64] The British and Canadian reforms were also protected somewhat by their association with national health insurance. Supporters of the NHS and Canada's Medicare program were ideologically opposed to increases in private funding and provision of a common medical procedure. By contrast, attacks on the use of "taxpayer's money" for abortion were quite successful in the United States. In Britain, pro-life activists not only refrained from attacking public provision, but also focused their attention on abuses by *private* providers outside the NHS whom they claimed were "racketeers" that loosely interpreted and enforced abortion law. In Canada, too, pro-life activists only rarely attacked public funding in the first two decades after reform.

In the United States, abortion was available on request and without any requirement of medical necessity. As such, pro-life activists were able to define it as an "elective" or voluntary procedure that was not worthy of public funding, or even private insurance.[65] Initially, abortions were funded by Medicaid, the public health insurance program for some of the

CHAPTER FOUR

poor. But soon after *Roe*, fourteen states restricted funding of "elective" abortions. Most states were ordered to end such restrictions by federal courts, but two, Pennsylvania and Connecticut, appealed to the Supreme Court. In Congress, pro-life legislators attached funding ban amendments to appropriations bills for the Department of Health, Education, and Welfare. Such an amendment failed in 1974, but another, the Hyde amendment, passed in 1976. Similar bans passed every year after that. The Supreme Court upheld the state funding bans in its 1977 *Maher v. Roe* and *Beal v. Doe* decisions and the federal funding ban in the 1980 *Harris v. McRae* decision. Some states continued to fund abortions using state rather than federal funds, usually because of decisions by state courts that to do otherwise violated state constitutions.[66] Low-income women have about half of abortions in the United States. After the federal funding ban, publicly funded abortions declined from 25 percent of all abortions to 13 percent.[67] The best study on the effects of funding bans found that about one-third of women who would have had abortions if public funding had been available ended up carrying their pregnancies to term.[68] The other two-thirds scraped together money for an abortion from friends or family members or by using money meant for food, utilities, or rent. This often took time. As a result, poor women tended to have abortions three weeks later than other women, and this, in turn, often increased their costs (in 2001, an abortion at 10 weeks' gestation was $370 while an abortion at fourteen weeks' gestation was $650).[69] I discuss the politics of the federal funding ban in more detail in chapter 6.

After Implementation: The Countries Converge on Gatekeeping and Clinics, but Diverge on Funding

There were several major changes in abortion provision in the forty years after implementation. In the United States, fewer states funded abortions, clinic abortions increased while hospital ones declined, and many states enacted policies restricting abortion services through spousal and parental consent and notification requirements, mandatory antiabortion counseling, and waiting periods. In Britain, interpretations of abortion grounds by NHS doctors continued to liberalize, clinic abortions increased, and some NHS regional health authorities began to fund clinic abortions—dramatically increasing the number of publicly funded abortions. In Canada, the Supreme Court struck down the 1969 abortion reform in 1988, and Parliament failed to replace it with a new one. Abortions became available on request for women's own reasons, and

Table 4.3 Provision and Funding of Abortions in the United States, England and Wales, and Canada, 1970s and 2000s

	United States		England and Wales		Canada	
Year	1976	2008[1]	1970	2006	1976	2005
Percent in clinics	61	95	45	61	20[2]	48
Percent publicly funded	26	20	50	89	80[3]	99
Percent out-of-pocket	64	57	50	11	20[2]	1[4]
Percent private insurance	10	12				
Percent private financial assistance[5]	6	13				

Sources: Robin F. Badgley, Denyse Fortin Caron, and Marion G. Powell, *Report of the Committee on the Operation of the Abortion Law* (Ottawa: Minister of Supply and Services Canada, 1977); Great Britain Office for National Statistics, *Abortion Statistics: Legal Abortions Carried Out under the 1967 Abortion Act in England and Wales,* vol. 28 (London: Stationery Office, 2007); Guttmacher Institute, "News in Context: Guttmacher Institute Memo on Insurance Coverage of Abortion," July 22, 2009; S. Henshaw and L. Finer, "The Accessibility of Abortion Services in the United States, 2001," *Perspectives on Sexual and Reproductive Health* 35 (2003): 16–24; R. K. Jones, M. R. Zolna, S. K. Henshaw, and L. B. Finer, "Abortion in the United States: Incidence and Access to Services, 2005," *Perspectives on Sexual and Reproductive Health* 40 (2008): 6–16; Rachel K. Jones, Lawrence B. Finer, and Susheela Singh, "Characteristics of U.S. Abortion Patients, 2008" (New York: Guttmacher Institute, 2010); Elizabeth Kathleen Lane, *Report of the Committee on the Working of the Abortion Act* (London: Her Majesty's Stationery Office, 1974); Barbara L. Lindheim, "Services, Policies, and Costs in U.S. Abortion Facilities," *Family Planning Perspectives* 11 (1979): 283–89; Statistics Canada, "Table 106-9005—Induced Abortions, by Area of Report and Type of Facility Performing the Abortion, Canada, Provinces, and Territories, Annual (number) (table)," 2008, CANSIM Database.

[1] Percent in clinics is for 2005.
[2] Abortions obtained by Canadian women in the United States.
[3] Roughly one-quarter of these abortions required a copayment equal to approximately half the price of a clinic abortion.
[4] Clinic abortions in New Brunswick.
[5] In all three countries, abortions were sometimes provided for reduced fees. Estimates for these abortions are available only for the United States. The 1976 figure includes abortions provided for reduced fees. The 2008 figure includes reduced-fee abortions as well as abortions funded by organizations such as the National Network of Abortion Funds (founded in 1993), the National Abortion Federation, and Planned Parenthood.

clinics became legal. Clinics now provide half of all Canadian abortions. Many provinces initially resisted funding clinic abortions, but all but New Brunswick eventually did so. Table 4.3 shows these changes in abortion provision in the three countries. In the 2000s, the percent of abortions paid out-of-pocket declined slightly in the United States but markedly in the other countries. Clinic abortions increased in all countries, but especially in Canada and the United States. In the United States, they almost completely replaced hospital abortions. In the 2000s, clinics provided 95 percent of American abortions, 61 percent of British ones, and 48 percent of Canadian ones.

In the United States, the number of clinics increased and the number of hospitals providing abortions declined. Clinics have provided the majority of abortions since 1974 (see appendix 4, table 2). The number of clinics almost quadrupled between 1973 and 1980, whereas the number of hospital providers grew slightly until 1976 and declined after that. In the 1980s, harassment, violence, and intentionally burdensome clinic regulations increased the costs, hassles, and fears of abortion providers.[70] Between 1982 and 2005 (the most recent year for which data are available), the number of facilities providing abortions fell 39 percent. This decline was most pronounced in hospitals. The number of hospitals providing abortions fell 59 percent while the number of clinics and doctors' offices providing abortions fell 21 percent. From 1978 to 2000, the proportion of counties with no abortion provider rose from 77 percent to 87 percent, and the percentage of women in counties with no provider rose from 27 percent to 34 percent. For the purpose of comparison, in 2000, regular obstetric and gynecological care was available in half of counties.[71]

At the same time, states enacted various restrictions on abortion, often with the intent of providing the test case that would allow the Supreme Court to overturn *Roe*. Until the late 1980s, the court struck most of these restrictions down. In 1976, the court disallowed spousal and parental consent requirements, but allowed spousal *notification* requirements. In 1981 and 1983, the court allowed parental notification and consent requirements if they included a judicial bypass, but disallowed waiting periods.[72] In *Webster v. Reproductive Health Services*,[73] the court allowed most of the above restrictions so long as they did not "unduly burden" the abortion choice. In *Planned Parenthood of Southeastern Pennsylvania v. Casey*,[74] the court reaffirmed this "undue burden" standard and upheld waiting periods and parental consent requirements, but struck down spousal notification requirements. I examine the *Webster* and *Casey* decisions in more detail in chapter 6.

There were two new developments in abortion funding. One was the founding of the National Network of Abortion Funds in 1993. The network now includes more than 100 private funds in 40 states and helps approximately 20,000 women pay for abortions each year.[75] Another was the health reform of 2010. The reform increases insurance coverage by requiring that all Americans be insured, expanding eligibility for Medicaid, and providing tax credits to help lower- and middle-income people without employer-based coverage buy private coverage in state insurance exchanges. On abortion, the act allows states to prohibit private plans from covering abortion. And in states that allow abortion coverage, insurers are required to collect two separate premiums—one for abortion and one for all other services—and set the abortion premiums aside to pay for abortions.[76] This is intended to ensure that no taxpayer funds pay for abortions.

The effects of these provisions on abortion coverage are hard to predict. Of women who had abortions in 2008, approximately a third had private insurance, a third had public insurance (Medicaid), and a third were uninsured. Of women with private insurance, most had coverage for medically necessary abortions—a 2002 study found that 87 percent of employer-provided plans cover such procedures.[77] However, only 37 percent of women with private insurance actually used it for their abortions. Of those who did not use it, some probably sought to keep the abortion private from employers, regular health-care providers, or family members; others may have judged that their insurers would not consider the abortion medically necessary; still others may have had high-deductible plans that made it impossible to use the insurance; and members of a final group may have been unaware that they were covered.[78]

Whether women have abortion coverage after reform will depend on how they obtain health insurance. Women with employer-provided coverage will most likely continue to be covered for medically necessary abortions (though many will still opt to pay out-of-pocket). Women who receive tax credits to buy insurance in the exchanges may or may not be able to purchase plans that provide abortion coverage. Some states will prohibit private insurers from selling such coverage, and in those states that allow it, insurers might decline to offer it because of the burdensome, and potentially controversial, requirement that they collect two separate premiums from each member (including men) and segregate all abortion funds. Among women receiving Medicaid, most will have abortion coverage only in the extreme cases allowed by the Hyde amendment (rape, incest, and to save the woman's life), but approximately a third will live in one of the seventeen states that use their own funds for Medicaid abortions and will thus be covered for medically necessary abortions.[79] Finally, analysts predict that some insurers that decline to offer abortion coverage in the exchanges may also decline to offer such coverage outside the exchanges (e.g., to large employers) for reasons of standardization and economies of scale.[80] Most of the fifteen million women buying insurance in the exchanges will be newly insured, but approximately five million will have been previously insured—either by themselves or by small employers.[81] Some portion of these women will exchange a policy that covered medically necessary abortions for one that does not.

There were also post-implementation changes in Britain. During the implementation period, doctors had gradually begun to interpret "mental health" grounds for abortions more liberally than most reformers had expected or intended. This trend continued in the post-implementation period. Eventually, abortion became available essentially on request. Private clinic interpretations of the abortion law had always been liberal, but, over time, they liberalized in NHS hospitals as well. Some of this liberalization was justified in terms of the "statistical argument" contained in the Abortion Act—because early abortions are safer than childbirth, all early abortions contribute to women's health. Pro-life activists repeatedly complained that Britain had developed a de facto policy of "abortion on demand."

Another major change was public funding of private clinic abortions. In 1981, NHS regional health authorities began contracting for clinic abortions through "agency agreements" with charitable providers such as the British Pregnancy Advisory Service. Such contracting was especially common in London, Trent, Wessex, Yorkshire, and West Midlands.[82] These "NHS agency" abortions were no more than 5 percent of all abortions for the next ten years. But in 1992, these abortions rose about 20 percent per year for the next five years, and 10 percent per year for the next ten years. By 2006 (the most recent year for which data are available), 61 percent of all abortions were provided in private clinics, and 89 percent of all abortions were publicly funded.[83] This change occurred for several reasons. First, NHS reforms gave health authority managers, rather than consultant gynecologists, responsibility for setting service levels. These managers were not doctors and were more likely to be younger and female—and thus more likely to support abortion rights.[84] The NHS reforms also emphasized cost savings, and the private sector abortions tended to be cheaper because they were performed earlier and with shorter lengths of stay. Another factor was the development in 2000 of new RCOG standards for abortion services. The standards were funded by the Department of Health and said that abortions should be carried out within three weeks of a woman's first contact with a GP. A later review found that 34 percent of NHS hospitals were out of compliance,[85] and since 2002, the health ministry has required Primary Care Trusts to meet performance targets both for the total number of abortions and for the number provided under ten weeks' gestation, and there are extra funds available to help them meet these goals.[86]

There were also major post-implementation changes in Canada. Clinic abortions were prohibited, but in 1968, Dr. Henry Morgentaler and his supporters began a civil disobedience campaign in Quebec that, by 1976, led the province to abandon its enforcement of the federal abortion law and eventually establish family planning clinics that provided abortion services.[87] In the 1980s, Morgentaler brought his clinic campaign to Ontario and Manitoba, and it lead to the Supreme Court's *Rex v. Morgentaler* (1988) decision, which struck down the 1969 Abortion Act. Parliament was unable to enact a new law, and abortion became available on request for any reason. I describe Morgentaler's campaign, the court's decision, and the ensuing parliamentary battle in chapter 6. After the court's decision, Morgentaler opened abortion clinics in several more provinces—Nova Scotia in 1989, Newfoundland in 1990, Alberta in 1991, and New Brunswick in 1995. By 2005 (the most recent year for which accurate data are available), clinics provided almost half of all abortions in Canada. Hospitals remained reluctant—only 16 percent provided abortions in 2006. Initially, some provinces (British Columbia, Manitoba, New Brunswick, and Nova Scotia) prohibited clinic abortions, but in 1993, the Supreme Court struck down these restrictions because the criminal law was reserved to the federal government.[88] Several provinces also declined to fund abortions under Medicare, but the Supreme Court also required this. In 1996, the Supreme Court allowed provinces to refuse funding for private clinic abortions, but the provinces have gradually yielded on this issue as well. Newfoundland began covering clinic abortions in 1998, Manitoba in 2004, and Quebec in 2006. The heavily Catholic Maritime provinces of New Brunswick and Prince Edward Island continue to hold out. New Brunswick covers hospital abortions only if they are deemed medically necessary and does not cover abortions in Morgentaler's clinic. Morgentaler is currently suing the province. Prince Edward Island has no hospital or clinic that provides abortions and will not fund out-of-province abortions. Saskatchewan has no clinic but covers clinic abortions provided in Alberta. Several suits against these provinces are pending.[89]

Conclusion

In this chapter, I examined cross-national differences in the organization, funding, and quality of abortion services during implementation—the first several years after reform—and in the forty years after that. A key difference among the countries was the development of freestanding abortion clinics in the United States and Britain that allowed women seeking abortions to evade reluctant and obstructive doctors and hospitals. In the United States, abortions were provided on request for women's own reasons and mainly in clinics. In Canada, abortions were subject to medical gatekeeping and provided mainly in hospitals. In Britain, abortions were subject to medical gatekeeping in hospitals but provided on request, or nearly so, in clinics. Britain and Canada publicly funded hospital abortions, but not clinic ones, whereas the United States publicly funded both hospital and clinic abortions but only for some of the poor. After implementation, there were several major changes in abortion provision in each country. In the United States, hospitals increased their avoidance of abortions, and many states imposed restrictions such as spousal and parental consent, waiting periods, and mandatory antiabortion counseling. In Britain, the government began to fund private abortions outside the NHS, and doctors' interpretations of the law continued to liberalize. In Canada, the Supreme Court struck down the country's abortion law, and Parliament failed to replace it. This left the country with publicly funded abortion on request for women's own reasons. Thus, Britain moved closer to Canada on public funding (funding most abortions), and both Canada and Britain moved closer to the United States on gatekeeping and clinics (providing abortions largely on request and mostly in clinics). But the United States moved away from the others on funding and access to abortion services, enacting various restrictions.

In the next two chapters, I examine the politics of abortion after reform. In Britain and Canada, many of the changes in abortion policy occurred outside electoral and partisan politics. But in the United States, abortion policy was at the very center of politics. The next chapter explains why.

FIVE

The Politicization of Abortion

This chapter and the next examine abortion politics and policy after the reforms of the Long 1960s. This chapter explains differences across the three countries in *abortion politics*—the positions of political parties on abortion and the degree to which abortion has been an issue in elections. The next chapter explains differences across the countries in *abortion policies*—the number and character of abortion regulations established by legislatures, courts, and government bureaucracies. This distinction between politics and policy is an artificial but useful one. It is artificial because parties and candidates typically campaign by touting policies that they have enacted or promise to enact, and because officials typically choose policy goals with an eye to how voters and party activists might respond to them. But the distinction is a useful one because intraparty battles, electoral campaigns, and policy making are driven by differing causal factors. In the next chapter, I argue that the degree to which political parties addressed the abortion issue was one of the main determinants of differences in abortion policies, but there were other determinants as well.

After the reforms of the Long 1960s, large movements faced off on both sides of the abortion issue in all three countries, and, at least initially, most parties and candidates were inclined to avoid the issue. But British and Canadian parties were more successful in doing so than American ones. In the United States, movements with abortion on their agenda—the feminist movement, the New Right, and the Christian Right—seized opportunities provided by open party and electoral systems to move abortion onto party and campaign agendas and, as I describe in the next chapter, policy agendas. Abortion eventually moved to the center of politics. The two major parties took firm and opposing positions, and abortion was a central issue in campaigns at all levels of government. Parties often imposed abortion litmus tests on potential nominees, and a candidate's position on abortion became a shorthand for whether he or she was a "real" Democrat or Republican or one "in name only." In Britain and Canada, by contrast, parties were reluctant to take positions on abortion and have successfully kept the issue out of electoral politics. In what follows, I describe abortion movement mobilization in each country. I then discuss the varying openness of party and electoral systems to new movements in each country and the implications of that openness for abortion movements. I close with a discussion of the American Christian Right, examining how it built its influence within the Republican Party and why its power within that party was so durable.

Opposing Movements Mobilize

After reform, pro-life and pro-choice movements faced off in all three countries, and the abortion issue became more visible and controversial. The movements were largest in the United States, followed by Canada and then Britain, but they were sizable in all three countries. In Britain, two formally nondenominational but predominantly Catholic groups, the Society for the Protection of Unborn Children (SPUC) and LIFE, spearheaded attempts to restrict abortion. Each group had more than 200 local affiliates. In the 1990s and 2000s, these groups were joined by several evangelical organizations, most notably Christian Action Research and Education (CARE), which runs more than 150 crisis pregnancy centers. In the 1980s, Rescue UK tried to bring American-style "rescues" to Britain, but this tactic was rejected by SPUC and LIFE.[1] The movement's largest protests occurred in 1971 (10,000) and 1975 (50,000).[2] The British pro-life movement was also aided by the dominance of the tabloid press, which had a strong appetite for stories of scandal and atrocity that were readily supplied by the movement. On the pro-choice side, the ALRA largely demobilized after the 1967 reform, but in 1970, "abortion on demand" became a primary goal of the British feminist movement. In 1975, feminist organizations formed the National Abortion Campaign (NAC), which eventually had 350 member organizations. NAC was especially successful at building links with unions—by 1986, more than 20 had pledged to defend abortion rights.[3] Beginning in 1978, the Co-ordinating Committee in Defence of the 1967 Act mobilized almost 60 pro-choice professional organizations.[4] The largest pro-choice rallies occurred in 1975 (20,000) and 1979 (100,000).

In Canada, the main pro-life groups were the Alliance for Life, the more radical Campaign Life, and approximately 200 local groups. These groups were mainly Catholic but were joined by members of churches represented by the Evangelical Fellowship of Canada.[5] In 1975, the Alliance for Life delivered one million signatures to Parliament—the largest petition in Canadian history. In the mid-1980s, pro-lifers protested at Henry Morgentaler's Toronto clinic, and at least one bombed the clinic. Abortion opponents also shot and wounded three doctors. In the late 1980s, activists mounted American-style clinic "rescues," resulting in hundreds of arrests.[6] In 1983, 40,000 protested in Toronto, and in 2006, 30,000 attended the annual March for Life. On the other side of the issue, the main groups were the Canadian Association for the Repeal of Abortion Laws (CARAL) and the National Action Committee on the Status of Women.[7] There were also strong local organizations in the cities where Morgentaler opened clinics, most notably Montreal, Toronto, Vancouver, and Winnipeg. In 1971, thousands protested at Parliament Hill, and in 1983 and 1985, 4,000 and 5,000 respectively protested in Toronto.[8]

In the United States, the largest group was the National Right to Life Committee (NRLC), officially nondenominational but predominantly Catholic.[9] The NRLC was supported in various ways by the National Conference of Catholic Bishops (NCCB) and developed close ties to the Republican Party leadership. The NRLC claims 3,000 local chapters and affiliates in every state. The next largest group was the explicitly Catholic and more radical American Life League. These mainly Catholic groups were joined by multi-issue evangelical groups such as Concerned Women for America, the Moral Majority, Focus on the Family, and later, the Christian Coalition. In the late 1980s and early 1990s, Operation Rescue mobilized evangelical pastors and their flocks to blockade clinics in several cities, resulting in more than 60,000 arrests.[10] During the 1990s, local and national direct action groups focused on picketing, "sidewalk counseling," and the harassment of providers and their patients. In the 1990s and 2000s, the Center for Bio-ethical Reform and Justice for All presented graphic displays of aborted fetuses on college campuses. Activists also established more than 3,000 crisis pregnancy centers. Beginning in 1997, the Susan B. Anthony List funded pro-life candidates, spending $6 million in 2010. During the 1980s and 1990s, violent activists

Table 5.1 Membership of Major Pro-Life and Pro-Choice Organizations, c. 1990

	United States	Britain	Canada
Pro-life organizations[2]	7,300,000	50,000	250,000
Multi-issue traditional values organizations[3]	3,300,000	100,000	264,000
Total	10,600,000	150,000	514,000
Total as % of population[1]	4.3%	0.3%	2.1%
Pro-choice organizations[4]	400,000	2,000	18,000
Feminist organizations[5]	310,000	20,000	750,000
Total	710,000	22,000	768,000
Total as % of population[1]	0.3%	0.04%	3.1%

[1]The 1990 populations were United States (249 million), Britain (56 million), and Canada (25 million). U.S. Bureau of the Census, International Database, Total Midyear Population, July 1990.

[2]The U.S. figure includes the National Right to Life Committee (7 million, 1990) and the American Life League (300,000, 1990). Gerald N. Rosenberg, *The Hollow Hope: Can Courts Bring About Social Change?* (Chicago: University of Chicago Press, 1991). The NRLC figure is likely an exaggeration—the organization sends out only 400,000 newsletters. Richard M. Skinner, *More Than Money: Interest Group Action in Congressional Elections* (Lanham, MD: Rowman and Littlefield, 2007). See also Myra Marx Ferree, William A. Gamson, Jurgen Gerhards, and Dieter Rucht, *Shaping Abortion Discourse: Democracy and the Public Sphere in Germany and the United States* (Cambridge: Cambridge University Press, 2002). The British figure includes the Society for the Protection of Unborn Children (SPUC) (30,000, 1984) and LIFE (20,000, 1979). Joni Lovenduski, "Parliament, Pressure Groups, Networks, and the Women's Movement: The Politics of Abortion Law Reform in Britain (1967–1983)," in *The New Politics of Abortion*, ed. Joni Lovenduski and Joyce Outshoorn (London: Sage Publications, 1986); J. Christopher Soper, "Political Structures and Interest Group Activism: A Comparison of the British and American Pro-Life Movements," *Social Science Journal* 31, no. 3 (1994): 319–34. The Canadian figure includes over one hundred pro-life groups. Lorna Kathleen Erwin, "The Politics of Anti-Feminism: The Pro-Family Movement in Canada" (PhD dissertation, York University, 1990).

[3]The U.S. figure includes the Christian Coalition (400,000, 1994), Christian Action Council (300,000, 1994), Concerned Women of America (600,000, 1992), and Focus on the Family (2 million, 1995). The Christian Coalition, founded in 1989, reported 2.8 million members in 1996, but critics and former employees reported that the Coalition failed to purge inactive members from its rolls and sent out only 400,000 copies of its magazine. I use that figure here. J. Christopher Soper, *Evangelical Christianity in the United States and Great Britain: Religious Beliefs, Political Choices* (New York: New York University Press, 1994); David Von Drehle and Thomas B. Edsall, "Life of the Grand Old Party: Energized Coalition Enters Another Political Phase," *Washington Post*, August 14, 1994, A1; Jeanne Cummings, "Religious Right Reviving Gospel of Political Activism," *Atlanta Journal and Constitution*, September 11, 1992, C1; Duane Murray Oldfield, *The Right and the Righteous: The Christian Right Confronts the Republican Party* (Lanham, MD: Rowman and Littlefield, 1996). The British figure is for Christian Action Research and Education (CARE), which claimed 100,000 supporters on its website. The Canadian figure includes Focus on the Family Canada (150,000, 1997), REAL Women (50,000, 1997), Renaissance Canada (50,000, 1983), and Evangelical Fellowship Council (EFC) (14,000, 1996). The EFC is an umbrella organization of Canada's evangelical congregations that represented 1.5 million evangelicals in 1991. The organization also had individual members, which is the figure used here. Dennis R. Hoover, "The Christian Right under Old Glory and the Maple Leaf," in *Sojourners in the Wilderness: The Christian Right in Comparative Perspective*, ed. Corwin Smidt and James M. Penning, 171–93 (Lanham, MD: Rowman and Littlefield, 1997); Harvey Shepherd. "Annual Spiritualism Conference Is Coming of Age," *Gazette* (Montreal), May 11, 1996, J4; David Howell, Spare the Rod, Don't Teach Kids Violence, *Toronto Star*, August 10, 1996, L1; George Egerton, "Trudeau, God, and the Canadian Constitution: Religion, Human Rights, and Government Authority in the Making of the 1982 Constitution," in *Rethinking Church, State, and Modernity: Canada between Europe and America*, ed. David Lyon and Marguerite Van Die (Toronto: University of Toronto Press, 2000).

bombed or burned more than 100 clinics and vandalized more than 400. They also killed seven clinic staff, including several doctors. The latest victim, in 2009, was Dr. George Tiller, the nation's leading provider of late-term abortions. The annual March for Life drew its largest crowds in 1976 (65,000), 1985 (71,000), 1990 (200,000), 1993 (75,000) and 1999 (100,000).[11]

On the pro-choice side, the main organizations were NARAL, the National Organization for Women (NOW), Planned Parenthood, and the ACLU.[12] EMILY's List PAC funded pro-choice women candidates—raising more than $200 million since its founding in 1984—and had close ties to the Democratic Party leadership. The largest pro-choice protests occurred in 1989 (300,000), 1992 (500,000), and 2004 (1 million)—the last two protests ranked as the largest in American history.[13] Table 5.1 shows membership figures for the leading movement organizations in each country. These figures should be taken with a grain of salt because most are self-reported and movement organizations have a tendency to exaggerate the size of their membership, but they do provide a rough indicator of the sizes of the movements in the three countries. As a

---

[4]The U.S. figure includes the National Abortion Rights Action League (NARAL). Gerald N. Rosenberg, *Hollow Hope*; Suzanne Staggenborg, *The Pro-Choice Movement: Organization and Activism in the Abortion Conflict* (New York: Oxford University Press, 1991). The British figure includes the National Abortion Campaign (NAC) and the Abortion Law Reform Association (ALRA). Soper estimates that no pro-choice organization had more than 1,000 members in 1985. I estimate a combined figure of 2,000 for these two groups. Soper, *Evangelical Christianity in the United States and Great Britain*. The Canadian figure includes the Canadian Abortion Rights Action League (CARAL), which had 18,000 individual members and 300 member groups in 1990. Melissa Hausman, "Gendering as a Variable and Process in Canadian Federal Abortion Policy Changes, 1969–1991" (Biennial Meeting of the Association for Canadian Studies in the United States, Pittsburgh, PA, 1999); "REAL Women Doing Favor for Feminists," *Toronto Star*, January 15, 1987, A23; Raymond Tatalovich, *The Politics of Abortion in the United States and Canada: A Comparative Study* (Armonk, NY: M. E. Sharpe, 1997), 125.

[5]The U.S. figure includes the National Women's Political Caucus (35,000, 1992) and the National Organization for Women (270,000, 1992). Catherine S. Manegold, "Women Advance in Politics by Evolution, Not Revolution," *New York Times*, October 21, 1992, A1. The British women's movement is quite decentralized. Most groups are small, local, and single-issue. Bouchier estimates that one-tenth of 1 percent of British women (20,000) are involved in feminist activities. Despite this small size, women have been organized and influential as pressure groups within trade unions and political parties. David Bouchier, *The Feminist Challenge: The Movement for Women's Liberation in Britain and the USA* (New York: Schocken Books, 1984), 178. See also Joyce Gelb, "Social Movement 'Success': A Comparative Analysis of Feminism in the United States and the United Kingdom," in *The Women's Movements of the United States and Western Europe: Consciousness, Political Opportunity, and Public Policy*, ed. Mary Fainsod Katzenstein and Carol McClurg Mueller (Philadelphia: Temple University Press, 1987). The Canadian figure is for 1993 and includes the 750,000 individual members of the National Action Committee on the Status of Women. NAC also has 573 organizational members representing 3 million women, but many of these affiliated organizations cannot be considered feminist. Hausman, "Gendering as a Variable and Process in Canadian Federal Abortion Policy Changes, 1969–1991"; Sylvia Bashevkin, *Women on the Defensive: Living through Conservative Times* (Toronto: University of Toronto Press, 1998).

percentage of the population, the pro-life (and pro-family) movement was largest in the United States, followed by Canada and then Britain. And the pro-choice (and feminist) movement was largest in Canada, followed by the United States and then Britain. A resource mobilization approach to social movement impacts suggests that abortion should be most controversial where movements are larger and richer, but the implications of this approach for policy change are not as clear. Large, rich movements should promote policy change, but when movements mobilize on both sides of an issue they might cancel each other out and produce gridlock. The large American movements help to explain the greater controversy and politicization of abortion in the United States, but they are not the end of the story. Pro-life movements were large and vocal in all of the countries, yet there was not just *less* party politicization of the abortion issue in Britain and Canada, but virtually none. As I show below, even if British and Canadian movements had been larger, it is unlikely that they would have influenced parties to the extent that American movements did.

Moreover, part of the reason that the American abortion movements were so large was because the issue was defined in a way that directly challenged moral traditionalists. Abortion was a "woman's right" rather than a "medical necessity." Kristin Luker argues that the abortion debate was so heated in the 1970s and 1980s because it was "a referendum on the place and meaning of motherhood," and pro-life activists were mainly homemakers who viewed *Roe* as a personal attack on their identities. Similarly, Gene Burns argues that the meaning of abortion shifted around 1970 from a limited medical-humanitarian frame to a contest between competing moral worldviews—women's rights and fetal rights. After this shift, abortion became highly controversial, and policy makers shied away.[14] In Britain and Canada, by contrast, abortion was defined as a medical necessity under the control of doctors and was not a similar threat to moral traditionalists.[15] The unique meaning of the American reform was facilitated in several ways by political institutions. As I showed in chapter 3, American medical organizations were more concerned about preserving fee-for-service medicine than abortion gatekeeping. They abandoned the field of abortion policy and left a definitional vacuum to be filled by alternative meanings. In Britain and Canada, by contrast, medical associations were heavily involved in the abortion issue, and medical meanings were central to the abortion debate. In addition, some of the controversy of American policy making sprang from the venue in which the initial reform was made. The abortion decisions of the American Supreme Court focused attention on the issue, went beyond public opinion, framed the issue in terms of competing "rights," and drew accusations of democratic illegitimacy. The abortion issue was also kept alive by the numerous venues available for contesting it. Settlement of the issue was impossible because losers could always move to a new arena. Finally, the ability of abortion movements to inject the abortion issue into parties and electoral politics only increased controversy and movement mobilization.

Parties and Politicians Avoid Abortion

In the face of large movements, frequent protests, and heated rhetoric, many parties and politicians in all three countries tried to avoid the abortion issue. They did so for many reasons. To begin, the parties were mainly organized around economic rather than religious cleavages and typically had members on both sides of the issue. This was especially true of the left-leaning parties—the American Democrats, the Canadian Liberals, and the British Labour Party—who all included both feminists and working-class Catholics among their ranks. For parties with members on both sides of the abortion issue, it was difficult to develop a position on abortion; and once they did, it was hard to impose that position on dissenting members since they usually held their positions with fervor. Party leaders preferred to focus on the economic issues that held their parties together rather than the social issues that divided them.[16] Some politicians were personally uncomfortable with an issue that provoked such strong emotions, and others wished to avoid confrontations with irate protestors. Finally, R. Kent Weaver argues that policy makers have weak incentives to enact policies on symbolic, winner-take-all issues. For this type of issue, every policy change creates both winners and losers, but voters are more sensitive to losses than gains. As a result, a new policy may please winners but will displease losers even more. And the incentives are even weaker when an issue involves strong opposing movements that mobilize the outrage of their supporters after every policy change, no matter how small.[17]

In all three countries, many politicians sought to avoid abortion. In Britain, Cabinets insisted that abortion was an "issue of conscience" that required private member's legislation and Government neutrality. The Canadian Government repeatedly tried to pass the buck—arguing that there was nothing wrong with abortion law, and if there was, it was the fault of the medical profession, hospitals, and the provinces. British and Canadian Governments also tried to defuse the issue by commissioning formal inquiries by nonpartisan experts with narrow mandates. In the United States of the 1970s, Presidents Ford and Carter sought to leave the issue with the courts or return it to the states. In the Democratic Congress, party leaders declined to take positions on abortion and committee chairs killed abortion bills before they came to the floor. State legislators ran from the issue as well. An Ohio legislator reported that his chamber included "ten strong pro-choice people, ten strong pro-life and 79 legislators who would rather the issue would go away."[18]

Of course, not all policy makers avoided abortion. Some took it on for personal or religious reasons, others for political ones. Those in the latter group were more likely to address the issue when they represented homogeneous constituencies that shared a common position on abortion, and this was more common in smaller districts. In the United States, state legislators and members of the House of Representatives, with their smaller districts, were more willing to address the issue than senators, governors, and presidents with statewide or national constituencies.[19] Politicians were also more willing to take up the issue during periods when the intensity of the two sides was asymmetric. During the 1970s and 1980s, abortion was more salient for pro-lifers than pro-choicers. The first group was freshly outraged by *Roe*, while the latter group felt reasonably well protected by the decision.[20] As a result, politicians worried more about offending pro-lifers than pro-choicers. After the 1989 *Webster* decision allowed greater restrictions on abortion, however, the issue became more salient for pro-choicers, and politicians' calculations changed.[21]

Why Are Some Parties More Open to New Movements than Others?

If parties and policy makers were initially inclined to avoid the abortion issue, why did they eventually embrace it in the United States? Mainly because American parties were more open to new movements than parties in the other countries. By new movements, I mean movements that are not currently members of the party coalition but wish to become one. This openness to new movements had three main dimensions: (1) broadly participatory systems for selecting candidates, party leaders, and policy goals; (2) expensive, low-turnout, candidate-centered elections; and (3) decentralized, coalitional parties.[22]

American party leaders and activists have much less control over who will represent them in elections than do their counterparts in Britain and Canada—and this makes it easier for candidates supported by new movements to win nominations. American candidates are chosen through state and local primaries and caucuses that allow extensive public participation, including participation by people who do not consider themselves members of the party.[23] In Britain, public participation in the nominating process is much narrower. Labour candidates are chosen by dues-paying members of the local party, most of whom are highly committed to the party and have been members for a long time. They reward those same characteristics in the candidates they select, making it almost impossible for newcomers to win nominations. Tory candidates are chosen by an even narrower group—a small committee of local party members. In Canada, candidates are also chosen by local party members, but the process is more open than in Britain because the memberships of the major parties swell at election time. As a result, new movements can sometimes win nominations by recruiting new party members.[24]

The parties in each country also vary in how they choose their leaders (i.e., their candidates for prime minister or president). Again, American party leaders and activists have less control over who will lead their party than do their British and Canadian counterparts, and this advantages new movements. In Britain's Conservative Party, the parliamentary party chooses the party leader. Until 1981, the Labour Party chose its leader the same way; afterwards, the parliamentary party, the local parties and the labor unions chose the leader jointly. In both British parties, party leaders must be sitting MPs—a significant barrier to newcomers. In Canada for most of the twentieth century, delegates to national conventions chose the leaders of both parties. Since the late 1990s, the major parties have begun holding a vote of the entire party membership—candidates need not be sitting MPs.[25] In the United States, the party is led by the president or presidential nominee, but during periods when there is no such person, the party is led by its top-ranking members of Congress. Congressional leaders are elected by their fellow members. Presidential nominees are chosen by the primary and caucus processes outlined above, and presidential candidates do not need to be sitting members of Congress. Leaders of new movements can and do campaign for the presidential nomination of their party—though few have won.[26]

Party goal setting is also more open to new movements in the United States than in the other countries. In the United States, delegates to state and national party conventions write and vote on party platforms. And in both parties, there are often large numbers of convention delegates who do not share the policy preferences of the nominee. This is especially a problem in the Republican Party where supporters of losing candidates may actually outnumber those of the nominee.[27] Convention delegates often adopt platform positions that the nominee does not share. The nominee may attempt to distance his- or herself from the platform or some of its planks, but this is easier said than done since the media report extensively on both the platform and any conflicts between the nominee and party factions. In Britain, parties campaign on "party manifestos" written by party leaders rather than party activists. The Labour Party holds annual conventions of the party membership that pass policy resolutions, but these are not campaign documents and are not binding on the PLP. The Tories do not allow members to pass resolutions but merely "listen" to their concerns. In Canada, the Liberals and Tories occasionally hold policy conventions of their members, but their resolutions are not binding on the parliamentary party and often do not make it into campaign platforms.[28]

New movements are also aided by the many low-turnout elections in the United States. Highly organized, intense minorities are more likely to vote than the average citizen, and when turnout is low, they start to become majorities. Intense minorities are also better at mobilizing their troops for events such as caucuses and conventions, which require both more time and interaction than voting. And church-based organizations are especially adept at eliciting high-commitment political action because they are cohesive communities central to their members' lives.[29] The United States has lower turnout for its most important elections than most other countries.[30] But more important, the United States has many more minor elections and meetings than other countries, and these typically have very low turnout. In the 2006 midterm election, average turnout was 37 percent, but in many states it was below 30 percent. Presidential primary turnout is lower still—in 2000 when both parties had contested primaries, most states had turnout rates between 10 and 20 percent, and caucus participation was often as low as 3 percent.[31]

American new movements also have a better chance of influencing individual candidates and legislators than do their counterparts in Britain and Canada. The key issues here are whether individual candidates need movement resources and whether individual legislators wield enough power to make them worth influencing. In the United States, elections are candidate centered. Voters often pay as much attention to the character and issue positions of candidates as they do to those candidates' party affiliations. In addition, individual candidates, rather than parties, fund and staff their campaigns. Candidates are typically more dependent on resources provided by movements and interest groups than those provided by parties.[32] In Britain and Canada, by contrast, campaigns are party centered. Voters choose a candidate mainly because he or she represents a particular party, and elections are funded and staffed mainly by the party and its members. This leaves little opportunity for new movements to contribute to the success of individual candidates.

There is also more value in influencing individual American legislators than British or Canadian ones. American legislators have a great deal of power—they can introduce legislation without party approval and usually vote against their party without penalty. If they are committee chairs, they can kill legislation. By contrast, in the Westminster parliamentary systems of Britain, and especially Canada, the principle of responsible government requires that the Government obtain support from the House of Commons for all major legislation. If it fails to do so, it must disband or call a new election. Consequently, party discipline is strict. The party leadership initiates most legislation and legislators are required to toe the party line.[33] As a result, there is usually little point in influencing legislators who are not members of the party leadership.[34] This difference gives American new movements more access points than their counterparts in Britain and Canada. They can attempt to influence any of hundreds of individual legislators rather than focusing on a small group of party leaders.

American new movements also have more influence because parties and candidates depend heavily on them for money and volunteers. American campaigns are longer, more expensive, more decentralized, more candidate centered, and use more paid media than those in Britain and Canada. American elections last a year or more while British and Canadian ones last one to two months. American electoral districts, especially for senators, are much larger in population and area. Voter registration requirements and low turnout make get-out-the-vote activities especially important. There is little public financing available and few restrictions on expenditures. At the same time, parties face restrictions on how much they can contribute to candidates' campaigns.[35] The resource intensity of American campaigns increases demand for campaign workers but, unlike their counterparts in Britain and Canada, American parties have no pool of dues-paying party members from which to draw this labor.[36] Instead, they rely on labor unions or movement organizations.

In Britain and Canada, on the other hand, movements have few opportunities to provide resources to parties or candidates. In Britain, there are no restrictions on national-level campaign contributions or expenditures and no public financing of campaigns, but campaigns are inexpensive because parties cannot buy television time and campaigns are short. Moreover, economic groups and large individual contributors provide ample funds, and there are no restrictions on how much money parties can provide to candidates.[37] Canadian campaigns are also short and inexpensive. The major parties get free time on television and radio. There are also strong restrictions on contributions and expenditures. Public campaign financing is extensive, and the major parties draw most of their campaign funding from business.[38] Parties in both Britain and Canada can draw on party members for campaign work.

Movements also have more access points in the decentralized and coalitional parties of the United States. The parties are divided between a presidentially oriented national committee and the congressional and senatorial legislative caucuses and campaign committees. In Congress, party leadership is broadly dispersed among committee and subcommittee chairs; state and local parties are similarly divided.[39] By contrast, parliamentary government in Britain and Canada translates into centralized parties without separate organizations for the legislative and executive branches. Britain is a unitary polity while Canada is a federal one.[40] But Canadian parties (with the exception of the New Democratic Party [NDP]) are not federations. Federal and provincial parties with the same name are in fact distinct entities with their own personnel, candidates, and issue positions, and only limited coordination. Thus, a movement that gains influence in a provincial party is not necessarily able to translate this into power within the national party.

Finally, movements have more influence in the coalitional parties of the United States and Canada. In Britain, the demands of large economic groups, such as unions, businesses, and farmers' associations, tend to drown out those of smaller noneconomic groups—though British parties have become more coalitional in recent years. In the United States and Canada, by contrast, where parties are coalitions of many groups, small groups have opportunities to ally with other party factions.[41]

Does the openness of American parties mean that all issues will be more politicized in the United States than in other countries? Not necessarily. Instead, it is easier for movements to bring *new* issues into politics in the United States than in the other countries. In all three countries, the left-right, labor-capital cleavage has been central, but this cleavage is stronger in Britain than in the United States. As a result, labor-capital issues are more important in British elections than American ones. And closed British parties have an easier time resisting new issues and movements that do not match this cleavage. Whether new movements are able to influence parties also depends on their size, resources, and strategies. Not all movements have the wherewithal to influence American parties, nor do all wish to do so. Below, I show how the strong abortion movements of all three countries fared when they encountered differing party and electoral systems.

Closed British Parties Avoid Abortion

In the face of daunting institutional obstacles, abortion activists never attained much power or influence in British parties. Labour and Liberal MPs tended to support abortion rights while Tories opposed them, but all three parties contained members on both sides of the issue and generally tried to avoid it. The Labour Party was in a particularly difficult position because it contained both feminists and working-class Catholics. As I detailed in chapter 2, the 1967 abortion reform occurred through a private member's bill with assistance from the Labour Government. This allowed the Government to avoid blame for the reform and responsibility for the issue. After reform, and the increased controversy that it brought, leaders of both parties maintained that abortion was an "issue of conscience" and thus a subject for private member's legislation. But in contrast to the initial reform, Governments no longer offered assistance to abortion bills.

Abortion activists had the most success in the Labour Party, but this was still quite limited. They had some influence with the party's rank-and-file membership and with labor unions, but little influence with the parliamentary party and its leaders. In 1975, the party conference passed a resolution calling for abortion on request, but it was not binding on the parliamentary party. In 1976, pro-choice activists formed the Labour Abortion Rights Campaign (LARC) to remind MPs of the party conference resolution, pressure MPs who voted against abortion rights, and raise the issue when the party reselected candidates. There is no evidence, however, that LARC ever succeeded in deselecting candidates. LARC also unsuccessfully lobbied the parliamentary party to establish a policy on abortion and firmly whip MPs on the issue.[42] In 1977, the party conference passed another resolution supporting abortion on request, but rejected a resolution requiring a firm whip on parliamentary abortion votes.[43] In 1985, the party conference finally passed a resolution requiring a firm whip on abortion, but party leaders would not enforce it. Party leaders rarely mentioned abortion in their campaign manifestos.[44]

Abortion activists had even less success in the other parties. The Liberal Party conference (the party joined with the Social Democratic Party to become the Liberal Democrats in 1988) passed resolutions supporting abortion rights in 1975, 1979, and 1992, but the parliamentary party would not discuss the issue. Conservative party conferences do not pass resolutions, and the parliamentary party considered abortion an "issue of conscience" on which the party should remain neutral.[45] Party leaders mentioned abortion in their 1974 campaign manifesto, pledging to introduce an abortion bill after the Lane Committee finished its deliberations, but never actually did so.

The British parliamentary parties have avoided initiating legislation or taking a position on abortion, instead confining the issue to private member's bills and free voting. Since the 1967 reform, MPs have initiated more than a dozen private member's bills on abortion, and none have passed. Since the 1967 reform, no Government has initiated a bill or taken a position on abortion. In 1990 and 2008, the Conservative and Labour Governments respectively, provided time for free votes on measures to reduce the upper time limit for abortions, but neither Government took a position on these measures and they both failed.

Because Catholics were a traditional Labour constituency, the Catholic hierarchy occasionally clashed with the party on abortion. For several years in the early 1990s, Labour for Life operated an information booth at the Scottish Labour conference, but in 1994 national party officials banned it. Cardinal Thomas Winning criticized the decision and demanded that Labour leader Tony Blair intervene. Blair passed the buck—arguing that party conventions were the responsibility of the party's general secretary.[46]

Blair, who converted to Catholicism after leaving office, said that he was personally opposed to abortion but supported a woman's right to decide for herself. He occasionally suggested that he would support a reduction in the upper time limit. At all times, however, he was clear that this was his personal opinion and that the abortion issue should be left to the individual consciences of MPs and kept out of electoral politics. Blair assured voters that he would not mix religion and politics, and cited the United States as a negative example: "I do not want to end up with an American-style of politics with us all going out there beating our chest about our faith."[47]

In 1996 and again in 1997, Cardinal Winning and Cardinal Basil Hume criticized Blair for "washing his hands" of abortion even though he personally opposed it.[48] But pro-choice activists, and many commentators, criticized the cardinals, arguing that abortion "has no place on the hustings [the stump]."[49] Blair agreed: "I intend to do everything in my power to keep abortion out of party politics."[50]

It appeared that abortion might finally become an election issue in 2005 when comments by Tory leader Michael Howard caused a weeklong media flap over abortion. A few weeks before Labour called an election, *Cosmopolitan* magazine asked the party leaders for their positions on abortion; Howard complained about "abortion on demand" and said that he would support a reduction in the upper time limit for abortion, while Blair said that he disliked "the idea of abortion" but would support the status quo.[51] Howard declared that if the Tories won the election, they would provide extra time to a private member's bill seeking to lower the limit. This was the first time that a party leader had ever offered extra time for a private member's bill during an election campaign. Cardinal Cormac Murphy-O'Connor hailed Howard's statement and warned Labour that it could no longer count on the support of Catholics. The middle-market tabloid the *Daily Mail* declared that abortion had become "a burning election issue."

Commentators were mixed on whether this was actually true and whether it was a good or bad thing. A columnist in the *Times* warned of "single-issue politics" dominated by "extremists" and of "threats and moral blackmail which have infected political campaigning in America."[52] Blair had no interest in debating the issue: "It would be a pity if this did become a party-political issue, or indeed a general election issue." Howard and his senior advisors denied that they were trying to campaign on abortion—Howard had simply responded honestly to a reporter's question. But journalists and Labour officials accused the Tories of waging an American-style campaign that focused on hot-button issues.[53] The abortion flap lasted only a week as the Tories turned to another hot-button issue—gypsy and traveler camps—and opposition to immigration soon became the centerpiece of the Tories' losing campaign.[54]

In the 2010 campaign, the Conservative Party revisited the abortion issue. In one of the first interviews of the campaign, party leader David Cameron told the *Catholic Herald* that he supported reducing the upper time limit for abortion, opposed assisted suicide, and thought that religious schools should be free to decide how they taught sex education. But Cameron stressed that "what's really important here is that members of Parliament are always allowed a free vote on this issue. This is an issue of conscience, so it would be wrong to put pressure on parliamentary colleagues when it comes to voting on this."[55]

A possible objection to my arguments about the ways that Britain's closed parties have handled the abortion issue is that some issues are just inherently "issues of conscience," and neither party could change that if

CHAPTER FIVE

it wanted to. In this view, parties avoided abortion not because they are closed to new movements, but because there was a social consensus that abortion was not a matter for party politics. The discussion above suggests that there is something to this, but it also suggests that the degree to which abortion should be a partisan issue is a matter of dispute. It is certainly the case that once an issue gets established as an "issue of conscience," as abortion was during the 1967 reform, it is difficult to change that definition. Politicians who wish to avoid the issue are glad of that, but there are no inherent "issues of conscience"; various issues, including capital punishment, gay rights, and Sunday commerce, have been whipped at some times and treated as "issues of conscience" at others.[56]

Closed Canadian Parties Avoid Abortion

As in Britain, Canadian abortion activists faced relatively closed parties and never gained much power or influence within them, and the parties avoided the abortion issue during the 1970s and 1980s. The Liberal Party enacted the 1969 abortion reform, but did so through an omnibus bill and a free vote on its abortion clauses; and after reform, Liberal Governments studiously avoided the issue. Liberal MPs were more likely to vote for abortion rights than Tories, but both parties had members on the other side, and the Liberals were heavily reliant on Catholic votes.[57] The year after the 1969 reform, a Liberal policy conference passed a resolution calling for increased abortion provision and the removal of abortion from the criminal code; and the next year, the party's task force on the status of women made a similar proposal, and this was approved by party activists; but the Liberal Government repeatedly refused to act.[58] As Henry Morgentaler was prosecuted and imprisoned by Quebec's Liberal Government in the early 1970s, the federal Liberal Government did nothing to aid him, and when the Parti Québécois announced that it would no longer enforce the federal abortion law in the province, the federal Government looked the other way. CMA president Bette Stephenson complained that the association's proposals to eliminate hospital abortion committees had been met by "the usual Ottawa activity—masterful inactivity."[59] In 1975, the Government appointed the Badgley Committee mainly to defuse the issue and get the CMA off its back, and in 1983, the Liberal Government began a review of the criminal code, but refused requests to include the abortion law in this review.[60]

The Progressive Conservatives (Tories) also avoided the issue during the 1970s and 1980s. Although there were more pro-lifers among the

Progressive Conservatives than among the Liberals, the Tories still did not have the strong antifeminist bent of the American Republicans. At a debate on women's issues during the 1984 election, the three parties barely differed. The Tory candidate said that the party would continue to allow a free vote on abortion and expressed support for the law as it stood. After the Supreme Court struck down the federal abortion law in January 1988, abortion was barely mentioned in that year's election. According to *MacLean's*:

Both [Progressive Conservative] Mulroney and [Liberal] Turner—their parties divided—have dodged the question, clearly loath to attract unwelcome attention from anti-abortion and pro-choice groups. Last August, Mulroney said that abortion should be allowed in cases of rape and incest and "certain personal situations." . . . Meanwhile, Turner last week refused to reveal how he would counsel his own daughter on abortion, arguing that it was "such a personal question."[61]

As I detail in the next chapter, when the Tory Government finally introduced an abortion bill in 1988, it did so only because the Supreme Court had struck down the abortion law, and the Government mainly tried to avoid offending either side. After the bill failed, the Government refused to introduce new legislation.[62]

Canada's main third party during the 1970s and 1980s, the NDP, was more supportive of abortion rights. The federal NDP adopted a resolution supporting the removal of abortion from the criminal code in 1971. NDP Governments in Ontario and British Columbia (1990–95 and 1991–2001, respectively) also supported abortion rights. But Manitoba's NDP Government (1981–88), which combined social democracy with conservative positions on social issues, opposed Morgentaler's 1983 attempt to open an abortion clinic there.[63]

After the failure of the Mulroney bill in 1990, abortion was occasionally a minor issue in Canadian elections.[64] In 1993, Liberals for Life sought party nominations in about 20 percent of ridings (districts). The campaign director of the Ontario Liberals privately urged Liberal leader Jean Chretien to disavow them, saying, "These Liberals for Life are nasty single-issue people who are prepared to try every trick in the book. They couldn't care less about the impact of adverse publicity on the Liberal party. In fact, they seek it out."[65] Chretien did not take this advice, instead simply saying that although he did not intend to introduce abortion legislation, the party had promised more power to backbench MPs and, as a result, Parliament would eventually vote on the issue. NDP leader Audrey McLaughlin called the Liberals "policy challenged" on abortion and criticized

Tory leader Kim Campbell for supporting the recriminalization of abortion when she was Mulroney's justice minister.[66] Chretien mocked McLaughlin's attempt to bring abortion into the campaign, saying, "This is not an issue." But after Liberal MPs criticized Chretien's vague statements, he clarified that "the position of the Liberal party is not to introduce a bill on abortion." Campbell insisted that she was pro-choice and that her preference was "not to legislate."[67]

After the 1993 election decimated the Progressive Conservatives, and the recently formed Reform Party made impressive gains, abortion became more prominent in Canadian politics. Reform and its successor, the Canadian Alliance, were populist Conservative parties originating in western Canada that had strong links with pro-life, pro-family, and antifeminist groups. During the 1997 campaign, Reform leader Preston Manning, an evangelical Christian, said that his party would hold a national referendum on abortion, but would not say whether he planned to recriminalize abortion. "All we're saying is in the future we will be forced to define the rights of the unborn."[68] In 2000, two candidates for the leadership of the Canadian Alliance, Preston Manning and Stockwell Day, both said that they were personally opposed to abortion and would support a referendum on the issue. Other candidates opposed such a referendum. Keith Martin said the party should avoid the perception "that we are going to legislate people's personal or moral values. . . . [W]e should stay away from these issues."[69] Once Day won the leadership with the support of pro-life activists, he assured the general electorate that he would not make abortion a top priority, but an Alliance campaign briefing said that signatures from a mere 3 percent of the electorate would trigger a referendum—this amounted to about 400,000 people, and the pro-life movement had already delivered a petition with one million signatures to the Government during the 1970s. Day disavowed the figure, but his opponents pounced. Tory leader Joe Clark claimed that Day had a "hidden agenda," and Liberal leader Jean Chretien said that "Canadians don't want a party that threatens a woman's right to choose."[70] Though the Liberal Party had never taken an official position on abortion, Chretien's statements certainly gave the impression that the party now supported abortion rights.[71]

In 2003, the Canadian Alliance merged with the Progressive Conservative Party to form the Conservative Party. Party members fought internally over abortion, but did not establish an official position. During the 2004 campaign, party leader Stephen Harper was repeatedly asked about abortion, but he insisted that the only social issue he would pursue would be a ban on same-sex marriage and he would give MPs a free vote.[72] Still, the Liberals attacked Harper for his refusal to say that he would discourage party MPs from introducing private member's bills on abortion.[73] Liberal leader Paul Martin boasted, "I will never infringe on a woman's right to choose. I will never infringe on the *Charter of Rights*."[74] He also claimed that he would discourage Liberal MPs from introducing abortion private member's bills and would whip any vote that sought to use the *Charter's* "notwithstanding clause" to trump the Supreme Court's abortion decision.[75]

In March 2005, the Conservative Party held its first policy convention since its founding. Party leaders first tried to suppress debates on abortion, same-sex marriage, and euthanasia, but eventually allowed them,[76] and by a vote of 55 to 45, the convention declared that "a Conservative Government will not initiate or support any legislation to regulate abortion." But during the 2006 campaign, the Liberals still claimed that Harper was a threat to abortion rights; during one debate, Martin pledged to abolish the "notwithstanding clause" and criticized Harper for refusing to do the same. He asked why Harper would not "stand up for a stronger *Charter of Rights and Freedoms*?" and said the answer was "obvious"—Conservatives had promised "right-wing conservative groups that if they are elected, they will ensure parliamentary votes on a woman's right to choose, on same-sex marriage and other social issues, and that these votes will not matter unless Mr. Harper retains the power to override the *Charter*. That is the hammer he wants to keep."[77] Martin also accused Harper of a secret plan to "pack" the Supreme Court with justices that would overturn rights to abortion and same-sex marriage. "Are we going to find ourselves in the same situation that they are in the United States, where in fact it is not only the competence of a judge that governs, but in fact it is a judge's social views?"[78] Once elected, the Harper Government, as promised, introduced an unsuccessful motion to reopen the debate on same-sex marriage but did not offer abortion legislation.

In 2010, the abortion issue heated up once again in advance of elections expected either at the end of the year or early in the next. Interestingly, both parties accused one another of reopening the abortion issue. In January, Harper announced that he would make maternal and child health in poor countries the main focus of his upcoming presidency of the Group of Eight (G8). But later that month, journalists and pro-life activists asked why the coalition supporting Harper's initiative included a pro-choice group. Liberal leader Michael Ignatieff seized on the issue, urging the Government to include abortion funding in his plan and bemoaning the George W. Bush administration's "global gag rule" that refused foreign aid to organizations that performed or promoted abortions.

(The policy was reversed by President Obama.) The Harper Government immediately accused Ignatieff of making abortion a "political football" but would not say whether it planned to fund abortions under the plan. In March, the Liberals upped the ante by sponsoring a parliamentary motion urging the Government to include "the full range of family planning, sexual and reproductive health options" in its plan. The motion did not mention abortion but implied it by decrying the "failed right-wing ideology" of the George W. Bush administration's "global gag rule." Ignatieff first claimed that the Liberal MPs would have a free vote on the motion, but eventually whipped them. The Liberals should have had enough votes to pass the motion (with the assistance of the NDP and the Bloc Quebecois) but fell embarrassingly short after fourteen Liberal MPs failed to show up for the vote and three voted nay. Ignatieff said that the MPs would be subject to "internal discipline." Conservatives whipped their members against the motion, decrying it as "a transparent attempt to reopen the abortion debate."[79]

Abortion remained on the front pages throughout the spring and summer. In late March, U.S. Secretary of State Hillary Clinton visited Canada and urged the Government to include abortion in the maternal health initiative,[80] and in April, Harper announced that the maternal health initiative would not fund abortions. "Canadians want to see their foreign aid money used for things that will help save the lives of women and children in ways that unite the Canadian people rather than divide them."[81]

In May, an unusually large number of demonstrators (15,000) attended the annual March for Life on Parliament Hill and hailed Harper's recent actions. Both pro-life and pro-choice activists claimed that a parliamentary debate on abortion was imminent and that Harper had signaled his intention to reopen the issue, but pundits could not decide whether Harper or Ignatieff had reopened the debate and whether Harper was avoiding it or embracing it; some said he had avoided it and then embraced it.[82] Ignatieff claimed that he knew who started it: "Recently, the Conservatives have accused us of trying to start a culture war, but let's be clear: we didn't end the 25-year consensus on a woman's right to choose. They did."[83]

Open American Parties Avoid and Then Embrace Abortion

The American story of political parties and the abortion issue is longer and more complicated than the British and Canadian ones. During the

1960s and early 1970s, the two parties mainly avoided the abortion issue, but during the seventies they gradually polarized on abortion, and by 1980, they had firmly embraced opposing positions. Catholics were the original abortion opponents, but they were joined by the New Right (with many Catholic leaders) in the mid-1970s and evangelical Christians at the end of the decade. With the rise of Ronald Reagan, social conservatives became key partners in the Republican coalition. At the same time, feminists gained influence in the Democratic Party.[84] American candidates and parties began to take firm positions on abortion in state and national party platforms, campaign speeches, and political advertising (see table 5.2 and appendix 1).[85]

Polarization on abortion was part of a broader party polarization on a wide range of issues. This was mainly the result of rightward movement by Republicans rather than leftward movement by Democrats, and it mainly involved legislators and activists rather than voters.[86] This polarization had several causes: The two parties became more purely ideological as southern conservatives started moving from the Democrats to the Republicans after the Civil Rights Act of 1964; gerrymandering increased the number of safe seats in Congress and caused legislators to pay more attention to primary voters than the general electorate; ideologically conservative activist groups, including the Christian Right, became an important source of campaign funding and voter mobilization, and they were willing to support primary challenges to moderate Republicans; and finally, increased campaign spending by the Republican Party and the personal campaign committees of its leaders provided another tool for disciplining moderates.[87]

In 1970, it was not obvious that either party would embrace the abortion issue or which side the parties might take. Most Catholics were Democrats, while well-to-do mainline Protestants, who generally supported contraception and abortion, formed the backbone of the Republican Party. Many Republicans supported family planning to defuse the "population bomb" and as a method of reducing crime and welfare spending. Republican President Richard Nixon, Vice President Gerald Ford, and National Security Advisor Henry Kissinger were all strong proponents of population control.[88] Finally, many Republicans supported women's rights—the party was the first to support the Equal Rights Amendment (ERA). A June 1972 Gallup poll that asked whether "the decision to have an abortion should be made solely by a woman and her doctor" found 68 percent of Republicans and 59 percent of Democrats in support.[89]

But there were also reasons to predict the partisan alignment on abortion that eventually emerged. Many feminist activists were veterans of

CHAPTER FIVE

the civil rights and antiwar movements that were building a home in the Democratic Party, and the party's support for African American rights suggested that it might support women's rights as well. In addition, Nixon aide Kevin Phillips had argued in 1970 that the party could steal white southerners and ethnic Catholics from the Democratic New Deal coalition by mobilizing a backlash against the racial, gender, and sexual changes of the 1960s—with abortion as a key symbol.[90] The racial backlash expressed in the campaigns of Barry Goldwater in 1964 and George Wallace in 1964 and 1968 is well known, but the Wallace campaign also include an incipient gender and sexual backlash.[91]

Throughout the 1970s, the parties gradually polarized on abortion. In October 1970, Jerry Brown, the Democratic candidate for attorney general in California, reported that the state Republican Party had recently sent representatives to half of the Catholic churches in Orange County to sign up new members by informing parishioners that the California Democratic Party had adopted a platform plank supporting "abortion on demand." Brown claimed that the national Republican Party was watching this experiment closely.[92]

That seemed to be true. At the advice of his conservative Catholic aide, Patrick (Pat) Buchanan, Nixon began to express opposition to abortion. In April 1971, he revoked a policy in which military hospitals provided therapeutic abortions regardless of state law, arguing that abortion was an "unacceptable form of population control" and announcing that "abortion on demand, I cannot square with my personal belief in the sanctity of human life—including the life of the yet unborn."[93] In March 1972, he distanced himself from the Rockefeller Commission on population control, which he had himself commissioned and which endorsed abortion reform. And in May 1972, he sent a letter to the archbishop of New York, Cardinal Terence Cooke, supporting his attempts to roll back New York's 1970 abortion repeal.[94]

In the 1972 general election, Nixon painted his Democratic opponent George McGovern as a supporter of "abortion on demand," though McGovern denied it. As the Democratic primaries were beginning in January, McGovern said, "in my judgment, abortion is a private matter which should be decided by a pregnant woman and her own doctor. Once the decision has been made, I do not feel the laws should stand in the way of its implementation. I do believe, however, that abortion is a matter to be left to state governments."[95] But in April, the *Washington Post* quoted an anonymous Democratic senator doubting McGovern's chances in the remaining primaries. "The people don't know McGovern is for amnesty, abortion and legalization of pot. Once middle America—Catholic middle

America, in particular—finds this out, he's dead."[96] Senate Republican leader Hugh Scott transformed this anonymous quote into a taunt—"the triple-A candidate—abortion, amnesty and acid"—and this was picked up by other Democratic candidates as well as by pro-life activists.[97]

Buchanan's "Assault Book" for the general election laid out the issues on which Nixon would campaign against McGovern. It began with "Social Issues—Catholic/Ethnic Concerns. 1. Abortion/ZPG [Zero Population Growth]/Contraceptives 2. Amnesty 3. Marijuana 4. Aid to Nonpublic Schools." He recommended that a flyer contrasting the abortion positions of the two candidates be distributed at the Right to Life Convention in June, that antiabortion groups include the flyer in their mailings, and that an October "position flyer" lay out "major issues of concern to Catholics—i.e., parochial schools, abortion, pornography, etc."[98] As Phillips put it, Republicans tried to portray McGovern as "a radical whose election could jeopardize the fabric and stability of American society."[99]

In May, McGovern tried to distance himself from his earlier abortion position: "I have proposed no action in this field. As president, I would propose no action. This is an issue in which the state has sole jurisdiction. I don't propose to enter this area."[100] But syndicated columnist Louis Cassels wasn't buying McGovern's line: "Catholics know—and Republicans won't let them forget it—that McGovern was saying only a few months ago that 'abortion is a private matter which should be decided by a pregnant woman and her own doctor.' In other words, he favored abortion-on-demand with no legal restrictions."[101]

As Nixon maneuvered on abortion, his party was still quite supportive of women's rights. In 1971 and 1972, bipartisan majorities enacted more women's rights legislation in a single Congress than in all previous ones combined, including the ERA, which then needed to be ratified by the states. At the 1972 conventions, neither party adopted a platform plank on abortion—though both included statements supporting family planning (see appendix 1). Reforms within the Democratic Party had increased women's representation at the convention from 13 percent of delegates in 1968 to 40 percent in 1972. Many of these new delegates were associated with NOW or the National Women's Political Caucus (NWPC).[102] These organizations had strong links to McGovern's campaign, and the platform addressed most of their key issues—the ERA, comparable worth, and tax deductions for child care. But McGovern balked at the inclusion of an abortion plank. Feminists forced a floor vote, but McGovern successfully whipped his delegates against it.[103]

Women were also better represented at the Republican convention.[104]

CHAPTER FIVE

As Republican feminist Tanya Melich put it, Nixon "was in bed with the new conservatives, but was flirting with us."[105] The Republican platform expressed support for a range of feminist initiatives including the ERA, equal pay, and women's full participation in politics. Feminists also managed to secure a plank supporting federally assisted child care, even though Nixon had just vetoed such a bill.[106] On abortion, feminists had enough votes to force a floor fight but decided against it; some did not want to embarrass Nixon; others worried that it might hurt the state repeals; still others heard rumors that Nixon wanted a floor fight because the sight of his party voting down an abortion plank on national television would help him in the general election.[107]

At the 1976 conventions, the two parties took their first formal, and opposing, positions on abortion—though these did not completely reflect the views of the presidential nominees.[108] During the primaries, Carter announced that he was personally opposed to abortion but would not seek a constitutional amendment banning it, and he opposed public funding. Some have suggested that his position was an unsuccessful attempt to appeal to both sides of the debate, while others convincingly argue that both his opposition to abortion and his commitment to the separation of church and state were based in his Southern Baptist faith.[109] The Democratic platform plank on abortion was mild, it acknowledged "religious and ethical" concerns about abortion, and said that it was "undesirable" to amend the Constitution to prohibit abortion.[110]

In the Republican Party, the New Right was on the rise behind its standard bearer Ronald Reagan, and abortion was becoming one of its key issues. After Congress passed the ERA in 1972 and the Supreme Court handed down *Roe* in 1973, long-time conservative activist Phyllis Schlafly launched a grassroots, antifeminist, pro-family movement. She mobilized many fellow Catholics as well as evangelical Christians, paving the way for later alliances between the New Right and the Christian Right. Schlafly repeatedly claimed that the ERA would liberalize abortion laws.[111] She framed abortion as an abandonment of motherhood rather than as murder, complaining that "women's libbers are promoting free sex instead of the 'slavery' of marriage. They are promoting Federal 'daycare centers' for babies instead of homes. They are promoting abortions instead of families."[112]

The nomination contest between Ford and Reagan had not been decided by the time of the convention. Though Reagan had signed the 1967 California abortion reform, he now said he would support a constitutional amendment to ban abortion. Ford's aides and his wife Betty, who was pro-choice, urged him to support abortion rights, but instead he took what he called a "moderate" position, declaring that the Supreme Court had "gone too far" and calling for a constitutional amendment to return the issue to the states.[113] At the convention, a New Right–dominated subcommittee passed a strong antiabortion plank. Feminists tried to remove it in the full committee and on the convention floor, but Ford's team blocked them.[114] During the general election, Carter tried to court Catholics on abortion, setting up a face-to-face meeting with the bishops, but Ford met with the bishops too and persuaded them that he was more opposed to abortion than Carter.[115]

The 1980 conventions solidified party positions on feminism and abortion. The Democratic convention was full of delegates supporting Massachusetts senator Edward Kennedy, and more than a fifth were members of the NWPC or NOW. They forced through several platform planks on feminist issues. One threatened to withhold party assistance from candidates who opposed the ERA, and another recognized "reproductive freedom as a fundamental human right." The abortion plank also supported public funding for the poor. President Carter tried but failed to kill the funding plank on the convention floor.[116] In the Republican Party, the Reagan Revolution had arrived. Since 1975, only one state (Indiana in 1977) had ratified the ERA. Congress extended the deadline in 1978, but now congressional Republicans had turned against it.[117] The New Right had gotten credit for electing scores of new conservatives to Congress during the 1978 midterm elections,[118] and the Christian Right was emerging as a force as Jerry Falwell, with the assistance of New Right leaders, founded the Moral Majority. The Republican platform failed to support the ERA for the first time since 1940 and called for an antiabortion constitutional amendment, a ban on public funding of abortions for the poor, and pro-life judicial appointments.[119] Reagan's campaign staff advised against such a strong antiabortion plank, but press secretary James Brady said the pro-lifers "were forces beyond our control."[120] Reagan became the first of many Republican presidential candidates to mention abortion in his acceptance speech, telling delegates "we believe in the sacredness of human life."[121]

The two parties remained polarized on abortion throughout the 1980s, but the Republicans were more willing to tout their position on the issue. Democrats were on the defensive; the pro-life movement was stronger than the pro-choice one; and abortion was more salient for pro-life voters than for pro-choice ones. But this changed in 1992: After the 1989 *Webster* decision allowed greater state restriction of abortion, Democratic gubernatorial candidates discovered a new phenomenon—the pro-choice single-issue voter. Now the Democrats not only supported abortion rights but placed them at the center of the campaign: The Democratic platform called for the legislative codification of *Roe* and the inclusion of abortion in a new national health insurance plan. Six pro-choice Republican women made the speaker's list at the convention, while pro-life Democratic governor of Pennsylvania Robert P. Casey was excluded,[122] and Bill Clinton became the first Democratic nominee to mention abortion in his acceptance speech (see table 5.2). There were also some stirrings of pro-choice sentiment in the Republican Party. In 1989, many congressional Republicans had crossed the aisle to override President George H. W. Bush's veto of a bill that mildly broadened the grounds for the funding of abortions for the poor, and in 1992, five East Coast state Republican parties declared their support for abortion rights. But pro-life forces continued to dominate platform committees and easily defeated their opponents. Convention organizers allowed Massachusetts governor William Weld to leave a pro-choice line in his speech, but some delegates booed him, and conservative Catholic presidential candidate Pat Buchanan told prime-time television viewers that there is "a religious war going on in our country for the soul of America."[123]

Journalist William Saletan argues that after 1992, candidates from both parties converged around a "pro-choice and antigovernment" position. They supported a basic right to abortion but opposed public funding, abortions for minors who did not have parental consent, and so-called partial-birth abortions (intact dilation and extraction). As House Speaker Newt Gingrich put it, the public was "pro-choice but antiabortion." In 1996, all of the leading Republican presidential candidates, with the exception of Pat Buchanan, favored increased abortion restrictions but not an antiabortion constitutional amendment.[124] Nominee Bob Dole tried to write "big tent" language into the party's abortion plank, but the Christian Right would not allow it. They had been instrumental in the 1994 Republican landslide that brought many social conservatives to office for the first time. As Wisconsin's party chairman put it, the Christian Right was "no longer trying to get a nose under the tent anymore. They are the tent."[125] Members of the Christian Coalition dominated state convention delegations in as many as eighteen states and had a large team assembled for any floor fight on abortion.[126]

For the rest of the 1990s and 2000s, the abortion positions of the two parties were virtually unchanged. The Republican nominee in 2000, George W. Bush, dissented slightly from his party's platform on abortion, saying that he would not seek an antiabortion constitutional amendment or pledge to appoint Supreme Court justices that opposed *Roe*. He said he dreamed of a world free of abortions but was "talking about an

Table 5.2 Statements on Abortion in U.S. Presidential Nomination Acceptance Speeches, 1972–2004

Year	Democratic Party	Republican Party
1972	McGovern—None.	Nixon—None.
1976	Carter—None.	Ford—None.
1980	Carter—None.	Reagan—None.
1984	Mondale—None.	Reagan—We believe in the sacredness of human life.
1988	Dukakis—None.	George H. W. Bush—Is it right to believe in the sanctity of life and protect the lives of innocent children? My opponent says no—but I say yes. We must change from abortion—to adoption. I have an adopted granddaughter. The day of her christening we wept with joy. I thank God her parents chose life.
1992	Clinton—George Bush won't guarantee a women's right to choose; I will. Listen. Here me now. I am not pro-abortion; I am pro-choice, strongly. I believe this difficult and painful decision should be left to the women of America. I hope the right to privacy can be protected and we will never again have to discuss this issue on political platforms. But I am old enough to remember what it was like before *Roe v. Wade*, and I do not want to return to the time when we made criminals of women and their doctors.	George H. W. Bush—I happen to believe very deeply in the worth of each individual human being, born or unborn.
1996	Clinton—We respect the individual conscience of every American on the painful issue of abortion, but believe as a matter of law that this decision should be left to a woman, her conscience, her doctor and her God. But abortion should not only be—abortion should not only be safe and legal, it should be rare. That's why I helped to establish and support a national effort to reduce out-of-wedlock teen pregnancy. And that is why we must promote adoption.	Dole—After decades of assault upon what made America great, upon supposedly obsolete values. What have we reaped? What have we created? What do we have? What we have in the opinion of millions of Americans is crime and drugs, illegitimacy, abortion, the abdication of duty, and the abandonment of children.
2000	Gore—And let there be no doubt: I will protect and defend a woman's right to choose. The last thing this country needs is a Supreme Court that overturns *Roe v. Wade*.	George W. Bush—I will lead our nation toward a culture that values life—the life of the elderly and the sick, the life of the young, and the life of the unborn. I know good people disagree on this issue, but surely we can agree on ways to value life by promoting adoption and parental notification, and when Congress sends me a bill against partial-birth abortion, I will sign it into law.
2004	Kerry—None.	George W. Bush—Because a caring society will value its weakest members, we must make a place for the unborn child. . . . And I will continue to appoint federal judges who know the difference between personal opinion and the strict interpretation of the law.
2008	Obama—We may not agree on abortion, but surely we can agree on reducing the number of unwanted pregnancies in this country.	McCain—We believe in a strong defense, work, faith, service, a culture of life, personal responsibility, the rule of law, and judges who dispense justice impartially and don't legislate from the bench.

Source: John Woolley and Gerhard Peters, American Presidency Project, http://www.presidency.ucsb.edu/platforms.php.

CHAPTER FIVE

ideal world and we don't live in an ideal world right now."[127] In 2008, the Democrats made overtures to pro-lifers. Nominee Barack Obama asked abortion opponent Senator Bob Casey Jr. (D-PA) to address the convention. Casey's father had been denied a speaking role because of his pro-life views sixteen years earlier, in an enduring slight to Catholics and pro-life Democrats.[128] In 2006, the Democrats had taken over the House in part by recruiting moderate and conservative candidates, many of them pro-lifers, to win formerly Republican seats in the West. Still, the Democratic platform was stronger than ever on abortion: It said the party "strongly and unequivocally supports *Roe v. Wade*" and opposes "any and all efforts to weaken or undermine" abortion rights, but it also expressed support for programs to reduce the number of abortions.

Republican nominee John McCain had a long pro-life record, but he had earlier battled pro-life groups over restrictions on "issue advocacy" advertising and the Christian Right over its attacks on him during the 2000 presidential campaign. He had also criticized President George W. Bush for supporting an abortion funding ban with no exception for life, rape, or incest. Before the convention, McCain floated the idea of choosing a pro-choice running mate, Connecticut senator Joseph Lieberman, but he quickly dropped the idea in the face of pro-life outrage. Instead, he chose Alaska governor Sarah Palin, an evangelical Christian who opposed abortion even in cases of rape or incest and who endeared herself to the pro-life movement by continuing a pregnancy after finding out that her child would be born with Down's syndrome.[129]

During the third presidential debate, McCain claimed that Obama was aligned "with the extreme aspect of the pro-abortion movement" while Obama called for "common ground" by preventing unwanted pregnancies, promoting adoption, and communicating to youth that "sexuality is sacred."[130] This approach won him the support of several prominent pro-life Catholics such as Pepperdine law professor and former Reagan appointee Douglas Kmiec.[131]

In sum, the two parties gradually polarized on abortion during the 1970s and then locked in those positions for the next three decades—though their candidates have varied in the degree to which they stressed the issue and have occasionally tolerated dissent within the party. Activists on both sides of the issue were quite successful at injecting the issue into party politics. They enshrined their positions in party platforms—often against the wishes of party nominees—and made abortion an issue in election campaigns. They were also successful in establishing litmus tests for presidential and vice presidential nominees, and in some cases, members of Congress. It is hard to distinguish "personal evolution" from "flip-flopping," but candidates typically brought their abortion positions into line with those of their party.[132]

Abortion was also an issue in campaigns below the presidential level. In 1990, abortion was a major issue in twenty of thirty-four gubernatorial campaigns.[133] Of the ninety-six Senate campaigns from 1988 to 1992, abortion was mentioned in the newspaper coverage of all but five.[134] In eighteen races, the percentage of articles mentioning abortion was more than 10 percent, and in four it was more than 20 percent.[135] State party platforms also polarized over abortion. In 1990, Republican parties took no position in twenty-three states, and two states supported abortion rights (New York and Maine). Among Democrats, twenty-two state parties took no position.[136] But in 2006, all Republican parties but one opposed abortion, and all Democratic parties but six supported abortion rights.[137]

The Christian Right and the GOP

Of the groups that sought to influence American political parties on abortion, the Christian Right was arguably the most successful. For a quarter century now, it has been a key player in the Republican Party coalition, and its power within the party has grown stronger with time. What explains this success? The Christian Right's main strengths have been gaining control of state party committees, sending delegates to state and national conventions, and mobilizing voters. A 1994 survey of state party officials found that the Christian Right held a majority in the Republican state party committees of eighteen states and had a substantial presence (more than 25 percent) in thirteen others.[138] A 2000 survey of Republican county chairs who reported being recruited to their positions found that almost half had been recruited by evangelical and pro-life groups while only a quarter had been recruited by business or farm groups.[139] The percentage of Republican National Convention delegates who were members of religious political organizations rose from 4 percent to 37 percent between 1976 and 1996, and the percentage who were members of pro-life organizations rose from 9 percent to 31 percent during the same period. The number of states in which more than 20 percent of delegates were members of religious-political or pro-life organizations was nine in 1988, eighteen in 1992, and twenty-four in 1996.[140] In the 1994 elections, Christian Right organizations spent about $20 million on voter contacting and mobilized about 200,000 volunteers.[141] The Christian Coalition alone distributed 30 million voter guides by mail and by hand in local organizations and churches. And a 1996 survey found that an astonishing 20 percent of Americans claimed that they had relied on Christian Right resources in deciding how to vote.[142]

Many of the Christian Right's strengths were facilitated by low-turnout elections and meetings. Texas provides a good example of the importance of low turnout. Its primaries typically drew only 10 percent of eligible voters. But after the polls closed, the parties held precinct conventions that elected delegates to the county convention. Any primary voter could attend, but less than 2 percent of voters usually did so. With the aid of such low turnout, the Christian Right accounted for 60 percent of the delegates to the 1994 Texas Republican convention and 50 percent of Texas's delegates to the 1996 and 2000 national Republican conventions.[143]

The Christian Right also excelled at matching its organizational structure to a federal polity. After being blamed for George H. W. Bush's loss in 1992, the Christian Coalition turned to the local level, increasing its local chapters from fewer than one hundred in 1990 to over two thousand in 1996, and providing training seminars for political candidates for state and local offices, including school boards. The Christian Coalition benefited from the low voter turnout in these state and local races. "In such contests," said the Coalition's director Ralph Reed, "boosting voter turnout was easy and competition from labor unions and pro-abortion groups tended to be lax. We discovered that our opponents on the left could target one or two school-board races and win, but it was impossible for them to focus on a thousand races at once." The Coalition used these state and local races as a training ground for political activism and campaigning at the federal level. Said Reed, "We needed practice. States and localities would become the 'laboratories' for testing our policy ideas, and for building a 'farm system' of future candidates, where locally elected religious conservatives could serve apprenticeships in government in a low-risk environment less exposed to the hostility of liberal lobby organizations." The Christian Coalition was often able to translate these local victories into power within the federated structure of the Republican Party.[144]

The success of the Christian Right within the GOP was not only impressive but durable in the face of several dangers. One was that the Christian Right would become disillusioned with the GOP when the party took moderate positions or dragged its feet on the social conservative agenda. Members of the Christian Right have sometimes made such complaints, but for the most part, Christian Right organizations have been loyal members of the Republican coalition, supporting conservative candidates in the primaries, but the party's nominee in the general election.[145] After losing the 1988 nomination, Pat Robertson lent his support to George H. W. Bush. And Christian Right leaders stuck with Bush in 1992 instead of joining Pat Buchanan's insurgency. The Christian Coalition put resources into defeating the Clinton health-care plan and campaigned for the GOP's 1994 "Contract with America," even though this meant its own "Contract with the American Family" would come second.[146]

The Christian Right remained loyal for several reasons. First, it made some important policy gains under Republican administrations: various policies restricting abortion, the funding of abstinence education, faith-based social welfare initiatives, court cases rolling back affirmative action, increased regulation of "indecent" television content, and the appointment of conservatives to the federal bureaucracy and the judiciary. The Christian Right also made numerous symbolic gains such as platform statements and presidential mentions of abortion, gay marriage, and family values, the impeachment of Bill Clinton, and federal intervention in the end-of-life medical care of Terri Schiavo. These were not very costly for the GOP since they did not require government expenditures and involved issues that did not especially interest economic conservatives. They also did not cost many votes, with the exception perhaps of the Schiavo case, because they were often small and incremental enough to anger liberal voters but not moderates.[147]

Some have argued that the economic right has used issues such as abortion and gay rights to appeal to Christian Right voters but without a sincere commitment to policy change.[148] This claim is slightly off target. No doubt the economic right is less concerned about abortion than the Christian Right, but this is typical of coalitions—not all members have the same priorities. In the 1970s, the mainly economic New Right recruited Christian Right leaders and donors using social issues such as abortion. They could plausibly be accused of "using" the Christian Right at that time, but it should be noted that many of the early New Right figures were religious themselves: Richard Viguerie, Paul Weyrich, Terry Dolan, and Phyllis Schafly were all devout Catholics.[149] More important, the Christian Right eventually established its own power base within the party. To say that the economic right of today is "using" evangelical voters on social issues assumes that the economic right controls the party when it is in fact only one part of a coalition.[150]

The Christian Right's satisfaction with the GOP was further aided by its hunger for legitimacy. The GOP incorporated Christian Right leaders into mainstream politics for the first time.[151] When evangelicals received mailings containing photos of their leaders with the president, they felt that they had become an accepted part of American culture.[152] Conservative movement leaders also made a concerted effort to build cohesion among the movements' main coalition members—the Christian Right, business elites and neoconservative intellectuals—and to cement ties between movement activists and Republican politicians. Since the early 1990s, activists from the various camps attended weekly "Wednesday meetings" convened by Grover Norquist of Americans for Tax Reform, where they exchanged resources and constructed a collective identity. Norquist regularly asked politicians where they stood on "babies, guns, and taxes." Norquist's main interest, of course, was taxes, but his question stressed the necessity of holding together the conservative coalition's multiple constituencies.[153] The Christian Right also tried to reach out to other factions within the party, as Reed explained: "Our goal was to unite social conservatives and economic conservatives by supporting traditional issues like welfare reform, a balanced budget, and tax cuts for families. We believed that most of the tension between moralists and libertarians was overstated. After all, conservative evangelicals who supported school prayer and pro-life laws were not in favor of higher taxes or deficit spending."[154]

Another danger was that the Christian Right would become an electoral liability for the GOP. Candidates that become too closely identified with the Christian Right tend to lose.[155] Christian Right leaders and activists tried to avoid such a backlash by practicing stealth politics—focusing on issues that were not clearly religious such as child tax credits, campaigning in churches rather than more traditional political venues, and supporting candidates that shared the movement's views but were not closely associated with it. During his presidential campaign, Pat Robertson identified himself as a businessman rather than a religious leader, and played down religious language. In the Christian Coalition, Robertson spoke to the insiders while the more worldly Ralph Reed spoke to outsiders.[156] As Reed said, "I want to be invisible. I do guerilla warfare. I paint my face and travel at night. You don't know it's over until you're in a body bag. You don't know until election night."[157] Unfortunately for Reed, these statements were widely publicized and were some of the least stealthy things he ever did.

Even when GOP leaders or candidates were embarrassed by links to the Christian Right, they found it hard to give up the grassroots activism that the Christian Right provided. Historically, Republicans lagged Democrats in grassroots mobilization: Republicans relied solely on local party organizations for campaign volunteers, while Democrats also drew volunteers from interest groups such as organized labor, and Republicans tended to win elections with money and connections rather than grassroots labor. The Christian Right, with its voter guides and dedicated troops, changed all this.[158] Some Republicans blamed the Christian Right and the intolerant rhetoric of Patrick Buchanan for the party's losses in 1992 (even though evangelical Christians mainly supported Bush rather than Buchanan). Those who worried about the electoral liabilities of the party's association with the Christian Right could not deny that the movement had brought a novel and critical resource to the party: It was hard not to become addicted.[159]

A final danger for the Republican coalition was the possibility that the Christian Right would simply run out steam, as most movements do. Scholars and journalists have proclaimed the death of the Christian Right again and again, but it has always revived. This endurance had three main causes: First, movement activists were kept in a continuous state of outrage by tales of their own persecution—the Christian Coalition's magazine *Religious Rights Watch* detailed monthly incidents of anti-Christian bigotry;[160] second, the Christian Right focused not only on politics, but on the broader culture and the individual morality of its members—when political victories were few, the movement sustained itself by spreading the gospel and following Christ's way; finally, the Christian Right's political, cultural, and religious missions were sustained by an extensive network of churches, schools, universities, broadcasters, bookstores, magazines, and book publishers that provided "abeyance structures" between moments of peak political activity.[161]

Religion and the Politicization of Abortion

In this chapter, I argued that abortion was a more important issue in parties and elections in the United States than in the other countries mainly because American parties were especially vulnerable to penetration by large new movements. Some journalists and scholars argue that religion is actually the key factor. The argument comes in two forms: One is that the main faith traditions that oppose abortion (Catholics and evangelical Christians) have more adherents in the United States than in other countries; the other is that Americans are more religious than citizens of other countries—they attend church more regularly, and are more likely to view religion as a central element in their lives.[162]

In other rich democracies, high levels of religiosity or Catholicism have typically not produced high levels of abortion politicization. As I discussed in chapter 1, rich democracies with large Catholic populations

CHAPTER FIVE

and/or Christian democratic parties mainly enacted "distress" abortion policies and did not experience much post-reform politicization or controversy afterward.[163] The main exceptions were Ireland, which never reformed its abortion laws, and Germany, where the issue was reopened twice by a constitutional court and once by reunification. (The East had a more liberal abortion policy than the West.)

Table 5.3 compares the Catholic and evangelical populations in the three countries under study: Canada has the highest percentage of Catholics, while the United States has the highest percentage of evangelicals; the United States has a higher proportion of the two groups combined, but the difference with Canada is small. There are three main ways in which these religious differences may have mattered to abortion politics: by affecting public opinion on abortion; by making religious and moral discourses and claims more publicly acceptable; and by providing recruits, resources, and elite allies for the pro-life movement.

The religious differences do not appear to have produced markedly different public opinion on abortion. As I described in chapter 2, at the time of the abortion reforms, strong majorities in all countries supported legal abortions for health grounds but opposed them for social grounds. This remained the case in the decades after the reforms. According to the World Values Survey (see appendix 5, table 1), in the early 1980s only about a quarter of Americans and Canadians and a third of Britons supported abortions because the "woman is not married" or because "a married couple does not want any more children." A decade later, support for these types of abortions was only at 30 percent in all three countries. Gallup polls (see appendix 5, table 2) show a similar result for the United States and Canada and bring the trend to 2001. The American General Social Survey (GSS) and the British Survey of Attitudes (BSA) (see appendix 5, table 3) show a similar pattern of strong support for health grounds and weaker support for social and economic grounds. But they also show that by 1994, Britons were more supportive of "soft" grounds than were Americans. Finally, the World Values Survey (see appendix 5, table 4) asked respondents to choose on a scale of 1 to 10 whether abortion was "never" justifiable or "always" justifiable. Responses from the three countries were quite similar (in the middle but tilted toward the "never" end) and converged over time. These similarities should not be completely surprising as some studies have shown that the abortion attitudes of American Catholics do not differ markedly from those of the general public—though this is not true for American evangelicals.[164]

Some have argued that the high religiosity of Americans has made religious and moral discourses and claims more acceptable and resonant

Table 5.3 Antiabortion Religious Groups as Percentage of Population

	United States	Britain	Canada
Catholics	23	13	37
Evangelicals	26	2	10
Total	49	15	47

Sources: European Values Study Group and World Values Survey Association, *European and World Values Surveys Four-Wave Integrated Data File, 1981–2004*, vol. 20060423 (Madrid, Spain; Tilburg, The Netherlands; Cologne, Germany: Análisis Sociológicos Económicos y Políticos, JD Systems, Zentralarchiv fur Empirische Sozialforschung, 2006); "U.S. Religious Landscape Survey" (Washington, DC: Pew Forum on Religion and Public Life, 2008); Sam Reimer, "A Generic Evangelicalism? Comparing Evangelical Subcultures in Canada and the United States." in *Rethinking Church, State, and Modernity*, ed. David Lyon and Marguerite Van Die (Toronto: University of Toronto Press, 2000); Rosie Waterhouse and Sarah Strickland, "Hungry for Souls," *Independent* (London), Sunday Review, January 13, 1991, 3.

Notes: British evangelical percentage is the 1991 membership of the Evangelical Alliance divided by the 1990 population. The Alliance is an umbrella organization of congregations but also has individual members. Member churches come from a variety of denominations including Anglican, Baptist, Methodist, Pentecostal, Presbyterian, Church of Scotland, and small house churches. Catholic figures are for 1999. Evangelical figures are for 2008 (United States), 1991 (Britain), and 1996 (Canada).

in the United States.[165] This seems plausible but is a matter of dispute as others have argued that the United States is marked by individualist and libertarian values that actually inhibit such moral claims making.[166] Myra Marx Ferree and her coauthors argue that specifically religious discourses are actually a liability in the American context because of religious pluralism, the separation of church and state, the absence of religious parties, and the Supreme Court's rejection of any consensus on when life begins. Catholic and evangelical abortion activists have in fact often taken pains to make their arguments in nonreligious terms.[167]

A final possibility is that high levels of Catholicism and evangelicalism produced both larger pro-life movements and clergies with more political clout. This seems likely, but it should be noted that the mere presence of Catholics and evangelicals did not mean that they would be mobilized into the pro-life movement or that their clergy would devote themselves to pro-life advocacy. Catholics and evangelicals have had to decide both that abortion was an important priority and that political action was the best way to address it. These decisions have varied over time and across countries and, as a result, so has the mobilization of these groups.

The American Catholic clergy has been opposed to abortion since it first hit the agenda in the late 1950s, and it has been more active on abortion, and more supportive of the pro-life movement, than the clergy in any other country. But its attention to the abortion issue has varied over time. The church played a strong role in the early pro-life movement, but its commitment seemed to wane during the Reagan administration, only to revive again in the 1990s and 2000s. When the Catholic clergy threw its resources into the abortion debate, it was a powerful actor. The U.S. Conference of Catholic Bishops employs more than four hundred people in its Washington office, and there are Catholic Conferences in thirty-three states. The bishops also provided extensive support to the pro-life movement.[168]

This fluctuation largely resulted from the fact that the church's policy preferences cut across party lines; the church is closer to the Republicans on abortion but closer to the Democrats on social welfare, nuclear weapons, peace, and immigration. As a result, the bishops have debated constantly about which issues should have greatest priority and which party is most hospitable to Catholic concerns. In addition, Catholic voters were solidly Democratic during the first half of the twentieth century, but as they became more prosperous and as the Republicans embraced the abortion issue, they increasingly voted Republican. Since 1972, Catholic voters have been up for grabs. The two parties have taken turns winning the most Catholic votes, and the margin of victory has usually been less than 15 percent.[169] Just as the bishops have argued about which party best serves Catholic interests, so have lay Catholics. Within the pro-life movement as well, some conservative Catholics have been extremely critical of liberal bishops, whom they accuse of being soft on abortion.

The bishops supported the Republican Ford over the Democrat Carter during the 1976 election because they believed that Ford was more opposed to abortion. But Reagan's 1980 election prompted a debate among the bishops over what priority to give abortion. In 1983, the bishops issued a highly publicized pastoral letter that criticized Reagan's nuclear weapons policies and supported a nuclear freeze. Archbishop Joseph Bernardin, the chair of the committee that drafted the letter, soon outlined a "consistent ethic of life" or "seamless garment" that treated abortion as one of many "life" issues; he argued that pro-lifers must be "equally visible in support of the quality of life of the powerless among us: the old and the young, the hungry and the homeless, the undocumented immigrant and the unemployed worker"[170] and that "no one is called to do everything, but each of us can do something."[171] This position seemed to condemn alliances between Catholics and Reagan, while letting liberal Catholics and Democrats off the hook for inactivity on abortion. If liberal Catholics did not work to oppose abortion, they could work to diminish some other threat to life. Archbishops Bernard Law of Boston and John O'Connor of New York were not convinced. Said O'Connor, "if the unborn in a mother's womb is unsafe it becomes ludicrous for the bishops to address the threat of nuclear war."[172] In 1986, the bishops followed up their antinuclear letter with one on economic justice.

Many Catholic conservatives were outraged by Bernardin's "consistent ethic of life." Liberal and conservative Catholics have been at war within the church at least since Vatican II. One source of this conflict was Pope Paul VI's 1968 encyclical *Humanae Vitae*, which reinforced the church's position against contraception and abortion. Many Catholics had expected the Pope to allow contraception and were shocked and disappointed when he did not,[173] and some, especially liberal academics in Catholic colleges and universities, publicly dissented. Many Catholics today ignore the church's teachings on divorce, contraception, and extramarital sex.[174] Even on abortion, the opinions of Catholics are not that different from those of Protestants.[175]

Catholic conservatives, led by groups such as Catholics United for the Faith, have defended *Humanae Vitae*, and conservatives also have their own wing within the pro-life movement. Organizations such as the American Life League, Human Life International, and the Pro-Life Action League have sometimes squared off against the bishops and the NRLC. The NRLC has focused on legislation and education, has compromised at times, has attempted to argue in secular terms, and has focused only on abortion, remaining neutral on contraception. The conservative Catholic pro-life groups, by contrast, have used direct action tactics and civil disobedience, have refused all compromise, have based their arguments and protests on Catholic faith and rituals, and have argued that the "contraceptive mentality" leads to abortion.[176]

The cross-cutting agenda of the Catholic Church was not the only reason that the bishops' antiabortion commitment seemed to wane. According to Father Edward Bryce, who ran the NCCB's Office of Pro-Life Activities during the late 1970s and early 1980s, some bishops had privately concluded that the church was wasting political and social capital on a losing battle. Said Bryce, "These were people who could build cathedrals, and they knew that you don't do something like this halfheartedly. The skills were there. But some of them made a determination early on that this battle was lost, and decided they would not devote extraordinary resources to it."[177] Some of the bishops' reticence also had to do with concerns about the church's tax-exempt status.[178] Indeed, pro-choice activists sued the church over its electioneering, and the case lasted nine years and went to the Supreme Court three times before a federal appeals court ruled that the activists lacked standing to sue.[179]

In November 1989, in the wake of the *Webster* decision that further restricted abortion, the bishops renewed their commitment to the abortion fight, declaring that Catholic politicians were obligated to take a pro-life stand. Some bishops denied Holy Communion to public officials or threatened them with excommunication. In 1990, the NCCB announced that it would spend several million dollars on an antiabortion public relations campaign. Timothy Byrnes argues that there were still differences between bishops who considered abortion the most important of all issues and those who advocated a "seamless garment," but the bishops would no longer let pro-choice Catholic politicians hide behind this disagreement.[180]

In the 2000s, the bishops became more involved with the abortion issue once again. In 2003, one week before the thirtieth anniversary of *Roe v. Wade*, the Vatican released a document reiterating that Catholic lawmakers had a "grave and clear obligation" to oppose "any law that attacks human life."[181] That same year, lay Catholics picketed the bishops' annual meeting and demanded that they deny communion to pro-choice Catholic politicians. Several bishops obliged, and one even denied communion to Democratic presidential candidate John Kerry. In 2004, the bishops made a statement on "Catholics in Political Life" that prohibited Catholic institutions from honoring pro-choice political officials. In 2009, some Catholics objected when the University of Notre Dame invited President Obama to give the commencement address and receive an honorary degree, but an editorial in the Jesuit magazine *America* complained that such criticism was motivated by political partisanship.[182]

Of the three countries, Canada has the highest percentage of Catholics. In Canada too the involvement of the Catholic Church in abortion politics has varied over time. The pro-life movement was dominated by lay Catholics, individual parishes, and groups such as the Catholic Women's League and the Knights of Columbus, but bishops, priests, and members of religious orders have provided only minimal support.[183] During the late 1960s, the bishops distinguished between divine and civil law on such issues as contraception, divorce, and abortion. The Canadian Catholic Conference (CCC) opposed the 1969 abortion reform but did "not believe that our moral principle must be enshrined in criminal law."[184] Many newspapers agreed, arguing that opposition to abortion was a doctrinal position that the bishops should not try to force on other Canadians.[185] During the 1970s, the Coalition for the Protection of Life tried to present its arguments in a nondenominational way and thus preferred that the bishops stay out of the fray. But once the more radical Campaign Life came to dominate the movement at the end of the 1970s, it was increasingly critical of the bishops, and they returned fire.[186]

In 1981, Campaign Life criticized the archbishop of Toronto, Cardinal Emmett Carter, for endorsing the *Charter of Rights and Freedoms* despite the fact that it did not contain protections for the unborn, and suggested that he had done so in exchange for public funding of Catholic schools. In reply, Carter prohibited parishes from distributing Campaign Life literature or mentioning the organization in church bulletins. In February 1985, Carter made a brief foray into pro-life activism, instructing pastors to turn out parishioners for four days of protest. But only about two thousand of the one million Catholics in the diocese showed up, and two days later, a pro-choice protest drew five thousand participants. The cardinal was embarrassed by the low turnout, and both the media and non-Catholic clergy criticized his involvement.[187] Six months later, Carter made a deal with the Ontario attorney general to limit the number of protesters in front of the Morgentaler clinic to five. Campaign Life denounced this "sleazy agreement" and refused to abide by it. One protestor complained that "it seems that the unborn are close to the bottom of the bishops' list of priorities. As for us, they probably just wish we'd piss off into the wind, and that way save them a lot of aggravation and embarrassment."[188] During their 1990 testimony on the Mulroney Government's abortion bill, the bishops again distinguished between divine and civil law. They restated the Catholic position on abortion, but "recognized that there are strongly held views which differ from ours" and argued that "authentic pluralism" means "that no one group has the right to impose its particular point of view."[189]

Just as the involvement of the Catholic Church with abortion varied over time in the United States and Canada, so did the involvement of American evangelicals. Most evangelicals retreated from politics after the repeal of prohibition and the humiliating 1925 Scopes trial over the teaching of evolution; it was not until the 1970s that they began to engage either politics or the abortion issue.[190] Many saw politics as a distraction from spiritual life, distrusted worldly governments, or did not wish to interfere with the chaos to come before the Rapture. "We became so heavenly-minded," said Operation Rescue leader Flip Benham, "that we were no worldly good."[191] Initially, many evangelicals saw abortion mainly as a concern of the heretical Catholic Church, and some avoided the issue precisely for that reason. Theologian O. J. Brown said many evangelicals felt that "if the Catholics are for it, we should be against it."[192] But beginning in the mid-1970s, evangelicals began to join campaigns against the ERA, gay rights, abortion, and especially the taxation of racially segregated religious schools.

The first evangelical pro-life organization, the Christian Action Council (later Carenet), was founded by Brown and future surgeon general C. Everett Koop in 1975. Koop had delivered a commencement address against abortion at Wheaton College in 1973, and Brown had written editorials on abortion for *Christianity Today*.[193] Many evangelicals also reentered politics for the first time when they supported fellow evangelical Jimmy Carter in the 1976 presidential elections—though many were badly disappointed by his presidency.[194] Another key event was the book and film *Whatever Happened to the Human Race?* by Koop and evangelical theologian Francis Schaeffer, who toured twenty cities in 1979, drawing thousands. Said Koop, "I think it was the first time that most Christians even knew what the issue was."[195] Schaeffer preached a turn away from "rapture theology" that isolated evangelicals from politics and American culture and argued that Christians had a duty to engage in civil disobedience to stop abortion. Many evangelicals, including Jerry Falwell and Southern Baptist leader Richard Land, credited Schaeffer and Koop with opening their eyes about abortion.[196] Phyllis Schlafly was also an important bridge between Catholics, the New Right, and evangelicals. Once evangelicals mobilized on abortion, they focused mainly on education and crisis pregnancy centers in the late 1970s and early 1980s, and turned to street protest only later, most notably with the founding of Operation Rescue in 1986.[197]

This discussion of the role of Catholics in the United States and Canada and evangelicals in the United States suggests that religious explanations for the stronger politicization of abortion in the United States are not fully convincing. Differences in the religious makeup of the three countries did not produce strong differences in public opinion, and the claim that the United States is more open to religious and moral claims than the other countries is a matter of dispute. The presence of Catholics and evangelicals in the United States and Canada contributed to the larger pro-life movements in these countries, but religious denominations did not automatically mobilize against abortion; there were strong variations in mobilization over time and across countries. In addition, the larger movements in the United States cannot alone explain the higher levels of politicization and controversy there. First, politicization and controversy of abortion were much weaker in Canada than in the United States, even though Canada had a larger Catholic population. Second, the differences in the size of religious populations across the countries were differences of degree while the differences among abortion politicization and controversy were absolute; there was not just *less* politicization in Britain and Canada, but virtually none. Finally, the particular way in which the abortion issue was constructed in the United States probably contributed to the higher level of controversy and religious mobilization over abortion in the United States. Abortion on request for a woman's own reasons and on grounds of privacy was more threatening to conservative Catholics and evangelicals than abortion with medical gatekeeping for grounds of medical necessity.

Conclusion

In this chapter, I examined abortion *politics* (in parties and elections) after the reforms of the Long 1960s. I argued that the openness of American political parties allowed feminists, the New Right, and especially the Christian Right to gain influence within the Democratic and Republican parties and move abortion to the center of American politics. By contrast, the sizable pro-choice and pro-life movements in Britain and Canada never made much headway in closed party and electoral systems.

In the next chapter, I examine post-reform abortion *policy making*. There were many more policy changes in the United States than in the other countries, and these mainly reduced the quality and availability of abortion services. In Britain and Canada, policy change was rare and mainly expanded the quality and availability of abortion services. Most of this difference is the result of the American politicization of abortion and the electoral success of the Republican Party outlined in this chapter, but there were some other factors at play as well, in particular the differing policy venues of abortion policy making and the differing involvement of medical associations in the abortion issue.

SIX

Policy Change after Reform

After the reforms of the Long 1960s, the three countries changed their abortion policies in various ways and with varying frequency. In Britain and Canada, abortion policies rarely changed, but when they did, they typically expanded the quality and availability of abortion services. Both countries reduced medical gatekeeping and increased public funding. In the United States, policy changed frequently, and mainly reduced the quality and availability of abortion services through spousal and parental consent requirements, waiting periods, mandatory counseling, and reductions in public funding. Another way of stating these differences is that the three countries converged on abortion availability and quality (Britain and Canada became more liberal while the United States became less so) but diverged on public funding (Britain and Canada expanded it while the United States cut it back).

This chapter explains these differences. The previous chapter examined the party and electoral politicization of abortion and showed that parties avoided the abortion issue in Britain and Canada but eventually embraced it in the United States. That difference was the main cause of the policy differences that are examined in this chapter. But there were other factors as well. Agenda control and nonpartisan policy processes helped British and Canadian policy makers avoid the abortion issue, while federalism and judicial policy making increased access points and controversy in the United States. Medical associations defended abortion rights and sought the expansion of abortion services in Britain and Canada but sought to avoid the issue in the United

POLICY CHANGE AFTER REFORM

Table 6.1 Major Changes in Abortion Policies of the United States, Britain, and Canada, 1967–2008

Britain		
	1970–2000s	Doctors and clinics loosen interpretations of abortion grounds.
	1991	NHS increases funding of abortions provided by private charitable agencies.
Canada		
	1976	Quebec stops enforcing federal abortion law.
	1988–90	Supreme Court strikes down federal abortion law. Parliament fails to enact new law. Abortion available on request for women's own reasons. Clinics become legal.
	1988–2008	Clinic abortions expand. Courts strike down clinic bans and funding restrictions.
United States		
	1973–80	Some states, then federal government, ban public funding of most abortions for the poor. Supreme Court upholds. Some states fund with own money.
	1973–83	States enact waiting periods and husband/parent consent requirements. Supreme Court strikes down waiting periods and husband consent, but allows husband notification and parent consent requirement with judicial bypass.
	1980s and 1990s	Number of abortion providers declines as result of state regulation and harassment by pro-life movement.
	1988	Executive order prohibits organizations receiving federal funding from discussing abortion ("the gag rule"). Supreme Court upholds.
	1989	*Webster v. Reproductive Health Services.* Supreme Court allows more state restrictions, deviates from *Roe*, but does not overturn it. States enact parent consent requirements, waiting periods, and mandatory counseling.
	1992	*Planned Parenthood v. Casey.* Supreme Court reaffirms *Roe*, but abandons trimester framework and replaces "compelling state interest" standard with "undue burden" standard. Strikes down husband notification requirement.
	1994	Federal legislation prohibits clinic blockades.
	2010	Health-care reform legislation reduces private health insurance coverage of abortion.

States. Finally, two major changes in Canadian policy were prompted by institutional changes outside of abortion politics—the changing nature of Canadian federalism and the enactment of a new Canadian bill of rights.

Table 6.1 lists major changes in the abortion policies of the three countries after the reforms of the Long 1960s. I described these changes in chapter 4; here I explain how they came about. In Britain, the Abortion Act of 1967 remained unchanged despite more than a dozen private member's bills and two parliamentary commissions aimed at amending it. Two major changes, however, occurred outside Parliament—doctors gradually interpreted mental health grounds more liberally, and in the 1980s and 1990s, Conservative and Labour governments expanded the public funding of abortions in private clinics. In Canada, Governments introduced only two post-reform bills, in 1988 and 1990, and did so only because the Supreme Court had struck down the 1969 reform. After these failed, Governments backed off again. The three most important policy changes occurred outside Parliament. In 1976, Quebec's Government announced that it would no longer enforce the federal abortion law—allowing abortion on request in the province. In 1988, the Supreme Court struck down the federal abortion law as procedurally unfair—allowing abortions on request. And in the years after the court's decision, abortion clinics opened in most provinces and soon provided half of all abortions.

In the United States, there were hundreds of policy changes—the table lists only several of the most consequential. Between 1973 and 1989, states enacted more than three hundred separate pieces of abortion legislation, and every state did so. Congress enacted another eighteen abortion statutes.[1] Most of these state and federal changes reduced the quality and availability of abortion services. They included the elimination of federal funding for most abortions for the poor, requirements of parent or husband consent, waiting periods, mandatory antiabortion counseling, and restrictions on the discussion of abortion by federally funded organizations.[2] In the first two years after *Roe*, state legislatures considered about 450 bills restricting abortion and almost 60 were enacted.[3] Between 1974 and 1993, 37 states enacted spousal and parental consent or notification requirements, 19 required waiting periods, 25 enacted limitations on abortion funding and 17 required husband consent or notification.[4] By 2010, 34 states required spousal and parental consent or notification, 24 required waiting periods, and 17 mandated counseling meant to discourage abortion.[5]

Most of the state-level policy innovations eventually reached the Supreme Court. It considered more than forty abortion cases after *Roe* (see appendix 2). Before 1989, the court struck down most abortion restrictions with the exception of funding bans and parental notification with a procedure to let minors avoid such notification with a judge's approval. But in the 1989 *Webster* decision and the 1992 *Casey* decision, the court gave the states more leeway to restrict abortion. As I mentioned in chapter 4, state regulation and protest also helped reduce the number of abortion providers. A few policy changes made abortions easier to obtain, but these were largely attempts to recover lost ground rather than to expand abortion services beyond the initial reform. These included state and federal bans on clinic blockades and approval of the abortion medication mifepristone.[6] There were also many failed proposals—most notably, attempts to enact an antiabortion constitutional amendment, to legislatively establish abortion rights, and to fund abortions under the national health insurance plan proposed by President Clinton. In the remainder of the chapter, I explain these patterns of change in the three countries.

British Governments Avoid Abortion with the Aid of Agenda Control and Nonpartisan Legislative Processes

British Governments, both Labour and Conservative, refused to amend the 1967 Abortion Act either to expand or reduce abortion services. British Governments had strong agenda control: Backbenchers could introduce legislation only through the highly restrictive private member process; and attempts to force the issue onto the Government's agenda typically failed because the Government declared that abortion was an "issue of conscience" best handled by private member's bills. Table 6.2 lists the seven major post-reform abortion bills and amendments in Britain. Most were private member's bills, and as I discussed in chapter 1, such bills, if controversial, cannot come to a final vote unless the Government provides extra time. Although the Labour Government provided extra time for the 1967 abortion reform, subsequent Governments refused to do so.[7]

The 1988 Alton bill is a good example of the procedural obstacles faced by abortion bills. In 1988, David Alton, a Liberal MP from Liverpool, introduced a private member's bill to reduce the abortion time limit from twenty-eight to eighteen weeks. The Liberal Party was split on abortion, and many party members, including the author of the 1967 reform, David Steel, attempted to dissuade Alton from pursuing his bill. Some members said that Alton should resign his position as chief party whip because the divisive abortion bill was incompatible with his duty to ensure party unity; and Alton agreed to do so.[8] Tory Prime Minister Margaret Thatcher and several other ministers supported a reduction in the time limit, but as individuals rather than as party representatives.[9] As Alton's bill began to run out of time, its supporters pleaded with the Government for extra time. Tory MP Sir Bernard Braine argued that the Government was morally bound to provide extra time since the Labour Government had done so for the 1967 reform, but leader of the House, John Wakeham, said that it was not Government practice to provide extra time for private member's bills and that it would be a grave step to intervene in behalf of one.[10] Alton expressed the frustration of abortion opponents with their difficult institutional position: "If no controversial Private member initiative is to be allowed to complete its stages it will set the 1967 Abortion Act in concrete. This places it in a unique constitutional position. It becomes a great untouchable."[11]

Labour Party leaders also refused to take a position despite a 1985 party conference resolution requiring a firm whip in support of abortion rights.

Table 6.2 Major British Abortion Bills and Amendments

Sponsor	Year	Content	Outcome
Norman St. John Stevas (Conservative)	1969	Consultant clause	Defeated at First Reading
Bryant Godman Irvine (Conservative)	1970	Consultant clause	Ran out of time at First Reading
James White (Labour)	1975	Narrower abortion grounds, residency requirement, 20-week upper time limit, burden of proof on doctors	Passed at Second Reading; referred to Select Committee
John Corrie (Conservative)	1979	Narrower abortion grounds, 20-week upper time limit, easier conscience clause, tighter licensing of clinics, separation of referral agencies and clinics	Passed at Second Reading; ran out of time at Report stage
David Alton (Liberal)	1988	Eighteen-week upper time limit	Passed at Second Reading; ran out of time at Report stage
Amendments to Conservative Government's embryology bill	1990	Upper time limits of 18, 20, 22, 24, 26, and 28 weeks; early abortions with single doctor's approval; doctors required to register conscientious objections	All amendments defeated except 24-week upper time limit
Amendments to Labour Government's embryology bill	2008	Upper time limits of 12, 16, 20, and 22 weeks; approval from three doctors; seven-day waiting period; antiabortion counseling; early abortions with single doctor's approval; early abortions by midwives and nurses; abortions in GP offices or family planning clinics; extension of abortion law to N. Ireland	Upper time limits defeated; other proposals not debated

Sources: Colin Francome, *Abortion Freedom: A Worldwide Movement* (Winchester, MA: Allen and Unwin, 1984); Victoria Greenwood and Jock Young, *Abortion in Demand* (London: Pluto Press, 1976); Keith Hindell and Madeline Simms, *Abortion Law Reformed* (London: Peter Owen, 1971); John Keown, *Abortion, Doctors, and the Law: Some Aspects of the Legal Regulation of Abortion in England from 1803 to 1982* (Cambridge: Cambridge University Press, 1988); David Marsh and Joanna Chambers, *Abortion Politics* (London: Junction Books, 1981); Sally Sheldon, *Beyond Control: Medical Power and Abortion Law* (London: Pluto Press, 1997); *Times*, May 21, 2008; *Guardian*, October 22 and October 23, 2008.

Note: Successful bills go through five stages in the House of Commons: First Reading (introduction), Second Reading (initial debate and vote), Committee (amendment), Report (amendment), and Third Reading (final debate and vote).

Thirty-five Labour MPs voted in favor of a reduced time limit, and twenty abstained. The Labour Women's Action Committee launched an unsuccessful campaign to deselect those MPs for the next general election.[12]

After the Alton bill died, pro-life MPs (most of them Tories) threatened to hijack debate on the Government's embryology bill. The Government was tired of the annual disruption caused by abortion and wanted to avoid jeopardizing its bill. It considered offering its own proposal to reduce the time limit to 24 weeks, but this was essentially the status quo, and many members of the Cabinet wanted to go lower.[13] The Government decided against introducing a bill and denied that it had ever considered doing so. Instead, it provided time for a debate on the upper time limit and allowed free votes on several different time limits (18, 20, 22, 24, 26 and 28 weeks). Tory MP Ann Widdecombe claimed that the pro-life MPs had "come to a tacit agreement with government business managers that if we can get a vote to lower the limit for a legal abortion freely and fairly, we will remove the dreadful pressure we have been placing on Parliament. For a while."[14] Because the votes took place during consideration of a Government bill, filibustering was impossible and the status quo 24-week time limit prevailed.[15]

In 2008, Gordon Brown's Labour Government sought to update the twenty-year-old embryology law, and according to parliamentarians, abortion amendments would be in order. All would be decided by a free vote.[16] Pro-choice amendments allowed early abortions with a single doctor's approval, let midwives and nurses perform first-trimester abortions, authorized abortions in GPs offices and family planning clinics, and extended the 1967 Abortion Act to Northern Ireland. A pro-life amendment reducing the upper time limit for abortion was defeated in May, with most Labour MPs, including Brown, voting against it. In response, pro-life MPs tabled a number of additional amendments that required the approval of three doctors rather than two, a seven-day waiting period, and antiabortion counseling. The embryology bill was supposed to come to a final vote in July, but the Government postponed the vote—possibly because of upcoming elections in Catholic Glasgow East.

In October, Parliament finally considered the final bill and was scheduled to vote on the abortion amendments. The pro-choice amendments had good odds until the Government defeated them by severely restricting the time for debate. The Government claimed that the abortion amendments might hurt the chances of the embryology bill in the House of Lords, but this seemed unlikely since most members of the Lords were supportive of both the embryology bill and abortion rights. Some speculated that the Government had lost its nerve in the face of upcoming

CHAPTER SIX

Scottish elections. Others claimed that the Government opposed extending the 1967 Abortion Act to Northern Ireland because all of its political parties were opposed to the extension and it might jeopardize the peace process. Finally, some claimed that Brown had earlier assured Northern Ireland's Democratic Unionist Party that he would maintain the abortion status quo in exchange for crucial votes on a bill allowing police to hold suspected terrorists for forty-two days without charge.[17]

Other than the two votes on the abortion time limit, the only other major parliamentary actions on abortion were the Lane Committee of 1971–74 and the Select Committee of 1975–76 (see chapter 4). Both made relatively mild recommendations. The Lane Committee opposed changing the abortion law and said any problems with the law could be resolved through administrative, professional, and educational action.[18] The Select Committee suggested reducing the upper time limit to twenty weeks, restricting the gatekeeping powers of partners in the same medical practice, and licensing commercial referral agencies.[19] None of these recommendations became law.

Canadian Governments with Strong Agenda Control Avoid Abortion Policy Making

In Canada, the initial reform occurred through Government legislation with free voting. After reform, Liberal Governments refused to introduce new abortion legislation and kept private member's bills off the agenda as well. The few major changes in abortion law took place outside of the federal legislature and national electoral politics, mainly because of exogenous changes in political institutions and federal-provincial relations. There were only two moments of major federal action between the 1969 reform and the 1988 *Morgentaler* decision—the Liberal Government's 1974 appointment of a committee to investigate abortion law and its attempts to deal with the abortion issue through its family planning division. Neither of these produced major changes in abortion law or practice.

In 1974, the CMA successfully lobbied the Government to appoint the Committee on the Operation of the Abortion Law, chaired by Robin Badgley. The Government required the committee to focus on the "operation" of the law and prohibited it from analyzing or providing recommendations about the law itself.[20] As one government official put it: "There was blood in the halls over what [the committee] would actually do. No way would Justice allow it to find fault with the law. The Government was not about to blame itself."[21] As the committee deliberated, Justice Minister Ron Basford suggested that the Government would initiate a parliamentary debate on abortion once the report was complete,[22] but two months later and three months before the report was released, the Cabinet privately resolved that it would "make no offer to entertain a debate" and would blame problems in the law on the provinces.[23] The committee's report documented broad inequities in the operation of abortion law but blamed everyone except the Liberal Government or the law itself. "It is not the law that has led to the inequities. . . . It is the Canadian people, their health institutions, and the medical profession who are responsible for this situation."[24]

The Government's main response to the Badgley report was a proposal by Minister of Health Marc Lalonde to increase pregnancy prevention through the Family Planning Division (FPD). This constrained and underfunded agency had until that point tried to please both sides of the abortion debate. It tried to compensate for the problems of the abortion law by increasing family planning, but stressed that abortion was not an acceptable form of birth control.[25] After the Badgley report, Lalonde announced that the FPD would no longer wait patiently for requests from clients but would actively promote family planning in the media and the schools; Lalonde asked the provinces to review age of consent laws for contraceptive counseling and proposed provincial women's clinics that would provide family planning services, including abortions.[26]

Pro-life forces lobbied against the proposal, and the provinces were opposed or afraid. As one FPD official put it, "the Feds were up to the old game of putting responsibility on the provinces. [Lalonde] made it sound like the government was about to set up street clinics where 14-year-olds could get abortions on demand. We received over a half million pieces of mail over that speech, most of it negative."[27] After this outcry, the Government abandoned Lalonde's proposal and told the FPD to return to its previous practice of providing contraceptive information only when requested. The FPD soon came under constant attack from pro-life forces. In 1977, the new health minister, Monique Begin, considered a review of the abortion law, but backed off after criticism by pro-life groups. Instead, she began to dismantle the FPD.[28]

Not only did Canadian Governments avoid the abortion issue, but in contrast to Britain, there was not much private member activity on the issue either. Until 2003, the parliamentary subcommittee on private member business was responsible for choosing a small number of "votable" bills each session. Only one abortion bill was ever chosen: a 1987 bill calling on the Government to amend the *Charter* to give fetuses a right to life, but the Government opposed it and it did not progress past its first introduction.[29] After 2003, all private member's bills were "votable" by default unless they violated the *Charter*, lay outside federal jurisdiction, or involved issues that had already been considered that session or were already the subject of a Government bill.[30] In October 2003, Parliament voted for the first time since 1990 on abortion legislation, defeating a bill authorizing a study of the "medical necessity" of abortion so that it could be defunded under Medicare. There have been other bills on abortion since 2003, but only one progressed notably—a 2008 bill that made it a separate offense to harm a fetus in the course of a crime. Before that bill could reach its final stage, the Conservative Harper Government removed it from Parliament's agenda by claiming that it wanted to introduce its own bill. Most observers thought the Government had become interested in the issue only so that it could keep the bill off Parliament's agenda as elections approached.[31]

Institutional Change Outside Abortion Politics

As Governments avoided the abortion issue, the two most important changes in post-reform Canadian abortion policy occurred outside Parliament: Quebec's 1976 decision to end its enforcement of the federal law and the Supreme Court's 1988 decision to strike down that law. Both of these changes were strongly colored by changes in federal-Quebec relations and the constitution. The late 1960s to the early 1980s were a period of intense conflict between Pierre Trudeau's Liberal Government and Quebec sovereignists. Secularization and economic reforms during Quebec's 1960s Quiet Revolution led to increased nationalist feeling in the province, and French President Charles de Gaulle aggravated matters when he cried "Vive le Québec libre!" in a speech at Montreal's Expo 67. The next year, René Lévesque created the sovereignist Parti Québécois (PQ). When, in 1970, the Marxist Front de libération du Québec (FLQ) kidnapped a British diplomat and Quebec's labor minister and murdered the minister, Trudeau invoked war powers—suspending civil liberties and sending the army to Quebec.

The murder discredited the FLQ but unified sovereignists behind the PQ. In 1976, the party defeated Quebec's Liberals—sending shock waves across Canada. It was the first time that a sovereignist party held Government, and the PQ had promised a referendum on Quebec's sovereignty. In 1980, it made good on its promise, asking voters for permission to negotiate both sovereignty and an economic association with Canada.

Trudeau campaigned against the referendum, promising constitutional reform and "renewed federalism," and after it failed, he began constitutional talks, which ended with a constitutional reform approved by all provinces except Quebec. It included a new *Charter of Rights and Freedoms* that gave the Supreme Court expanded powers of judicial review.[32] These developments had little to do with abortion politics but strongly affected them as they intersected with Dr. Henry Morgentaler's campaign against the 1969 abortion act. Morgentaler opened up an abortion clinic in Montreal in 1968 and was arrested by Quebec's Liberal Government in 1970 (clinics were prohibited by the 1969 act). Morgentaler asked Quebec to designate his clinic as an authorized abortion facility, but it refused and charged him with thirteen counts of illegal abortion. Morgentaler's case drew national attention, especially after he performed a Mother's Day abortion on national television. Supporters and opponents protested nationwide, and Morgentaler defense committees formed in most major cities. In November 1973, a Montreal jury acquitted Morgentaler. Flashing his trademark "V-for-victory," he claimed that "no jury will ever convict me" and reported later that year in the CMA journal that he had performed more than five thousand illegal abortions.[33]

But his legal troubles were not over. In Canada, unlike the United States and Britain, jury acquittals can be appealed. In April 1974, the Quebec Court of Appeal set aside Morgentaler's acquittal and imposed its own guilty verdict—a rarely used procedure that set off a national debate on the right to trial by jury. In March 1975, the federal Supreme Court rejected Morgentaler's appeal, and he began serving an eighteen-month prison term. Morgentaler, a survivor of Nazi concentration camps, suffered anxiety and depression in prison and eventually had a heart attack.[34] At the end of the year, Parliament enacted legislation prohibiting appeals courts from substituting convictions for jury acquittals. Trudeau's federal Liberal Government set aside Morgentaler's conviction. He was released after serving ten months and acquitted again, but the province scheduled yet another trial.

In November 1976, the PQ defeated the Liberals and, a month later, Quebec's justice minister. Marc-André Bédard dropped all charges against Morgentaler, arguing that the federal abortion law was unenforceable and urging the Government to modify the criminal code.[35] Federal Justice Minister Ron Basford said he could not respond immediately to Bédard's call for changes to the abortion law, but he did not complain about the PQ's decision. "I have maintained throughout that this is properly a decision for the provincial authorities. I think in light of all the circumstances, most people should regard it as a fair and just decision."[36]

CHAPTER SIX

The PQ Government tried to strike a delicate balance on abortion. On the one hand, the party membership, and especially its left wing, supported abortion rights. On the other hand, the Cabinet had only one female member, it was often in conflict with feminist members of the party, and its top priority was the referendum on sovereignty association—it sought to avoid any controversy that might reduce support for the referendum.[37]

In May 1977, the PQ held its first policy convention since taking power. PQ leaders, unlike those of many Canadian parties, were committed to taking the policy positions of their members seriously. But after Lévesque tried and failed to defeat a resolution endorsing "abortion on demand," he told the convention that he would not be bound by it. He explained that he was not opposed to abortion but that the public was not ready to discuss the issue and that it "tore many consciences." He received a standing ovation from both supporters and opponents of the resolution. When asked by a reporter if his position was related to the planned referendum, he replied, "You keep reasoning on that and I think you've got your answer."[38] As the PQ Government avoided the abortion issue, the federal government ignored the province's failure to enforce the federal abortion law. Neither government wanted to alienate potential supporters before the referendum.

But feminists were not happy with this arrangement. It was very difficult to obtain hospital abortions in Quebec. Francophone hospitals refused to establish abortion committees, and, as a result, the province had only about eight abortion providers—Morgentaler's clinic and some Anglophone hospitals.[39] In April 1977, one thousand women demonstrated for "avortement libre et gratuit" (on demand and free)—calling on the Government to establish abortion clinics and fund abortions under Medicare. "We are not fooled by the Quebec government," said one of the organizers. "The decision not to prosecute doctors performing abortions hasn't changed the abortion situation in Quebec. . . . [I]t is not enough for the Quebec government to look the other way when private doctors perform abortions."[40]

In response to this pressure, Social Affairs Minister Denis Lazure announced in May 1978, to the objections of the province's Catholic bishops, that the province would soon open approximately twenty hospital-based family planning clinics that would provide abortions.[41] But pro-choice activists argued that there were too few of these clinics and that they did provide enough abortions. In 1980, feminist activists reported that their survey of twenty-seven major hospitals had found that only six had established Lazure clinics. "We must conclude," said one activist, "that the only advantage of the Lazure clinics is to furnish the Parti Quebecois government with a good 'policy.'"[42] Later in the year, a Planned Parenthood spokesperson agreed that the PQ's attitude toward abortion was "hypocritical": The party had set up the clinics to please its more radical members, but then restricted them to avoid a voter backlash.[43] Abortion opponents were upset about the clinics as well. In 1980, Lazure denied allegations that the clinics were providing "abortion on demand" and said they approved abortions only for grounds of physical or mental health.[44]

During this time, the PQ Government also established approximately one hundred community service centers (CLSCs) that provided public health and outpatient hospital services, including family planning. Beginning in 1978, some CLSCs began to ask the Government if they could provide abortions. The Government first ignored this request and then said it was studying the issue. In April 1981, five Montreal CLSCs began providing abortions without provincial approval. Federal Justice Minister Jean Chretien called on the province to prosecute the CLSCs. Now that the sovereignty-association referendum had failed, the federal government no longer needed to tread lightly in Quebec. But the PQ Government declined to prosecute, arguing that in light of the Morgentaler acquittals and the lack of clarity in the federal law, such a prosecution would be unlikely to succeed.[45] The PQ Government denied that it had "a policy of tolerating illegalities," but the director of one CLSC disagreed, claiming that the Government wanted the centers "to go further than we're technically supposed to. They don't officially support us but they haven't told us to stop, only to keep quiet."[46] After this, the abortion issue largely receded in Quebec.

In 1983, Morgentaler and feminist pro-choice activists brought their clinic campaign to Toronto and Winnipeg.[47] As he had in Quebec, Morgentaler asked the provincial governments to designate his clinics as authorized abortion facilities, but they refused. He and his colleagues were arrested and charged by Ontario's Progressive Conservative Government and Manitoba's NDP Government.[48] The legal context of the clinic campaign had changed since Quebec. Then, Morgentaler had relied on jury acquittals that made it impossible for provincial officials to enforce the law, but now, at the urging of his attorney Morris Manning, Morgentaler mounted a constitutional challenge.

When the *Charter* had been negotiated a few years before, both sides of the abortion debate tried to incorporate their positions within it. Lobbying centered around Section 7 of the *Charter*—"Everyone has the right to life, liberty and the security of the person and the right not to be

CHAPTER SIX

deprived thereof except in accordance with the principles of fundamental justice."[49] Pro-choice groups lobbied to replace the word "everyone" with "every person" to prevent the Supreme Court from extending rights to fetuses, and also promoted explicit language that declared that the *Charter* did not extend rights to fetuses or in any way compromise the right of women to medically safe abortions. Pro-life groups lobbied for language declaring that "everyone from conception until natural death has the right to life." In response, the Government declared that the abortion question was the proper jurisdiction of Parliament and that the *Charter* did not speak to the question of abortion.[50]

In November 1984, a Toronto jury acquitted Morgentaler, but in May 1985, Ontario's Progressive Conservative Government won on appeal, and Morgentaler appealed to the Supreme Court. In September 1987, the Liberals took office in Ontario and, fulfilling a promise to the National Action Committee on the Status of Women, dropped the charges against Morgentaler.[51] But the Supreme Court appeal remained. On January 1988, the Supreme Court ruled by a margin of 5 to 2 in *Rex v. Morgentaler* that the 1969 abortion reform violated Section 7 of the *Charter*.[52] The court's majority produced three separate opinions, so there was no common rationale for the decision.[53] All five justices agreed that the protection of fetal life was a legitimate and an important state interest, but found that the abortion law was arbitrary and unfair, was too broadly drawn, and did not strike the proper balance between state interests and the liberty and security of the person.[54] Chief Justice Dickson and Justice Lamer found the statute infringed on "bodily integrity" guaranteed by the "security of the person" because it forced a woman to carry a pregnancy to term unless she met "criteria unrelated to her own priorities and aspirations" and because delays increased the physical risk and emotional trauma of abortions. Justices Beetz and Estey found that the statute violated "security of the person" because it prevented women whose health was endangered by pregnancy from "obtaining effective and timely medical treatment."[55] Justice Wilson argued that the statute violated "liberty" because the *Charter* guarantees Canadians "a degree of personal autonomy over important decisions intimately affecting their private lives."[56] She also argued that the statute violated "the security of the person" because it gave the state rather than the pregnant woman control over her reproductive capacity.[57] The court did not create an explicit constitutional right to abortion. Instead, it left it up to Parliament to establish a new abortion law that was procedurally fair.

Later in the chapter, I argue that judicial policy making increased controversy in the United States. But for several reasons, this effect was much weaker in Canada. The ruling did contain several controversial elements: It was the most dramatic case in which the court had overruled an Act of Parliament; it occurred only six years after the court gained new powers of judicial review; and it appeared to interpret the phrase "the principles of fundamental justice" to offer substantive, not just procedural, protection of individual rights—in direct opposition to the intentions of the *Charter*'s framers.[58] In their dissent, La Forest and McIntyre argued that a constitutional right to abortion had no support in the language or history of the *Charter*, nor in the history and traditions of Canadian society, and like the *Roe* dissenters, criticized the court for usurping parliamentary prerogatives.[59]

But the ruling, and Canadian judicial review more generally, contained several elements that reduced controversy. First, the *Charter* contained a "notwithstanding clause" that allowed Parliament to designate legislation that is not subject to the *Charter*. This made it more difficult for opponents of the decision to accuse the court of usurping Parliament's prerogatives.[60] Second, the Canadian court ruled quite narrowly. Dickson and Lamer discussed the limits of judicial review at length. The three opinions did not establish an explicit right to abortion, but left it up to Parliament to draft fairer, less arbitrary abortion legislation. The opinions also did not impose quasi-legislative requirements such as the American trimester system.[61] In the end, Canada was left with abortion on request and for women's own reasons, not because the court required this but because Parliament failed to enact a new abortion law. As Daniel Conkle puts it, Canada's lack of an abortion law is a "product of democratic choice, not judicial compulsion."[62] The Canadian court also did not move abortion from provincial to federal jurisdiction, as did the American court, because criminal law (which has historically included abortion law) had always been reserved to the federal government. Finally, the decision was not a "bolt from the blue" that suddenly brought the abortion issue to public attention, as in the United States. The civil disobedience campaign that brought abortion to the court was long-standing and well known.[63]

In 1988, the Tories embarked on the seemingly impossible task of enacting a new abortion law without actually taking a position on abortion. They had a strong majority in Parliament, but it was divided over abortion. Prime Minister Brian Mulroney offered free votes on liberal, moderate, and conservative abortion *resolutions*.[64] After votes on these resolutions, Mulroney would introduce a bill identical to the winning resolution and whip his party behind it. Through this strategy, Mulroney hoped that Parliament could choose one of the options without having to achieve a majority. But when the opposition parties refused to agree to a ban on amendments to the resolutions, Mulroney introduced only the moderate resolution, and it was defeated by a coalition of MPs on both sides of the issue.[65] Further action was postponed until after the November 1988 elections, which were fought mainly over free trade. A year later, the Government tried again with a narrowed majority, introducing a bill allowing abortions for grounds of life or health with health defined as "physical, mental and psychological." Pro-lifers feared that doctors would interpret the word "psychological" to include social factors. Mulroney whipped the forty members of the Cabinet but not the backbenchers. He also announced that he would not seek new abortion legislation if the bill failed. Pro-lifers, though unhappy with the bill, realized that it would be their last chance to restrict abortion, and it passed 140 to 131. In the Senate, the Tories had a slim majority, but Mulroney allowed a free vote and seven of the party's own senators (on both sides of the issue) defected. The bill was defeated on a 43 to 43 tie. Other than the Progressive Conservative defections, voting was along party lines, with the Liberals and NDP opposing the bill.[66]

True to his word, Mulroney refused to seek new legislation, and subsequent Governments followed suit. This left Canada with no federal abortion law—no gatekeeping, no restrictions on clinics, and no gestational limits. After the Morgentaler decision, most provinces banned public funding of clinic abortions, and Nova Scotia banned clinics entirely. Courts struck down the clinic ban and most of the funding bans. Eventually all of the provinces except New Brunswick, Nova Scotia, and Prince Edward Island yielded on the funding issue. Litigation continues in those provinces.[67]

American Federalism and Judicial Review Increase Access Points and Controversy but Constrain Major Change

In the United States, the initial abortion reforms occurred through state-level policy making and Supreme Court decisions, and these remained the main venues in the post-reform period. The White House and Congress were also involved, but, aside from bans on public funding and the prohibition on abortion counseling by federally funded organizations, their main policy contributions were Supreme Court nominations.[68] Most state policy innovations were examined at least once by the Supreme Court. Initially, the court struck down most of these, but with the

Webster decision of 1989, the court began to allow more state restrictions. The court was not willing, however, to strike down *Roe*.

Institutionalists typically argue that political fragmentation (multiple venues of political authority) hinders policy change by creating a large number of "veto points" where opponents of a given policy can kill it.[69] But a few scholars have argued that such fragmentation actually promotes policy change by providing more access points for policy advocates. In the case of American abortion policy, political fragmentation had both of these effects—it promoted frequent, incremental policy change but hindered major change. Federalism and judicial review contributed both to the large number of abortion enactments and to never-ending contention over abortion, as courts and state legislatures tossed the issue back and forth.[70] Any settlement of abortion policy seemed impossible. But at the same time, federalism and judicial review narrowed the scope of abortion policy making. Abortion restrictions, though many, fell far short of the aspirations of pro-life activists, whose strategic options were strongly constrained by the Supreme Court. Pro-life activists were left with the unpalatable choices of pursuing a constitutional amendment, nominating sympathetic justices, and enacting restrictive legislation that tested the limits of the law.[71] Pro-life activists failed miserably in their attempts to enact a constitutional amendment. They had some success with judicial nominations, but this was a slow process and did not produce the final prize, the overturn of *Roe*. It should also be noted that the court's ruling offered fewer opportunities for pro-choice activists to expand abortion access than in the other countries because its gatekeeping requirements were already the most liberal.

Reform through the Supreme Court had several other effects on subsequent policy making. As I argued in chapter 2, because the justices did not worry about reelection, they were free to establish an abortion policy in *Roe* that went further than the public and state legislatures desired, and this provoked a backlash. Some scholars, most notably Mary Ann Glendon and Justice Ruth Bader Ginsburg, have argued that the court would have produced less conflict if it had ruled more narrowly, or stayed out of the debate entirely and let the states gradually find democratic compromises.[72] But other scholars argue that such compromises were unlikely because abortion had already become a winner-take-all conflict between fetal rights and women's rights by 1970, making it too hot for legislators to handle.[73]

Both views are probably correct. Abortion was already polarized and controversial before *Roe*, and further legislation was unlikely. But the decision also made the controversy worse. The court ruled broadly, allowing abortion on request in the first trimester even though public opinion opposed this, and justified its ruling through a "right of privacy" that is not explicitly mentioned in the Constitution.[74] Justice White complained that the court "simply fashions and announces a new constitutional right" and, as a result, "the people and the legislatures of the 50 States are constitutionally disentitled to weigh the relative importance of the continued existence and development of the fetus, on the one hand, against a spectrum of possible impacts on the mother, on the other hand."[75] *Roe* became a key symbol for conservatives of judicial overreach and insufficient deference to democratically elected legislatures.[76] Some also criticized the court for ruling on the issue too quickly, before it had been adequately aired in state legislatures and lower courts.[77] For many Americans the ruling appeared as a "bolt from the blue." The court also increased controversy by nationalizing what had previously been a state issue—suddenly presidential candidates were required to have a position on abortion.

Because the right to privacy was not explicitly mentioned in the Constitution and had been articulated for the first time only eight years before in *Griswold v. Connecticut*, it provided a much weaker foundation for abortion rights than did the social right to medical care in Britain and Canada. The court's definition of abortion as a right of privacy also weakened claims for abortion as a right of gender equality.[78] Abortion opponents were also outraged that the court gave so little consideration to the potential rights of fetuses: Blackmun merely wrote, "We need not resolve the difficult question of when life begins. When those trained in the respective disciplines of medicine, philosophy, and theology are unable to arrive at any consensus, the judiciary, at this point in the development of man's knowledge, is not in a position to speculate as to the answer."[79] Finally, "rights talk" polarized the debate. The court attempted to balance women's interests with state ones, but activists on both sides of the debate found this balancing intolerable.[80]

American Parties Avoid Abortion and Then Embrace It

As chapter 5 explained, American parties gradually polarized over abortion during the 1970s; by 1980 they fully embraced opposing positions. Abortion policy making showed a similar pattern. During the Ford and Carter administrations, most policy changes involved legislators from both parties in almost equal measure, and party leaders wanted no part of the issue. The Democratic Party controlled Congress and kept many abortion bills off the agenda, but its agenda control was incomplete and some bills slipped through. Beginning with the Reagan administration, however, legislators from the two parties strongly diverged on abortion, and party leaders—initially Republicans but later Democrats too—began to let abortion bills reach the floor through normal committee processes.

During the Ford and Carter administrations, the Democratic Party was split not just between northerners and southerners, but also between traditional and liberal northerners on such issues as the environment, energy, foreign policy, busing, and abortion. Republicans were also divided between moderate, often northeastern Republicans, and a rising conservative faction. In the House, leaders for both sides of the abortion debate came from both parties, but in the Senate, leaders of both sides came from the Republican Party. Left-right ideology and Catholicism, rather than party, were the best predictors of abortion voting. A majority of House Republicans opposed abortion rights, but Senate Republicans and both House and Senate Democrats were divided. As I mentioned in the last chapter, President Ford wanted to return the issue to the states and President Carter opposed both an antiabortion constitutional amendment and public funding of abortion.[81]

The Democratic Party controlled Congress, and its leaders typically sought to avoid the abortion issue because it reduced party unity at a time when it was hard to come by.[82] Party discipline is notoriously weak in Congress, but things were worse than usual in the late 1970s. Congressional reforms had distributed the power of the approximately twenty committee chairs to more than one hundred subcommittee chairs. And new legislators, elected in the Democratic landslide after Watergate, challenged party leaders. They were unwilling to defer to committees, and, as a result, bills were often amended on the floor and voting was unpredictable.

Struggles over bans on public funding for the poor illustrate the bipartisan nature of abortion policy making in the 1970s and the inability of Democratic Party leaders to keep them off the agenda. Pro-life legislators from both parties introduced the bans as floor amendments (riders) to must-pass appropriations bills rather than as freestanding bills in order to keep them from being killed in committee.[83] The riders had to be reapproved every year, subjecting Congress to a divisive annual battle. Tables 6.3 and 6.4 examine the positions of party members on the funding bans from 1974 to 1997 in the House and Senate, respectively. During the 1970s, Republicans were the main supporters of the bans in the House, but Democrats were quite supportive as well. In the Senate, majorities of

Table 6.3 U.S. House of Representatives, Percentage of Each Party Voting to Increase Restrictions on Public Funding of Abortions, 1974–97

Year	Issue	Dem.	Rep.
1974	Include funding ban in appropriations bill, no exceptions	26	42
1976	Include funding ban in appropriations bill, no exceptions	46	73
1976	Final vote, funding ban with life endangerment exception	62	82
1977	Include funding ban in appropriations bill, no exceptions	40	82
1978	Oppose addition of rape and incest to life endangerment exception	48	78
1978	Retain funding ban with life endangerment exception	61	87
1979	Oppose addition of rape and incest to life endangerment exception	39	80
1988	Oppose addition of rape and incest to life endangerment exception	21	83
1989	Oppose addition of rape and incest to life endangerment exception	29	77
1993	Retain ban with life endangerment, rape, and incest exceptions	38	91
1995	Eliminate rape and incest exceptions, retain life endangerment exception	21	77
1997	Extend funding ban to publicly funded but privately provided health insurance plans for the poor	30	95

Sources: Barbara Hinkson Craig and David M. O'Brien, *Abortion and American Politics* (Chatham, NJ: Chatham House, 1993), 151nn21, 23; Douglas W. Jaenicke, "Abortion and Partisanship in the US Congress, 1976–2000: Increasing Partisan Cohesion and Differentiation," *Journal of American Studies* 36 (2002): 1–22.

Table 6.4 U.S. Senate, Percentage of Each Party Voting to Increase Restrictions on Public Funding of Abortions, 1974–97

Year	Issue	Dem.	Rep.
1974	Include funding ban with life endangerment exception in appropriations bill	58	61
1975	Include funding ban with life endangerment exception in appropriations bill	31	54
1976	Include funding ban with life endangerment exception in appropriations bill	27	41
1976	Final vote, funding ban with life endangerment exception	69	69
1977	Include funding ban with life endangerment endangerment, health, rape, and incest exception in appropriations bill	57	57
1978	Allow rape exception only if reported in 48 hours	23	21
1984	Oppose addition of rape and incest exceptions to life endangerment exception	32	74
1988	Remove exceptions for rape and incest, retain life endangerment exception	33	68
1993	Retain funding ban	38	86
1997	Extend funding ban to Children's Health Insurance Program	24	91

Sources: Barbara Hinson Craig and David M. O'Brien, *Abortion and American Politics* (Chatham, NJ: Chatham House, 1993), 117; Douglas W. Jaenicke, "Abortion and Partisanship in the US Congress, 1976–2000: Increasing Partisan Cohesion and Differentiation," *Journal of American Studies* 36 (2002): 1–22.

both parties opposed the bans. In the 1980s, however, the positions of the parties began to polarize—House Democrats became less supportive of the bans, and Senate Republicans became more supportive.[84]

Although the bans had supporters in both parties. Democratic congressional leaders were vexed by lengthy debates over the bans. In 1977, it took Congress five months to reach a compromise between the House version with no exceptions and the Senate version with exceptions for life, health, rape, and incest. When this dispute delayed funding for two federal departments and almost delayed the paychecks of federal employees, the Carter administration asked Democratic congressional leaders to broker a compromise.[85] After doing so, they began exploring ways to remove the issue from the agenda by restricting substantive amendments to appropriations bills, but the rules were hard to change because they had the support of both conservatives, who used them to subvert the agenda control of the Democratic leadership, and liberals, who had previously used them to deny funding for the Vietnam War. In the end, the leaders did not need to change the rules because newly elected conservative Republicans provided the Senate votes to eliminate the health exception throughout the 1980s. The parties continued to polarize on the funding bans throughout the 1980s—though most of this was the result of Republican movement. Democratic support for the ban declined slightly over time while Republican support increased strongly. In 1980, the Supreme Court upheld the federal funding ban in *Harris v. McRae*.[86] It found that although the government could not impose obstacles to abortion rights, it was not required to remove obstacles (such as poverty) that were not of its own creation.[87]

With the 1980 election of Ronald Reagan and Republican control of the Senate, abortion policy making became more partisan, and Republican Party leaders and committee chairs lent their support to antiabortion proposals—though beyond the funding bans, they had little success. Republican committee chairs scheduled hearings for constitutional amendment proposals and reported some out of committee. Senator Orrin Hatch (R-UT) proposed a constitutional amendment returning the abortion question to the states while Senator Jesse Helms (R-NC) proposed a statute declaring that fetuses are "persons" entitled to due process and equal protection under the Fourteenth Amendment. Hatch's proposal was a constitutional amendment and thus needed a two-thirds majority, while Helm's proposal was a regular bill and needed only a simple majority, but most observers thought it was unconstitutional because it changed the Constitution by statute rather than amendment. In August 1982, Helms and Hatch attached their proposals to a must-pass bill increasing the government debt limit, but pro-choice Republican Bob Packwood successfully filibustered both proposals despite attempts by President Reagan to bring several reluctant Republicans on board. In June 1983, the full Senate voted on Hatch's proposal, and it fell eighteen votes short of the required two-thirds majority.[88]

Table 6.5 Party Control of U.S. State Legislatures Enacting Restrictions on Minors' Powers of Consent and Partial-Birth Abortions, 1973–2007

Party Control of State Legislature	Restrictions on Minors' Powers of Consent (Parental Consent and Notification)			Restrictions on Partial-Birth Abortions
	1973–80	1981–92	1993–2006	1997–2007
Republican	8	9	14	15
Southern Democrat	10	14	4	11
Non-Southern Democrat	10	8	0	3
Divided	3	6	4	6
Total	31	37	22	35

Sources: Guttmacher Report on Public Policy, Family Planning Perspectives, State Reproductive Health Monitor, *State Policies in Brief* (New York: Alan Guttmacher Institute, v.d.); Carl Klarner, State Partisan Balance, 1959 to 2007, Data file, 2007; Jon F. Merz, Catherine A. Jackson, and Jacob A. Klerman, "A Review of Abortion Policy: Legality, Medicaid Funding, and Parental Involvement, 1967–1994," *Women's Rights Law Reporter* 17 (1995): 1–61; National Abortion Rights Action League, *Who Decides? A State-by-State Review of Abortion Rights* (Washington, DC: NARAL, v.d.); National Abortion Federation, *State Legislative Report* (Washington, DC: NAF, v.d.).

Notes: Party control means control of both houses of the legislature. Divided control means that one party controlled each house. Nebraska is excluded because it had a unicameral, nonpartisan legislature. The state enacted restrictions on minors' powers of consent in 1973, 1977, 1981, 1991, and 2004. It did not enact restrictions on partial-birth abortions.

Not only did abortion policy making become more partisan over time in Congress, but also in the states.[89] Table 6.5 shows the party control of legislatures enacting restrictions on minors' powers of consent (parental consent and notification) and so-called partial-birth abortions (intact dilation and extraction) from 1973 to 2007.[90] From 1973 to 1980, state legislatures controlled by Republicans, Southern Democrats, and non-Southern Democrats were equally likely to restrict minors' consent powers. From 1980 to 1992, legislatures controlled by Southern Democrats were most likely to enact such restrictions, and Republican and non-Southern Democratic legislatures were equally likely. But after 1992, Republican legislatures were much more likely to enact consent restrictions than Southern Democratic ones, and legislatures controlled by non-Southern Democrats did not enact a single restriction. This does not mean that individual Democratic legislators did not vote for consent restrictions. They often did. But Democratic party leaders and committee chairs often tried to keep such restrictions from coming to a vote.[91] There were also strong partisan and regional patterns in partial-birth abortion restrictions: Republican and Southern Democratic legislatures enacted twenty-six of the thirty-five restrictions while non-Southern Democratic legislatures enacted only three.

Judicial Appointments

The executive branch also got into the action: Republican President Reagan first prohibited discussion of abortion by federally funded organizations, and his order was renewed by subsequent Republican presidents and rescinded by Democratic ones. Democratic President Bill Clinton vetoed bans on so-called partial-birth abortions while Republican President George W. Bush signed them. But the main contributions of the presidents to abortion policy were appointments to the federal courts, and especially the Supreme Court. From 1980 to 2010, Republican presidents appointed seven Supreme Court justices while Democrats appointed four. Table 6.6 shows the votes of the justices on key abortion cases since *Roe*. For justices appointed before the Reagan presidency, the relationship between partisan affiliation and support for abortion rights was not particularly strong. Brennan, Blackmun, and Stevens were all appointed by Republican presidents (though Brennan was a Democrat) and were all strong proponents of abortion rights. White, appointed by a Democrat, opposed abortion rights. But for the nine nominees since Reagan's first appointment, Sandra Day O'Connor, the relationship between partisan affiliation and abortion voting was much stronger. This was also true in lower courts. Federal judges appointed by Reagan took antiabortion positions in 77 percent of their cases while Carter appointees did so in only 13 percent.[92]

Republican attempts to secure antiabortion Supreme Court rulings by changing the composition of the court, while impressive, were not as fruitful as pro-life activists had hoped. Changing Supreme Court decisions through a series of nominations is no easy task: Nominees must be confirmed by the Senate, they are not required to reveal their views on the issues they will address, and once they reach the court there is no guarantee that they will vote as expected. Presidents Reagan and George H. W. Bush appointed Justices Sandra Day O'Connor, Antonin Scalia, Anthony Kennedy, David Souter, and Clarence Thomas with the hope that they would help overturn *Roe*, but all but Scalia and Thomas were disappointments. Though O'Connor, Kennedy, and Souter supported greater restrictions on abortion, they would not agree to overturn *Roe*. This failure was a combination of vetting errors, political constraints, the unpredictability of Supreme Court justices, and the failure to secure the confirmation of Robert Bork. O'Connor was nominated during Reagan's first year in office while the administration was still developing its procedures for vetting nominees. Justice Department officials overlooked several of her votes in favor of abortion rights while an Arizona legislator and had

Table 6.6 Voting by U.S. Supreme Court Justices in Abortion Cases, 1973–2007

Justice	Year of Appointment and Party of President	Roe and Doe 1973 7-2	McRae 1980 5-4	Akron 1983 6-3	Thornburgh 1986 5-4	Webster 1988 5-4	Rust 1991 5-4	Casey 1992 4-3-2	Carhart 2007 5-4
Douglas	1939 D	+							
Brennan	1956 R	+	+	+	+	+			
Stewart	1958 R	+	(-)						
White	1962 D	(-)	(-)	(-)	(-)	(-)	(-)	(-)	
Marshall	1967 D	+	+	+	+	+	+		
Burger	1969 R	+	(-)	+	(-)				
Blackmun	1970 R	+	+	+	+	+	+	+	
Powell	1972 R	+	(-)	+	+				
Rehnquist	1972 R	(-)	(-)	(-)	(-)	(-)	(-)	(-)	
Stevens	1975 R		+	+	+	+	+	+	+
O'Connor	1981 R			(-)	(-)	Mixed	+	Mixed	
Scalia	1986 R					(-)	(-)	(-)	(-)
Kennedy	1988 R					(-)	(-)	Mixed	(-)
Souter	1990 R						(-)	Mixed	+
Thomas	1991 R							(-)	(-)
Ginsburg	1993 D								+
Breyer	1994 D								+
Roberts	2005 R								
Alito	2006 R								(-)
Sotomayor	2009 D								
Kagan	2010 D								

Source: Oyez Project, http://www.Oyez.org.

Note: For summaries of the cases, see appendix 2.

+ Supports abortion rights (opposes increased restrictions).
(-) Opposes abortion rights (supports increased restrictions).
Mixed Upholds abortion rights but increases restrictions.
R Appointed by a Republican president. Justice Brennan was a Democrat, but was appointed by Republican President Dwight Eisenhower.
D Appointed by a Democratic president.

difficulty determining her views because, as a midtier state judge, she had written little on federal constitutional issues.[93]

President Reagan's unsuccessful 1987 nomination of Robert Bork was also a key moment in the failure to overturn *Roe*. Antonin Scalia's nomination the previous year had drawn little opposition because Scalia was replacing Burger, another conservative, and because the concurrent elevation of Rehnquist to chief justice drew the most opposition. But Reagan's nomination of Bork to replace Justice Lewis Powell, a moderate and *Roe* supporter, would tip the court toward the conservatives. Bork had written critiques of *Roe*, and his opponents dubbed him a "walking constitutional amendment." He rejected any constitutional right of privacy—not just on abortion but on birth control, private schools, and guns. His nomination drew unprecedented opposition, in particular from pro-choice and civil rights activists. Conservative Southern Democrats were the key to his defeat, and many had very personal reservations about his "strange lifestyle" and "refusal to discuss his belief in God."[94] Bork's defeat demonstrated for the first time that effective opposition could derail a Supreme Court nomination, and this raised the stakes and controversy for later confirmation battles.[95] As Laurence Tribe notes, it also increased public attention to and support for a general "right of privacy" that applied to abortion, but also went beyond it.[96]

Reagan nominated Kennedy and George H. W. Bush nominated Souter at moments of political vulnerability. Reagan was a lame-duck president with sagging approval ratings and a Senate minority. He was also under investigation for illegal arms shipments to Nicaraguan rebels and had watched his two previous nominations (Robert Bork and Douglas Ginsburg) go down in flames. He needed a nominee that could be easily confirmed and chose Kennedy despite serious concerns about his conservatism, and especially his views on privacy rights.[97] Bush had a Senate minority as well, and memories of the Bork debacle were still fresh. He wanted a quick and trouble-free confirmation. Chief of staff John Sununu and pro-choice Republican senator Warren Rudman urged Bush to appoint fellow New Hampshirite Souter, but administration officials had difficulty determining his judicial philosophy because he had not written much on federal constitutional issues and refused to answer questions about abortion or any other issue on which he might rule. Conservatives were shocked by how liberal he sounded during his confirmation hearings.[98]

In 1988, after Reagan had made three appointments to the court (O'Connor, Scalia, and Kennedy), he asked it to overturn *Roe v. Wade* in *Webster v. Reproductive Health Services*.[99] That case, and *Planned Parenthood* of *Southeastern Pennsylvania v. Casey*[100] three years later, illustrate the extreme difficulty of the Republican's judicial nomination strategy. In *Webster*, the court considered the constitutionality of a Missouri statute that declared that life began at conception, outlawed abortions in public hospitals, and required amniocentesis to establish whether fetuses were viable, as postviability abortions were illegal under Missouri law. It appeared that there were five votes for overturning *Roe*—Reagan appointees O'Connor, Scalia, and Kennedy along with *Roe* dissenters White and Rehnquist. Instead, the court upheld most of the Missouri statute but did not overturn *Roe*. Rehnquist (joined by Scalia, White, and Kennedy) argued that states have an interest in protecting potential life at any point during pregnancy. He approved Missouri's viability test and said this required the abandonment of *Roe*'s trimester framework: Some viability tests would have negative results and would thus amount to previability regulation to protect potential life. But O'Connor argued that the viability test was consistent with *Roe* because it did not impose an "undue burden" on women's abortion decisions.[101] Scalia decried O'Connor's refusal to overturn *Roe*: "Given the Court's newly contracted abstemiousness, what will it take, one must wonder, to permit us to reach that fundamental question?"[102] Though the decision maintained *Roe*, it clearly signaled that the court would accept increased state regulation of abortion.

Three years later, the court considered abortion once again in *Casey*. Bush nominees David Souter and Clarence Thomas had replaced liberal justices William Brennan and Thurgood Marshall. If either joined the *Webster* majority, *Roe* would fall. In conference, five justices, including Thomas, agreed to uphold all of Pennsylvania's abortion restrictions and overturn *Roe*.[103] But at the last moment, Kennedy changed his mind and joined O'Connor and Souter to reaffirm "the core holding of *Roe*."[104] The trio replaced the previous "strict scrutiny" standard of judicial review with an "undue burden" standard and eliminated the trimester framework. They also found that postviability restrictions must have an exception for life or health.[105]

The decision was not a clear victory for either side—in fact, both claimed defeat.[106] But most media commentators, and the Clinton and Bush presidential campaigns, declared it an acceptable compromise. The ruling was hailed by some as a triumph of the "robes on" model of judicial decision making: Legal theorist Ronald Dworkin claimed the ruling "refuted the cynics who insist that since Supreme Court appointments are politically motivated the Court is inevitably just another political institution."[107] But more political explanations are also possible; one is that the three nominees were more liberal on abortion than the presidents who nominated them; another is that they were acting as good Republicans. In the wake of *Webster*, pro-choice forces appeared ascendant—money was flowing into their organizations, their voters were paying attention, and pro-choice Democrats were winning congressional and gubernatorial elections—a presidential election was approaching, and some argued that the court would grievously harm the Republicans if it overturned *Roe*.[108]

Another political explanation, expressed by the trio themselves, is that they sought to preserve the court's institutional legitimacy in the face of state resistance.[109] The trio wrote that *Roe*, like *Brown*, had called "the contending sides of a national controversy to end their national division." They argued that such a decision required a "rare precedential force to counter the inevitable efforts to overturn it and to thwart its implementation" and that to "overrule under fire" "would subvert the Court's legitimacy beyond any serious question."[110] Scalia bitingly refuted this rationale: "I cannot agree with, indeed I am appalled by, the Court's suggestion that the decision whether to stand by an erroneous constitutional decision must be strongly influenced—*against* overruling, no less—by the substantial and continuing public opposition the decision has generated."[111]

Abortion and the Obama Health-Care Reform

In 2010, the enactment of health-care reform legislation reduced private health insurance coverage of abortion. Initially, pro-choice and pro-life Democrats agreed on the general principle of maintaining the status quo on abortion funding—federal funds would not be used to pay for abortions except in the extreme cases contained in the Hyde amendment—rape, incest, or to save the life of the woman.[112] But the two sides soon disagreed about what it meant to maintain the status quo. Some thought that any insurance plan receiving federal dollars should not be allowed to pay for abortions. Others thought that plans receiving both private and federal funds should be allowed to pay for abortions so long as they used only the private funds. Still others argued that applying the Hyde amendment's funding restrictions to millions of women beyond current Medicaid recipients did not preserve the status quo.

The proposed health reform increased insurance coverage by requiring everyone to sign up for insurance, expanding eligibility for Medicaid, and providing subsidies to lower- and middle-income people who did not have employer-provided insurance. These people (and some small businesses) would buy coverage in an insurance exchange that included private plans and, in early proposals, a public plan.[113] The House health reform bill initially allowed these plans to pay for abortions (beyond the extreme cases laid out in the Hyde amendment—this is what I mean by "abortion coverage" in the remainder of the discussion), but required them to set aside private premiums for this purpose. The bill also required that the national insurance exchange include at least one plan that covered abortions and one that did not.[114] But a group of pro-life Democrats led by Representative Bart Stupak (D-MI) refused to vote for the bill unless the House leadership allowed a vote on a more restrictive amendment: It prohibited any plan in the exchange, public or private, from paying for abortions. The House leadership reluctantly allowed the vote—they needed the votes of the pro-lifers—and the amendment passed with the support of all Republicans and 25 percent of Democrats. In the last two elections, the Democratic Party had won seats in swing districts by recruiting more conservative candidates, and this had brought more pro-life legislators into the party.[115]

As the Senate took up health reform, Obama and pro-choice legislators argued that the Stupak amendment did not preserve the status quo because many women would lose their abortion coverage if they or their employers bought coverage in the exchange—and the problem would worsen once large employers became eligible for the exchange.[116]

The Senate majority leader, Harry Reid (D-NV), developed a compromise similar to the one in the initial House bill—private premiums would be set aside to pay for abortions. But Senator Ben Nelson (D-NE), the last Democratic senator to endorse health reform, forced more restrictive language. It required private plans that covered abortion to collect two separate premiums—one for abortion and one for all other services.[117] The Nelson language also allowed states to prohibit all plans in their exchanges, including those purchased without subsidies, from providing abortion coverage. Stupak and his supporters initially opposed Nelson's language, but eventually accepted it after Obama agreed to issue an executive order reiterating his earlier promise that federal funds would not pay for abortions.[118]

The Nelson language caused a split among Catholic pro-lifers. The bishops had long advocated universal health insurance, but withdrew their support because although Nelson's amendment prohibited the use of federal funds to pay for abortions, it did not prohibit the use of federal funds for *plans* that covered abortions. The bishops also worried that pro-life families might be faced with a moral dilemma if a plan addressed their needs better than other plans but forced them to pay an extra premium for other people's abortions. They also claimed that new funds for community health centers would be used to provide abortions, protested that conscience protections for hospitals and health workers were inadequate, and opposed the exclusion of undocumented immigrants from the exchanges.[119]

Pro-life supporters of health reform, including Catholic nuns and hospitals, disputed the bishops' claims. The progressive Catholic opinion magazine *Commonweal* published an analysis by Timothy Stoltzfus Jost, a Mennonite pro-life law professor, who argued that the Senate and House bills were equally pro-life and both were more pro-life than the status quo. He predicted that the vast majority of plans in the exchanges would not offer abortion coverage, and that those that did would likely offer an identical plan without it. He also argued that, for reasons of cost or stigma, few people would actually purchase plans with abortion coverage and, as a result, the total number of people with abortion coverage would decline. He disputed the claim that new funds for community health centers would be used for abortions. Finally, he argued that the health reform would save 45,000 lives per year and that the Senate bill had pro-life features that the House bill did not: it allowed states to ban all plans in their exchanges from covering abortion; it was stronger on euthanasia and assisted suicide; and it provided new funds to support pregnant teens, teenage mothers, and adoptive parents.[120] Finally, Jost faulted the bishops for acting as if they had a choice between the House and Senate bills when in fact they had a choice between the Senate bill and the much worse status quo.[121] Pro-lifers in Congress were also divided: Democrats claimed that the reform ensured that no federal funds would pay for abortions while Republicans called it the "largest expansion of publicly-funded abortion in history."[122]

Pro-choice groups also criticized the abortion provisions of health reform. The Alan Guttmacher Institute predicted, like Jost, that most insurers would refuse to offer abortion coverage in the exchanges, and perhaps, for reasons of standardization, in the employer-provided market as well. But the Institute noted with approval that the reform's Medicaid expansion would increase the number of low-income people with abortion coverage in the seventeen states that cover medically necessary Medicaid abortions with their own funds. NARAL Pro-Choice America refused to support the bill because of its abortion funding restrictions, but the group did not oppose it because it had other positive reproductive health provisions.[123]

To sum up this section, British Governments refused to introduce abortion legislation, insisting that abortion was an "issue of conscience" and confining abortion policy making to occasional private member's bills with little chance of enactment. Canadian Governments also refused to legislate on abortion until the Supreme Court forced the Mulroney Government's hand, and after failing to enact legislation, it avoided the issue again. Private member's bills had even worse chances in Canada than in Britain. The few major policy changes in Britain and Canada occurred outside Parliament and partisan politics and generally expanded abortion provision. By contrast, American policy making was frequent, touched every level of government, and produced some important restrictions. These differences in the frequency and direction of policy change flowed mainly from the differences in the party politicization of abortion that I explained in chapter 5, but they also stemmed from differing policy venues and the degree of agenda control that parties had within them. In Britain and Canada, most policy making was confined to Parliament, and Governments had strong control over its agenda. In the United States, the Supreme Court established a more liberal reform than the other countries, justified it in particularly controversial terms, and prompted accusations of democratic usurpation. This helped stimulate pro-life mobilization. Political parties had little control over the agenda or the decisions of the court, though they tried to shape its views through appointments. Party leaders also had limited control over Congress's agenda. Even before abortion became a partisan issue, pro-life activists had some success in Congress. Finally, the American polity offered numerous access points for contention over abortion—fifty state legislatures, the White House, two houses of Congress, and the courts. Back and forth between the Supreme Court and these other venues hindered settlement of the abortion issue and promoted frequent policy making. But the Supreme Court was also a brake on major policy change. Its purported respect for precedent, its concern for institutional legitimacy, its relative insulation from direct political pressure, and its unpredictable justices deeply frustrated pro-life activists. I now turn to a final crucial factor—the involvement of medical associations in abortion politics and policy.

British and Canadian Doctors Defend and Promote Abortion Services; American Doctors Ignore Them

As I showed in chapter 3, British and Canadian medical associations were heavily involved in abortion reforms while American ones were only minimally involved. And medical associations in all three countries initially opposed abortion on request, but the AMA eventually accepted it. The orientations of the medical associations during reform had implications for their orientations after. British and Canadian medical associations remained active on abortion, while the AMA continued to keep it at arm's length. And the positions of the British and Canadian associations gradually liberalized until they came to support abortion on request, or something approaching it, and advocated the expansion of abortion services.

During the struggle over the 1967 reform, the BMA and the RCOG had attempted to ensure that doctors were not faced with patients who "demanded" abortions and thus opposed social grounds and grounds of rape, incest, mental disability, and underage pregnancy.[124] After reform, mainstream doctors were heavily involved in abortion services since half of abortions were provided in NHS hospitals. They also had wide discretion: Doctors who opposed abortion could interpret the law strictly, while doctors who supported abortion rights could interpret the law liberally and take comfort in the fact that women unable to get abortions in NHS hospitals could get them in private clinics.

In 1970, the BMA and RCOG supported unsuccessful private member's bills to restrict abortion gatekeeping to NHS consultants, and they supported the creation of the ostensibly antiabortion Lane Committee in 1971.[125] In its testimony to the committee, the BMA said that the 1967 reform was a welcome piece of legislation but that the general public and the profession needed to understand that the act did not allow "abortion on demand." But when the Lane Committee finally issued its report in 1974, the BMA and RCOG agreed with its recommendations for modest changes in administrative and professional practice rather than the law. By then, medical associations' concerns about "abortion racketeering" had subsided as European women seeking abortions began traveling to the Netherlands rather than Britain, and the Lane Committee also revealed that the health ministry had increased its oversight of private providers.

Beginning in 1976, the BMA and RCOG routinely opposed private member's bills restricting abortion, and in 2008, the BMA testified in favor of an amendment to the embryology bill that allowed first-trimester abortions with only a single doctor's approval. Moreover, the BMA argued that because first-trimester abortions were now safer than pregnancy, they automatically met the criteria of the 1967 Abortion Act. The requirement of medical necessity for early abortions should be eliminated.[126] In other words, the BMA now supported abortion on request for early abortions.

In Canada, the CMA quickly turned against the 1969 abortion reform—opposing hospital abortion committees and narrowly supporting social grounds in 1971. It lobbied Parliament for changes to the law throughout the 1970s and 1980s. The association's change of position appeared to result from both the inconsistency of the hospital committees, which interpreted health in widely varying ways, and overbearing enforcement by the federal health minister. Still, the association was badly divided over social grounds and abortion on request. It also opposed abortion clinics and offered little support to Dr. Morgentaler's civil disobedience campaign. The association did not support clinics and abortion on request until after the *Morgentaler* decision of 1988, and it denied that it supported "abortion on demand." But when the Mulroney Government tried to enact a new abortion law, the CMA was its most influential opponent.

In Canada, the CMA had put abortion reform on Parliament's agenda and strongly influenced its content, but it quickly became disenchanted with the reform. Few hospitals established abortion committees, and those that did were swamped with requests. The CMA also had not expected hospital committees to interpret the law so variably.[127] In 1970, the Canadian Psychiatric Association and the Alberta Medical Association called for repeal of the abortion law, and the CMA established a committee to reconsider the reform. The committee recommended abolition of the abortion committees, the restriction of abortion to hospitals, a twenty-week upper time limit (there was no such time limit in the original reform), a conscientious objector clause with an obligation to refer patients to a willing doctor, and a statement that abortion is not an appropriate method of birth control. It also asked the Government to provide additional facilities and staff if it ever widened the grounds for abortion. All of these recommendations had broad support at the CMA annual meeting, but one passed by only four votes (78 to 74): "The CMA recognizes that there is justification on non-medical, social grounds for the deliberate termination of pregnancy."[128] This recommendation was put forward by the CMA board of directors because it felt that the association's acceptance of the other resolutions "implies acceptance of the concept that abortion should be permitted for other than purely medical reasons."[129]

The press said the CMA had liberalized its position, but an editorial in the association's journal contested this. It claimed that although the CMA now opposed hospital abortion committees, it also supported a twenty-week upper time limit and "gave the impression" that doctors would "perform abortions only when there are clear medical grounds."[130]

CMA opposition to hospital abortion committees hardened in 1974 when the new Liberal Justice Minister Otto Lang, an abortion opponent, declared that abortion law was to be applied "strictly" and that "social and economic considerations were not to be taken into account."[131] A *Globe and Mail* editorial claimed that the abortion reform "designedly gave doctors considerable latitude within which to exercise their medical judgement," but now the justice minister had threatened them with "legal action if they exercise their judgement. No wonder they have become fearful about what they should do."[132] Bette Stephenson, the first woman president of the CMA, accused Lang of intimidation and asked Prime Minister Trudeau to clarify the meaning of "health" either through the courts or "the frequently promised parliamentary debate."[133] Trudeau assured Stephenson that no threat was intended and said it was too early to reconsider the abortion law, but the Government did establish the Badgley Committee to examine it. Lang soon backtracked, noting that "health is a broad word and a medical term that can certainly include mental and other factors," and he was moved to another ministry.[134]

At its June 1975 annual meeting, the association again called for an end to abortion committees.[135] But Communications Director Douglas Geekie noted that the "the association *has steadfastly rejected* the philosophy and position of abortion on demand." He also said that although CMA had recognized that there were social grounds for abortion, it rejected the idea that CMA should develop such grounds and present them to the Government—"the prerogative and responsibility for providing leadership in this area rest with the country's duly elected legislators—the representatives of Canadian society as a whole."[136]

Thus, the CMA had a complicated position on abortion. It recognized the need for abortions on social grounds but saw it as Parliament's job to specify what those grounds should be, and it opposed "abortion on demand." It opposed both hospital abortion committees and abortion clinics. This complex position seemed to reflect differences within the profession itself. According to the 1977 Badgley report's survey of gynecologists and family practitioners, 40 percent thought the existing law was too restrictive, 20 percent thought it was too liberal, and 30 percent thought it was just right, and only half of doctors thought that hospital committees should consider social and family health when approving abortions.[137] Doctors also opposed abortion clinics—only 20 percent thought abortions could be safely provided in them,[138] and medical organizations were not particularly supportive of Morgentaler's clinic campaigns. Provincial Colleges of Physicians and Surgeons revoked Morgentaler's license or threatened to do so in Quebec, Ontario, Manitoba, New Brunswick, and Alberta,[139] and when Morgentaler was in prison, the CMA general council refused to condemn either his conviction or Quebec's substitution of a guilty verdict for his jury acquittal.[140]

By 1983, a CMA poll suggested that doctors' abortion attitudes were liberalizing somewhat: Half of doctors now supported abortion on request for women's own reasons during the first trimester while the other half supported abortions only for medical or economic grounds.[141] When the 1988 *Morgentaler* decision finally struck down the abortion law, the CMA immediately reiterated its opposition to "abortion on demand" and abortion clinics, but at its annual meeting that summer, it adopted a new policy that supported licensed clinics and said that the abortion decision was "a medical one, made privately between the patient and her physician, within the confines of existing Canadian law, and after conscientious examination of all other options." The drafting committee for the policy claimed that it simply reaffirmed the CMA's existing policy, but pro-life members called it "abortion on demand." The new policy also supported public funding of abortions and an upper time limit of twenty weeks.[142]

Eighteen months later, the CMA was the main, and most influential, opponent of the Mulroney Government's attempt to recriminalize abortion. The CMA testified against the bill in the House of Commons and in the Senate and mounted a media campaign against it. The association said it was especially worried about third-party prosecutions of doctors by jilted boyfriends and pro-life activists and claimed that a survey of members had found that fear of such lawsuits would cause 20 percent of doctors currently providing abortions to stop doing so.[143] After the bill passed the House of Commons, the CMA stepped up its attack, reporting that as many as fifty doctors had already stopped performing abortions in anticipation of the bill's passage, and "things are going to get measurably worse."[144] Justice Minister Kim Campbell said she was outraged by the association's hardball tactics, essentially an abortion strike, and assured the CMA that the Government would amend the law if such lawsuits actually became a problem; it could not, however, amend the bill at hand because that would require sending it back to the House of Commons, where it might be defeated.[145]

In the United States, the AMA avoided the abortion issue much as it had prior to *Roe*. It signed on to various amicus briefs supporting abortion rights but put few resources into lobbying on the issue. After *Roe*, the AMA and the American Hospital Association successfully lobbied Congress for a conscientious objector statute.[146] In June 1973, the AMA brought its abortion policy into agreement with *Roe*, removing requirements that doctors consult with two colleagues and that abortions be performed in accredited hospitals, but it also enacted a resolution declaring the "traditional favorable attitude of the medical profession toward pregnancy and motherhood."[147] When Congress enacted bans on federal funding of abortions for the poor, the AMA took no action.[148] State medical organizations were not particularly responsive either: Only seventeen state medical societies released statements on the post-*Roe* situation or offered practice guidelines. Only fifteen state hospital associations took action, and this amounted mainly to declaring the rights of conscientious objectors and providing legal guidance.[149]

As I explained in chapter 4, the private, fee-for-service medical system allowed individual doctors and hospitals to escape contact with abortion. Most hospitals and private practices chose not to provide abortions. In those that did, individual doctors could opt out. With the emergence of abortion specialists and single-purpose clinics, abortion became segregated from mainstream medical care: It became the exception rather than the rule that ob/gyns provided abortions.[150] Doctors who did provide abortions were often stigmatized by other members of the profession, and some were denied surgical positions in hospitals and leadership positions in medical societies.[151] Meanwhile, pro-choice activists such as Judith Mears of the ACLU pleaded for the support of the medical profession. "If we are to avoid the disheartening prospect of history repeating itself, *a la Brown*, with twenty years of legislative and litigative battles ahead . . . we must have the cooperative and active assistance of physicians who can assert the primacy of their medical judgement in this sphere."[152]

Because most hospitals and mainstream ob/gyns were not involved in abortion services, and because the initial reform gave doctors little discretion to protect in the first place, the AMA had little reason to involve itself with abortion;[153] besides, it had other worries as the medical profession lost power in the face of managed care.[154] The founding of the National Abortion Federation (NAF) in 1977 further reduced the AMA's responsibility for representing the interests of doctors that provided abortion. The AMA opposed antiabortion constitutional amendments during the 1970s and 1980s, but as conservatives and the pro-life movement gained prominence, the AMA tried to stay out of the debate. In 1982, AMA chief executive Dr. James Sammons told the editor of the association's journal to avoid the abortion issue along with other sensitive issues such as nuclear war and tobacco.[155] The AMA was slow to oppose prohibitions on the discussion of abortion by federally funded organizations,[156] and NARAL criticized the AMA for its failure to file an amicus brief in *Planned Parenthood of Southeastern Pennsylvania v. Casey*. In 1997, ACOG and the *New England Medical Journal* opposed the partial-birth abortion ban, but the AMA supported it. The association had exchanged this support for a guarantee that the Republican Congress would not cut Medicare reimbursements—the press accused the AMA of following the "Hypocritic Oath."[157] Once again, the AMA had traded clinical autonomy for economic power. AMA chief executive James S. Todd summed up the AMA's position: "The pro-lifers pick on us, but so do the pro-choice people. We're being attacked by both sides. That puts us in a neutral position doesn't it? We can't win no matter what we do. And on this subject I think the less the AMA says [the better]."[158]

While AMA provided only minimal support for abortion rights, other medical organizations were more active. After the *Roe* decision, ACOG and the American Public Health Association published guidelines on abortion services and lobbied against the federal funding ban. ACOG also issued a statement defending Kenneth Edelin, a Boston doctor convicted of manslaughter for performing a late-term abortion in 1975.[159] In the early 1990s, several mainstream medical organizations such as ACOG and the Accreditation Council for Graduate Medical Education (ACGME) met with NAF to discuss strategies for increasing the supply of abortion providers. In 1995, after lobbying by Medical Students for Choice, ACGME required abortion training during residency for doctors and hospitals that did not have moral objections to abortion. In response, congressional pro-lifers enacted legislation allowing residency programs to obtain accreditation even if they did not meet all ACGME requirements. The AMA, ACOG, and other medical organizations opposed this interference with the profession's control over its educational requirements. Around the same time, two programs based at the University of California, San Francisco, established postresidency fellowships in family planning (including abortion) in more than twenty universities and offered financial and technical assistance to residencies that incorporated abortion training.[160] In 2007, ACOG established an obligation for providers who invoke abortion conscience clauses to make referrals to providers who will provide the service, but the Bush administration criticized the policy and the association backtracked.[161]

Conclusion

This chapter explained differences in the frequency and direction of postreform policy change. In Britain and Canada, policy changes were rare, mainly expanded the quality and availability of abortion services, and generally occurred outside Parliament. Parties avoided the issue and easily kept it off Parliament's agenda, partly by confining it to nonpartisan parliamentary processes such as private member's bills and free voting. Medical associations in both countries were deeply involved in both the initial reform and post-reform policy making; they gradually broadened their interpretations of abortion grounds, advocated the expansion of abortion services, and eventually supported the elimination of medical gatekeeping.

In the United States, policy changes were frequent and mainly reduced the quality and availability of abortion services. Abortion movements successfully injected their issue into open political parties, and once this was accomplished, the pro-life movement benefited from the electoral success of the Republican Party. The policy venue of the initial reform, the Supreme Court, increased controversy but also imposed a significant constraint on the scope of policy change—attempts to roll back *Roe* through judicial nominations were only moderately successful. At the same time, the many policy venues for abortion contention resulted in continuous back and forth between courts and legislatures. The absence of mainstream medicine from the abortion debate left the issue to other actors and meanings—and in particular to feminist and fetal rights meanings that heightened controversy and mobilized opposing movements.

SEVEN

Political Institutions and Abortion Policy

This book examined the abortion policies of Britain, Canada, and the United States: three countries that shared "secular majoritarian" abortion politics and "gatekeeping" policies during the 1960s but eventually diverged as the United States moved to an "own reasons" policy and "negotiated" abortion politics. During the Long 1960s, Britain, Canada, and the United States all reformed their abortion laws, but the American national reform was more liberal than those in the other countries—allowing abortion on request for women's own reasons. The British reform allowed abortions only for reasons of health, fetal abnormality, or limited social grounds and only with the approval of two doctors. The Canadian reform was the most restrictive, allowing abortions only for reasons of health and only with the approval of a hospital abortion committee. After the reforms of the Long 1960s, abortion sparked controversy and movement mobilization in all three countries, but only the American movements succeeded in moving abortion to the center of politics and only the United States experienced frequent policy changes that reduced the quality and availability of abortion services. In Britain and Canada, Governments and political parties successfully avoided the abortion issue. Abortion policies changed infrequently and usually outside of partisan politics, and most of these changes expanded abortion services. These differences among the countries prompted me to pose several questions at the beginning of the book: How did the United States, founded by Puritans, with high levels of religious belief and observance, and typically backward in social and sexuality policies, end up with one of the most liberal abortion policies in the West? Why did abortion become a party political issue in the United States but not in the other countries? And why was the American pro-life movement more successful that its counterparts in the other countries?

My answers to these questions focused on the ways in which macro-level political institutions mediated the actions of meso-level actors. I showed that political institutions such as health-care policies, electoral and party systems, and policy venues strongly influenced the understandings and actions of medical interest groups, political parties, and social movements. My institutional approach suggests several modifications of theories meant to explain the actions of these groups. For example, interest group theories argue that powerful interest groups routinely translate their preferences into policy and that similarly situated groups typically have similar preferences. But I showed that the preferences, and especially the priorities, of similar groups can vary because they are constructed within differing political institutions. Medical associations in all three countries shared common interests on abortion. They opposed "abortion on demand" because it threatened their clinical autonomy. Instead, they wanted to maintain their role as abortion gatekeepers—"diagnosing" the "medical necessity" of abortions. They agreed that abortions should be available only in legally defined circumstances such as health or fetal abnormality rather than for a woman's own reasons and that doctors should determine when women meet these circumstances. But though the medical associations shared these common preferences, they did not pursue them with equal vigor or persistence. American doctors were located in a system of private, fee-for-service medicine that gave them great wealth and power. Preserving that system was their highest priority, and, as a result, they were more concerned with protecting their economic power than their clinical autonomy, in part because they believed that the former was their best guarantee of the latter. In addition, at the very moment that abortion reforms hit the political agenda, the AMA faced an imminent threat to fee-for-service medicine—an alliance of powerful actors pushing for national health insurance that seemed likely to win. Moreover, by observing developments in a few states that had repealed their abortion laws, American doctors realized that even if abortion laws were repealed, they could easily avoid unpleasant abortion work and "demanding" patients by simply refusing to provide abortions. Women seeking abortion would have to find them in single-purpose clinics rather than in the hospitals and offices of mainstream medicine.

For all of these reasons, American doctors eventually ceded their role as abortion gatekeepers. In 1970, the AMA passed a policy resolution that said abortion should be provided when it was "in the best interests" of patients, but unlike earlier resolutions, this one did not specify legally defined grounds for which doctors should approve abortions—a policy of de facto abortion on request.

By contrast, British and Canadian doctors were located in medical systems in which the government funded, and in Britain provided, medical care. Doctors had fought but failed to prevent these systems of health care. In the process, they reached accommodations with the state in which they were compensated for reduced control over the economics and organization of medical care through a guarantee of extensive clinical autonomy. As a result, they guarded their clinical prerogatives jealously including when they were threatened by abortion reforms. During consideration of abortion reforms, the BMA, the RCOG, and the CMA lobbied Parliament to ensure that abortion reforms maintained doctors' gatekeeping authority over abortions. They sought to ensure that abortions were allowed only for reasons of health or fetal abnormality and only with the approval of multiple doctors. In sum, doctors were similarly situated with regard to abortion and shared some common interests, but their priorities differed in the context of differing health-care systems.

Theories of social movement impacts suggest that movements will be more successful when they are large and rich, when they match their tactics to the contexts in which they contend, and when they develop meanings that resonate with policy makers and the public. I showed that political institutions mediated each of these factors. The American pro-choice movement was the largest and most radical of the three, but this was largely a result of the pace and timing of the reforms in the three countries. For many years, American states made abortion reforms one by one. This slow, state-level policy making provided opportunities for policy learning and the development of new coalitions and claims. Early reformers were disappointed with the implementation of the first state reforms because they did not markedly increase the availability of abortions. They began to call for the complete repeal of abortion laws and were joined in these calls by civil liberties lawyers and an emerging second-wave feminist movement. In Britain and Canada, by contrast, policy making was quick and reforms were early. There was no similar opportunity for early reformers to revise their claims after policies were implemented, and the reforms occurred well before second-wave feminism had gained strength. The relative success of the American pro-choice movement was not just a function of its greater numbers, however. Abortion became more controversial around 1970 as feminists and pro-lifers faced off. As a result, policy makers shied away and state-level reforms stalled. If state legislatures had been the only venue available, pro-choice activists probably would have been best off taking assertive actions against them. But there were other, more favorable, venues available—the courts. The pro-choice movement moved contention to them and developed new "privacy rights" meanings for abortion that resonated there. This meaning construction was aided by the failure of the AMA to defend more medical understandings of abortion.

Partisanship theories suggest that left-wing governments will establish the most liberal abortion policies (usually after internal party pressure from feminists) and that Christian democratic parties will establish more conservative policies. As I showed in chapter 1, partisanship seems to explain differences in the abortion policies of OECD countries pretty well. But in the case of Britain, Canada, and the United States, the governments in the three countries were broadly centrist, and none was especially committed to feminism; but they still varied in their support for abortion reform. The British and Canadian center-left governments were mildly supportive of reform while the American state and federal governments sought to avoid the issue after it became polarized around women's rights and fetal rights. This difference among the governments is best explained by the combination of timing and policy venues. As I mentioned above, the campaigns for abortion reform in Britain and Canada preceded the emergence of second-wave feminism in those countries, and thus did not include controversial claims for abortion on request. The British and Canadian governments, like state governments in the United States, approved gatekeeping reforms that delegated the issue to the medical profession rather than reforms that allowed abortion on request for women's own reasons. In addition, any reticence that the British and Canadian Governments might have felt about legislating in such a controversial policy area was ameliorated by the availability of nonpartisan parliamentary processes that helped them avoid blame.

Another crucial difference between the abortion reforms in the three countries was the policy venues in which they were made—the Supreme Court in the United States and Parliament in Britain and Canada. The American justices delivered a reform that was more liberal than the public and elected policy makers probably wanted—though neither was exactly sure what they wanted. This occurred for a few reasons. The justices noted that the AMA no longer favored the specification of legal grounds by which doctors should approve abortions. Moreover, because the justices were appointed rather than elected and did not regularly interact with constituents, they underestimated the breadth and depth of opposition to abortion on request. And they were supposed to rely mainly on the law rather than public opinion to guide their decisions anyway. In Britain and Canada, members of Parliament were both more attuned to mass and elite opinion and more constrained by it. They deferred to medical elites who urged caution, and they used nonpartisan parliamentary processes that helped them avoid blame for the reforms.

The abortion reforms left several questions of implementation unresolved. Who would provide and pay for abortions? And how would doctors interpret legal grounds? By the end of the 1970s, the three countries had answered these questions. American women could obtain abortions without the approval of medical gatekeepers and for their own reasons, but usually had to pay for those abortions themselves, even when they could not afford to do so. The vast majority of abortions were provided in specialized clinics segregated from hospitals and other mainstream medical institutions. Canadian women could obtain abortions only with medical approval for reasons of medical necessity, but abortions were paid for by the state. The vast majority of abortions were provided in hospitals. Specialized clinics were illegal in Canada, but about 20 percent of abortions were provided in American clinics and paid for by patients. British women needed medical approval for abortions, but the grounds were broader than in Canada and doctors interpreted them more liberally, especially in private clinics. The state paid for the half of abortions provided in NHS hospitals, but patients paid for the half provided in specialized clinics.

These differences in implementation sprang from the differing medical-care systems and meanings of abortion reform in the three countries. Britain and Canada had national health insurance systems, and their abortion reforms constructed abortion as a medical necessity. As such, few suggested that the state should refuse to pay for abortions. Still, many doctors and hospitals resisted providing them. In Britain, the law allowed for private provision outside hospitals, which gave women an alternative source of provision, but they had to pay for those "private" abortions themselves. Canadian women had no domestic alternative to hospital gatekeeping, but many women sought clinic abortions in the United States. The United States had national health insurance only for the poor and elderly. Abortion on request allowed pro-lifers to construct abortions as "elective," and thus made it easier for them to deny coverage to the poor. In many years, Congress denied coverage to the poor even for "medically necessary" abortions. This provoked little outrage in a country where health rights were less entrenched and where the main victims of the policy lacked political power.

After the abortion reforms, pro-life movements tried to roll them back in all three countries, but only the American movement succeeded in moving abortion to the center of politics and bringing about reductions in the quality and availability of abortion services through public funding bans, spousal and parental consent requirements, waiting periods, and mandatory counseling. British and Canadian parties and governments avoided the issue and kept it out of politics and off Parliament's agenda. Changes in abortion policy in these countries were rare and mainly expanded abortion services through increased public funding and reduced gatekeeping. These differences are best explained by party and electoral systems, and in particular, the relative openness of American political parties to social movements. In the United States, large movements concerned about abortion—such as the New Right, the Christian Right, and the feminist movement—took advantage of party openness to gain power within the Republican and Democratic parties. The parties took increasingly polarized positions on abortion. Low-turnout, expensive, candidate-centered elections gave abortion movements influence disproportionate to their numbers. Decentralized, coalitional parties provided them with multiple points of access. And party democracy welcomed their input when parties chose candidates, leaders, and policy goals. The closed parties of Britain and Canada denied such influence to similar movements; and party discipline, agenda control, and nonpartisan parliamentary processes helped parties to keep the issue out of elections and policy making. In the United States, once abortion movements became attached to parties, the pro-life movement benefited from the electoral successes of the Republican Party.

The relative success of the pro-life movement was also shaped by the policy venues of both the initial reforms and later policy making. The American reform occurred through a Supreme Court decision that was especially controversial. The court went farther than the public and most elected policy makers desired, justified its decision in arcane and unusual terms, focused attention on the issue, and inspired claims of judicial overreach and the usurpation of democracy. The court's decision did not settle the issue but instead kicked off a never-ending back and forth with state and federal legislatures. The decentralized American polity offered numerous access points for movement activists to press for advantage. By contrast, the British and Canadian reforms occurred in a Parliament that was more responsive to public opinion, and especially elite opinion. The

British and Canadian reforms were narrower, less visible, and made by elected officials. After reform, successive Governments kept abortion out of politics and policy making through party discipline, agenda control, and the use of private member's bills and free voting. Finally, the patterns of medical involvement established during reform continued after it: American medicine continued to avoid the abortion issue. It failed to vigorously defend the abortion reforms or fight for abortion access, and its absence from the debate cleared the field for nonmedical constructions of the issue relating to fetal and women's rights, increasing controversy and promoting the mobilization of pro-choice and pro-life movements. By contrast, British and Canadian medical associations remained heavily involved in abortion policy; they defended abortion services, sought their expansion, and gradually came to support abortion on request for women's own reasons. Their continued involvement helped ensure that abortion was constructed largely as an issue of health, and this reduced controversy.

At several points in this book, I contrasted my institutional explanations for differences among the three countries with the most prominent alternative explanation: national values. I found explanations based on the classical liberalism of the United States unpersuasive. All three countries have strong traditions of classical liberalism, and there were strong similarities between American state-level reforms of the late 1960s and the national reforms of Britain and Canada. The United States did not suddenly become more classically liberal in the three years between the last state-level reform and the national reform. The liberalism argument also suggests that the *Roe* decision was foreordained by values enshrined in American law by Oliver Wendell Holmes, but as my discussion of the *Roe* decision in chapter 3 showed, its outcome was actually highly contingent and depended on a complex intersection of political institutions, strategy, and biography.

Another national values argument suggests that abortion is so controversial and politicized in the United States because so many Americans belong to antiabortion faiths and because Americans are, in general, more religious than Britons or Canadians. As a percentage of the population, the United States has more evangelical Protestants than either of the other countries while Canada has more Catholics, but the United States has the most of the two groups combined. Proponents of this argument must first deal with the fact that the United States, counter to this religiosity thesis, enacted the most liberal abortion reform of the three countries during the Long 1960s. Religious differences also did not lead to substantially different public opinion on abortion. In all three countries, majorities supported abortion for health grounds but opposed abortion for social ones. The religious differences probably did contribute to the higher levels of pro-life mobilization in the United States and Canada, but this is not enough to explain the high levels of politicization in the United States. All of the countries had substantial pro-life movements, but these movements made inroads only within American political parties. A difference in degree, the size of the movements, cannot explain the virtual absence of abortion party politicization in Britain and Canada. Finally, the mere presence of evangelicals or Catholics in a country should not be taken to mean that those groups will automatically mobilize on abortion. Religious mobilization on abortion had to be constructed, and it varied over time and across countries. Finally, I argued that the liberal American reform and its construction of abortion as a woman's right, as opposed to Britain's and Canada's medical construction of the issue, contributed to the heavy mobilization on abortion in the United States.

Rethinking American Abortion Politics

This account of differences between the abortion policies and politics of Britain, Canada, and the United States challenges conventional understandings of American abortion policy and politics in several ways. In particular, it highlights the unusual breadth, controversy, and politicization of the American reform of the Long 1960s and the relative absence of the medical profession from the American abortion debate. My comparative approach highlights how liberal the 1973 American reform was in comparison with the reforms in Britain and Canada. In the United States, abortions were available on request for women's own reasons while the other countries required medical or social necessity and the approval of gatekeepers. Single-country studies, and even some comparative ones, often ignore this crucial difference, perhaps because the three countries have converged on abortion gatekeeping in recent years. But this initial difference should not be forgotten because it helps explain the controversy and fragility of the American reform. I explained the relative breadth of the American reform through the differing positions of medical associations, policy making through courts versus legislatures, and the timing of the reforms. Lengthy state-level policy making allowed American reformers to learn from earlier reforms, radicalize their claims, and ally with civil liberties lawyers and an emerging second-wave feminist movement. In the other countries, reforms preceded second-wave feminism and demands for abortion on request.

In addition, many observers do not recognize that high levels of post-reform controversy and politicization in the United States are unique. Many abortion reforms in rich countries during the 1970s and 1980s were highly controversial, but after these reforms, controversy died down and abortion became a marginal issue. Many observers explain the politicization and controversy of the abortion issue in the United States through what they view as the intrinsic characteristics of the issue (its relationship to life and death and its bearing on the social status of motherhood) or through the high religiosity of Americans. These factors are certainly important, but the first two are common to all three countries, and, as I mentioned above, religiosity cannot explain American politicization on its own. Instead, I argued for the importance of two factors—a policy venue, the Supreme Court, that produced a broad reform and heightened controversy; and political parties that were unusually open to newly organized social movements. Britain and Canada established moderate reforms through Parliament, and their closed, disciplined parties kept abortion off political and policy agendas afterward.

Finally, few have noticed the glaring absence of mainstream medicine from the American abortion debate.[1] I showed that the disengagement of American doctors from the abortion issue had its roots in the AMA's priority construction during the late 1960s. But it was accentuated and legitimated by the establishment of an "own reasons" reform, by the social construction of abortion as an "elective" procedure, and by the refusal of the federal government to fund abortions. After reform, the medical profession continued to avoid the issue and organized abortion out of hospitals and the mainstream practice of obstetrics and gynecology. This has forced women to receive abortions from practitioners other than their usual ob/gyn, in segregated clinics where they are more likely to encounter harassment. The medical profession has only grudgingly defended abortion services from political attacks. Things were different in Britain and Canada. Medical organizations were heavily involved in abortion reforms and remained involved after reform as well. As in the United States, many mainstream hospitals and doctors resisted providing abortions, but the level of mainstream provision was always much higher than in the United States. The abortion reforms constructed abortion as "medical necessity" to be diagnosed by doctors and justified abortion services in terms of a right to health. Over time, medical organizations liberalized their positions on abortion. They defended abortion laws against attacks by pro-life activists and even lobbied for the expansion of abortion services. Gradually, they came to support abortion on request.

It seems possible that if the Supreme Court had established a gatekeeping reform instead of an "own reasons" reform, this might have reduced some of the controversy of abortion while eventually leading to abortion on request or something approaching it.[2] A reform that retained medical control over abortion might have encouraged the medical profession to engage with abortion services rather than segregating them from mainstream medicine. If the profession had been more involved in abortion provision, it might have defended it against its opponents. A "medical necessity" framing of abortion might have increased public support for abortion services and reduced pro-life mobilization. Though such a reform would have initially produced worse abortion access than the "own reasons" one in *Roe*, the British experience suggests that access might have improved over time as doctors broadened their interpretations of abortion grounds. Of course, the medical paternalism of such a reform would not have satisfied feminist activists, and perhaps, as Gene Burns argues, it was already too late by 1973 to retain a medical construction of the issue as fetal and women's rights ones became prominent. And as I showed, the American medical profession was never particularly eager to involve itself in abortion anyway.[3]

Rethinking Politics

This study also challenges some conventional understandings of politics. I argued not only that institutions *matter*, but that they matter in three particular ways. First, the goals of social groups are not pre-given but are constructed in particular political-institutional contexts, and part of this construction involves *prioritizing* among multiple goals. Second, the policy impacts of movements depend not just on their resources and strategies, but on the openness of political parties to newly organized groups. Third, policy venues leave distinct marks on the policies that emerge from them.

Many theorists of politics (Marx is the most obvious example) treat the "interests" of groups as naturally occurring and self-evident. But like many historical and political institutionalists, I argued that group interests and identities are constructed in specific historical and institutional contexts and that these constructions leave legacies for future political struggles. As a result, similar groups often perceive and articulate their interests differently. I also focused on the multiple, often cross-cutting, goals of social actors and the ways in which they *prioritize* among these

CHAPTER SEVEN

goals in particular institutional and strategic contexts. Rational choice theorists speak of actors' "rank-ordered preferences" but treat these rankings as fixed for the period of contention. I focused on the ways in which priorities change along with facts on the ground. I also argued that party and electoral systems strongly affect the success of newly organized social movements within political parties. Decentralized parties, candidate-centered elections, and weak party discipline provide more points of access. Intraparty democracy means that movements can help choose party candidates, leaders, and policies. Low-turnout elections and meetings are easier to capture; expensive campaigns offer opportunities to provide money and labor; and coalitional parties give movements a chance to join the dominant coalition. My arguments here resemble "political opportunity" theory in the social movements literature. But the political opportunity literature typically focuses on a large number of potential political opportunities such as the openness of the political system, the stability of elite alignments, alliances with elites, and the repressive capacities of the state. My argument is much more specific than this. I focus only on the openness of the political system and on one particular dimension of that openness—the receptivity of *parties* to movements.

Finally, I argued that policy venues strongly shape the policies that emerge from them. I focused on three specific venues: constitutional courts, state-level policy making, and nonpartisan parliamentary processes. Constitutional courts tend to produce winner-take-all policies articulated through "rights talk" and arcane language. Such policies are often insensitive to public opinion, provoke accusations of nondemocracy, and strongly focus the attention of the media and the public. As a result, court decisions are often more controversial than legislative ones. Subnational policy making provides access points for policy change and demonstration, but it also produces gradual national reforms that give the public and opponents more time to take notice and mobilize. The availability of multiple venues hinders the settlement of issues because losers simply move to new battlegrounds. Finally, parliamentary governments are able to use agenda control and nonpartisan parliamentary processes such as private member's bills and free voting to avoid difficult issues and blame for their actions.

Scope Conditions

Many of the arguments in this book are applicable to countries, policies, and social actors other than those examined here, but some have more limited scope. The arguments rely on contrasts between national and subnational policy making, candidate- and party-centered elections, judicial review and parliamentary supremacy, private and public medical systems, strong and weak agenda control, and partisan and nonpartisan legislative processes; and thus they will be most useful for comparing countries that vary along these dimensions. In addition, arguments about the relative openness of political parties to new movements are mainly relevant to issues and movements of a certain type: issues that are not already organized into the party system, and movements that are large enough to take advantage of open parties. Arguments about nonpartisan legislative processes are mainly applicable to issues that could be defined as "issues of conscience." My argument about the construction of interest group preferences and priorities is a general one, but the specific application to the medical profession is limited to issues affecting the economic, organizational, or clinical autonomy of doctors (e.g., contraception, preventive medicine, and evidence-based medicine). The argument that radical policies framed in expansive ways tend to be more controversial than moderate policies framed in narrow ways is a general one, but my distinction between medical and women's rights framings of the abortion issue is limited to the case at hand. My arguments about venue shopping and evasive action by social movements are mainly applicable to polities where this is possible. As I discuss below, the arguments in this book should be especially applicable to abortion policy and politics in other rich democracies, to policies of moral regulation, and to other American movements.

Abortion Policy and Politics in Rich Democracies

My arguments are useful, with some key limitations, for explaining abortion policies and politics in other rich countries. In most of these countries, partisanship (itself related to social cleavages and cultural differences) probably offers the best explanation for the timing and form of abortion policies. Left-wing parties tended to support abortion liberalization (often after lobbying by party feminists), liberal (free-market) parties also supported abortion liberalization (though in a more moderate form), and Christian Democratic parties tended to oppose such liberalization. In countries where left-wing parties dominated, abortion reforms came earlier, often allowed abortion on request for women's own reasons, and were fairly stable afterward. In countries where there was greater balance between parties, and especially where multiparty coalitions were common, reforms came later, were usually of the "distress" type, and were followed by more pro-life mobilization and post-reform controversy than in the countries where left-wing parties dominated. Abortion reforms also came later and were more moderate in countries with late democratization and women's suffrage—though these policies often became more liberal over time.

But partisanship is a less useful guide to abortion policy in majoritarian, two-party systems with weak left-wing parties and no religious party—in other words, in most of the rich, English-speaking countries. Here, relationships between abortion positions and particular political parties were not automatic and political institutional factors were central. The openness of political parties, the priorities of the medical profession, and the venues of policy making helped color abortion policies. In these countries, most parties sought to avoid the abortion issue and were usually able to do so by pawning it off on the medical profession or the courts. When party leaders did act, they tended to do so through nonpartisan legislative mechanisms such as free voting and private member's bills. The one exception, of course, is the United States, where permeable political parties and the many access points provided by federalism and the separation of powers helped strong pro-life and pro-choice movements to politicize the abortion issue.

Even in countries where political partisanship explains much of the timing and form of abortion policies, political institutional factors are still relevant. In particular, they help to explain the low level of controversy over abortion in most rich countries. Most of these countries have national systems of health insurance or health-care provision, and, as a result, abortion has usually been defined as a medical necessity rather than as a moral issue involving competition between women's rights and fetal rights. Moreover, in such countries, mainstream medicine is typically heavily involved in abortion provision—abortion is not segregated from mainstream medicine as in the United States, and, as a result, medical associations often defend (a medicalized form of) abortion rights. In addition, most rich countries, not just the secular-majoritarian ones, combined free voting on abortion with party-centered elections, and this reduced controversy by helping parties and individual legislators to avoid blame for their actions and remove the abortion issue from electoral politics. Finally, most countries enacted abortion policies through legislatures rather than courts, and this reduced controversy by promoting compromise policies that carried more democratic legitimacy than court-made policies. Countries, such as Germany, where courts weighed in on abortion, experienced more post-reform controversy.

Moral Regulation

Most political institutionalist work to date has focused on policies of social provision such as pensions, health care, and aid to the poor. This book examines legal regulation and especially moral regulation and should be useful for examining other issues of that type—contraception, assisted suicide, pornography, gay rights, divorce, gun control, and capital punishment, to name just a few. These are issues which usually do not line up with the dominant economic cleavages on which many party systems are based, and as such, party positions on these issues must be constructed and the permeability of parties to new movements becomes quite important. In many countries, elected officials seek to avoid these types of issues and are able to keep them out of party and electoral politics through agenda control and the use of nonpartisan legislative mechanisms such as free voting and private member's bills. Sometimes judges fill the policy void, and often produce controversial, winner-take-all policies. Whether made through nonpartisan legislative processes or judicial review, these policies are subject to limited democratic accountability, and, as a result, the views of political and professional elites often prevail: In many European countries and in Canada, for example, public opinion is quite supportive of the death penalty, and yet none of these countries allow it because political elites are opposed.[4]

Other American Movements

This book suggests that American political parties are especially permeable to upstart and outsider movements. But this raises the question of why more movements have not achieved the influence within political parties that the Christian Right and feminists have within the Republican and Democratic parties respectively. One answer is that such influence requires strong sustained mobilization. It is possible that groups with symbolic goals might be better able to sustain this level of commitment than groups with material goals: Given the many veto points in American political system, groups with material goals may become discouraged after they fail to achieve their goals. Groups with symbolic goals may experience more victories and thus stay motivated and persistent. In the case of feminists, and the abortion rights movement in particular, gains have been few, but defensive mobilization against the pro-life movement has helped to sustain, and periodically renew, pro-choice mobilization.

My arguments also suggest that American movements may last longer than those in other countries because the American political system has difficulty settling issues: Given multiple access points, policy gains are frequent, but limited and unsatisfying; and losers can always move the fight to new venues.

The Future of Abortion Policy

In his provocative book, Mark Graber argues that the party politicization of abortion in the United States makes abortion rights less secure. When abortion is a party political issue, abortion policies and judicial nominations depend on which party controls the government. When Democrats take office, abortion rights are secure, but when Republicans do so, abortion rights are threatened. And economic conditions rather than abortion politics mainly determine which party holds office. Graber argues that removing abortion from party politics would preserve the abortion status quo—elected officials would avoid the issue, and judges would protect abortion rights because the vast majority of legal elites, like other American elites, support abortion rights. Graber argues that judges oppose abortion rights only when they are selected for that reason, a practice that would end if abortion was no longer central to party politics. To accomplish this, Graber argues that pro-choice activists should give more support to their allies in the Republican Party than those in the Democratic Party, and focus on defeating those who strongly oppose abortion rights rather than electing those who strongly support them.[5] Graber's arguments are certainly interesting, but the question becomes, as one reviewer puts it, "how to get the toothpaste back in the tube."[6] My arguments about the openness of American parties suggest that parties probably cannot keep abortion out of politics even if they want to. And though the pro-choice movement may have an incentive to depoliticize abortion, the pro-life movement does not.

Barack Obama has sought a truce in the abortion wars. This seemed to work during the 2008 elections, but not once Obama took office: The abortion issue almost derailed his central domestic policy initiative, healthcare reform. Abortion remains a central issue for the Christian Right. Some observers have recently noted the emergence of young "liberal" evangelicals, but despite their liberal positions on the environment and poverty, they remain strongly opposed to abortion. The Christian Right remains a key member of the Republican Party's conservative coalition, and the party remains dependent on its grassroots mobilization. Party polarization on abortion will likely continue, despite Obama's calls for a new politics. The permeability of American political parties and the many access points in the American polity mean that abortion will be a central political issue for as long as movements continue to mobilize over it—in other words, for a very long time. Mobilization against same-sex marriage could reduce the resources available to the pro-life movement and displace some attention to the abortion issue. Alternatively, such mobilization could actually increase attention to "moral" issues in general. And even if the same-sex marriage issue crowds out the abortion issue to some degree, it is unlikely that it will displace it completely: Abortion will remain a key issue for Christian conservatives and thus for the Republican Party. Obama's Supreme Court appointees, Sonia Sotomayor and Elena Kagan, followed the recent practice of declining to state their abortion positions during their confirmation hearings, but they will likely protect the *Roe* and *Casey* decisions, especially as these are considered "superprecedents" by many. The real battle will be fought over which burdens are "undue." The medical profession will probably not be much help to pro-choice activists as it continues to segregate abortion services and stay out of abortion politics.

In Britain and Canada, abortion will likely remain out of politics and policy will change little. In Britain, Parliament will periodically take free votes on the upper time limit for abortion. When Conservatives again gain a majority in Parliament, the limit will probably be reduced from twenty-four to twenty-two weeks, but neither the Conservative Party nor its individual MPs will be held accountable for this change. Pro-choice activists will continue to advocate for the elimination of abortion gatekeeping. They now have the support of the medical associations for this change, but they should be careful what they wish for. The medicalization of abortion in Britain has been a valuable protection for abortion services. On the other hand, there are already so many protections for the status quo in Britain that perhaps they need not worry. Pro-choicers will not be able to eliminate gatekeeping through a private member's bill since neither Labour nor the Tories are willing to provide extra time. Instead, they will need to change the law through a free vote on an amendment to a Government bill, perhaps the next revision of the embryology laws in about ten years time. By then, maybe public and elite opinion may have changed enough, and the Labour Government may believe that it is in a strong-enough position to allow such a vote. The elimination of formal gatekeeping requirements will have little effect on abortion provision since so much gatekeeping is already pro forma, but it will be a victory for women's claims to equal citizenship.

In Canada, the Liberals will likely remain committed to their "pro-choice" "position" of avoiding the abortion issue. They may continue to accuse the Conservatives of a "secret agenda" on abortion, but those claims will become less credible the longer that the Conservatives avoid the issue, and they do not seem inclined to take it up. As this book has shown, the pro-life movement has little capacity to force them to do so. Attempts to limit public funding of abortion have mainly failed, though the Maritime provinces will continue to resist funding and providing abortions. The increased provision of abortions in clinics will likely continue. As in the United States, many hospitals are reluctant to provide abortion services, and single-purpose clinics do offer some real advantages to patients. Importantly, however, these clinic abortions, in contrast to those in the United States, will be funded by national health insurance.

Things may play out differently, of course. Much about politics is unpredictable: Actors creatively build new understandings, discourses, and strategies, and respond to changing contexts and random events. But one thing is certain: Abortion politics will continue to be enabled and constrained by political institutions.

References

Archival Sources

The archival data for this study are from the following sources: in the United States, the American Medical Association, the National Organization for Women, the National Religious Coalition for Abortion Rights, the Women's Collection at Northwestern University, Planned Parenthood of California, the California History Library, and the State of California Government Documents Archive. In Britain, the Royal College of Obstetricians and Gynaecologists, the National Archives, the Wellcome Institute for the History of Medicine, the Birth Control Trust, and the National Abortion Campaign. In Canada, the National Archives, the Canadian Abortion Rights Action League, the Archives of the Canadian Medical Association, and Planned Parenthood of Canada.

Cases Cited

UNITED STATES

Akron v. Akron Center for Reproductive Health, 462 U.S. 416 (1983)
Ayotte v. Planned Parenthood of Northern New England, 546 U.S. 320 (2006)
Beal v. Doe, 432 U.S. 438 (1977)
Bellotti v. Baird, 428 U.S. 132 (1976)
Bellotti v. Baird (*Baird II*), 443 U.S. 622 (1979)
Brown v. Board of Education of Topeka, 347 U.S. 483 (1954)
Cooper v. Aaron, 358 U.S. 1 (1958)
Danforth v. Rodgers, 414 U.S. 1035 (1973)
Doe v. Bolton, 410 U.S. 179 (1973)

REFERENCES

Eisenstadt v. Baird, 405 U.S. 438 (1972)
Gonzales v. Carhart, 550 U.S. 124 (2007)
Griswold v. Connecticut, 381 U.S. 479 (1965)
H. L. v. Matheson, 450 U.S. 398 (1981)
Harris v. McRae, 448 U.S. 297 (1980)
Maher v. Roe, 432 U.S. 464 (1977)
Marbury v. Madison, 5 U.S. (1 Cranch) 137 (1803)
People v. Belous, 458 P.2d 194 (Cal. 1969)
Planned Parenthood Association of Kansas City, Missouri v. Ashcroft, 462 U.S. 476 (1983)
Planned Parenthood of Central Missouri v. Danforth, 428 U.S. 52 (1976)
Planned Parenthood of Southeastern Pennsylvania v. Casey, 505 U.S. 833 (1992)
Poelker v. Doe, 432 U.S. 519 (1977)
Roe v. Wade, 410 U.S. 113 (1973)
Rust v. Sullivan, 500 U.S. 171 (1991)
Stenberg v. Carhart, 530 U.S. 914 (2000)
Thornburgh v. American College of Obstetricians & Gynecologists, 476 U.S. 747 (1986)
Webster v. Reproductive Health Services, 492 U.S. 490 (1989)

BRITAIN

Rex v. Bourne, (1939) 1 K.B. 687

CANADA

Rex v. Morgentaler, (1988) 1 S.C.R. 30
Tremblay v. Daigle, (1989) 2 S.C.R. 530
Borowski v. Canada, (1989) 1 S.C.R. 342

APPENDIX 1

Statements on Abortion in American Party Platforms, 1972–2008

Year	Democratic Party	Republican Party
1972	Family planning services, including the education, comprehensive medical and social services necessary to permit individuals freely to determine and achieve the number and spacing of their children, should be available to all, regardless of sex, age, marital status, economic group or ethnic origin, and should be administered in a non-coercive and non-discriminatory manner.	Since 1969, we have increased the Federal support for family planning threefold. We will continue to support expanded family planning programs and will foster research in this area so that more parents will be better able to plan the number and spacing of their children should they wish to do so. Under no circumstances will we allow any of these programs to become compulsory or infringe upon the religious conviction or personal freedom of any individual.
1976	We fully recognize the religious and ethical nature of the concerns which many Americans have on the subject of abortion. We feel, however, that it is undesirable to attempt to amend the U.S. Constitution to overturn the Supreme Court decision in this area.	The question of abortion is one of the most difficult and controversial of our time. It is undoubtedly a moral and personal issue but it also involves complex questions relating to medical science and criminal justice. There are those in our Party who favor complete support for the Supreme Court decision which permits abortion on demand. There are others who share sincere convictions that the Supreme Court's decision must be changed by a constitutional amendment prohibiting all abortions. Others have yet to take a position, or they have assumed a stance somewhere in between polar positions.

(continues)

APPENDIX 1

Year	Democratic Party	Republican Party
1980	Reproductive Rights—We fully recognize the religious and ethical concerns which many Americans have about abortion. We also recognize the belief of many Americans that a woman has a right to choose whether and when to have a child. The Democratic Party supports the 1973 Supreme Court decision on abortion rights as the law of the land and opposes any constitutional amendment to restrict or overturn that decision. The Democratic Party recognizes reproductive freedom as a fundamental human right. We therefore oppose government interference in the reproductive decisions of Americans, especially those government programs or legislative restrictions that deny poor Americans their fight to privacy by funding or advocating one or a limited number of reproductive choices only. Specifically, the Democratic Party opposes . . . restrictions on funding for health services for the poor that deny poor women especially the right to exercise a constitutionally-guaranteed right to privacy.	The Republican Party favors a continuance of the public dialogue on abortion and supports the efforts of those who seek enactment of a constitutional amendment to restore protection of the right to life for unborn children. There can be no doubt that the question of abortion, despite the complex nature of its various issues, is ultimately concerned with equality of rights under the law. While we recognize differing views on this question among Americans in general—and in our own Party—we affirm our support of a constitutional amendment to restore protection of the right to life for unborn children. We also support the Congressional efforts to restrict the use of taxpayers' dollars for abortion. We will work for the appointment of judges at all levels of the judiciary who respect traditional family values and the sanctity of innocent human life.
1984	There can be little doubt that a Supreme Court chosen by Ronald Reagan would radically restrict constitutional rights and drastically reinterpret existing laws. Today, the fundamental right of a woman to reproductive freedom rests on the votes of six members of the Supreme Court—five of whom are over 75. That right could easily disappear during a second Reagan term. The Democratic Party recognizes reproductive freedom as a fundamental human right. We therefore oppose government interference in the reproductive decisions of Americans, especially government interference which denies poor Americans their right to privacy by funding or advocating one or a limited number of reproductive choices only. We fully recognize the religious and ethical concerns which many Americans have about abortion. But we also recognize the belief of many Americans that a woman has a right to choose whether and when to have a child.	The unborn child has a fundamental individual right to life which cannot be infringed. We therefore reaffirm our support for a human life amendment to the Constitution, and we endorse legislation to make clear that the Fourteenth Amendment's protections apply to unborn children. We oppose the use of public revenues for abortion and will eliminate funding for organizations which advocate or support abortion. We commend the efforts of those individuals and religious and private organizations that are providing positive alternatives to abortion by meeting the physical, emotional, and financial needs of pregnant women and offering adoption services where needed. We applaud President Reagan's fine record of judicial appointments, and we reaffirm our support for the appointment of judges at all levels of the judiciary who respect traditional family values and the sanctity of innocent human life.

STATEMENTS ON ABORTION

Year	Democratic Party	Republican Party
1988	We further believe . . . that the fundamental right of reproductive choice should be guaranteed regardless of ability to pay.	We do believe . . . that the unborn child has a fundamental individual right to life which cannot be infringed. We therefore reaffirm our support for a human life amendment to the Constitution, and we endorse legislation to make clear that the Fourteenth Amendment's protections apply to unborn children. We oppose the use of public revenues for abortion and will eliminate funding for organizations which advocate or support abortion. We commend the efforts of those individuals and religious and private organizations that are providing positive alternatives to abortion by meeting the physical, emotional, and financial needs of pregnant women and offering adoption services where needed. We applaud President Reagan's fine record of judicial appointments, and we reaffirm our support for the appointment of judges at all levels of the judiciary who respect traditional family values and the sanctity of innocent human life.
1992	Democrats stand behind the right of every woman to choose, consistent with *Roe v. Wade*, regardless of ability to pay, and support a national law to protect that right. It is a fundamental constitutional liberty that individual Americans—not government—can best take responsibility for making the most difficult and intensely personal decisions regarding reproduction. The goal of our nation must be to make abortion less necessary, not more difficult or more dangerous. We pledge to support contraceptive research, family planning, comprehensive family life education, and policies that support healthy childbearing and enable parents to care most effectively for their children. We will enact a uniquely American reform of the health care system to control costs and make health care affordable; . . . provide for the full range of reproductive choice—education, counseling, access to contraceptives, and the right to a safe, legal abortion.	We believe the unborn child has a fundamental individual right to life which cannot be infringed. We therefore reaffirm our support for a human life amendment to the Constitution, and we endorse legislation to make clear that the Fourteenth Amendment's protections apply to unborn children. We oppose using public revenues for abortion and will not fund organizations which advocate it. We commend those who provide alternatives to abortion by meeting the needs of mothers and offering adoption services. We reaffirm our support for appointment of judges who respect traditional family values and the sanctity of innocent human life.
1996	The Democratic Party stands behind the right of every woman to choose, consistent with *Roe v. Wade*, and regardless of ability to pay. President Clinton took executive action to make sure that the right to make such decisions is protected for all Americans. Over the last four years, we have taken action to end	The unborn child has a fundamental individual right to life which cannot be infringed. We support a human life amendment to the Constitution and we endorse legislation to make clear that the Fourteenth Amendment's protections apply to unborn children. Our purpose is to have legislative and judicial protec-

(continues)

APPENDIX 1

Year	Democratic Party	Republican Party
	the gag rule and ensure safety at family planning and women's health clinics. We believe it is a fundamental constitutional liberty that individual Americans—not government—can best take responsibility for making the most difficult and intensely personal decisions regarding reproduction. The Democratic Party is a party of inclusion. We respect the individual conscience of each American on this difficult issue, and we welcome all our members to participate at every level of our party. Our goal is to make abortion less necessary and more rare, not more difficult and more dangerous. We support contraceptive research, family planning, comprehensive family life education, and policies that support healthy childbearing. For four years in a row, we have increased support for family planning. The abortion rate is dropping. Now we must continue to support efforts to reduce unintended pregnancies, and we call on all Americans to take personal responsibility to meet this important goal.	tion of that right against those who perform abortions. We oppose using public revenues for abortion and will not fund organizations which advocate it. We support the appointment of judges who respect traditional family values and the sanctity of innocent human life. Our goal is to ensure that women with problem pregnancies have the kind of support, material and otherwise, they need for themselves and for their babies, not to be punitive towards those for whose difficult situation we have only compassion. We oppose abortion, but our pro-life agenda does not include punitive action against women who have an abortion. We salute those who provide alternatives to abortion and offer adoption services. Republicans in Congress took the lead in expanding assistance both for the costs of adoption and for the continuing care of adoptive children with special needs. Bill Clinton vetoed our adoption tax credit the first time around—and opposed our efforts to remove racial barriers to adoption—before joining in this long overdue measure of support for adoptive families. Worse than that, he vetoed the ban on partial-birth abortions, a procedure denounced by a committee of the American Medical Association and rightly branded as four-fifths infanticide. We applaud Bob Dole's commitment to revoke the Clinton executive orders concerning abortion and to sign into law an end to partial-birth abortions.
2000	The Democratic Party stands behind the right of every woman to choose, consistent with *Roe v. Wade*, and regardless of ability to pay. We believe it is a fundamental constitutional liberty that individual Americans—not government—can best take responsibility for making the most difficult and intensely personal decisions regarding reproduction. This year's Supreme Court rulings show to us all that eliminating a woman's right to choose is only one justice away. That's why the stakes in this election are as high as ever. Our goal is to make abortion less necessary and more rare, not more difficult and more dangerous. We support contraceptive research, family planning, comprehensive family life education, and policies that support healthy childbearing. The abortion rate is dropping. Now we must continue to support efforts to reduce unintended pregnancies,	The Supreme Court's recent decision, prohibiting states from banning partial-birth abortions—a procedure denounced by a committee of the American Medical Association and rightly branded as four-fifths infanticide—shocks the conscience of the nation. As a country, we must keep our pledge to the first guarantee of the Declaration of Independence. That is why we say the unborn child has a fundamental individual right to life which cannot be infringed. We support a human life amendment to the Constitution and we endorse legislation to make clear that the Fourteenth Amendment's protections apply to unborn children. Our purpose is to have legislative and judicial protection of that right against those who perform abortions. We oppose using public revenues for abortion and will not fund organizations which advocate it. We support the appointment of judges

STATEMENTS ON ABORTION

Year	Democratic Party	Republican Party
	and we call on all Americans to take personal responsibility to meet this important goal. The Democratic Party is a party of inclusion. We respect the individual conscience of each American on this difficult issue, and we welcome all our members to participate at every level of our party. This is why we are proud to put into our platform the very words which Republicans refused to let Bob Dole put into their 1996 platform and which they refused to even consider putting in their platform in 2000: "While the party remains steadfast in its commitment to advancing its historic principles and ideals, we also recognize that members of our party have deeply held and sometimes differing views on issues of personal conscience like abortion and capital punishment. We view this diversity of views as a source of strength, not as a sign of weakness, and we welcome into our ranks all Americans who may hold differing positions on these and other issues. Recognizing that tolerance is a virtue, we are committed to resolving our differences in a spirit of civility, hope and mutual respect."	who respect traditional family values and the sanctity of innocent human life. Our goal is to ensure that women with problem pregnancies have the kind of support, material and otherwise, they need for themselves and for their babies, not to be punitive towards those for whose difficult situation we have only compassion. We oppose abortion, but our pro-life agenda does not include punitive action against women who have an abortion. We salute those who provide alternatives to abortion and offer adoption services, and we commend congressional Republicans for expanding assistance to adopting families and for removing racial barriers to adoption. The impact of those measures and of our Adoption and Safe Families Act of 1997 has been spectacular. Adoptions out of foster care have jumped forty percent and the incidence of child abuse and neglect has actually declined. We second Governor Bush's call to make permanent the adoption tax credit and expand it to $7,500.
2004	Because we believe in the privacy and equality of women, we stand proudly for a woman's right to choose, consistent with *Roe v. Wade*, and regardless of her ability to pay. We stand firmly against Republican efforts to undermine that right. At the same time, we strongly support family planning and adoption incentives. Abortion should be safe, legal, and rare.	As a country, we must keep our pledge to the first guarantee of the Declaration of Independence. That is why we say the unborn child has a fundamental individual right to life which cannot be infringed. We support a human life amendment to the Constitution and we endorse legislation to make it clear that the Fourteenth Amendment's protections apply to unborn children. Our purpose is to have legislative and judicial protection of that right against those who perform abortions. We oppose using public revenues for abortion and will not fund organizations which advocate it. We support the appointment of judges who respect traditional family values and the sanctity of innocent human life. Our goal is to ensure that women with problem pregnancies have the kind of support, material and otherwise, they need for themselves and for their babies, not to be punitive towards those for whose difficult situation we have only compassion. We oppose abortion, but our pro-life agenda does not include punitive action against women who have an abortion. We salute those who provide alternatives to abortion and offer adoption

(continues)

APPENDIX 1

Year	Democratic Party	Republican Party

services, and we commend Congressional Republicans for expanding assistance to adopting families and for removing racial barriers to adoption. We join the President in supporting crisis pregnancy programs and parental notification laws. And we applaud President Bush for allowing states to extend health care coverage to unborn children.

We praise the President for his bold leadership in defense of life. We praise him for signing the Born Alive Infants Protection Act. This important legislation ensures that every infant born alive—including an infant who survives an abortion procedure—is considered a person under federal law.

We praise Republicans in Congress for passing, with strong bipartisan support, a ban on the inhumane procedure known as partial-birth abortion. And we applaud President Bush for signing legislation outlawing partial-birth abortion and for vigorously defending it in the courts.

In signing the partial-birth abortion ban, President Bush reminded us that "the most basic duty of government is to defend the life of the innocent. Every person, however frail or vulnerable, has a place and a purpose in this world."

We praise President Bush and Republicans in Congress for the measures they have taken to protect pregnant women from violent crime by passing Laci and Conner's law, which recognizes the common-sense proposition that when a crime of violence against a pregnant woman kills or injures her unborn child, there are two victims and two offenses that should be punished.

Year	Democratic Party	Republican Party
2008	The Democratic Party strongly and unequivocally supports *Roe v. Wade* and a woman's right to choose a safe and legal abortion, regardless of ability to pay, and we oppose any and all efforts to weaken or undermine that right. The Democratic Party also strongly supports access to comprehensive affordable family planning services and age-appropriate sex education which empower people to make informed choices and live healthy lives. We also recognize that such health care and education help reduce the number of unintended pregnancies and thereby also reduce the need for abortions.	Faithful to the first guarantee of the Declaration of Independence, we assert the inherent dignity and sanctity of all human life and affirm that the unborn child has a fundamental individual right to life which cannot be infringed. We support a human life amendment to the Constitution, and we endorse legislation to make clear that the Fourteenth Amendment's protections apply to unborn children.

We oppose using public revenues to promote or perform abortion and will not fund organizations which advocate it. We support the appointment of judges who respect traditional |

STATEMENTS ON ABORTION

Year	Democratic Party	Republican Party
	The Democratic Party also strongly supports a woman's decision to have a child by ensuring access to and availability of programs for pre- and post-natal health care, parenting skills, income support, and caring adoption programs.	family values and the sanctity and dignity of innocent human life. We have made progress. The Supreme Court has upheld prohibitions against the barbaric practice of partial-birth abortion. States are now permitted to extend health-care coverage to children before birth. And the Born Alive Infants Protection Act has become law; this law ensures that infants who are born alive during an abortion receive all treatment and care that is provided to all newborn infants and are not neglected and left to die. We must protect girls from exploitation and statutory rape through a parental notification requirement. We all have a moral obligation to assist, not to penalize, women struggling with the challenges of an unplanned pregnancy. At its core, abortion is a fundamental assault on the sanctity of innocent human life. Women deserve better than abortion. Every effort should be made to work with women considering abortion to enable and empower them to choose life. We salute those who provide them alternatives, including pregnancy care centers, and we take pride in the tremendous increase in adoptions that has followed Republican legislative initiatives.

Source: The American Presidency Project, http://www.presidency.ucsb.edu/platforms.php.

APPENDIX 2

U.S. Supreme Court Cases on Abortion

Roe v. Wade	410 U.S. 113 (1973)	Prohibited "life" grounds; allowed regulation to protect women's health after first trimester and regulation to protect potential life after viability
Doe v. Bolton	410 U.S. 179 (1973)	Prohibited "health" grounds, residency, gatekeeping, and hospital requirements
Danforth v. Rodgers	414 U.S. 1035 (1973)	Prohibited abortion ban
Louisiana State Board of Medical Examiners v. Rosen	419 U.S. 1098 (1975)	Prohibited doctor's license revocation
Bigelow v. Virginia	421 U.S. 809 (1975)	Prohibited advertising ban
Connecticut v. Menillo	423 U.S. 9 (1975)	Allowed physician-only requirement
Planned Parenthood of Central Missouri v. Danforth	428 U.S. 52 (1976)	Prohibited husband consent, parent consent, ban on specific late-term procedure
Singleton v. Wulff	428 U.S. 106 (1976)	Gave doctors standing to challenge funding ban
Bellotti v. Baird	428 U.S. 132 (1976)	Remanded parent consent law to determine if it had a judicial bypass
Gerstein v. Coe	428 U.S. 901 (1976)	Prohibited husband and parent consent
Sendak v. Arnold	429 U.S. 968 (1976)	Prohibited hospital requirement
Guste v. Weeks	429 U.S. 1056 (1977)	Prohibited advertising ban, husband consent, parent consent, gag rule
Bowen v. Gary- Northwest Indiana Women's Services	429 U.S. 1067 (1977)	Prohibited parent consent

(continues)

U.S. SUPREME COURT CASES

Case	Citation	Holding
Beal v. Doe	432 U.S. 438 (1977)	Allowed state funding ban
Maher v. Roe	432 U.S. 464 (1977)	Allowed state funding ban
Poelker v. Doe	432 U.S. 519 (1977)	Allowed public hospital ban
Colautti v. Franklin	439 U.S. 379 (1979)	Prohibited viability tests, care standards, and requirement to save fetal life
Ashcroft v. Freiman	440 U.S. 941 (1979)	Prohibited biased counseling requirement
Bellotti v. Baird (*Baird II*)	443 U.S. 622 (1979)	Allowed parent consent with judicial bypass
Harris v. McRae	448 U.S. 297 (1980)	Allowed federal funding ban
Williams v. Zbaraz	448 U.S. 358 (1980)	Allowed federal funding ban
H. L. v. Matheson	450 U.S. 398 (1981)	Allowed parent notice
Akron v. Akron Center for Reproductive Health	462 U.S. 416 (1983)	Prohibited parent consent, biased counseling, waiting period, second-trimester hospital requirement, and fetal disposal requirement
Planned Parenthood Association of Kansas City, Missouri v. Ashcroft	462 U.S. 476 (1983)	Prohibited hospital requirement, allowed parent consent with judicial bypass, second doctor after viability to care for surviving child
Simopoulos v. Virginia	462 U.S. 506 (1983)	Allowed clinic licensing for second trimester
Thornburgh v. American College of Obstetricians & Gynecologists	476 U.S. 747 (1986)	Prohibited biased counseling, reporting, preservation of viable fetal life, second-doctor requirement; reaffirmed *Roe*
Babbitt v. Planned Parenthood of Central and Northern Arizona	479 U.S. 925 (1986)	Prohibited gag rule
Hartigan v. Zbaraz	484 U.S. 171 (1987)	Prohibited waiting period for minors
Webster v. Reproductive Health Services	492 U.S. 490 (1989)	Allowed fetal viability test, public employee/facility ban; did not apply *Roe*, but did not explicitly overturn it
Hodgson v. Minnesota	497 U.S. 417 (1990)	Allowed parent notice with judicial bypass, minor waiting period
Ohio v. Akron Center for Reproductive Health	497 U.S. 502 (1990)	Allowed parent notice with bypass
Rust v. Sullivan	500 U.S. 171 (1991)	Allowed ban on public funds for counseling organizations
Planned Parenthood of Southeastern Pennsylvania v. Casey	505 U.S. 833 (1992)	Allowed biased counseling, waiting period, reporting, parent consent; prohibited husband notice; abandoned trimester framework; replaced "compelling state interest" standard with "undue burden" standard; reaffirmed "central" holding of *Roe*
Bray v. Alexandria Women's Health Clinic	506 U.S. 263 (1993)	Clinic blockades not a conspiracy to deprive women of equal protection of the law
Madsen v. Women's Health Center	512 U.S. 753 (1994)	Allowed buffer zone around clinic entrances
Schenck v. Pro-Choice Network of Western New York	519 U.S. 357 (1997)	Prohibited "floating" buffer zone
Lambert v. Wicklund	520 U.S. 292 (1997)	Allowed parent notice with bypass
Mazurek v. Armstrong	520 U.S. 968 (1997)	Allowed physician-only requirement

APPENDIX 2

Hill v. Colorado	530 U.S. 703 (2000)	Allowed eight-foot floating buffer zone near clinic entrance
Stenberg v. Carhart	530 U.S. 914 (2000)	Prohibited state ban on partial-birth procedure
Scheidler v. National Organization for Women	537 U.S. 393 (2003)	Racketeering laws do not apply to clinic blockades
Ayotte v. Planned Parenthood of Northern New England	546 U.S. 320 (2006)	Allowed parent notice
Schiedler v. National Organization for Women (*NOW II*)	547 U.S. 9 (2006)	Racketeering laws do not apply to clinic violence
Gonzales v. Carhart	550 U.S. 124 (2007)	Allowed federal ban on partial-birth procedure

Sources: Arlen Specter, "Supreme Court Decisions Upholding *Roe v. Wade*," 2005; Life Legal Defense Fund, "Senator Specter's 35 Mistakes," October 20, 2005; "What the Supreme Court Has Said About Abortion," *National Right to Life News*, January 2006, 11; Right to Life of Michigan, "Supreme Court Decisions on Abortion Since 1973," 2007, http://www.rtl.org/prolife_issues/overturningroe.html; The Oyez Project, http://www.Oyez.org; Raymond Tatalovich, *The Politics of Abortion in the United States and Canada: A Comparative Study* (Armonk, NY: M. E. Sharpe, 1997).

APPENDIX 3

Abortion Attitudes in the United States and Britain

Table 1. Abortion Attitudes in the United States and Britain, Gallup, 1966

Percent approving when asked, "Do you think abortion should or should not be legal in the following cases?"	United States	Britain
Where the health of the mother is in danger?	77	79
Where the child may be born deformed?	54	71
Where the family does not have enough money to support another child?	18	33

Source: Connie de Boer, "The Polls: Abortion," *Public Opinion Quarterly* 41 (1977): 553–64.

Table 2. Abortion Attitudes in the United States, NORC

Percent approving when asked, "Please tell me whether or not you think it should be possible for a pregnant woman to obtain a legal abortion if . . ."	1965	1972
Health: If the woman's health is seriously endangered by the pregnancy	73	87
Defect: If there is a strong chance of serious defect in the baby	57	79
Rape: If she became pregnant as result of rape	60	79
Money: If the family has a very low income and cannot afford more children	22	49
Unmarried: If she is not married and does not want to marry the man	18	44
No more: If she is married and does not want any more children	16	40

Source: M. Evers and J. McGee, "The Trend and Pattern in Attitudes toward Abortion in the United States, 1965–1977," *Social Indicators Research* 7 (1980): 251–67.

Note: Respondents answering "don't know" or "no answer" are excluded from percentages.

APPENDIX 4

Abortion Funding and Provision in the United States, Britain, and Canada, 1970s–2000s

Table 1. Prices of First-Trimester Clinic Abortions as Percent of Median Weekly Income in the United States, Britain, and Canada, 1970s–2000s

	1970s	1980s	1990s	2000s
United States	65 ($165, 1976)	45 ($200, 1983)	38 ($325, 1997)	38 ($413, 2005)
Britain	176 (£60, 1972)	61 (£140, 1985)	96 (£300, 1997)	115 (£575, 2008)
Canada	73 ($200, 1976)	52 ($250, 1983)	48 ($350, 1998)	56 ($550, 2008)

Sources: Robin F. Badgley, Denyse Fortin Caron, and Marion G. Powell, *Report of the Committee on the Operation of the Abortion Law* (Ottawa: Minister of Supply and Services Canada, 1977); British Pregnancy Advisory Service, *Price List* (London: British Pregnancy Advisory Service, 2008); Catherine Dunphy, *Morgentaler: A Difficult Hero* (Toronto: Random House of Canada, 1996); R. B. Gold and B. Nestor, "Public Funding of Contraceptive, Sterilization, and Abortion Services, 1983," *Family Planning Perspectives* 17 (1985): 25–30; Great Britain Office for National Statistics, *Abortion Statistics: Legal Abortions Carried Out under the 1967 Abortion Act in England and Wales*, vol. 28 (London: Stationery Office, 2007); S. Henshaw and L. Finer, "The Accessibility of Abortion Services in the United States, 2001," *Perspectives on Sexual and Reproductive Health* 35 (2003): 16–24; J Frederick S. Jaffe, Barbara L. Lindheim, and Philip R Lee, *Abortion Politics: Private Morality and Public Policy* (New York: McGraw-Hill, 1981); R. K. Jones, M. R. Zolna, S. K. Henshaw, and L. B. Finer, "Abortion in the United States: Incidence and Access to Services, 2005," *Perspectives on Sexual and Reproductive Health* 40 (2008): 6–16; Elizabeth Kathleen Lane, *Report of the Committee on the Working of the Abortion Act* (London: Her Majesty's Stationery Office, 1974); Barbara L. Lindheim, "Services, Policies, and Costs in U.S. Abortion Facilities," *Family Planning Perspectives* 11 (1979): 283–89; Statistics Canada, "Table 106-9005—Induced Abortions, by Area of Report and Type of Facility Performing the Abortion, Canada, Provinces, and Territories, Annual (number) (table)," 2008, CANSIM Database.

Notes: In 1976, U.S. hospital abortions were $300 (outpatient) and $415 (inpatient). The 1972 British price (£60) is for nonprofit clinics. Abortions in for-profit clinics were £100, and private abortions by NHS consultants were £85. For 1972 and 1985, the British price is a percent of average weekly income rather than median weekly income (median weekly income was not available). The price would be higher as a percent of median weekly income. Canadian prices are for the Morgentaler clinics in Quebec (1976 and 1983) and New Brunswick (1998 and 2008).

Table 2. Abortion Facilities in the United States, 1973–2005

Year	Hospital Providers	Nonhospital Providers[1]	Nonhospital Abortions (%)
1973	1,281	346	48
1974	1,471	557	54
1975	1,629	769	60
1976	1,695	872	65
1977	1,654	1,055	70
1978	1,626	1,127	75
1979	1,526	1,208	77
1980	1,504	1,254	78
1982	1,405	1,503	83
1985	1,191	1,489	87
1988	1,040	1,542	90
1992	855	1,525	93
1996	703	1,339	93
2000	603	1,216	95
2005	604	1,183	95

Sources: Trends in Abortion in the United States, 1973–2003 (New York: Alan Guttmacher Institute, 2003); L. B. Finer and S. K. Henshaw, "Abortion Incidence and Services in the United States in 2000," *Perspectives on Sexual and Reproductive Health* 35, no. 1 (2003): 6–15; S. K. Henshaw, "Abortion Incidence and Services in the United States, 1995–1996," *Family Planning Perspectives* 30, no. 6 (1998): 263–87; R. K. Jones, M. R. Zolna, S. K. Henshaw, and L. B. Finer, "Abortion in the United States: Incidence and Access to Services, 2005," *Perspectives on Sexual and Reproductive Health* 40 (2008): 6–16; Gerald N. Rosenberg, "The Real World of Constitutional Rights: The Supreme Court and the Implementation of the Abortion Decisions," in *Contemplating Courts,* ed. by Lee Epstein (Washington, DC: Congressional Quarterly Press, 1995).

[1] Includes single-purpose abortion clinics, multiservice clinics, and doctor's offices. Only a small percentage (2–4%) of abortions were provided in doctors' offices.

APPENDIX 5

Abortion Attitudes in the United States, Britain, and Canada, 1975–2004

Table 1. Abortion Attitudes in the United States, Britain, and Canada, WVS

Percent approving abortion when asked, "Do you approve or disapprove of abortion under the following circumstances..."	1982	1990	1982	1990	1981	1990
	United States		Canada		Britain	
Where the mother's health is at risk by the pregnancy?	89	86	91	92	93	93
Where it is likely that the child would be born physically handicapped?	60	55	64	64	82	80
Where the woman is not married?	26	29	23	32	34	33
Where a married couple does not want to have any more children?	25	26	24	30	35	35

Source: European Values Study Group and World Values Survey Association, *European and World Values Surveys Four-Wave Integrated Data File, 1981–2004*, vol. 20060423 (Madrid, Spain; Tilburg, The Netherlands; Cologne, Germany: Análisis Sociológicos Económicos y Políticos, JD Systems, Zentralarchiv fur Empirische Sozialforschung, 2006).

Table 2. Attitudes toward Abortion in the United States and Canada, Gallup

Percent approving when asked, "Do you think abortions should be..."	1975		1983		1992		2001	
	United States	Canada	United States	Canada	United States*	Canada	United States*	Canada
Legal under any circumstances?	21	23	23	23	33	31	26	32
Legal under certain circumstances?	54	60	58	59	50	57	55	52
Illegal in all circumstances?	22	16	16	17	14	10	17	14

Sources: "Gallup's Pulse of Democracy: Abortion," vol. 2008 (Gallup, 2008); Neil Nevitte, William P. Brandon, and Lori Davis, "The American Abortion Controversy: Lessons from Cross-National Evidence," *Politics and the Life Sciences* 12 (1993): 19–30.

* Figures are averages of three separate polls taken that year.

Table 3. Abortion Attitudes in the United States and Britain, GSS and BSA

Percent approving abortion...	1984		1994		2004	
	United States	Britain	United States	Britain	United States	Britain
For any reason	38		46		40	
Married woman—no more children	42		48		41	
Woman decides on own does not want		28		55		55
Couple does not want		31		63		63
Woman is unmarried	43	31	47	54	41	50
Couple cannot afford	49	36	50	60	40	52
Birth defect	80	81	82	84	72	79
Health	90	91	90	91	85	90
Rape	79	88	83	92	75	88

Sources: James A. Davis, Tom W. Smith, and Peter V. Marsden, *General Social Surveys, 1972–2006* [Cumulative file], vol. ICPSR04697-v2 (Chicago: National Opinion Research Center, 2007); J. Scott, "Generational Changes in Attitudes to Abortion: A Cross-National Comparison," *European Sociological Review* 14 (2002): 177–90; Social and Community Planning Research, *British Social Attitudes Survey, 1991* [Computer file] (London: Social and Community Planning Research, 2004).

Notes:
General Social Survey (GSS)
Please tell me whether or not you think it should be possible for a pregnant woman to obtain an abortion if:
There is a strong chance of a serious defect in the baby? (ABDEFECT)
If she is married and does not want any more children? (ABNOMORE)
If the woman's health is seriously endangered by the pregnancy? (ABHLTH)
If the family has a low income and cannot afford any more children? (ABPOOR)
If she became pregnant as a result of rape? (ABRAPE)
If she is not married and does not want to marry the man? (ABSINGLE)
Is she wants an abortion for any reasons? (ABANY)

APPENDIX 5

British Social Attitudes Survey (BSA)
Here are a number of circumstances in which a woman might consider an abortion. Please say whether or not you think the law should allow an abortion in each case.
The woman decides on her own she does not want to have the child. (abort1)
The couple agrees that they do not wish to have the child. (abort2)
The woman is not married and does not wish to marry the man. (abort3)
The couple cannot afford any more children. (abort4)
There is a strong chance of defect in the baby. (abort5)
The woman's health is seriously endangered by the pregnancy. (abort6)
The woman became pregnant as a result of rape. (abort7)

Table 4. Abortion Attitudes in the United States, Britain, and Canada, WVS

Is abortion "never justifiable" (1) or "always justifiable" (10)?[1]

	United States	Britain	Canada
1981–82[2]	3.52	4.16	3.77
1990	4.00	4.37	4.95
1999–2000[3]	4.36	4.62	4.49

Source: European Values Study Group and World Values Survey Association, *European and World Values Surveys Four-Wave Integrated Data File, 1981–2004*, vol. 20060423 (Madrid, Spain; Tilburg, The Netherlands; Cologne, Germany: Análisis Sociológicos Económicos y Políticos, JD Systems, Zentralarchiv fur Empirische Sozialforschung, 2006).

[1] Question: "Please tell me for each of the following statements whether you think it can always be justified, never be justified, or something in between. . . ."
[2] The British question was asked in 1981; the others were asked in 1982.
[3] The Canadian question was asked in 2000; the others were asked in 1999.

Notes

CHAPTER ONE

1. Ann Shola Orloff, "Gender and the Social Rights of Citizenship: The Comparative Analysis of Gender Relations and Welfare States," *American Sociological Review* 58 (1993): 303–28; Julia S. O'Connor, Ann Shola Orloff, and Sheila Shaver, "Body Rights, Social Rights, and Reproductive Choice," in *States, Markets, Families: Gender, Liberalism, and Social Policy in Australia, Canada, Great Britain and the United States* (Cambridge: Cambridge University Press, 1999), 157–85.
2. James Trussell and B. Vaughan, "Aggregate and Lifetime Contraceptive Failure in the United States," *Family Planning Perspectives* 21, no. 5 (1989): 224–26; James Trussell, "Contraceptive Failure in the United States," *Contraception* 70, no. 2 (2004): 89–96; Guttmacher Institute, "Facts on Induced Abortion in the United States," May 2010, http://www.guttmacher.org/pubs/fb_induced_abortion.html.
3. Kristin Luker, *Abortion and the Politics of Motherhood* (Berkeley: University of California Press, 1984); Joni Lovenduski and Joyce Outshoorn, eds., *The New Politics of Abortion* (London: Sage, 1986); Marianne Githens and Dorothy McBride Stetson, *Abortion Politics: Public Policy in Cross-Cultural Perspective* (New York: Routledge, 1996); Dorothy McBride Stetson, ed., *Abortion Politics, Women's Movements, and the Democratic State: A Comparative Study of State Feminism* (Oxford: Oxford University Press, 2001).
4. Arthur Marwick suggests the term "the Long 1960s" for the period ranging from the late 1950s (rising prosperity, increased youth power, Elvis Presley, new sexual mores, and the civil rights movement) to the mid-1970s (the OPEC oil crisis, the end of the Vietnam War, and Nixon's resignation).

Arthur Marwick, *The Sixties: Cultural Revolution in Britain, France, Italy, and the United States, c. 1958–c. 1974* (Oxford: Oxford University Press, 1998). I use the terms "pro-choice" and "pro-life" to identify groups as they wish to be identified. The phrase "right to life" was used in a 1951 speech by Pope Pius XII in which he reiterated the Catholic Church's opposition to birth control and abortion. Jimmye Kimmey, the executive director of the Association for the Study of Abortion in the United States, developed the phrase "right to choose" in December 1972 to counter this phrase. The terms "pro-life" and "pro-choice" have been used widely in all three countries in this study. Other common terms include "abortion rights," "reproductive rights," "pro-abortion," "anti-abortion," and "anti-choice." In 2010, historian Nancy L. Cohen suggested replacing "pro-choice" with "pro-freedom." *Los Angeles Times*, May 29, 2010. See Pope Pius XII, *Moral Questions Affecting Married Life* (addresses given October 29, 1951, to the Italian Catholic Union of Midwives and November 26, 1951, to the National Congress of the Family Front and the Association of Large Families, National Catholic Welfare Conference, Washington, DC); Jimmye Kimmey, "Right to Choose Memorandum" in *Before* Roe v. Wade*: Voices That Shaped the Abortion Debate before the Supreme Court's Ruling*, ed. Linda Greenhouse and Reva Siegel (New York: Kaplan, 2010).

5. Among other things, the restrictions banned abortion provision in public hospitals and required fetal viability tests for late abortions (abortions after viability were illegal in Missouri).

6. Webster v. Reproductive Health Services, 492 U.S. 490, 557 (1989) (Blackmun, J., dissenting in part and concurring in part). See also *New York Times*, July 4, 1989, p. 1; November 11, 1988, p. A20; April 16, 1989, p. 28; David J. Garrow, *Liberty and Sexuality: The Right to Privacy and the Making of* Roe v. Wade (New York: Macmillan, 1994); G. Halva-Neubauer, "Abortion Policy in the Post-*Webster* Age," *Publius: The Journal of Federalism* 20, no. 3 (1990): 27.

7. *Financial Times*, May 7, 1988, 1; *Independent*, January 23, 1988; *Guardian*, April 4, 1988; April 25, 1988; May 7, 1988; Norman Willis, "Message from Norman Willis, TUC General Secretary, to Fight Alton's Bill Campaign Meeting" (London: Birth Control Trust Library, April 26, 1988); National Abortion Campaign, "A Brief and Partial History of the National Abortion Campaign," in *A Celebration of 25 Years of Safe Legal Abortion* (London: National Abortion Campaign, 1992), 16–22; J. Christopher Soper, "Political Structures and Interest Group Activism: A Comparison of the British and American Pro-Life Movements," *Social Science Journal* 31, no. 3 (1994): 319–34.

8. *Toronto Star*, November 13, 1989, A19; November 29, 1989, ME2; November 29, 1989, A22; May 30, 1990, A1; January 30, 1991, A13; February 2, 1991, A7; Mary Ann Glendon, "A Beau Mentir Quie Vient De Loin: The 1988 Canadian Abortion Decision in Comparative Perspective," *Northwest-*

ern University Law Review 83, no. 3 (1989): 569–91; Raymond Tatalovich, *The Politics of Abortion in the United States and Canada: A Comparative Study* (Armonk, NY: M. E. Sharpe, 1997); Marilyn J. Field, *The Comparative Politics of Birth Control: Determinants of Policy Variation and Change in the Developed Nations* (New York: Praeger, 1983); Frederick Lee Morton, *Pro-Choice vs. Pro-Life: Abortion and the Courts in Canada* (Norman: University of Oklahoma Press, 1992).

9. Joyce Arthur, "Abortion in Canada: History, Law and Access," Pro-Choice Action Network, October 1999, http://www.prochoiceactionnetwork-canada.org/articles/canada.shtml.

10. Some cross-national studies of abortion policy are mainly oriented to conceptualizing differences in abortion policies while others seek to explain them. These studies rely on explanatory factors common in research on the welfare state: economic development, social inequality, democracy, left-party strength, Catholicism, Christian Democracy, feminist movements, medical interest groups; classically liberal political culture, the meaning of the abortion issue, the political opportunity structures of movements and countermovements, and the diffusion of regional or world models. Most of these studies compare the United States with one other country—Britain, Canada, Australia, Germany, or Sweden. Jane Brodie, "Health vs. Rights: Comparative Perspectives on Abortion Policy in Canada and the United States," in *Power and Decision: The Social Control of Reproduction*, ed. Gita Sen and Rachel C. Snow (Cambridge, MA: Harvard University Press, 1994), 123–46; Lisa DeLorme, "Gaining a Right to Abortion in the United States and Canada: The Role of Judicial Capacities," *Berkeley Journal of Sociology* 36 (1991): 93–114; David S. Meyer and Suzanne Staggenborg, "Countermovement Dynamics in Federal Systems: A Comparison of Abortion Politics in Canada and the United States," *Research in Political Sociology* 8 (1998): 209–40; Tatalovich, *Politics of Abortion*; J. Christopher Soper, *Evangelical Christianity in the United States and Great Britain: Religious Beliefs, Political Choices* (New York: New York University Press, 1994); Mildred Schwartz, "Politics and Moral Causes in Canada and the United States," in *Comparative Social Research*, ed. Richard F. Tomasson (Greenwich, CT: JAI Press, 1981); Alvin Cohan, "Abortion as a Marginal Issue: The Use of Peripheral Mechanisms in Britain and the United States," in Lovenduski and Outshoorn, *New Politics of Abortion*, 27–48; Myra Marx Ferree et al., *Shaping Abortion Discourse: Democracy and the Public Sphere in Germany and the United States* (Cambridge: Cambridge University Press, 2002); Myra Marx Ferree, "Resonance and Radicalism: Feminist Framing in the Abortion Debates of the United States and Germany," *American Journal of Sociology* 109, no. 2 (2003): 304–44; Annulla Linders, "Abortion as a Social Problem: The Construction of Opposite Solutions in Sweden and the United States," *Social Problems* 45, no. 4 (1998): 488–509; Annulla Linders, "Victory and Beyond: A Historical Comparative Analysis of the Outcomes of the Abortion

Movements in Sweden and the United States," *Sociological Forum* 19, no. 3 (2004): 371–404; Kerry A. Petersen, *Abortion Regimes* (Sudbury, MA: Dartmouth, 1993); Ian Mylchreest, "'Sound Law and Undoubtedly Good Policy': *Roe v. Wade* in Comparative Perspective," *Journal of Policy History* 7, no. 1 (1995): 53–71; Ellie Lee, *Abortion, Motherhood, and Mental Health: Medicalizing Reproduction in the United States and Great Britain*, Social Problems and Social Issues (New York: Aldine de Gruyter, 2003); Ted G. Jelen and Marthe A. Chandler, *Abortion Politics in the United States and Canada: Studies in Public Opinion* (Westport, CT: Praeger, 1994); Colin Francome, *Abortion Practice in Britain and the United States* (London: Allen and Unwin, 1986).

Other studies compare three to five countries. Melissa Haussman, *Abortion Politics in North America* (Boulder, CO: Lynne Rienner, 2005); O'Connor, Orloff, and Shaver, *States, Markets, Families*; Sheila Shaver, "Body Rights, Social Rights, and the Liberal Welfare State," *Critical Social Policy* 13 (1993–94): 66–93; Michael Minkenberg, "The Policy Impact of Church-State Relations: Family Policy and Abortion in Britain, France, and Germany," *West European Politics* 26, no. 1 (2003): 195–217; Yael Yishai, "Public Ideas and Public Policy: Abortion Politics in Four Democracies," *Comparative Politics* 25, no. 2 (1993): 207–28; Dorothy McBride Stetson, "Abortion Policy Triads and Women's Rights in Russia, the United States, and France," in *Abortion Politics: Public Policy in Cross-Cultural Perspective*, ed. Marianne Githens and Dorothy McBride Stetson (New York: Routledge, 1996); Kim Lane Scheppele, "Constitutionalizing Abortion," in Githens and Stetson, *Abortion Politics*; Merike Blofield, *The Politics of Moral Sin: Abortion and Divorce in Spain, Chile, and Argentina* (London: Routledge, 2006).

Several studies compare abortion policies across a larger number of cases in western Europe, eastern Europe, or among the rich democracies. Marianne Githens, "Reproductive Rights and the Struggle with Change in Eastern Europe," in Githens and Stetson, *Abortion Politics*; T. Alexander Smith and Raymond Tatalovich, *Cultures at War: Moral Conflicts in Western Democracies* (Peterborough, Ontario: Broadview Press, 2003); Michael Minkenberg, "Religion and Public Policy: Institutional, Cultural, and Political Impact on the Shaping of Abortion Policies in Western Democracies," *Comparative Political Studies* 35, no. 2 (2002): 221; Joel E. Brooks, "Abortion Policy in Western Democracies: A Cross National Analysis," *Governance: An International Journal of Policy and Administration* 5, no. 3 (1992): 342–57; Mary Ann Glendon, *Abortion and Divorce in Western Law* (Cambridge, MA: Harvard University Press, 1987); Albin Eser, "Abortion Law Reform in Germany in International Comparative Perspective," *European Journal of Health Law* 1 (1994): 15; Field, *Comparative Politics of Birth Control*; Joyce Outshoorn, "The Stability of Compromise: Abortion Politics in Western Europe," in Githens and Stetson, *Abortion Politics*; Evert Ketting and Philip van Praag, "The Marginal Relevance of Legislation Related to Induced

Abortion," in *The New Politics of Abortion*, ed. Joni Lovenduski and Joyce Outshoorn (London: Sage, 1986).

Three studies are edited volumes that offer case studies of several countries written by different authors that are then analyzed by volume editors in introductory or concluding chapters. Joni Lovenduski and Joyce Outshoorn, "Introduction," in Lovenduski and Outshoorn, *New Politics of Abortion*; Stetson, *Abortion Politics, Women's Movements, and the Democratic State*; Bill Rolston and Anna Eggert, *Abortion in the New Europe: A Comparative Handbook* (Westport, CT: Greenwood Press, 1994).

Finally, several authors compare abortion policies worldwide. Albin Eser and Hans Georg Koch, *Abortion and the Law: From International Comparison to Legal Policy* (The Hague: Asser Press, 2005); Francisco O. Ramirez and Elizabeth H. McEneaney, "From Women's Suffrage to Reproduction Rights? Cross-National Considerations," *International Journal of Comparative Sociology*, 38, no. 1–2 (1997): 6–24; Andrzej Kulczycki, *The Abortion Debate in the World Arena* (London: Routledge, 1999); Victor Asal, Mitchell Brown, and Renee Gibson Figueroa, "Structure, Empowerment and the Liberalization of Cross-National Abortion Rights," *Politics and Gender* 4, no. 02 (2008): 265–84.

11. Previous studies have attended to such factors as the access points provided by federalism and the separation of powers; party discipline; unusual political procedures such as court decisions, free voting, and private member's bills; and multiparty compromise. Several studies also note comparative differences in the ability of social movements and interest groups to influence political parties—mainly through campaign funding and institutionalized linkages between feminist movements and the state. Some have also focused on the differential openness to movements of patronage-oriented and programmatic parties. Haussman, *Abortion Politics in North America*; Schwartz, "Politics and Moral Causes in Canada and the United States"; Soper, *Evangelical Christianity in the United States and Great Britain*; Meyer and Staggenborg, "Countermovement Dynamics in Federal Systems"; Tatalovich, *Politics of Abortion*; Scheppele, "Constitutionalizing Abortion"; Glendon, *Abortion and Divorce in Western Law*; Cohan, "Abortion as a Marginal Issue"; DeLorme, "Gaining a Right to Abortion"; Outshoorn, "Stability of Compromise"; Stetson, *Abortion Politics, Women's Movements, and the Democratic State*; Rosemary Nossiff, *Before* Roe: *Abortion Policy in the States* (Philadelphia: Temple University Press, 2000).

12. There are various definitions of institutions. John Campbell defines them as "formal and informal rules, monitoring and enforcement mechanisms, and systems of meaning that define the context within which individuals, corporations, labor unions, nation-states, and other organizations operate and interact with each other." John L. Campbell, *Institutional Change and Globalization* (Princeton, NJ: Princeton University Press, 2004), 1. Elisabeth Clemens and James Cook write that "institutions exert

patterned higher-order effects on the actions, indeed the constitution, of individuals and organizations without requiring repeated collective mobilization or authoritative intervention to achieve these regularities." Elisabeth S. Clemens and James M. Cook, "Politics and Institutionalism: Explaining Durability and Change," *Annual Review of Sociology* 25 (1999): 444–45. Peter Hall defines institutions as "the formal or informal procedures, routines, norms and conventions embedded in the organizational structure of the polity or political economy. These can range from the rules of a constitutional order or standard operating procedures of a bureaucracy to the conventions governing trade union behavior or bank-firm relations." Peter A. Hall and Rosemary C. R. Taylor, "Political Science and the Three New Institutionalisms," *Political Studies* 44 (1996): 938. John Campbell notes that sociological and popular uses of the term differ. What most people call institutions, sociologists call organizations as in "Lou's Restaurant is a local institution." "From an institutionalist's point of view, Lou's is really an organization, a group of people that produces goods or services. It exists within a set of institutions that make up its surrounding environment, such as the rules established and enforced by the government regarding the restaurant's health, accounting, labor and other practices as well as the taken-for-granted local customs regarding the appropriate way to treat customers, employees and suppliers." Campbell, *Institutional Change and Globalization*, 4n5.

13. James M. Jasper, "A Strategic Approach to Collective Action: Looking for Agency in Social-Movement Choices," *Mobilization: An International Quarterly* 9, no. 1 (2004): 1–16.
14. Gosta Esping-Andersen, *Three Worlds of Welfare Capitalism* (Princeton, NJ: Princeton University Press, 1990); Greg M. Olsen, *The Politics of the Welfare State: Canada, Sweden, and the United States* (Oxford: Oxford University Press, 2002).
15. O'Connor, Orloff, and Shaver, "Body Rights, Social Rights, and Reproductive Choice."
16. Harold Wilensky, *The Welfare State and Equality* (Berkeley: University of California Press, 1975); Anthony King, "Ideas, Institutions, and Policies of Governments," *British Journal of Poltical Science* 3, no. 4 (1974): 291–313.
17. Walter Korpi, *The Working Class in Welfare Capitalism* (London: Routledge and Kegan Paul, 1978); Walter Korpi, *The Democratic Class Struggle* (London: Routledge and Kegan Paul, 1983); Francis Castles, "The Impact of Parties on Public Expenditure," in *The Impact of Parties: Politics and Policies in Democratic Capitalist States*, ed. Francis Castles (London: Sage, 1982); John D. Stephens, *The Transition from Capitalism to Socialism* (London: Macmillan, 1979).
18. Ann Shola Orloff and Theda Skocpol, "Why Not Equal Protection? Explaining the Politics of Public Social Spending in Britain, 1900–1911 and in the United States, 1880s–1920s," *American Journal of Sociology* 49 (1984):

726–50; Theda Skocpol, *Protecting Soldiers and Mothers* (Cambridge, MA: Harvard University Press, 1992); Evelyne Huber, Charles Ragin, and John D. Stephens, "Social Democracy, Christian Democracy, Constitutional Structure, and the Welfare State," *American Journal of Sociology* 99 (1993): 711–49; Edwin Amenta, *Bold Relief: Institutional Politics and the Origins of Modern American Social Policy* (Princeton, NJ: Princeton University Press, 1998); Theda Skocpol and Edwin Amenta, "States and Social Policies," *Annual Review of Sociology* 12 (1986): 131–57. For a discussion of these generations, see Skocpol, *Protecting Soldiers and Mothers*.

19. Faye Ginsburg, *Contested Lives: The Abortion Debate in an American Community* (Berkeley: University of California Press, 1998); James Davison Hunter and Joseph E. Davis, "Cultural Politics at the Edge of Life," *Journal of Policy History* 7, no. 1 (1995): 103–27; Luker, *Abortion and the Politics of Motherhood*; Rosalind Pollack Petchesky, *Abortion and Woman's Choice: The State, Sexuality, and Reproductive Freedom* (New York: Longman, 1984); Sally Sheldon, *Beyond Control: Medical Power and Abortion Law* (London: Pluto Press, 1997); Laura Grindstaff, "Abortion and the Popular Press: Mapping Media Discourse from *Roe* to *Webster*," in *Abortion Politics in the United States and Canada: Studies in Public Opinion*, ed. Ted G. Jelen and Marthe A. Chandler (Westport, CT: Praeger, 1994), 57–88; Kurt W. Back, "Why Is Abortion a Public Issue? The Role of Professional Control," *Politics and Society* 15 (1986–87): 197–206; Carole E. Joffe, *The Regulation of Sexuality: Experiences of Family Planning Workers*, Health, Society, and Policy (Philadelphia: Temple University Press, 1986).

20. Edwin Amenta, "State-Centered and Political Institutional Theory," in *The Handbook of Political Sociology: States, Civil Societies, and Globalization*, ed. Thomas Janoski et al. (New York: Cambridge University Press, 2005). For political institutionalism, see Skocpol, *Protecting Soldiers and Mothers*; Orloff and Skocpol, "Why Not Equal Protection?"; Amenta, *Bold Relief*; Theda Skocpol, "Bringing the State Back In: Strategies of Analysis in Current Research," in *Bringing the State Back In*, ed. Peter B. Evans, Dietrich Rueschmeyer, and Theda Skocpol (Cambridge: Cambridge University Press, 1985); Jeff Goodwin, *No Other Way Out: States and Revolutionary Movements, 1945–1991*, Cambridge Studies in Comparative Politics (Cambridge: Cambridge University Press, 2001); Sven Steinmo, *Taxation and Democracy: Swedish, British, and American Approaches to Financing the Modern State* (New Haven, CT: Yale University Press, 1993). For historical institutionalism, see Sven Steinmo, Kathleen Thelen, and Frank Longstreth, *Structuring Politics: Historical Institutionalism in Comparative Analysis* (Cambridge: Cambridge University Press, 1992); Ellen M. Immergut, *Health Politics: Interests and Institutions in Western Europe* (Cambridge: Cambridge University Press, 1992); Ellen M. Immergut, "The Theoretical Core of the New Institutionalism," *Politics and Society* 26, no. 1 (1998): 5–34; Hall and Taylor, "Political Science and the Three New Institutionalisms."

21. Skocpol, *Protecting Soldiers and Mothers*; Steinmo, *Taxation and Democracy*; Ira Katznelson, *City Trenches* (Chicago: University of Chicago Press, 1981).
22. See Paul DiMaggio and Walter Powell, "Introduction," in *The New Institutionalism in Organizational Analysis*, ed. Walter Powell and Paul DiMaggio (Chicago: University of Chicago Press, 1991); Walter Powell and Paul DiMaggio, *The New Institutionalism in Organizational Analysis* (Chicago: University of Chicago Press, 1991); James G. March and Johan P. Olsen, *Rediscovering Institutions: The Organizational Basis of Politics* (New York: Free Press, 1989).
23. Hugh Heclo, *Modern Social Politics in Britain and Sweden* (New Haven, CT: Yale University Press, 1974); Skocpol, *Protecting Soldiers and Mothers*.
24. Charles Tilly, *From Mobilization to Revolution* (Reading, MA: Addison-Wesley, 1978); Herbert Kitschelt, "Political Opportunity Structures and Political Protest: Anti-nuclear Movements in Four Democracies," *British Journal of Political Science* 16 (1986): 57–85; David S. Meyer, "Protest and Political Opportunities," *Annual Review of Sociology* 30, no. 1 (2004): 125–45.
25. Kitschelt, "Political Opportunity Structures and Political Protest"; Hanspeter Kriesi, *New Social Movements in Western Europe: A Comparative Analysis* (Minneapolis: University of Minnesota Press, 1995); Amenta, *Bold Relief*; Nossiff, *Before* Roe.
26. Frank R. Baumgartner and Bryan D. Jones, *Agendas and Instability in American Politics* (Chicago: University of Chicago Press, 1993).
27. Petchesky, *Abortion and Woman's Choice*.
28. Orloff, "Gender and the Social Rights of Citizenship."
29. Previous typologies of abortion policies have added up the number of abortion restrictions in a given place—treating all as equally consequential. Others have focused on particular aspects of policy such as the legal grounds for abortion, time limits for obtaining abortions, parental consent requirements, or public funding. Others have compared abortion rates. Glendon, *Abortion and Divorce in Western Law*; Marilyn J. Field, "The Determinants of Abortion Policy in Developed Nations," *Policy Studies Journal* 7 (1979): 771–81; Ketting and Praag, "Marginal Relevance of Legislation Related to Induced Abortion"; Glen Halva-Neubauer, "The States after *Roe*: No Paper Tigers," in *Understanding the New Politics of Abortion*, ed. Malcolm L. Goggin (Newbury Park, CA: Sage, 1993), 167–89; Jeffrey E. Cohen and Charles Barrileaux, "Public Opinion, Interest Groups, and Public Policy-Making: Abortion Policy in the American States," in Goggin, *Understanding the New Politics of Abortion*; Susan B. Hansen, "Differences in Public Policies toward Abortion: Electoral and Policy Context," in Goggin, *Understanding the New Politics of Abortion,* 222–48; Kenneth J. Meier and Deborah R. McFarlane, "Abortion Politics and Abortion Funding Policy," in Goggin, *Understanding the New Politics of Abortion*, 249–67; Michael B. Berkman and Robert E. O'Connor, "Do Women Legislators Matter? Female Legislators and State Abortion Policy," in Goggin, *Understanding the New Politics of*

Abortion, 268–84; Matthew E. Wetstein, *Abortion Rates in the United States* (Albany: State University of New York Press, 1996); Eser, "Abortion Law Reform in Germany"; Minkenberg, "Religion and Public Policy"; Roland Boland and Laura Katzive, "Developments in Laws on Induced Abortion: 1998–2007," *International Family Planning Perspectives* 34, no. 3 (2008): 110–20; Brooks, "Abortion Policy in Western Democracies"; Petersen, *Abortion Regimes*. In 1990, the United States had the highest abortion rate among rich Western democracies. But abortion rates pose some problems for comparing abortion policies. They are mainly influenced by nonpolicy factors such as contraception, attitudes of the population toward abortion, labor force and educational participation of women, and various measures of social and economic development. Wetstein, *Abortion Rates in the United States*; Ketting and Praag, "Marginal Relevance of Legislation Related to Induced Abortion." In addition, abortion policies have implications that go beyond the mere ability of women to obtain or not obtain abortions, such as monetary and temporal costs and physical and emotional discomfort. They also affect women's claims to reproductive and bodily self-determination and, in turn, their status as citizens. Finally, contention over abortion is not particularly oriented toward reducing or increasing abortion rates. Abortion rights proponents seek to make abortion more available as an element of reproductive self-determination. Most would be quite content with a decline in abortion rates if this resulted from increased contraceptive services. Pro-lifers find legal abortion unacceptable no matter how low the rate. See Anika Rahman, Laura Katzive, and Stanley K. Henshaw, "A Global Review of Laws on Induced Abortion, 1985–1997," *International Family Planning Perspectives* 24, no. 2 (1998): 56–64; Ketting and Praag, "Marginal Relevance of Legislation Related to Induced Abortion"; Field, "Determinants of Abortion Policy in Developed Nations"; Glendon, *Abortion and Divorce in Western Law.*
30. The limit is shorter in Turkey and Portugal (ten weeks), and longer in Sweden (eighteen weeks), West Australia (twenty weeks), Victoria, Australia (twenty-four weeks), and the United States (many states have no limit or the limit is viability—about twenty-four weeks). In the Netherlands, the limit is viability. There are no legal time limits in Canada and the Australian Capital Territory.
31. Glendon, *Abortion and Divorce in Western Law*; Eser, "Abortion Law Reform in Germany"; Minkenberg, "Religion and Public Policy."
32. Glendon, *Abortion and Divorce in Western Law*. German law contains a unique twist on this model—early abortions are illegal but unpunishable.
33. Counseling is neutral in France and the Netherlands, but aimed at protecting life in Italy. In Germany, continuation of pregnancy is one of the many goals of counseling, but the counseling itself must be neutral as to the final outcome and leave it to the woman to make the decision. In some countries, counselors are required to inform women about available social

assistance for mothers. The length of waiting or reflection periods is seven days in France and Italy, six days in Belgium, five days in the Netherlands, three days in Germany, and usually one day in the approximately twenty-five American states that have such waiting periods. Eser and Koch, *Abortion and the Law*; Guttmacher Institute, "Mandatory Counseling and Waiting Periods for Abortion" (New York: Alan Guttmacher Institute, 2007).

34. Strict gatekeeping countries include Ireland, Mexico, and Poland. In Ireland, abortions are legal only if necessary to protect a woman's life. In Mexico (outside of Mexico City), abortion is legal only in cases of rape or fetal abnormality. In Poland, abortions are legal only to protect physical health and in cases of rape, incest, or fetal impairment. Eser offers a typology distinguishing between "permission models based on third party evaluation," "conflict oriented discourse models," and "time terminated models on a self-determination basis." He does not, however, distinguish between countries in which third parties interpret abortion grounds liberally or strictly. He also erroneously places England/Wales, Luxembourg, and Mexico within the conflict-oriented discourse model. Eser, "Abortion Law Reform in Germany." My typology is similar to that of Michael Minkenberg, who, following Eser, distinguishes between "period," "distress," and "indication" models. Minkenberg also does not distinguish between liberal and strict interpretations of indication models. Instead, he incorporates countries such as New Zealand and the United Kingdom where legal grounds are liberally interpreted into the "distress" model. Minkenberg, "Religion and Public Policy."

35. Most countries in this category allow abortions for physical or mental health and for social grounds. South Korea, Spain, and New Zealand do not allow abortions for social grounds, but doctors often import social grounds into the law under mental health grounds. Although Britain's law contains a social ground (the health of existing children in the family), this ground is rarely used. Instead, most abortions are approved on mental health grounds.

36. Currently, the gatekeepers are doctors in every country except Hungary, where they are family welfare nurses.

37. The Netherlands, Greece, Switzerland, and some Australian states are examples of places that abandoned earlier gatekeeping laws. Rolston and Eggert, *Abortion in the New Europe*. The Netherlands is an interesting example of the liberal interpretation of a narrow abortion statute. In 1966, an influential law review article suggested that because the country's 1920 abortion law had delegated abortion decisions to the medical profession, this allowed doctors to bring modern (broad) conceptions of health to bear. Doctors began to broaden their interpretations of the law and, within seven years, interpreted it so broadly that abortion became available on request, and the Netherlands became an abortion center for women from

all over Europe. The country did not change its abortion laws legislatively for another eight years and then merely codified the new broader practice.
38. In addition to gatekeeping by doctors, some countries require consent from parents or husbands. Nine countries require parental consent. Five of these have judicial bypass procedures (Denmark, France, Italy, Norway, and the United States) while the others do not (Turkey, Greece, the Czech Republic, and Slovakia). Two countries (Japan and Turkey) require husband consent. Rahman, Katzive, and Henshaw, "Global Review of Laws on Induced Abortion, 1985–1997"; United Nations Population Division, *Abortion Policies: A Global Review* (New York: United Nations, 2002); F. M. Tedesco, "Rites for the Unborn Dead: Abortion and Buddhism in Contemporary Korea," *Korea Journal* 36, no. 2 (1996): 61–74; Boland and Katzive, "Developments in Laws on Induced Abortion: 1998–2007." These countries are mainly clustered in the own reasons (Denmark, United States, Turkey, Greece, the Czech Republic, and Slovakia) and distress types (France, Italy, Norway). Japan is the only country in the gatekeeping type that requires consent from parents or husbands.
39. Iceland and Luxembourg are excluded due to their small size. The subnational units of Australia and Mexico fall into more than one type. Women may obtain abortions without gatekeeping and for their own reasons in West Australia, the Australian Capital Territory, and Victoria, but they must obtain doctors' approvals in the other five states and territories. Women may obtain abortions without gatekeeping and for their own reasons in Mexico's Federal District (Mexico City), but the thirty-one states strongly restrict abortions. In Italy, the required reason for obtaining an abortion is not distress or emergency but danger to women's health "in view of their state of health, their economic, social or family circumstances, [and] the circumstances in which conception occurred." Italy, "Law No. 194 of 22 May 1978 on the Social Protection of Motherhood and the Voluntary Termination of Pregnancy," *Gazzetta Ufficiale della Repubblica Italiana*, no. 140 (1978). This resembles the grounds typically contained in gatekeeping models, but women do not need a gatekeeper's approval. They decide for themselves whether they meet the legally defined grounds for abortion.
40. Lewis A. Coser, *Masters of Sociological Thought: Ideas in Historical and Social Context* (New York: Harcourt, 1977).
41. Guttmacher Institute, "Mandatory Counseling and Waiting Periods for Abortion"; National Abortion Rights Action League, "Who Decides? A State-by-State Review of Abortion and Reproductive Rights" (Washington, DC: National Abortion Rights Action League, 2007).
42. For a similar argument about the United States, see Udo Werner, "Convergence of Abortion Regulation in Germany and the United States: A Critique to Glendon's Rights Talk Thesis," *Loyola of Los Angeles International and Comparative Law Review* 18 (1995): 571.

43. Yishai distinguishes between "enabling," "hindering," "intrusive," and "restrictive" policies that result from the ability of women to choose abortion without restriction and the degree to which the state facilitates abortion access through health-care funding and provision. Yishai, "Public Ideas and Public Policy." Minkenberg criticizes this typology because it confuses two independent policy areas—abortion and health care. Though the two policy areas obviously are not identical, they are only rarely independent. For example, one could argue that there is little public funding of abortion in the United States because there is little public health care in general. But this does not explain why abortion has been excluded from public health insurance for the poor. Minkenberg, "Religion and Public Policy."
44. For example, Germany, Austria, and the Czech Republic fund abortions only if they are provided for medical reasons, and Germany does so only for the poor. The American Hyde amendment allows federal funding of abortions only for grounds of life, rape, or incest, but seventeen states use their own money to fund abortions for grounds of physical or mental health or fetal abnormality. These are Alaska, Arizona, California, Connecticut, Hawaii, Illinois, Maryland, Massachusetts, Minnesota, Montana, New Jersey, New Mexico, New York, Oregon, Vermont, Washington, and West Virginia. Six additional states use their own funds for a narrower set of circumstances: Indiana (physical health), Iowa (fetal abnormality), Mississippi (fetal abnormality), Utah (physical health and fetal abnormality), Virginia (fetal abnormality), and Wisconsin (physical health). *Abortion Facts: Public Funding for Abortion: Medicaid and the Hyde Amendment* (Washington, DC: National Abortion Federation, 2008), http://www.prochoice.org/about_abortion/facts/public_funding.html.
45. This includes Spain, Greece, Turkey, South Korea, and Britain before 1991.
46. A final unusual path occurs in Japan where abortion grounds are interpreted liberally but both birth and abortion are considered private matters ineligible for public health insurance coverage. H. P. David, "Abortion in Europe, 1920–91: A Public Health Perspective," *Studies in Family Planning* 23, no. 1 (1992): 1–22; United Nations Population Division, *Abortion Policies*; National Abortion Rights Action League, "Who Decides?"; B. Pinter et al., "Accessibility and Availability of Abortions in Six European Countries," *European Journal of Contraception and Reproductive Health Care* 10, no. 1 (2005): 51–58; Tedesco, "Rites for the Unborn Dead"; Tomoko Furukawa, "Health Care Puzzles," *Japan Times*, November 4, 2004; Eser and Koch, *Abortion and the Law*.
47. The types are based on my reading of case studies of abortion reforms in OECD countries as well as my own knowledge of the British, Canadian, and American cases. The types are also inspired by scholars who have attempted to explain similarities in "families" or "worlds" of welfare capitalism through such factors as left-wing power, Catholicism and Christian Democracy, women's suffrage and mobilization, policy makers' imitation

of policy models, and the legacies of previous policies. Finally, the types are inspired by scholars who have classified parties and party systems on the basis of such factors as the number of parties and their polarization, whether decisions are made through consensus or majority rule, and the degree to which parties prioritize policies, votes, or spoils of office.

For case and cross-national studies of abortion policies, see Outshoorn, "Stability of Compromise"; Lovenduski and Outshoorn, *New Politics of Abortion*; Stetson, *Abortion Politics, Women's Movements, and the Democratic State*; Githens and Stetson, *Abortion Politics: Public Policy in Cross-Cultural Perspective*; Eugenia Georges, "Abortion Policy and Practice in Greece," *Social Science and Medicine* 42, no. 4 (1996): 509–19; Paul Christopher Manuel, "Roman Catholicism, Secularization, and the Recovery of Traditional Communal Values: The 1998 and 2007 Referenda on Abortion in Portugal," *South European Society and Politics* 13, no. 1 (2008): 117–29; D. Bradley, "Equality and Patriarchy: Family Law and State Feminism in Finland," *International Journal of the Sociology of Law* 26, no. 2 (1998): 197–216; Linders, "Victory and Beyond"; Mylchreest, "'Sound Law and Undoubtedly Good Policy'"; Karen Coleman, "The Politics of Abortion in Australia: Freedom, Church and State," *Feminist Review* 29 (1988): 75–97; M. J. Rankin, "Contemporary Australian Abortion Law: The Description of a Crime and the Negation of a Woman's Right to Abortion," *Monash University Law Review* 27 (2001); Mark J. Rankin, "Recent Developments in Australian Abortion Law: Tasmania and the Australian Capital Territory," *Monash University Law Review* 29 (2003): 229; Noah Riseman, "An Unfinished Job? Abortion Law Reform in Australia 1967-80," *Australia and New Zealand Law and History E-Journal*, Other Paper No. 4 (2006); Petersen, *Abortion Regimes*; Marilyn Pryor, *The Right to Live: The Abortion Battle of New Zealand* (Auckland: Harlen Books, 1986); Abortion Law Reform Association New Zealand, "A Brief History of Abortion Laws in New Zealand," 2008, http://www.alranz.org/nzabortionlaws.htm; Deirdre McKeown and Rob Lundie, "Free Votes in Australian and Some Overseas Parliaments," *Current Issues Brief: Parliament of Australia*, no. 1 (2002); Ferree et al., *Shaping Abortion Discourse*. The Lovenduski and Outshoorn volume includes case studies of Belgium, Britain, France, Ireland, Italy, Netherlands, Norway, and the United States. The Rolston and Eggert volume includes case studies of Austria, Belgium, Britain, Bulgaria, the Czech and Slovak Republics, Denmark, Finland, France, Germany, Hungary, Ireland, the Netherlands, Norway, Poland, Portugal, Spain, Sweden, Switzerland, and the United States. The Stetson volume includes case studies of Austria, Belgium, Britain, Canada, France, Germany, Ireland, Italy, the Netherlands, Spain, and the United States. Another edited volume by Githens and Stetson contains comparative studies involving Canada, eastern Europe, France, Germany, Hungary, Ireland, Japan, Russia, the United States, and western Europe, but also case studies of Japan and the United States.

For work on "families" of nations, see Wil A. Arts and John Gelissen, "Three Worlds of Welfare Capitalism or More? A State-of-the-Art Report," *Journal of European Social Policy* 12, no. 2 (2002): 137; Esping-Andersen, *Three Worlds of Welfare Capitalism*; Gøsta Esping-Andersen, *Social Foundations of Postindustrial Economies* (Oxford: Oxford University Press, 2000); Alan Siaroff, "Work, Welfare, and Gender Equality: A New Typology," in *Gendering Welfare States*, ed. Diane Sainsbury (London: Sage, 1994), 82–100; Francis Castles, ed., *Families of Nations: Patterns of Public Policy in Western Democracies* (Brookfield, VT: Dartmouth, 1993); Francis G. Castles, "On Religion and Public Policy: Does Catholicism Make a Difference?," *European Journal of Political Research* 25, no. 1 (1994): 19–40. See also H. Obinger and U. Wagschal, "Families of Nations and Public Policy," *West European Politics* 24, no. 1 (2001): 99–114.

Esping-Andersen famously theorized "three worlds of welfare capitalism"—social democratic, conservative, and liberal—which he based on the degree to which welfare states promoted decommodification (the independence of citizens from labor markets and employers), economic equality, and state (rather than market) provision of benefits and services. Ann Orloff criticized Esping-Andersen's scheme for its inattention to gender and proposed that welfare states be judged on five main dimensions: (1) the ways in which they divide responsibilities for social provision between states, markets and families, and within families between men and women; (2) the ways in which they are stratified, including their treatment of paid and unpaid labor; (3) the degree to which they "decommodify" workers by providing sources of income that emancipate men and women from markets and individual employers; (4) the degree to which they promote women's access to paid work—thus emancipating women from dependence on families; and (5) the degree to which they promote women's ability to form and maintain autonomous households. Siaroff's gender-sensitive welfare regimes are based on spending on family benefits (family allowances, day care, and parental leave) and the degree to which paid work is attractive to women (e.g., less discrimination in wages and positions). He calls the four resulting types protestant social-democratic, advanced Christian Democratic, protestant liberal, and late female mobilization. Finally, Castles's "families of nations" include the English-speaking, Continental, Scandinavian, and Southern. Esping-Andersen, *Three Worlds of Welfare Capitalism*; Orloff, "Gender and the Social Rights of Citizenship." See also Julia S. O'Connor, "Gender, Class, and Citizenship in the Comparative Analysis of Welfare State Regimes: Theoretical and Methodological Issues," *British Journal of Sociology* 44 (1993): 501–18; O'Connor, Orloff, and Shaver, *States, Markets, Families*. For Esping-Andersen's response, see Gosta Esping-Andersen, *Social Foundations of Postindustrial Economies* (New York: Oxford University Press, 1999); Siaroff, "Work, Welfare and Gender Equality"; Castles, *Families of Nations*.

For comparisons of political party systems, see Robert A. Dahl, *Political Oppositions in Western Democracies* (New Haven, CT: Yale University Press, 1966); Giovanni Sartori, *Parties and Party Systems: A Framework for Analysis* (Colchester, UK: ECPR Press, 2005); Richard Gunther and Larry Diamond, "Species of Political Parties: A New Typology," *Party Politics* 9, no. 2 (2003): 167; Martin Rhodes, "Southern European Welfare States: Identity, Problems, and Prospects for Reform," in *Southern European Welfare States: Between Crisis and Reform*, ed. Martin Rhodes (London: Frank Cass, 1997); Otto Kirchheimer, "The Transformation of the Western European Party Systems," in *Political Parties and Political Development*, ed. Joseph LaPalombara and Myron Weiner (Princeton, NJ: Princeton University Press, 1966), 177–200; Steven B. Wolinetz, "Classifying Party Systems: Where Have All the Typologies Gone?" (paper presented at the Annual Meeting of the Canadian Political Science Association, Winnipeg, Manitoba, 2004); Peter Mair, *The West European Party System* (Oxford: Oxford University Press, 1990); Jean Blondel, "Party Systems and Patterns of Government in Western Democracies," *Canadian Journal of Political Science* 1, no. 2 (1968): 180–203; Steven B. Wolinetz, "Beyond the Catch-All Party: Approaches to the Study of Parties and Party Organization in Contemporary Democracies," in *Political Parties: Old Concepts and New Challenges*, ed. Richard Gunther, J. R. Montero, and Juan J. Linz (Oxford: Oxford University Press, 2002), 136–65; Arend Lijphart, *Patterns of Democracy: Government Forms and Performance in Thirty-Six Countries* (New Haven, CT: Yale University Press, 1999).

48. This is instead of assigning the reforms based on the overall or cumulative nature of abortion politics in each country. The long-term fortunes of political parties are less relevant to abortion policy than other types of policy because many parties have been reluctant to reopen the issue once reforms have been made. This is especially true in the negotiated and nonpartisan types. Outshoorn, "Stability of Compromise."

49. Abortion votes were whipped only in Austria, Norway, and the Netherlands. Only the Austrian social democratic party whipped its members (after pressure from feminists and after a nonwhipped bill failed). Above, I noted that the Austrian reform fell somewhere between the own reasons and distress models since its health insurance system does not fund abortions for nonmedical reasons. Austria's reform is probably more restrictive than others in the "social democratic" type because of the presence of a large Christian democratic party and more liberal than others in the "negotiated" type because the reform was not the product of a coalition government. Though social democratic governments enacted the Norwegian and Finnish reforms, they established gatekeeping and distress models respectively rather than own reasons models like the other countries in the "social democratic" type. This may be because Norway is the only Nordic country with a sizable Christian democratic party and Finland is the only Nordic country where the social democrats are not the dominant party.

Moreover, although the Finnish reform involved gatekeeping, the grounds were broad and were interpreted liberally from the beginning. Outshoorn, "Stability of Compromise."

50. West Germany's 1974 reform was introduced by the parliamentary caucuses of the governing social democrats and liberals while the opposition Christian democrats opposed it. Germany's 1992 reform was introduced by a cross-party group of women MPs, but after it was struck down by the Supreme Court, social democrats and liberals forced the Christian democrats to compromise. In Switzerland, social democrats allied with other parties behind the 2001 reform while Christian democrats gathered signatures for an unsuccessful 2002 referendum to rescind it. In Belgium and Italy, members of left and liberal parties used private member initiatives to enact reforms over the opposition of Christian democratic cabinets. In the Netherlands, governing coalitions of Christian democrats and liberals introduced abortion reform bills in 1971 and 1980. This is one of the few cases in which Christian democrats were behind abortion reform proposals. These were aimed at preventing broader reforms supported by social democrats and also sought to narrow liberal medical interpretations of the 1920 abortion law. In France, the 1975 reform was introduced by the center-right modernizer Giscard d'Estaing, but more than half of his party voted against it while virtually all social democrats and communists voted for it. This was also the pattern when the law was renewed after its expiration in 1979.

51. Although Britain and Canada contain major third parties, the Liberal Democrats (formerly the Liberals) and the New Democratic Party respectively, these countries are commonly classified as two-party systems since third parties have not been particularly influential (with the exception of the Liberal Democrats in 2010). Canada is sometimes referred to as a two-and-a-half party system because of its small left party, the NDP, but the NDP would have a greater effect on Canadian politics if it was between the two major parties rather than to the left of them. This is the case in the other main cases of two-and-a-half parties in Germany, Belgium, and Luxembourg. Blondel, "Party Systems and Patterns of Government in Western Democracies."

52. The British party system is usually classified as being moderately polarized, though polarization was higher during the Thatcher and Major years (1979–97). Scholars also note that the British Conservative and the American Republican parties were less "catch-all" during the Thatcher, Reagan, and Bush (father and son) years. Wolinetz, "Classifying Party Systems"; Wolinetz, "Beyond the Catch-All Party."

53. Of the countries in which courts have ruled on abortion, four liberalized abortion laws (the United States (1973), Australia, Canada, and Italy), four restricted abortion (Ireland, Germany, Spain, and the United States (1988 and 1992)), and three upheld legislative liberalizations (Austria, France, Portugal). Eser and Koch, *Abortion and the Law*.

54. Outshoorn, "The Stability of Compromise"; Stetson, *Abortion Politics, Women's Movements, and the Democratic State*; Blofield, *Politics of Moral Sin*; Pierre Bréchon, "Integration into Catholicism and Protestantism in Europe: The Impact on Moral and Political Values," in *Religion and Secularizing Society: The Europeans' Religion at the End of the 20th Century*, ed. Loek Halman and Ole Riis (Boston: Brill-Leiden, 2003), 114–61.
55. In Germany, unification and two Supreme Court decisions reopened the abortion issue. In Austria, antiabortion forces took the 1974 abortion reform to the Supreme Court, which upheld it. In Italy, abortion opponents brought abortion to the public agenda through a 1981 referendum, 1999 private member's legislation, and the 2008 election. Parliaments voted on, but rejected, antiabortion legislation in Austria in 1978 and 1999, and in the Netherlands in 1984.
56. Robert Dahl, *Who Governs? Democracy and Power in an American City* (New Haven, CT: Yale University Press, 1961); Korpi, *Democratic Class Struggle*; Castles, "Impact of Parties on Public Expenditure"; Frank Wilson, "Interest Groups and Politics in Western Europe: The Neo-Corporatist Approach," *Comparative Politics* 16, no. 1 (1983): 105–23; James Alt, "The Evolution of Tax Structures," *Public Choice* 41 (1984): 181–222.
57. Immergut, "Theoretical Core of the New Institutionalism"; Immergut, *Health Politics*; Peter A. Hall, *Governing the Economy: The Politics of State Intervention in Britain and France* (Oxford: Oxford University Press, 1986); Steinmo, *Taxation and Democracy*; Frank Dobbin, *Forging Industrial Policy: The United States, Britain, and France in the Railway Age* (New York: Cambridge University Press, 1994); Skocpol, *Protecting Soldiers and Mothers*; Joseph R. Gusfield, *The Culture of Public Problems: Drinking-Driving and the Symbolic Order* (Chicago: University of Chicago Press, 1981); Aaron Wildavsky, "Choosing Preferences by Constructing Institutions: A Cultural Theory of Preference Formation," *American Political Science Review* 81, no. 1 (1987): 3–21; James G. March and Johan P. Olsen, "The New Institutionalism: Organizational Factors in Political Life," *American Political Science Review* 78 (1984): 734–49; Steinmo, Thelen, and Longstreth, *Structuring Politics*; Elisabeth S. Clemens, *The People's Lobby: Organizational Innovation and the Rise of Interest Group Politics in the United States, 1890–1925* (Chicago: University of Chicago Press, 1997); James M. Jasper, *Nuclear Politics: Energy and the State in the United States, Sweden, and France* (Princeton, NJ: Princeton University Press, 1990).
58. Peter Swenson, *Capitalists against Markets: The Making of Labor Markets and Welfare States in the United States and Sweden* (Oxford: Oxford University Press, 2002).
59. Drew Halfmann, "Historical Priorities and the Responses of Doctors' Associations to Abortion Reform Proposals in Britain and the United States, 1960–1973," *Social Problems* 50, no. 4 (2003): 567–91.
60. Esping-Andersen, *Three Worlds of Welfare Capitalism*; Stephens, *Transition*

from Capitalism to Socialism; Korpi, *Working Class in Welfare Capitalism*; Castles, "Impact of Parties on Public Expenditure"; Francis G. Castles and Peter Mair, "Left-Right Political Scales: Some "Expert" Judgements," *European Journal of Political Research* 12 (1984): 73–88.

61. Alexander Hicks, Joya Misra, and Tang Nah Ng, "The Programmatic Emergence of the Social Security State," *American Sociological Review* 60 (1995): 329–49.

62. This is a narrower usage than that of "new social movement" theory, which focuses on an allegedly new set of post-industrial, post-Marxist movements such as the feminist, gay rights, and environmental movements that are mainly concerned with quality of life rather than economic issues. Alberto Melucci, *Challenging Codes: Collective Action in the Information Age* (Cambridge: Cambridge University Press, 1989); Enrique Laraña, Hank Johnston, and Joseph R. Gusfield, *New Social Movements: From Ideology to Identity* (Philadelphia: Temple University Press, 1994); Jurgen Habermas, "New Social Movements," *Telos* 49 (1981): 33–37; C. Offe, "New Social Movements: Changing Boundaries of the Political," *Social Research* 52 (1985): 817–68. Critics of the term have argued that "new social movements" have been present throughout American history, that economic movements have hardly subsided, and that many of the new social movements have economic interests as well. Nelson A. Pichardo, "New Social Movements: A Critical Review," *Annual Reviews in Sociology* 23, no. 1 (1997): 411–30; Craig Calhoun, "'New Social Movements' of the Early Nineteenth Century," *Social Science History* 17, no. 3 (1993): 385–427.

63. V. O. Key, *Politics, Parties, and Pressure Groups*, 5th ed. (New York: Crowell, 1964); Geoffrey K. Roberts, *Political Parties and Pressure-Groups in Britain* (London: Weidenfeld and Nicolson, 1970).

64. Meyer and Staggenborg, "Countermovement Dynamics in Federal Systems"; Soper, "Political Structures and Interest Group Activism"; R. Kent Weaver, "The Politics of Blame Avoidance," *Journal of Public Policy* 6, no. 4 (1986): 371–98; Lisa Young, *Feminists and Party Politics* (Vancouver: UBC Press, 2000); Leon D. Epstein, *Political Parties in the American Mold* (Madison: University of Wisconsin Press, 1986); Earl H. Fry, *The Canadian Political System*, ACSUS Papers (Washington, DC: Association for Canadian Studies in the United States, 1996); Frank J. Sorauf, *Money in American Elections* (Glenview, IL: Scott, Foresman, 1988); Clive S. Thomas, "The United States: The Paradox of Loose Party-Group Ties in the Context of American Political Development," in *Political Parties and Interest Groups: Shaping Democratic Governance*, ed. Clive S. Thomas (Boulder, CO: Lynne Rienner, 2001); Duane Murray Oldfield, *The Right and the Righteous: The Christian Right Confronts the Republican Party*, Religious Forces in the Modern Political World (Lanham, MD: Rowman and Littlefield, 1996); William J. Crotty, *Party Reform* (New York: Longman, 1983); John C. Green, James L. Guth, and Clyde Wilcox, "Less Than Conquerors: The Christian Right in State

Republican Parties," in *Social Movements and American Political Institutions*, ed. Anne N. Costain and Andrew S. McFarland (Lanham, MD: Rowman and Littlefield, 1998); William P. Cross, *Political Parties* (Vancouver: UBC Press, 2004); E. E. Schattschneider, *The Semi-Sovereign People* (Hinsdale, IL: Dryden Press, 1975).

65. Oldfield, *Right and the Righteous*; Thomas Frank, *What's the Matter with Kansas?* (New York: Macmillan, 2005).

66. Kenneth T. Andrews and Bob Edwards, "Advocacy Organizations in the U.S. Political Process," *Annual Review of Sociology* 30 (2004): 479–506; Marco Giugni, Doug McAdam, and Charles Tilly, *How Social Movements Matter* (Minneapolis: University of Minnesota Press, 1999); Edwin Amenta, *When Movements Matter: The Townsend Plan and the Rise of Social Security* (Princeton, NJ: Princeton University Press, 2006).

67. Frances Fox Piven and Richard Cloward, *Poor People's Movements: Why They Succeed, How They Fail* (New York: Random House, 1977); Michael Lipsky, "Protest as a Political Resource," *American Political Science Review* 62, no. 4 (1968): 1144–58; William A. Gamson, *The Strategy of Social Protest* (Homewood, IL: Dorsey Press, 1975); Kenneth T. Andrews, *Freedom Is a Constant Struggle: The Mississippi Civil Rights Movement and Its Legacy* (Chicago: University of Chicago Press, 2004).

68. Doug McAdam, "Political Opportunities: Conceptual Origins, Current Problems, Future Directions," in *Comparative Perspectives on Social Movements*, ed. Doug McAdam, John D. McCarthy, and Mayer N. Zald (Cambridge: Cambridge University Press, 1996), 23–40; Sidney Tarrow, *Power in Movement: Social Movements, Collective Action and Politics* (New York: Cambridge University Press, 1994); Jack Goldstone, "The Weakness of Organization: A New Look at Gamson's *The Strategy of Social Protest*," *American Journal of Sociology* 85 (1980): 1017–42; Kitschelt, "Political Opportunity Structures and Political Protest." For a critique of this approach, see Jeff Goodwin and James M. Jasper, "Caught in a Winding, Snarling Vine: The Structural Bias of Political Process Theory," *Sociological Forum* 14, no. 1 (1999): 27–54; Edwin Amenta and Drew Halfmann, "Opportunity Knocks: The Trouble with Political Opportunity and What You Can Do About It," in *Contention in Context: New Opportunities in Social Movement Research*, eds. Jeff Goodwin and James M. Jasper (Palo Alto: Stanford University Press, forthcoming); David S. Meyer and Debra C. Minkoff, "Conceptualizing Political Opportunity," *Social Forces* 82, no. 4 (2004): 1457–92; Jeff Goodwin and James M. Jasper, eds., *Contention in Context: New Opportunities in Social Movement Research* (Palo Alto: Stanford University Press, forthcoming).

69. Amenta also notes several more permanent political institutional factors that provided context for the American Townsend movement: the underdemocratized polities of the South, the patronage parties of the Northeast, the fragmentation of political authority, the difficulty of building third

parties in a winner-take-all electoral system, and the rightward skew of the major political parties. Amenta, *When Movements Matter*.

70. As Amenta defines them, assertive tactics include public protests and electoral challenges as opposed to educational and letter-writing campaigns. Ibid.

71. Gene Burns, *The Moral Veto: Framing Contraception, Abortion, and Cultural Pluralism in the United States* (Cambridge: Cambridge University Press, 2005).

72. In Canada, the 1960s reform was led by medical and legal interest groups—social movement organizations were not much of a factor. After reform, abortion became more controversial in all three countries as opposing movements expanded. Pro-life and pro-choice movements combined assertive and less assertive actions in all three countries. Initially, elected officials in all three countries sought to avoid the abortion issue. Institutions were key because, as I mentioned in the last section, American parties offered more opportunities for new movements to persuade, benefit, and sanction political parties and candidates. Both major American parties eventually embraced the issue. Once this occurred, partisanship, rather than movement tactics, became the best explanation for movement gains. The pro-life movement made significant policy gains mainly because of the electoral success of the Republican Party. Amenta argues that ballot initiatives are assertive actions because they usurp the prerogatives of elected officials. The move to the courts could perhaps be viewed similarly, but some legislators were probably happy to have the court take over the issue. Amenta does not pay much attention to courts as they were not particularly relevant to the Townsend movement, but he does note that they are often a veto point for social policies. Here, however, they were an access point. Amenta, *When Movements Matter*.

73. Jasper has criticized the framing concept in the social movement literature for its overemphasis on the strategic and intentional aspects of meaning making. And Skrentny argues that framing analysts ignore the numerous ways in which issue definitions and meanings result from the unconscious and uncoordinated activities of multiple actors. James M. Jasper, "The Emotions of Protest: Affective and Reactive Emotions in and around Social Movements," *Sociological Forum* 13, no. 3 (1998): 395–424; John D. Skrentny, *The Minority Rights Revolution* (Cambridge, MA: Belknap Press, Harvard University, 2002). See also John Kingdon, *Agendas, Alternatives, and Public Policies* (Boston: Little, Brown, 1984); Baumgartner and Jones, *Agendas and Instability in American Politics*; Joel Best, *Images of Issues: Typifying Contemporary Social Issues* (New York: Aldine de Gruyter, 1995); Deborah Stone, "Causal Stories and the Formation of Policy Agendas," *Political Science Quarterly* 104 (1989): 281–300; William H. Riker, *The Art of Political Manipulation* (New Haven, CT: Yale University Press, 1986); Gusfield, *Culture of Public Problems*; David A. Snow et al., "Frame Alignment Processes,

Micromobilization, and Movement Participation," *American Sociological Review* 51, no. 4 (1986): 464–81; William Gamson, *Talking Politics* (New York: Cambridge University Press, 1992); Margaret Weir, *Politics and Jobs: The Boundaries of Employment Policy in the United States* (Princeton, NJ: Princeton University Press, 1992); Erving Goffman, *Frame Analysis: An Essay on the Organization of Experience* (New York: Harper and Row, 1974).

74. Daniel M. Cress and David A. Snow, "The Outcomes of Homeless Mobilization: The Influence of Organization, Disruption, Political Mediation and Framing," *American Journal of Sociology* 105 (2000): 1063–1104.

75. This is reminiscent of Gamson's claim that "displacement" goals are counterproductive. Gamson, *Strategy of Social Protest*.

76. Luker, *Abortion and the Politics of Motherhood*; Burns, *Moral Veto*; William Saletan, *Bearing Right: How Conservatives Won the Abortion War* (Berkeley: University of California Press, 2004). See also Ferree et al., *Shaping Abortion Discourse*; Shaver, "Body Rights, Social Rights, and the Liberal Welfare State."

77. Frank R. Baumgartner and Bryan D. Jones, "Agenda Dynamics and Policy Subsystems," *Journal of Politics* 53, no. 4 (1991): 1044–74; Frank R. Baumgartner and Bryan D. Jones, eds., *Policy Dynamics* (Chicago: University of Chicago Press, 2002); Schattschneider, *Semi-Sovereign People*; Jasper, *Nuclear Politics*.

78. The conflict between constitutional courts and democracy can be overstated. Decisions made by elected officials may not be any more representative of majority views than those of courts. And much research shows that courts stay fairly close to the views of the majority as well as to those of the incumbents of other branches of government. Constitutional court judges are usually appointed by elected officials, and the constitutions on which they base their decisions are usually approved through democratic processes. Barry Friedman, "The Counter-Majoritarian Problem and the Pathology of Constitutional Scholarship," *Northwestern University Law Review* 95 (2000): 933; Mark C. Miller and Jeb Barnes, *Making Policy, Making Law: An Interbranch Perspective* (Washington, DC: Georgetown University Press, 2004); Stephen Holmes, "Gag Rules or the Politics of Omission," in *Constitutionalism and Democracy*, ed. Jon Elster and Rune Slagstad (Cambridge: Cambridge University Press, 1988), 19–58; Lee Epstein and Jack Knight, *The Choices Justices Make* (Washington, DC: Congressional Quarterly Press, 1998).

79. Kingdon, *Agendas, Alternatives, and Public Policies*; Baumgartner and Jones, *Agendas and Instability in American Politics*; Roger Cobb, Jeannie-Keith Ross, and Marc Howard Ross, "Agenda-Building as a Comparative Political Process," *American Political Science Review* 70, no. 1 (1976): 126–38; Roger W. Cobb and Charles D. Elder, *Participation in American Politics; the Dynamics of Agenda-Building* (Boston: Allyn and Bacon, 1972); Jack L. Walker, "Setting the Agenda in the U.S. Senate: A Theory of Problem Selection," *British*

Journal of Political Science 7 (1977): 423–45; Roy B. Flemming, John Bohte, and B. Dan Wood, "One Voice among Many: The Supreme Court's Influence on Attentiveness to Issues in the United States, 1947–92," *American Journal of Political Science* 41 (1997): 1224–50.

80. Jasper, "Emotions of Protest"; Edward J. Walsh, "Resource Mobilization and Citizen Protest in Communities around Three Mile Island," *Social Problems* 29 (1981): 1–21; Jeff Goodwin, James M. Jasper, and Francesca Polletta, "The Return of the Repressed: The Fall and Rise of Emotions in Social Movement Theory," *Mobilization* 5, no. 1 (2000): 65–84.

81. Paul Burstein, "Is the Welfare State a Bad Idea?," *Contemporary Sociology* 21, no. 4 (1992): 451–53; Cass R. Sunstein, *After the Rights Revolution: Reconceiving the Regulatory State* (Cambridge, MA: Harvard University Press, 1990); Scheppele, "Constitutionalizing Abortion."

82. Scheppele, "Constitutionalizing Abortion." The constraints and limitations of constitutional discourse should not be overstated since judges reshape and reinterpret constitutional texts over time and creatively use them in ways that might have shocked the founders. Mary Ann Glendon argues that Americans are especially likely to frame issues in terms of rights and that they speak a particular dialect of rights talk. This dialect is characterized by absolute, exaggerated formulations; silence about responsibilities; overattention to individual independence and self-sufficiency; neglect of the intermediate institutions of civil society; and insulation from legal discourses in other countries. She also suggests that Anglo-American law is less pedagogical and communitarian than continental European law. The former produces morally neutral, absolutist law while the latter produces morally engaged, compromise law. Mary Ann Glendon, *Rights Talk* (New York: Free Press, 1991). For a critique, see Samuel Walker, *The Rights Revolution: Rights and Community in Modern America* (New York: Oxford University Press, 1998); Holmes, "Gag Rules or the Politics of Omission"; Glendon, *Abortion and Divorce in Western Law*. Court decisions can have both positive and negative effects on social movement mobilization. They can serve as discursive resources for the construction of injustice claims and collective identities. But movement litigation can also inhibit other types of mobilization by sucking up scarce resources and hindering the development of broad-based, multi-issue movements. Litigation also requires the involvement of professionals who may inhibit disruptive action. Finally, court "victories" may lead to movement demobilization, as winners consider an issue settled, while court "losses" may lead to movement mobilization, as losers are motivated to action. Stuart A. Scheingold, *The Politics of Rights: Lawyers, Public Policy, and Political Change* (Ann Arbor: University of Michigan Press, 2004); Piven and Cloward, *Poor People's Movements*; Gerald N. Rosenberg, *The Hollow Hope: Can Courts Bring About Social Change?* (Chicago: University of Chicago Press, 1991); Michael McCann, *Rights at Work: Reform and the Politics of Legal Mobilization* (Chicago: University of Chicago

Press, 1994); Nicholas Pedriana and Robin Stryker, "Political Culture Wars 1960s Style: Equal Employment Opportunity-Affirmative Action Law and the Philadelphia Plan," *American Journal of Sociology* 103, no. 3 (1997): 633–91.

83. For an excellent discussion of conflicts between constitutionalism and democracy, see Jon Elster and Rune Slagstad, *Constitutionalism and Democracy*, Studies in Rationality and Social Change (Cambridge: Cambridge University Press, 1988).

84. Since 1988, British courts have also had the power to declare that an Act of Parliament is incompatible with human rights. Such a declaration does not invalidate the Act but puts pressure on Parliament to change it. The Constitutional Reform Act of 2005 created the Supreme Court of the United Kingdom, which began operation in 2009. Lord Irvine of Lairg, "Sovereignty in Comparative Perspective: Constitutionalism in Britain and America," in *The Unpredictable Constitution*, ed. Norman Dorsen (New York: New York University Press, 2002); James T. McHugh, *Comparative Constitutional Traditions*, Teaching Texts in Law and Politics, vol. 27 (New York: P. Lang, 2002).

85. Alexis de Tocqueville, *Democracy in America*, ed. and trans. Harvey C. Mansfield and Delba Winthrop (Chicago: University of Chicago Press, 2000), 257.

86. Robert A. Kagan, *Adversarial Legalism: The American Way of Law* (Cambridge, MA: Harvard University Press, 2001); Charles R. Epp, *The Rights Revolutions: Lawyers, Activists, and Supreme Courts in Comparative Perspective* (Chicago: University of Chicago Press, 1998).

87. Rosenberg further argues that significant change occurs only when there is ample precedent, when other branches of government support it, when some of the public supports it or nobody opposes it, and when one of the following methods of implementation is available: The court offers inducements or imposes sanctions, markets promote implementation, or other branches of government wish to leverage or hide behind court decisions. Rosenberg, *Hollow Hope*.

88. Neal Devins, "Judicial Matters," *California Law Review* 80 (1992): 1027–69. For a response to his critics, see Gerald N. Rosenberg, *Ideological Preferences and Hollow Hopes: Responding to Criticism* (Chicago: University of Chicago Press, 2008).

89. Paul Frymer, *Black and Blue: African Americans, the Labor Movement, and the Decline of the Democratic Party* (Princeton, NJ: Princeton University Press, 2007); Paul Frymer, "Acting When Elected Officials Won't: Federal Courts and Civil Rights Enforcement in U.S. Labor Unions, 1935–85," *American Political Science Review* 97, no. 03 (2003): 483–99; Mark A. Graber, "The Nonmajoritarian Difficulty: Legislative Deference to the Judiciary," *Studies in American Political Development* 7, no. 1 (1993): 35–73; Cohan, "Abortion as a Marginal Issue."

90. Glendon, *Rights Talk*.

91. Huber, Ragin, and Stephens, "Social Democracy, Christian Democracy, Constitutional Structure and the Welfare State"; Samuel P. Huntington, *Political Order in Changing Societies* (New Haven, CT: Yale University Press, 1968); Orloff and Skocpol, "Why Not Equal Protection?"; Immergut, *Health Politics*.
92. Amenta, *Bold Relief*.
93. New State Ice Co. v. Liebmann, 285 U.S. 262, 280 (1932) (Brandeis, J., dissenting); Jack L. Walker, "The Diffusion of Innovations among the American States," *American Political Science Review* 63 (1969): 880–99; Pierre Trudeau, "The Practice and Theory of Federalism," in *Federalism and the French Canadians*, ed. Pierre Trudeau (Toronto: Macmillan of Canada, 1968); Alan G. Cairns, "The Government and Societies of Canadian Federalism," *Canadian Journal of Political Science* 10, no. 4 (1977): 695–725; Alan G. Cairns, "The Other Crisis in Canadian Federalism," *Canadian Public Administration* 22 (1979): 175–95; Gwendolyn Gray, *Federalism and Health Policy: The Development of Health Systems in Canada and Australia* (Toronto: University of Toronto Press, 1991); Meyer and Staggenborg, "Countermovement Dynamics in Federal Systems"; Tatalovich, *Politics of Abortion*; Schattschneider, *Semi-Sovereign People*.
94. Private member's bills exist in both Britain and Canada, but are far more important in the former.
95. These bills are usually technical and uncontroversial and pass without objection. Though introduced by backbenchers, these bills usually originate within the Government or are based on Government reports or the findings of the Law Commission (an independent body of lawyers appointed to advise the Lord Chancellor on legal reform). Private member's bills cannot be mainly concerned with government expenditure, and if they involve incidental expenditures, these must be approved by a minister. David Marsh and Melvyn Read, *Private Member's Bills* (Cambridge: Cambridge University Press, 1988).
96. In Britain, debate for all private member's bills is limited to Fridays and thus a mere sixty hours. MPs who are opposed to a specific private member's bill will often try to filibuster. The sponsor can call for a closure vote, but one hundred votes are required. There are three types of private member's bills—Balloted, Standing Order 39, and ten-minute-rule. Bills go through five stages in the House of Commons—First Reading (introduction), Second Reading (initial debate), Committee, Report, and Third Reading (final debate). Balloted bills are introduced by about twenty backbenchers who win a private member's bill lottery. Standing Order 39 bills may be introduced by any backbencher, but can only receive their Second Reading after all of the balloted bills for a given day have been considered. Ten-minute-rule bills may also be introduced by any backbencher. Upon introduction (First Reading) of these bills, the sponsor is entitled to make a ten-minute speech in favor of the bill, which may be followed by

a ten-minute opposing speech. If an opposing speech is given, a vote is taken on whether the bill should be given a Second Reading. Like Standing Order 39 bills, ten-minute-rule bills may receive their Second Reading only after consideration of the balloted bills for a given day. Bills automatically move to Committee stage unless a single member objects. Once a member objects, however, the bill must gain a majority in a Second Reading vote to proceed. But such a vote can occur only if there is time available in a given day. Otherwise, it will be held over for another day. Given these rules, Standing Order 39 and ten-minute-rule bills usually run out of time unless they are completely unopposed. In Britain, since 1959, no private member's bill has passed that was opposed by a single MP at Second or Third Reading and that did not receive extra time from the Government. In Canada, most private member's bills get only an hour of debate. If no decision is made within an hour, the bill falls to the bottom of the list and usually never returns to the chamber. There are less than one hundred hours for debate on private member's bills in each session. During the twenty-eighth Parliament (1968–72), there were 639 private member's bills. Only 22 were enacted, and all involved naming such things as electoral districts, banks, and "national pollution week." R. V. Stewart Hyson, "The Role of the Backbencher: An Analysis of Private Members' Bills in the Canadian House of Commons," *Parliamentary Affairs* 3, no. 3 (1974): 262–72; Philip Cowley, *Conscience and Parliament* (London: Frank Cass, 1998); Marsh and Read, *Private Member's Bills*. In Britain's House of Lords, any member can introduce a private member's bill (there is no lottery) and there is no time limit for debate, but such a bill can become law only if it is taken up by a member of the Commons who has won a place in the lottery. *Promoting a Private Member's Bill in the House: A Guide for Members* (London: Public Bill Office, House of Lords, October, 2001).

97. Cowley, *Conscience and Parliament*; Keith Hindell and Madeline Simms, *Abortion Law Reformed* (London: Peter Owen, 1971); Colin Francome, *Abortion Freedom: A Worldwide Movement* (Winchester, MA: Allen and Unwin, 1984); Barbara Brookes, *Abortion in England, 1900–1967* (London: Croom Helm, 1988); Marsh and Read, *Private Member's Bills*; Hyson, "The Role of the Backbencher"; McKeown and Lundie, "Free Votes in Australian and Some Overseas Parliaments"; Philip Cowley, "Unbridled Passions? Free Votes, Issues of Conscience and the Accountability of British Members of Parliament," *Journal of Legislative Studies* 4, no. 2 (1998): 70–88.
98. Peter G. Richards, *Parliament and Conscience* (London: George Allen and Unwin, 1971); Cohan, "Abortion as a Marginal Issue"; Cowley, *Conscience and Parliament*.
99. Roger Freeman, quoted in Cowley, *Conscience and Parliament*, 181.
100. Even within the context of a free vote, the Government has extensive power to defeat private member's bill legislation that it opposes without utilizing formal party machinery. It can orchestrate opposition among

members of the Government, arrange a filibuster, urge a member to withdraw his or her measure in exchange for some concession such as the creation of a commission, or seek amendments to a bill in the Committee stage. In the postwar period, only seven private member's bills that were opposed by the Government passed. Richards, *Parliament and Conscience*; Marsh and Read, *Private Member's Bills*.

101. The Government can even go so far as to solicit an MP to introduce a private member's bill, aid its passage by providing extra time, and then disclaim responsibility—the party did not introduce the bill, remained neutral, allowed free voting, and gave extra time only to guarantee full consideration of the issue.
102. Marsh and Read, *Private Member's Bills*; Keith Archer, *Parameters of Power: Canada's Political Institutions* (Toronto: Nelson Canada, 1995); Cowley, "Unbridled Passions?"
103. Liberal Democrat MP Evan Harris in *Guardian*, July 11, 2008.
104. As Philip Cowley puts it, "in a system in which voters overwhelmingly vote for parties and not MPs . . . free votes allow controversial issues to become detached from the electoral process. However controversial they are, free vote issues vanish from the political radar at election time." As a result, "free votes effectively allow the party in government to enact controversial legislation while simultaneously denying all responsibility for that legislation." Philip Cowley, "Party Rules," *Progress*, May 14, 2008, http://www.progressonline.org.uk/articles/article.asp?a=2776.
105. James Mahoney, "Nominal, Ordinal, and Narrative Appraisal in Macro-Causal Analysis," *American Journal of Sociology* 104, no. 4 (1999): 1155. See also James Mahoney and Dietrich Rueschmeyer, *Comparative Historical Analysis in the Social Sciences* (Cambridge: Cambridge University Press, 2003); Theda Skocpol and Margaret Somers, "The Uses of Comparative History in Macro-Social Research," *Comparative Studies in Society and History* 22 (1980): 174–97.
106. I also seek to develop concepts that are equivalent across cases. These need to be abstract enough to serve my analytical purposes across cases and, at the same time, particular enough to be meaningful within cases. Julia Adams, Elisabeth Clemens, and Ann Shola Orloff, "Social Theory, Modernity, and the Three Waves of Historical Sociology" (Working Paper #206, Russell Sage Foundation, New York, 2003); Clifford Geertz, *The Interpretation of Cultures* (New York: Basic Books, 1973); Dietrich Rueschmeyer, "Can One or a Few Cases Yield Theoretical Gains?," in *Comparative Historical Analysis in the Social Sciences*, ed. James Mahoney and Dietrich Rueschmeyer (Cambridge: Cambridge University Press, 2003), 305–36.
107. O'Connor, Orloff, and Shaver, "Body Rights, Social Rights, and Reproductive Choice."
108. James Mahoney, "Strategies of Causal Assessment in Comparative and Historical Analysis," in Mahoney and Rueschmeyer, *Comparative Historical*

Analysis in the Social Sciences, 337–72; Adam Przeworski and Henry Teune, *The Logic of Comparative Social Inquiry* (New York: John Wiley, 1970); Carsten Anckar, "On the Applicability of the Most Similar Systems Design and the Most Different Systems Design in Comparative Research," *International Journal of Social Research Methodology* 11, no. 5 (2008): 389–401.
109. Castles, *Families of Nations*.
110. See also Esping-Andersen, *Three Worlds of Welfare Capitalism*.
111. Ibid. O'Connor, Orloff, and Shaver, *States, Markets, Families*; Mary Ruggie, *Realignments in the Welfare State: Health Policy in the United States, Britain, and Canada* (New York: Columbia University Press, 1996); Siaroff, "Work, Welfare, and Gender Equality."
112. Donald T. Campbell, "'Degrees of Freedom' and the Case Study," *Comparative Political Studies* 8 (1975): 178–93; Andrew Bennett, "Lost in the Translation: Big (N) Misinterpretations of Case Study Research" (paper presented at the thirty-eighth Annual Convention of the International Studies Association, Toronto, March 1997); Henry E. Brady and David Collier, *Rethinking Social Inquiry: Diverse Tools, Shared Standards* (Lanham, MD: Rowman and Littlefield, 2004); Michael Coppedge, "Thickening Thin Concepts and Theories: Combining Large N and Small in Comparative Politics," *Comparative Politics* 31, no. 4 (1999): 465–76.
113. Coppedge, "Thickening Thin Concepts and Theories," 472.
114. Jack A. Goldstone, "Comparative Historical Analysis and Knowledge Accumulation in the Study of Revolutions," in Mahoney and Rueschmeyer, *Comparative Historical Analysis in the Social Sciences*, 47.
115. Mahoney and Rueschmeyer, *Comparative Historical Analysis in the Social Sciences*; Alexander L. George and Timothy J. McKeown, "Case Studies and Theories of Organizational Decision-Making," *Advances in Information Processing in Organizations* 2 (1985): 21–58; Charles Tilly, *Mechanisms in Political Processes* (New York: Columbia University, 2000); Peter Hedstrom and Richard Swedberg, *Social Mechanisms: An Analytical Approach to Social Theory* (Cambridge: Cambridge University Press, 1998); Bennett, "Lost in the Translation"; Charles Tilly, "To Explain Political Processes," *American Journal of Sociology* 100 (1995): 1594–610; Peter A. Hall, "Aligning Ontology and Methodology in Comparative Research," in Mahoney and Rueschmeyer, *Comparative Historical Analysis in the Social Sciences*, 373–404; Coppedge, "Thickening Thin Concepts and Theories," 472. I pursue pattern matching and process tracing through "strategic narrative." According to Jack Goldstone, "Strategic narrative differs from a straightforward narrative of historical events by being structured to focus attention on how patterns of events relate to prior theoretical beliefs about social phenomena. . . . Sometimes such narratives are designed to demonstrate strict causal connections between elements in a sequence of events . . . , sometimes they are designed to demonstrate the impact of contingency or path dependency in producing divergent or unexpected outcomes. Either way, the

NOTES TO PAGES 32–36

narrative marshals evidence that particular sequences or patterns unfolded in a particular way, for particular reasons, and it relates those data to our confidence in the existing theory." Goldstone, "Comparative Historical Analysis and Knowledge," 50–51. See also Robin Stryker, "Beyond History Versus Theory: Strategic Narrative and Sociological Explanation," *Sociological Methods and Research* 24, no. 3 (1996): 304–52.

116. Coppedge, "Thickening Thin Concepts and Theories," 472.
117. For exemplars of this approach, see Theda Skocpol, *States and Social Revolutions: A Comparative Analysis of France, Russia, and China* (Cambridge: Cambridge University Press, 1979); Orloff and Skocpol, "Why Not Equal Protection?"

CHAPTER TWO

1. In Britain and Canada, abortions for reasons of health were allowed by the 1938 English court decision *Rex v. Bourne*. In the United States, abortions were permissible to preserve the life of the mother in forty-two states. Five states and the District of Columbia had broader grounds: to preserve the life or health of the mother (Alabama, District of Columbia, Oregon), to save the life of the mother or to prevent serious or permanent bodily injury to her (Colorado, New Mexico), when a physician was "satisfied that the fetus is dead, or that no other method will secure the safety of the mother (Maryland). Finally, in three states, physicians violated the law only if they performed an abortion "unlawfully" (Massachusetts, Pennsylvania) or "maliciously or without lawful justification" (New Jersey). Precedents suggested that these latter statutes would be applied liberally to a licensed physician acting in good faith to preserve the life or health of the pregnant woman. Even in states that allowed abortions only to protect the mother's life, doctors often argued that the preservation of health extended life or that abortions for mental health grounds prevented suicide. J. M. Kummer and Z. Leavy, "Criminal Abortion—a Consideration of Ways to Reduce Incidence," *California Medicine* 95, no. 3 (1961): 170.
2. Carole E. Joffe, *Doctors of Conscience: The Struggle to Provide Abortion: Before and After* Roe v. Wade (Boston: Beacon Press, 1995); Elizabeth Kathleen Lane, *Report of the Committee on the Working of the Abortion Act*, Great Britain. Parliament. (London: Her Majesty's Stationery Office, 1974); Robin F. Badgley, Denyse Fortin Caron, and Marion G. Powell, *Report of the Committee on the Operation of the Abortion Law* (Ottawa: Minister of Supply and Services Canada, 1977).
3. In general, social grounds include such things as being poor, unmarried, too young or too old, or having too many children. The specific British social grounds are detailed below.
4. With no good tests for pregnancy, doctors could not distinguish between pregnancy and menstrual blockage, and the treatment for the latter was

NOTES TO PAGES 37-38

identical to abortion. Doctors could not know with certainty whether they were treating menstrual blockage or providing an early abortion, but in the interest of keeping their patients, they were wise not to ask too many questions. Michael Thomson, "The Doctor, the Profession, His Patient, and Her Abortion," in *Reproducing Narrative: Gender, Reproduction, and Law* (Hants, England: Ashgate, 1998); James C. Mohr, *Abortion in America: The Origins and Evolution of National Policy* (New York: Oxford University Press, 1978).

5. Thomson, "The Doctor, the Profession, His Patient, and Her Abortion"; Mohr, *Abortion in America*.
6. The death penalty was reserved for abortions after quickening. In addition, only abortions by drugs, not surgical ones, were illegal after quickening. This apparently unintentional loophole was corrected in 1828.
7. Victoria Greenwood and Jock Young, *Abortion in Demand* (London: Pluto Press, 1976); Keith Hindell and Madeline Simms, *Abortion Law Reformed* (London: Peter Owen, 1971); Anthony Hordern, *Legal Abortion: The English Experience* (Oxford: Pergamon Press, 1971); Thomson, "The Doctor, the Profession, His Patient, and Her Abortion"; John Keown, *Abortion, Doctors, and the Law:Some Aspects of the Legal Regulation of Abortion in England from 1803 to 1982* (Cambridge: Cambridge University Press, 1988); Barbara Brookes, *Abortion in England, 1900–1967* (London: Croom Helm, 1988); Mohr, *Abortion in America*.
8. Gayle Davis and Richard Davidson, "'Big White Chief,' 'Pontius Pilate,' and The 'Plumber': The Impact of the 1967 Abortion Act on the Scottish Medical Community, c. 1967–1980," *Social History of Medicine* 18, no. 2 (2005): 283–306; Gayle Davis and Roger Davidson, "'A Fifth Freedom' or 'Hideous Atheistic Expediency'? The Medical Community and Abortion Law Reform in Scotland, c. 1960–1975," *Medical History* 50, no. 1 (2006): 29–48.
9. By Joseph Reeves in 1953, Lord Amulree in 1954, Kenneth Robinson in 1961, Renee Short in 1965, Lord Silkin in 1965, and Simon Wingfield Digby in 1966.
10. Silkin's bills allowed abortions with the approval of a single doctor for grounds of physical or mental health, economic hardship, rape, mental disability, or underage pregnancy.
11. Only a few people recognized the possible consequences of the amendment at the time. ALRA leader Diane Munday was one of them: "The real implications hit me as soon as the amendment was proposed and I nearly fell out of the gallery of the House of Lords with excitement and disbelief." Some abortion opponents also recognized this potential, arguing that the amendment might lead to "abortion on demand" if abortion later became safer than childbirth. Greenwood and Young, *Abortion in Demand*; Diane Munday, "Talking about Abortion," in *A Celebration of 25 Years of Safe Legal Abortion, 1967–1992* (London: National Abortion Campaign, 1992), 9.
12. British Medical Association, "Proceedings of Council: Therapeutic Abortion," *British Medical Journal Supplement*, January 22, 1966; "Leading

Articles: Therapeutic Abortion," *British Medical Journal*, January 29, 1966; "Leading Articles: Legislation on Abortion," *British Medical Journal*, March 5, 1966; "B.M.A.'s Views on Abortion," *Lancet*, July 2, 1966; Hindell and Simms, *Abortion Law Reformed*; Keith Cuninghame, "Research Note: Abortion (Amendment) Bill 1987–88" (London: House of Commons Library Research Division, 1988); Keown, *Abortion, Doctors, and the Law*.

13. Maureen Muldoon, *The Abortion Debate in the United States and Canada: A Source Book* (New York: Garland, 1991); Janine Brodie, Shelley A. M. Gavigan, and Jane Jenson, *The Politics of Abortion* (Toronto: Oxford University Press, 1992).

14. Ian Wahn's (Liberal) 1966 bill allowed abortion for grounds of life and health. Grace MacInnis's (NDP) 1967 bill allowed abortion for life, health, mental health, fetal abnormality, and rape or incest. H. W. Herridge's (NDP) 1967 bill mimicked the British Abortion Act, allowing abortion for life, health, mental health, fetal abnormality, and the health of existing children in the family. When the standing committee issued its report in December 1967, it supported Wahn's more conservative bill. The Government's bill included the grounds suggested by the committee but substituted the word "likely" for "seriously," thus liberalizing it slightly.

15. Alphonse de Valk, "Abortion in Canada, 1960–66," in *Death before Birth*, ed. E. J. Kremer and E. A. Synan (Toronto: Griffin House, 1974); Jane Jenson, "Getting to Morgentaler: From One Representation to Another," in Brodie, Gavigan, and Jenson, *Politics of Abortion*; Eleanor Wright Pelrine, *Abortion in Canada* (Toronto: New Press, 1971); Frederick Lee Morton, *Pro-Choice vs. Pro-Life: Abortion and the Courts in Canada* (Norman: University of Oklahoma Press, 1992).

16. Criminal Code, 1968–69 (Eliz. II) (1969), 17–18, ch. 38, s. 18 (Can.).

17. The president of the Ontario Medical Association, Dr. John Walters, agreed, "[Abortion committees] will base their decisions on a conservative interpretation of what constitutes a danger to life and health. Doctors are not trained to weigh economic or social factors." *Toronto Star*, July 5, 1969; Canada House of Commons, House of Commons Debates (Hansard) (Ottawa: v.d.), 8397, May 6, 1969.

18. Sharon Walls, "Abortion Law and Improved Abortion Services: Discussion Paper" (Ottawa: National Association of Women and the Law, National Archives of Canada, Record Group 29, 1990-91/248, Box 31, File 0154-A1 vol. 2, 1982).

19. Even the most ardent antiabortion physicians resisted attempts to better specify therapeutic exceptions or monitor doctors' compliance with it. The writings of prominent antiabortion physicians as well as various accounts of abortion in medical journals indicate that the exception was often defined broadly, for example, to include threats to women's physical or mental health, as well as cases of rape, incest, or "fetal deformity." Kristin Luker, *Abortion and the Politics of Motherhood* (Berkeley: University of

NOTES TO PAGES 39–40

California Press, 1984); U.S. Public Health Service, *Family Planning Evaluation: Abortion Surveillance Report—Legal Abortions, United States, Annual Summary, 1970* (Atlanta: U.S. Public Health Service, Center for Disease Control, Department of Health, Education, and Welfare, 1970).

20. Mohr, *Abortion in America*; Luker, *Abortion and the Politics of Motherhood*; Gene Burns, *The Moral Veto: Framing Contraception, Abortion, and Cultural Pluralism in the United States* (Cambridge: Cambridge University Press, 2005); Thomson, "The Doctor, the Profession, His Patient, and Her Abortion."

21. Mohr, *Abortion in America*; "Abortion: The Doctor's Dilemma," *Modern Medicine*, April 24, 1967; Luker, *Abortion and the Politics of Motherhood*; Jonathan B. Imber, *Abortion and the Private Practice of Medicine* (New Haven, CT: Yale University Press, 1986); Leslie J. Reagan, *When Abortion Was a Crime: Women, Medicine, and Law in the United States, 1867–1973* (Berkeley: University of California Press, 1997); Rosalind Pollack Petchesky, *Abortion and Woman's Choice: The State, Sexuality, and Reproductive Freedom* (New York: Longman, 1984); Jenson, "Getting to Morgentaler."

22. Joseph W. Dellapenna, *Dispelling the Myths of Abortion History* (Durham, NC: Carolina Academic Press, 2005).

23. In 1952, the ALI began drafting a model penal code. Its council considered abortion provisions in 1956, and its membership approved them in 1959 and 1962. American Law Institute, Model Penal Code: Council Draft No. 10 (Philadelphia: American Law Institute, 1956); American Law Institute, Model Penal Code: Tentative Draft No. 9 (Philadelphia: American Law Institute, 1959); Herbert Wechsler, "Codification of Criminal Law in the United States: The Model Penal Code," *Columbia Law Review* 68, no. 8 (1968): 1425–49; Lee Epstein and Joseph F. Kobylka, *The Supreme Court and Legal Change: Abortion and the Death Penalty* (Chapel Hill: University of North Carolina Press, 1992); Mary Calderone, *Abortion in the United States* (New York: Paul Hoeber, 1958).

24. "American Law Institute Abortion Policy" in *Before* Roe v. Wade: *Voices That Shaped the Abortion Debate before the Supreme Court's Ruling*, ed. Linda Greenhouse and Reva Siegel (New York: Kaplan, 2010), 25; American Law Institute, Model Penal Code: Tentative Draft No. 9; Wechsler, "Codification of Criminal Law in the United States"; American Law Institute, *Model Penal Code and Commentaries, Part II* (Philadelphia: American Law Institute, 1980); American Law Institute, *Model Penal Code and Commentaries, Part I* (Philadelphia: American Law Institute, 1985); Reagan, *When Abortion Was a Crime*; Charles M. Cook, *The American Codification Movement: A Study of Antebellum Legal Reform* (Westport, CT: Greenwood Press, 1981); Joseph W. Dellapenna, *Dispelling the Myths of Abortion History* (Durham, NC: Carolina Academic Press, 2005).

25. The author of the ALI's sexual offenses provisions, University of Pennsylvania Law Professor Louis B. Schwartz, later criticized the ALI abortion provisions. He argued that the ALI's general approach to morality laws and

unenforceable criminal liabilities supported a broader revision of abortion law along the lines of Danish and Swedish law, which allowed abortions for grounds of economic hardship. Schwartz suggested that the ALI had sacrificed a broader abortion reform to avoid offending the Catholic Church and jeopardizing the legislative prospects of the code as a whole. The code's language on abortion said: "A licensed physician is justified in terminating a pregnancy if he believes there is substantial risk that continuance of the pregnancy would gravely impair the physical or mental health of the mother or that the child would be born with grave physical or mental defect, or that the pregnancy resulted from rape, incest, or other felonious intercourse. All illicit intercourse with a girl below the age of 16 shall be deemed felonious for purposes of this subsection. Justifiable abortions shall be performed only in a licensed hospital except in case of emergency when hospital facilities are unavailable." American Law Institute Model Penal Code, 230.3 Proposed Official Draft, 1962; Louis B. Schwartz, "Morals Offenses and the Model Penal Code," *Columbia Law Review* 63 (1963): 669.

26. The 1961 New Hampshire bill merely added a life endangerment ground, which had perhaps been omitted by a printer's mistake from the nineteenth-century law. The bill was introduced at the behest of the state medical society and passed both houses, but was vetoed by the governor after opposition from the Catholic Church. David J. Garrow, *Liberty and Sexuality: The Right to Privacy and the Making of* Roe v. Wade (New York: Macmillan, 1994).

27. In 1966 California medical examiners attempted to discipline nine doctors who performed abortions on grounds of fetal abnormality, but backed off after public objections by prominent figures in academic medicine. *Los Angeles Times*, November 18, 1966, 11B; Garrow, *Liberty and Sexuality*.

28. *Wall Street Journal*, November 9, 1972, 4; May 15, 1972, 24; Mary C. Segers and Timothy A. Byrnes, "Introduction: Abortion Politics in American States," in *Abortion Politics in American States*, ed. Mary C. Segers and Timothy A. Byrnes (Armonk, NY: M. E. Sharpe, 1995), 1–15; Burns, *Moral Veto*; Lawrence Lader, *Abortion II: Making the Revolution* (Boston: Beacon Press, 1973).

29. Greenhouse and Siegel, *Before* Roe v. Wade.

30. Oregon's reform included language from a May 1968 resolution of the American College of Obstetricians that was itself borrowed from the British reform. As doctors assessed the pregnant woman's health, they could take account of "the mother's total environment, actual or reasonably forseeable." Garrow, *Liberty and Sexuality*.

31. Raymond Tatalovich and Byron W. Daynes, *The Politics of Abortion: A Study of Community Conflict in Public Policy Making* (New York: Praeger, 1981).

32. Burns, *Moral Veto*; U.S. Public Health Service, *Family Planning Evaluation*.

33. United States v. Vuitch, 402 U.S. 62 (1971). *Vuitch* was actually a victory for the pro-choice movement because the Supreme Court ruled that "health" included mental health.

34. Roe v. Wade, 410 U.S. 113 (1973); Doe v. Bolton, 410 U.S. 179 (1973). See Eva R. Rubin, *Abortion Politics and the Courts* (New York: Greenwood Press, 1987); Garrow, *Liberty and Sexuality*; Mark A. Graber, *Rethinking Abortion: Equal Choice, the Constitution, and Reproductive Politics* (Princeton, NJ: Princeton University Press, 1996); Leon Epstein, "British Mass Parties in Comparison with American Parties," *Political Science Quarterly* 71, no. 1 (1956): 97–125; Burns, *Moral Veto*; Lader, *Abortion II*.
35. Greenhouse and Siegel, *Before* Roe v. Wade, 226.
36. The designation of the second trimester as the "compelling" point where the state could begin to regulate abortion rested on the fact that mortality rates for first trimester abortions were lower than those for childbirth.
37. Roe v. Wade, 410 U.S. at 164–65.
38. Doe v. Bolton, 410 U.S. at 192.
39. Betty Friedan's *The Feminine Mystique* (New York: Norton, 1963) was especially influential.
40. Greenhouse and Siegel, *Before* Roe v. Wade; Hindell and Simms, *Abortion Law Reformed*; Lader, *Abortion II*; Alphonse de Valk, *Morality and Law in Canadian Politics: The Abortion Controversy* (Montreal: Palm, 1974).
41. Abortion reached the governmental agenda in Canada in part because of the 1967 British reform. The U.S. Supreme Court's *Roe* decision referred to the treatment of abortion under English common law and to the 1967 British abortion reform. British and Canadian movements borrowed the designations "pro-choice" and "pro-life" from the United States.
42. Here, I mean the classical liberalism of Locke and Hobbes rather than the American usage in which "liberal" is one side of the conservative-liberal, left-right, Democratic-Republican divide. Anthony King, "Ideas, Institutions, and Policies of Governments," *British Journal of Poltical Science* 3, no. 4 (1974): 291–313; Gaston Rimlinger, *Welfare Policy and Industrialization in Europe, America, and Russia* (New York: Wiley, 1971); Samuel P. Huntington, *American Politics: The Promise of Disharmony* (Cambridge, MA: Belknap Press, 1981); Seymour Martin Lipset, *American Exceptionalism* (New York: W. W. Norton, 1996); John W. Kingdon, *America the Unusual* (New York: Worth, 1999).
43. Laurence Tribe critiques Glendon's suggestion that European-style abortion compromises are applicable to the United States, arguing that such compromises would violate American traditions of individual rights and the rule of law, and that discretion in the American context often produces race and class inequality. Laurence H. Tribe, *Abortion: The Clash of Absolutes* (New York: W. W. Norton, 1990).
44. All three countries were heavily influenced by the thought of Thomas Hobbes, John Locke, and John Stuart Mill. But Glendon argues that U.S. Supreme Court Justices Oliver Wendell Holmes Jr. and Louis Brandeis imported liberal legal values from England in a particularly radical form. Mary

Ruggie, *Realignments in the Welfare State: Health Policy in the United States, Britain, and Canada* (New York: Columbia University Press, 1996); Gosta Esping-Andersen, *Three Worlds of Welfare Capitalism* (Princeton, NJ: Princeton University Press, 1990); Julia S. O'Connor, Ann Shola Orloff, and Sheila Shaver, *States, Markets, Families: Gender, Liberalism, and Social Policy in Australia, Canada, Great Britain, and the United States* (Cambridge: Cambridge University Press, 1999); Mary Ann Glendon, *Abortion and Divorce in Western Law* (Cambridge, MA: Harvard University Press, 1987). Tatalovich, following Lipset, suggests that because Canadians are more collectivist and defer more to elites (i.e., are less classically liberal than Americans) they might show greater deference to abortion laws. But he rejects this hypothesis when he finds that Canadian and American hospitals were equally slow to provide abortions. What is most interesting here is that liberal values can be used to explain both support for permissive abortion laws (Glendon) and resistance to them (Tatalovich). This underscores the multivocality of liberal values and the difficulty of using them to explain policy differences. Raymond Tatalovich, *The Politics of Abortion in the United States and Canada: A Comparative Study* (Armonk, NY: M. E. Sharpe, 1997); S. M. Lipset, *Continental Divide* (New York: Routledge, 1990).

45. Social movements also shape public opinion and issue salience and communicate this information to policy makers. Activists try to convince policy makers of the intensity of their members, the utility of their issue for building electoral coalitions, and the potential of particular policy proposals to mobilize their members. Susan Herbst, *Reading Public Opinion: How Political Actors View the Democratic Process*, Studies in Communication, Media, and Public Opinion (Chicago: University of Chicago Press, 1998).
46. Connie de Boer, "The Polls: Abortion," *Public Opinion Quarterly* 41, no. 4 (1977): 553–64.
47. Mark Evers and Jeanne McGee, "The Trend and Pattern in Attitudes toward Abortion in the United States, 1965–1977," *Social Indicators Research* 7, no. 1 (1980): 251–67.
48. "Do you believe that there should be no legal restraint on getting an abortion—that is, if a woman wants one she need only consult her doctor, or do you believe that the law should specify what kinds of circumstances justify abortion." J. Blake, "The Supreme Court's Abortion Decisions and Public Opinion in the United States," *Population and Development Review* 3, no. 1/2 (1977): 50.
49. Monica Boyd and Dierdre Gillieson, "Canadian Attitudes on Abortion: Results of the Gallup Polls," *Canadian Studies in Population* 2 (1975): 53–64.
50. Ann Shola Orloff and Theda Skocpol, "Why Not Equal Protection? Explaining the Politics of Public Social Spending in Britain, 1900–1911 and in the United States, 1880s–1920s," *American Journal of Sociology* 49 (1984): 726–50; Herbert McClosky and John Zaller, *The American Ethos* (Cambridge, MA: Harvard University Press, 1984).

51. Sven Steinmo, "American Exceptionalism Reconsidered: Culture or Institutions?," in *The Dynamics of American Politics: Approaches and Institutions*, ed. Lawrence C. Dodd and Calvin Jillson (Boulder, CO: Westview Press, 1993), 106–31; Ann Swidler, "Culture in Action: Symbols and Strategies," *American Sociological Review* 51, no. 2 (1986): 273–86; Lawrence R. Jacobs and Robert Y. Shapiro, *Politicians Don't Pander: Political Manipulation and the Loss of Democratic Responsiveness*, Studies in Communication, Media, and Public Opinion (Chicago: University of Chicago Press, 2000).

52. Kingdon, *America the Unusual*; Steinmo, "American Exceptionalism Reconsidered: Culture or Institutions?"; Theda Skocpol, *Protecting Soldiers and Mothers* (Cambridge, MA: Harvard University Press, 1992).

53. Edwin Amenta, *When Movements Matter: The Townsend Plan and the Rise of Social Security* (Princeton, NJ: Princeton University Press, 2006).

54. Reeves and Robinson both drew tenth place. Short introduced her bill under the ten-minute rule. Steel drew third place. Hindell and Simms, *Abortion Law Reformed*; Peter G. Richards, *Parliament and Conscience* (London: George Allen and Unwin, 1971); Brookes, *Abortion in England, 1900–1967*.

55. Hindell and Simms, *Abortion Law Reformed*; David Marsh and Melvyn Read, *Private Member's Bills* (Cambridge: Cambridge University Press, 1988); Richards, *Parliament and Conscience*.

56. Incrementalism might have been expected in Canada since it also had a federal system, but the British North America Act of 1867 gave the federal government sole jurisdiction over the criminal code where abortion statutes were found. The relative powers of the provinces and the federal government have varied over time. Initially, the federal government had unlimited powers of taxation while the provinces were limited to direct taxation. The federal government could disallow provincial legislation, even in areas that had been reserved to the provinces. But over time, the provinces gained more power. In the postwar period, federal and provincial governments engaged in "cooperative federalism." But in the 1960s, many provinces, led by Quebec, demanded more independence and took a greater role in social, economic, and taxation policy. Gwendolyn Gray, *Federalism and Health Policy: The Development of Health Systems in Canada and Australia* (Toronto: University of Toronto Press, 1991).

57. David J. Garrow, *Liberty and Sexuality: The Right to Privacy and the Making of Roe v. Wade* (New York: Macmillan, 1994).

58. Pat Vergata, Charlyn Buss, Barbara Schain, and Donna Greenfield, "Abortion Cases in the United States," *Women's Rights Law Reporter* 1 (1972): 50–55.

59. Francome, *Abortion Freedom*; Lesley Hoggart, "Socialist Feminism, Reproductive Rights, and Political Action," *Capital and Class* 24, no. 1 (2000): 95; Hindell and Simms, *Abortion Law Reformed*.

60. Jenson, "Getting to Morgentaler"; Association for the Modernization of Canadian Abortion Laws, "Presentation to the Honorable John N. Turner,

P.C., M.P., Minister of Justice and Attorney General of Canada," Ottawa, National Archives of Canada, December 9, 1968; de Valk, *Morality and Law in Canadian Politics*. AMCAL had about three hundred members in 1968.
61. The organization was originally called the Citizen's Committee for Humane Abortion Laws. Maginnis was out of California in 1963 and 1964, but revived the organization in 1965 and started distributing Hardin's speeches. Garrow, *Liberty and Sexuality*, 293–95.
62. Ibid.
63. Ibid., 304.
64. In its first few years, ASA was called the Committee for Humane Abortion Law and then the Association for Humane Abortion. Ibid. Luker, *Abortion and the Politics of Motherhood*.
65. Garrow, *Liberty and Sexuality*, 292.
66. Anthony Beilenson, the sponsor of the California reform bill, said in 1965 that his "deliberately restrictive and conservative" reform bill would have "absolutely no effect on the great majority of abortions." Similarly, the California Committee on Therapeutic Abortion (CCTA), founded and funded by contraceptive manufacturer Joseph Sunnen, was established in 1966 with the short-term goal of enacting the Beilenson bill but the long-term goal of repealing the abortion laws. Ibid., 299–300.
67. The implementation of reform was different in California where abortion soon became available virtually on request. Legal abortions increased from less than 600 in 1967 to 5,000 in 1968, 15,000 in 1969, 60,000 in 1970, and 117,000 in 1971. E. W. Jackson, M. Tashiro, and G. C. Cunningham, "Therapeutic Abortions in California," *California Medicine* 115, no. 1 (1971): 28; Luker, *Abortion and the Politics of Motherhood*; Garrow, *Liberty and Sexuality*.
68. Garrow, *Liberty and Sexuality*, 347.
69. Ibid., 359.
70. Ibid.
71. Jo Freeman, "The Origins of the Women's Liberation Movement," *American Journal of Sociology* 78, no. 4 (1973): 792–811; Suzanne Staggenborg, *The Pro-Choice Movement: Organization and Activism in the Abortion Conflict* (New York: Oxford University Press, 1991).
72. Abortion was listed after such issues as the Equal Rights Amendment (ERA), employment discrimination, maternity leave, child-care tax credits, public day-care centers, educational equality, and job training. National Organization for Women, "Bill of Rights [1967]," in Greenhouse and Siegel, *Before Roe v. Wade*, 36–38.
73. Betty Friedan, "Abortion: A Woman's Civil Right—Speech to the First National Conference on Abortion Laws, Chicago, February 1969," in Greenhouse and Siegel, *Before Roe v. Wade*, 39; Steven M. Buechler, *Women's Movements in the United States: Woman Suffrage, Equal Rights, and Beyond* (New Brunswick, NJ: Rutgers University Press, 1990).

74. Judith Hole and Ellen Levine, *Rebirth of Feminism* (New York: Quadrangle Books, 1973); Jo Freeman, *The Politics of Women's Liberation* (New York: Longman Press, 1975); Freeman, "Origins of the Women's Liberation Movement"; Staggenborg, *Pro-Choice Movement*; National Organization for Women, "Bill of Rights [1967]."
75. Hole and Levine, *Rebirth of Feminism*; Greenhouse and Siegel, *Before* Roe v. Wade; Ruth Rosen, *The World Split Open: How the Modern Women's Movement Changed America* (New York: Viking, 2000); Garrow, *Liberty and Sexuality*.
76. Staggenborg, *Pro-Choice Movement*.
77. Another ASA member, Cyril Means, also advocated a judicial strategy but argued that *Griswold* could not be applied to abortion. Instead, he promoted a historical argument that nineteenth-century abortion laws had been designed to protect women's health (rather than fetuses) and had thus outlived their purpose. Garrow, *Liberty and Sexuality*.
78. Garrow, *Liberty and Sexuality*; Roy Lucas, "Federal Constitutional Limitations on the Enforcement and Administration of State Abortion Statutes," *North Carolina Law Review* 46 (1967): 730.
79. Mark P. Henriques, "Desuetude and Declaratory Judgment: A New Challenge to Obsolete Laws," *Virginia Law Review* 76, no. 5 (1990): 1057–97.
80. Garrow, *Liberty and Sexuality*, 354.
81. Ibid.
82. The *Belous* opinion argued that in determining whether an abortion was "medically necessary," physicians could weigh the statistical risks of childbirth against those of abortion. Since early abortion carries less risk than childbirth, some observers felt that the court had found that early abortions could always be considered "medically necessary." Ibid.
83. Ibid.; Rubin, *Abortion Politics and the Courts*; Amy Kesselman, "Women versus Connecticut: Conducting a Statewide Abortion Hearing," in *Abortion Wars: A Half Century of Struggle*, ed. Rickie Solinger (Berkeley: University of California Press, 1998); Greenhouse and Siegel, *Before* Roe v. Wade.
84. Garrow, *Liberty and Sexuality*; Marian Faux, *Roe v. Wade: The Untold Story of the Landmark Supreme Court Decision That Made Abortion Legal* (New York: Cooper Square Press, 2001).
85. Greenhouse and Siegel, *Before* Roe v. Wade; Luker, *Abortion and the Politics of Motherhood*; Burns, *Moral Veto*.
86. Greenhouse and Siegel, *Before* Roe v. Wade.
87. Ibid., 191–92.
88. Staggenborg, *Pro-Choice Movement*.
89. Garrow, *Liberty and Sexuality*. Colorado's Richard Lamm complained that conservative doctors turned his 5 percent law into a 3 percent one.
90. Ibid.
91. Rosalind Petchesky, for example, argues that the pro-choice movement was successful because of the combined pressure of the population control, abortion reform, and feminist movements but that the most important

factor was the refusal of women and feminist activists to comply with abortion laws—creating a crisis of legitimacy for the law. "These two factors—the militant organizing of feminists and the threat of 'alternative services' were crucial political influences toward loosening population establishment and medical abortion policy. The role of feminist activists as 'shock troops'—doing underground abortion referrals and counseling, conducting speakouts, sit-ins, and demonstrations—was critical for the timing of the Supreme Court decisions and earlier decriminalization statutes in several states." Petchesky, *Abortion and Woman's Choice*, 129. Luker explains the establishment of de facto abortion on request in California by arguing that the SHA raised the consciousness of California women, creating a rights-based mass movement for repeal, which the women reformers of the CCTA eventually joined after the 1967 reform. Male reformers, doctors especially, were generally satisfied with the reform and did not join the repeal movement. After the 1967 reform, women members of the CCTA, worried that doctors would implement the reform narrowly, established a service that referred women either to nonphysicians or physicians willing to go beyond the law. The combination of a new abortion rights frame, the referral service, the 1969 *Belous* decision, and efforts for legislative repeal led to expansive interpretations of the 1967 reform Luker, *Abortion and the Politics of Motherhood*. Garrow notes that Charles Munger also worked to ensure an expansive interpretation of the statute. Garrow, *Liberty and Sexuality*. As for the Supreme Court's *Roe* decision, Luker argues that the court took up the abortion cases and ruled the way that it did because the pro-choice movement was larger and had broader national support than the pro-life movement, because public opinion was supportive of reform, and because the court wished to resolve the confusion created by contradictory state laws. Her argument that abortion has become a referendum on the meaning of motherhood is mainly oriented to explaining why abortion has been so controversial after the *Roe* decision.

92. Tatalovich and Daynes, *Politics of Abortion*; Gerald N. Rosenberg, *The Hollow Hope: Can Courts Bring About Social Change?* (Chicago: University of Chicago Press, 1991).
93. Burns, *Moral Veto*.
94. Amenta, *When Movements Matter*.
95. ICBH Witness Seminar, "The Abortion Act 1967" (paper presented at the Witness Seminar, Institute of Contemporary British History, 2001).
96. Francome, *Abortion Freedom*; Sheldon, *Beyond Control*; ICBH Witness Seminar, "Abortion Act 1967"; Roy Jenkins, *A Life at the Center* (London: Random House, 1993); Hindell and Simms, *Abortion Law Reformed*; Marsh and Read, *Private Member's Bills*.
97. Hindell and Simms, *Abortion Law Reformed*.
98. Jenkins, *Life at the Center*, 198.
99. It had been the general practice of the Government in the 1960s to give

drafting assistance to private member's bills that had passed their Second Reading. However, the private member's bills on divorce, family planning, and abortion all received drafting assistance before their Second Reading. The family planning bill had the assistance of the Ministry of Health, and the abortion bill had the aid of the Home Office. Hindell and Simms, *Abortion Law Reformed*.

100. de Valk, "Abortion in Canada, 1960–66"; "Council of Women Asks Abortion Law Change," *Globe and Mail*, January 31, 1967; Pelrine, *Abortion in Canada*.
101. In this, it was inspired by the 1957 British Wolfenden Commission, which examined proposals for the decriminalization of homosexuality and prostitution.
102. Alphonse de Valk, *Abortion: Lang, Lalonde, Trudeau, Turner* (Toronto: Life Cycle Books, 1975), 16.
103. de Valk, *Morality and Law in Canadian Politics*, 104.
104. Beginning in 1963, the CBA began questioning the existing abortion law at its annual meetings. It eventually proposed provincial termination boards and the same three abortion grounds as the CMA. Ibid.
105. C. E. S. Franks, "Free Votes in the House of Commons: A Problematic Reform," *Policy Options*, November 1997.
106. *Globe and Mail*, March 11, 1968; Canada House of Commons (Hansard), May 8, 1969, 8503–5, 8589–91.
107. Canada House of Commons (Hansard), May 6, 1969, 8397; May 9, 1969, 8543–44; Marilyn J. Field, *The Comparative Politics of Birth Control: Determinants of Policy Variation and Change in the Developed Nations* (New York: Praeger, 1983); Jenson, "Getting to Morgentaler"; Pelrine, *Abortion in Canada*; Tatalovich, *Politics of Abortion*; Morton, *Pro-Choice vs. Pro-Life*.
108. The New York abortion repeal had bipartisan support and was signed by Republican governor Nelson Rockefeller. *New York Times*, April 1, 1970, April 11, 1970, and May 11, 1972. But Hawaii's bill was an exception; it pitted Democratic supporters of repeal against Republicans. *New York Times*, February 11, 1970.
109. Burns, *Moral Veto*; Mary C. Segers and Timothy A. Byrnes, eds., *Abortion Politics in American States* (Armonk, NY: M. E. Sharpe, 1995).
110. Burns, *Moral Veto*.
111. Greenhouse and Siegel, *Before Roe v. Wade*, 213.
112. Lisa Young, *Feminists and Party Politics* (Vancouver: UBC Press, 2000); Christina Wolbrecht, *The Politics of Women's Rights: Parties, Positions, and Change* (Princeton, NJ: Princeton University Press, 2000); Donald T. Critchlow, *Intended Consequences: Birth Control, Abortion, and Federal Government in Modern America* (New York: Oxford University Press, 1999); *New York Times*, May 8, 1972.
113. Charles M. Lamb and Stephen C. Halpern, "The Political and Historical

Context of the Burger Court," in *The Burger Court: Political and Judicial Profiles*, ed. Charles M. Lamb and Stephen C. Halpern (Urbana: University of Illinois Press, 1991), 1–34; Garrow, *Liberty and Sexuality*; Epstein and Kobylka, *Supreme Court and Legal Change*. Justice Brennan was a Democrat but was appointed by Republican president Dwight D. Eisenhower.

114. Dorothy E. Smith, *The Everyday World as Problematic: A Feminist Sociology* (Boston: Northeastern University Press, 1987).

115. In the 1960s, states had primary jurisdiction over such issues as property rights, utilities, education, land use, criminal law, family policy, and morality policy. The main exception to state jurisdiction over morality was the national prohibition of alcohol. This occurred only after most states had already instituted their own prohibitions and the federal prohibition implicitly recognized state jurisdiction in the policy area by its passage through constitutional amendment. William H. Riker, *Federalism: Origin, Operation, Significance* (Boston: Little, Brown, 1964); Jack L. Walker, "The Diffusion of Innovations among the American States," *American Political Science Review* 63 (1969): 880–99.

116. N. E. H. Hull and Peter Charles Hoffer, Roe v. Wade*: The Abortion Rights Controversy in American History*, Landmark Law Cases and American Society (Lawrence: University Press of Kansas, 2001); Raymond Tatalovich, "The Abortion Controversy in Canada and the United States," *Canadian-American Public Policy*, February 1996, 1–39. Several factors have caused the court to take up more individual rights cases in the last century: enactment of the Fourteenth Amendment, increased control of the court over its agenda, and the ascendance after 1937 of liberal majorities such as the Warren court. Another factor was the development of a support structure for legal mobilization including rights advocacy organizations and increased sources of funding for litigation. This was aided by the court's procedural decisions relaxing rules on standing and class-action suits, and allowing the award of attorney's fees to successful rights plaintiffs. Charles R. Epp, *The Rights Revolutions: Lawyers, Activists and Supreme Courts in Comparative Perspective* (Chicago: University of Chicago Press, 1998). The court also relaxed the standards by which it determined whether it could take a case as well as standards of evidence (e.g., amicus curiae briefs and historical and social science evidence). Rubin, *Abortion Politics and the Courts*; Lisa DeLorme, "Gaining a Right to Abortion in the United States and Canada: The Role of Judicial Capacities," *Berkeley Journal of Sociology* 36 (1991): 93–114.

117. Julie Conger, "Abortion: The Five-Year Revolution and Its Impact," *Ecology Law Quarterly* 3, no. 2 (1973): 311–47; Garrow, *Liberty and Sexuality*; Lader, *Abortion II*.

118. Hull and Hoffer, Roe v. Wade*: The Abortion Rights Controversy in American History*, 180.

119. David J. Garrow, "*Roe v. Wade* Revisited," *Green Bag* 9, no. 2 (2005): 80.

120. John C. Jeffries, *Justice Lewis F. Powell Jr.* (New York: Charles Scribner's Sons, 1994), 351.
121. Evers and McGee, "Trend and Pattern in Attitudes toward Abortion."
122. Jeffries argues that Powell's blind spot about the extent of opposition to *Roe* may have resulted from the fact that none of the justices, including the two dissenters, Rehnquist and White, were personally opposed to abortion. Nor were any of their clerks. He argues that "if Powell had had to override heartfelt objections from a clerk or colleague, he at least would have been alerted to something he entirely missed—the risk that the constitutionalization of abortion would be deeply and durably divisive." Jeffries, *Justice Lewis F. Powell Jr.*, 351.
123. *Roe v. Wade*, 410 U.S. at 115.
124. Harry A. Blackmun, *Justice Harry A. Blackmun Oral History Project Transcript* (Washington, DC: Library of Congress, 1995), 194.
125. Linda Greenhouse, *Becoming Justice Blackmun: Harry Blackmun's Supreme Court Journey* (New York: Times Books, 2005), 90; George Gallup, "Abortion Seen Up to Woman, Doctor" in Greenhouse and Siegel, *Before* Roe v. Wade, 207–9.
126. Blake, "Supreme Court's Abortion Decisions."
127. Greenhouse, *Becoming Justice Blackmun*, 93.
128. *Roe v. Wade*. Some analysts have argued that the defeats of abortion legislation in the early 1970s were a case of organized minorities vetoing majority preferences. As such, the court asserted majority preferences in *Roe*. This makes sense for the defeat of ALI-style reforms, but it is not the case that public opinion clearly favored abortion repeals (i.e., abortion on request), especially in light of state-by-state variations in public opinion. Neal Devins, *Shaping Constitutional Values: Elected Government, the Supreme Court, and the Abortion Debate*, Interpreting American Politics (Baltimore: Johns Hopkins University Press, 1996).
129. "No. 70-18—Roe v. Wade, No. 70-40—Doe v. Bolton" in Greenhouse and Siegel, *Before* Roe v. Wade, 247.
130. Ibid.

CHAPTER THREE

1. Some exceptions are Jonathan B. Imber, *Abortion and the Private Practice of Medicine* (New Haven, CT: Yale University Press, 1986); Frederick S. Jaffe, Barbara L. Lindheim, and Philip R. Lee, *Abortion Politics: Private Morality and Public Policy* (New York: McGraw-Hill, 1981); Carole E. Joffe, *Doctors of Conscience: The Struggle to Provide Abortion: Before and after* Roe v. Wade (Boston: Beacon Press, 1995); Lori Freedman, *Willing and Unable: Doctors' Constraints in Abortion Care* (Philadelphia: Temple University Press, 2010).
2. A large number of studies show that existing policies influence later political struggles and policies. Policy legacies can matter in a multitude of

ways. They can affect the resources, incentives, cognitions, emotions, and knowledge of government elites, interest groups, and mass publics. They can mobilize new groups and identities, determine how policy problems and solutions are defined, create cultural schemas and symbolic resources, and shape the legitimacy of organizations and practices. See John D. Skrentny, *The Ironies of Affirmative Action: Politics, Culture, and Justice in America* (Chicago: University of Chicago Press, 1996); John D. Skrentny, *The Minority Rights Revolution* (Cambridge, MA: Belknap Press, Harvard University, 2002); John David Skrentny, "State Capacity, Policy Feedbacks, and Affirmative Action for Blacks, Women, and Latinos," *Research in Political Sociology* 8 (1998): 279–310; Paul Pierson, *Dismantling the Welfare State? Reagan, Thatcher, and the Politics of Retrenchment* (New York: Cambridge University Press, 1994); James M. Jasper, "The Emotions of Protest: Affective and Reactive Emotions in and around Social Movements," *Sociological Forum* 13, no. 3 (1998): 395–424; Edward J. Walsh, "Resource Mobilization and Citizen Protest in Communities around Three Mile Island," *Social Problems* 29 (1981): 1–21; Jeff Goodwin, James M. Jasper, and Francesca Polletta, "The Return of the Repressed: The Fall and Rise of Emotions in Social Movement Theory," *Mobilization* 5, no. 1 (2000): 65–84; E. E. Schattschneider, *Politics, Pressures, and the Tariff* (New York: Prentice Hall, 1935); Edwin Amenta, *Bold Relief: Institutional Politics and the Origins of Modern American Social Policy* (Princeton, NJ: Princeton University Press, 1998); Peter Hall, *The Political Power of Economic Ideas: Keynesianism across Countries* (Princeton, NJ: Princeton University Press, 1989); Peter A. Hall, *Governing the Economy: The Politics of State Intervention in Britain and France* (Oxford: Oxford University Press, 1986); Sven Steinmo, Kathleen Thelen, and Frank Longstreth, *Structuring Politics: Historical Institutionalism in Comparative Analysis* (Cambridge: Cambridge University Press, 1992); Hugh Heclo, *Modern Social Politics in Britain and Sweden* (New Haven, CT: Yale University Press, 1974); Jacob S. Hacker, "The Historical Logic of National Health Insurance: Structure and Sequence in the Development of British, Canadian, and U.S. Medical Policy," *Studies in American Political Development* 12, no. 1 (1998): 57–130; Theda Skocpol, *Protecting Soldiers and Mothers* (Cambridge, MA: Harvard University Press, 1992); Nicholas Pedriana and Robin Stryker, "Political Culture Wars 1960s Style: Equal Employment Opportunity-Affirmative Action Law and the Philadelphia Plan," *American Journal of Sociology* 103, no. 3 (1997): 633–91; Chad. A. Goldberg, "Contesting the Status of Relief Workers during the New Deal: The Workers Alliance of America and the Works Progress Administration, 1935–1941," *Social Science History* 29, no. 3 (2005): 337–71.

3. Joffe, *Doctors of Conscience*; Keith Hindell and Madeline Simms, *Abortion Law Reformed* (London: Peter Owen, 1971); Colin Francome, *Abortion Practice in Britain and the United States* (London: Allen and Unwin, 1986); Julia S. O'Connor, Ann Shola Orloff, and Sheila Shaver, "Body Rights,

Social Rights, and Reproductive Choice," in *States, Markets, Families: Gender, Liberalism, and Social Policy in Australia, Canada, Great Britain and the United States* (Cambridge: Cambridge University Press, 1999), 157–85; Jane Brodie, "Health vs. Rights: Comparative Perspectives on Abortion Policy in Canada and the United States," in *Power and Decision: The Social Control of Reproduction*, ed. Gita Sen and Rachel C. Snow (Cambridge, MA: Harvard University Press, 1994), 123–46.

4. Kurt W. Back, "Why Is Abortion a Public Issue? The Role of Professional Control," *Politics and Society* 15 (1986–87): 197–206.

5. Jonathan B. Imber, *Abortion and the Private Practice of Medicine* (New Haven, CT: Yale University Press, 1986); Carole E. Joffe, Patricia Anderson, and Jody Steinauer, "The Crisis in Abortion Provision and Pro-Choice Medical Activism," in *Abortion Wars: A Half Century of Struggle*, ed. Rickie Solinger (Berkeley: University of California Press, 1997), 320–34; Raymond Tatalovich, *The Politics of Abortion in the United States and Canada: A Comparative Study* (Armonk, NY: M. E. Sharpe, 1997); Canadian Abortion Rights Action League, "Protecting Abortion Rights in Canada" (Ottawa: Canadian Abortion Rights Action League, 2003); Francome, *Abortion Practice in Britain and the United States*. Canada also has strong regional disparities as the result of the large number of hospitals that have refused to provide abortions and limited provision by clinics.

6. Eliot Freidson, *Professional Dominance: The Social Structure of Medical Care* (Chicago: Aldine, 1970); Eliot Freidson, *Profession of Medicine: A Study of the Sociology of Applied Knowledge* (New York: Dodd, Mead, 1970); Donald W. Light, "Countervailing Power: The Changing Character of the Medical Profession in the United States," in *The Changing Medical Profession*, ed. Frederic W. Hafferty and John B. McKinlay (Oxford: Oxford University Press, 1993), 69–79; Frederic W. Hafferty and Donald W. Light, "Professional Dynamics and the Changing Nature of Medical Work," *Journal of Health and Social Behavior* 35, extra issue (1995): 132–53; Marie R. Haug, "The Erosion of Professional Authority: A Cross-Cultural Inquiry in the Case of the Physician," *Milbank Quarterly* 54, no. 1 (1976): 83–106.

7. I use the phrase "abortion on demand" only in quotation marks. Feminist abortion rights activists first used the term, but doctors and abortion opponents eventually used it pejoratively. In practice, "abortion on demand" has never existed in the three countries examined here because individual doctors maintained the right to refuse to perform abortions.

8. In their testimony to Parliament, CMA delegates argued that abortion rates tended to be higher in smaller unaccredited hospitals and that the CMA had taken a "solid stand . . . that some form of control should be exercised in this regard by the medical profession." Canada House of Commons, *Minutes and Proceedings and Evidence of the Standing Committee on Health Welfare and Social Affairs*, October 31, 1967, 111–12.

9. Hindell and Simms, *Abortion Law Reformed*.

10. "Leading Articles: Abortion Law," *British Medical Journal*, April 17, 1965.
11. British Medical Association, "Annual Representative Meeting: Abortion," *British Medical Journal Supplement*, July 17, 1965; John Keown, *Abortion, Doctors, and the Law: Some Aspects of the Legal Regulation of Abortion in England from 1803 to 1982* (Cambridge: Cambridge University Press, 1988); Hindell and Simms, *Abortion Law Reformed*.
12. Hector MacLennan, Draft of President's Letter to the *Times* for Comment by Members of the Finance and Executive Committee, Royal College of Obstetricians and Gynaecologists, 1965, Archives of the RCOG A16/1; Sir Hector MacLennan, President, Royal College of Obstetricians and Gynaecologists, to Sir George Godber, Chief Medical Officer, Ministry of Health, December 15, 1965, Archives of the RCOG A16/1.
13. Vera Houghton, Memorandum to Executive Committee of Abortion Law Reform Association on Amendments to Medical Termination of Pregnancy Bill (London (SA/ALR/A6/9/38): Wellcome Institute for the History of Medicine, Contemporary Medical Archives Centre, January 3, 1967).
14. Baird also urged Steel to resist efforts to remove Scotland from the abortion act since abortion practice was liberal only in Baird's home of Aberdeen. Gayle Davis and Roger Davidson, "'A Fifth Freedom' or 'Hideous Atheistic Expediency'? The Medical Community and Abortion Law Reform in Scotland, c. 1960–1975," *Medical History* 50, no. 1 (2006): 29–48.
15. British Medical Association, "Therapeutic Abortion: Report by B.M.A. Special Committee," *British Medical Journal*, July 2 1966; British Medical Association and the Royal College of Obstetricians and Gynaecologists, "Medical Termination of Pregnancy Bill: Views of the British Medical Association and the Royal College of Obstetricians and Gynaecologists," *British Medical Journal*, December 31, 1966; Royal College of Obstetricians and Gynaecologists, "Legalized Abortion: Report by the Council of the Royal College of Obstetricians and Gynaecologists," *British Medical Journal* 1 (1966): 850–52; British Medical Association, "Proceedings of Council: Therapeutic Abortion"; "Leading Articles: Therapeutic Abortion"; "Leading Articles: Legislation on Abortion," *British Medical Journal*, March 5, 1966; "B.M.A.'s Views on Abortion," *Lancet*, July 2, 1966; Hindell and Simms, *Abortion Law Reformed*.
16. "Relaxation of Federal Abortion Law Is Asked by B.C. Doctor," *Globe and Mail*, August 31, 1961; "The Abortion Issue," *Globe and Mail*, September 1, 1961; Alphonse de Valk, "Abortion in Canada, 1960–66," in *Death before Birth*, ed. E. J. Kremer and E. A. Synan (Toronto: Griffin House, 1974). In 1962, a doctor with a law degree argued that Britain's *Bourne* decision did not actually apply to Canada and thus existing law did not allow abortions under any circumstances. The solicitor of the OMA immediately disagreed. J. J. Lederman, "The Doctor, Abortion, and the Law," *Canadian Medical Association Journal* 87 (1962): 216; J. J. Lederman and G. E. Parker, "Therapeutic Abortion and the Canadian Criminal Code," *Criminal Law Quarterly* 6

(1963): 36; Graham E. Parker, "Bill C-150: Abortion Reform," *Criminal Law Quarterly* 11 (1969): 267–74; Alphonse de Valk, *Morality and Law in Canadian Politics: The Abortion Controversy* (Montreal: Palm, 1974), 761ff.; *Ontario Medical Review*, September 1962.

17. Marilyn J. Field, "The Determinants of Abortion Policy in Developed Nations," *Policy Studies Journal* 7 (1979): 771–81; Jane Jenson, "Getting to Morgentaler: From One Representation to Another," in Brodie, Gavigan, and Jenson, *Politics of Abortion*; Eleanor Wright Pelrine, *Abortion in Canada* (Toronto: New Press, 1971).

18. The 1966 proposal allowed abortion for grounds of life, physical health, or mental health with approval by a hospital abortion committee and parental or husband consent when necessary. This resembled a proposal approved by the OMA the year before. The Council rejected a motion to add grounds for rape, incest, and fetal abnormality, and the resolution did not include grounds of economic hardship or abortion on request. Canadian Medical Association, *Transactions of the Ninety-eighth Annual Meeting of the Canadian Medical Association* (Ottawa: Canadian Medical Association Archives, 1965), 79; "A Long Overdue Reform," *Globe and Mail*, June 18, 1966; Ontario Medical Association, "Transactions of Council, May 10–11, 1963, No. 96, Section on Obstetrics and Gynecology—Proposed Study of Sterilization and Therapeutic Abortions," *Ontario Medical Review* 30, no. 7 (1963): 418; de Valk, "Abortion in Canada, 1960–66"; "Free the Doctor," *Globe and Mail*, May 18, 1965; Canadian Medical Association, *Transactions of the Ninety-ninth Annual Meeting of the Canadian Medical Association* (Ottawa: Canadian Medical Association Archives, 1966), 62–63.

19. Canadian Medical Association, *Transactions of the General Council at the One Hundredth Annual Meeting of the Canadian Medical Association* (Ottawa: Canadian Medical Association Archives, 1967).

20. Medical World News, "Rewriting the Law on Abortion," *Medical World News*, September 29, 1967.

21. The California Medical Association was an exception to the general pattern; it endorsed abortion reform as early as 1962. James M. Ingram, "Changing Aspects of Abortion Law," *American Journal of Obstetrics and Gynecology* 105 (1969): 35–45; Sagar C. Jain and Laurel Gooch, *Georgia Abortion Act 1968: A Study in Legislative Process* (Chapel Hill: School of Public Health, University of North Carolina at Chapel Hill, 1972); Sagar C. Jain and Steven Hughes, *California Abortion Act 1967: A Study in Legislative Process* (Chapel Hill: School of Public Health, University of North Carolina at Chapel Hill, 1968); Sagar C. Jain and Steven W. Sinding, *North Carolina Abortion Law 1967: A Study of Legislative Process* (Chapel Hill: School of Public Health, University of North Carolina at Chapel Hill, 1972); Raymond Tatalovich and Byron W. Daynes, *The Politics of Abortion: A Study of Community Conflict in Public Policy Making* (New York: Praeger, 1981).

22. Jain and Gooch, *Georgia Abortion Act 1968*; Kristin Luker, *Abortion and*

the Politics of Motherhood (Berkeley: University of California Press, 1984); Suzanne Staggenborg, *The Pro-Choice Movement: Organization and Activism in the Abortion Conflict* (New York: Oxford University Press, 1991).
23. Tatalovich and Daynes, *Politics of Abortion*.
24. Lawrence Lader, *Abortion II: Making the Revolution* (Boston: Beacon Press, 1973); Rosalind Pollack Petchesky, *Abortion and Woman's Choice: The State, Sexuality, and Reproductive Freedom* (New York: Longman, 1984).
25. *New York Times*, June 26, 1970. See also Anthony Hordern, *Legal Abortion: The English Experience* (Oxford: Pergamon Press, 1971); David J. Garrow, *Liberty and Sexuality: The Right to Privacy and the Making of Roe v. Wade* (New York: Macmillan, 1994); American Medical Association, *House of Delegate Proceedings, Annual Convention* (Chicago: American Medical Association, 1970).
26. Later, pro-choice activists asked the AMA to file an amicus brief in *Roe*, but it declined. The American College of Obstetricians and Gynecologists (ACOG) did provide a brief in behalf of the "vagueness" argument. Lee Epstein and Joseph F. Kobylka, *The Supreme Court and Legal Change: Abortion and the Death Penalty* (Chapel Hill: University of North Carolina Press, 1992).
27. The Royal Medico-Psychological Association endorsed a variety of grounds including fetal abnormality, rape, underage pregnancy, and economic hardship. However, it opposed abortion for grounds of "inconvenience" and warned against defining abortion grounds too exactly because this might introduce an element of "coercion" in which patients would "expect the doctor to acquiesce" and "the role of the surgeon or gynecologist would be reduced to that of a technician carrying out an objectionable task." In the same year, the Medical Women's Federation endorsed grounds of physical or mental health only. Royal Medico-Psychological Association, "The Royal Medico-Psychological Association's Memorandum on Therapeutic Abortion," *British Journal of Psychiatry* 112 (1966): 1071–72; Medical Women's Federation, "Abortion Law Reform: Memorandum Prepared by a Subcommittee of the Medical Women's Federation," *British Medical Journal*, December 17, 1966.
28. Rosemary Stevens, *Medical Practice in Modern England: The Impact of Specialization and State Medicine* (New Haven, CT: Yale University Press, 1966); Michael Moran and Bruce Wood, *States, Regulation, and the Medical Profession* (Buckingham: Open University Press, 1993); Hindell and Simms, *Abortion Law Reformed*.
29. Hindell and Simms, *Abortion Law Reformed*.
30. Carolyn J. Tuohy, *Accidental Logics: The Dynamics of Change in the Health Care Arena in the United States, Britain, and Canada* (New York: Oxford University Press, 1999); Christopher Hamm, *Health Policy in Britain: The Politics and Organization of the National Health Service* (London: MacMillan, 1982).
31. Hamm, *Health Policy in Britain*; Stevens, *Medical Practice in Modern England*.

32. Stevens, *Medical Practice in Modern England*; Donald Gould, *The Black and White Medicine Show: How Doctors Serve and Fail Their Customers* (London: Hamish Hamilton, 1985).
33. As Mary Ann Elston puts it: "In 1948, an "underlying concordat" between the state and the profession was established with respect to resource allocation. The state determined the overall resources devoted to medical care, leaving the profession largely free to determine the use of these resources, under the rubric of "clinical autonomy." This freedom extended to include a considerable level of representation as a matter of right on policymaking bodies at all levels as well as freedom from managerial supervision over patient care." Mary Ann Elston, "The Politics of Professional Power: Medicine in a Changing Health Service," in *The Sociology of the Health Service*, ed. Jonathan Gabe, Michael Calnan, and Michael Bury (London: Routledge, 1991), 67. See also Tuohy, *Accidental Logics*.
34. Elston, "Politics of Professional Power"; Hamm, *Health Policy in Britain*; Deal Chandler Brooks, "The Joint Commission on Accreditation of Healthcare Organizations," in *Providing Quality Care*, ed. Norbert Goldfield and David B. Nash (Ann Arbor, MI: Health Administration Press, 1995), 145–60; James Warner Bjorkman, "Politicizing Medicine and Medicalizing Politics: Physician Power in the United States," in *Controlling Medical Professionals: The Comparative Politics of Health Governance*, ed. Giorgio Freddi and James Warner Bjorkman (London: Sage, 1989), 28–73; Stephen Harrison and Rockwell I. Schulz, "Clinical Autonomy in the United Kingdom and the United States: Contrasts and Convergence," in Freddi and Bjorkman, *Controlling Medical Professional*, 198–209; Marian Dohler, "Physicians' Professional Autonomy in the Welfare State: Endangered or Preserved," in Freddi and Bjorkman, *Controlling Medical Professionals*, 178–97; Moran and Wood, *States, Regulation, and the Medical Profession*; Stevens, *Medical Practice in Modern England*; Paul Starr and Ellen Immergut, "Health Care and the Boundaries of Politics," in *The Politics of Health Care Reform: Lessons from the Past, Prospects for the Future*, ed. James A. Morone and Gary S. Belkin (Durham, NC: Duke University Press, 1994), 221–54; John Fry, *Medicine in Three Societies: A Comparison of Medical Care in the USSR, USA, and UK* (London: MTP Chiltern House, 1969); "Towards Medical Audit," *British Medical Journal*, 1, no. 5902 (1974): 255–57.
35. Elston, "Politics of Professional Power"; Bjorkman, "Politicizing Medicine and Medicalizing Politics"; Harrison and Schulz, "Clinical Autonomy in the United Kingdom and the United States"; Dohler, "Physicians' Professional Autonomy in the Welfare State"; Moran and Wood, *States, Regulation, and the Medical Profession*; Starr and Immergut, "Health Care and the Boundaries of Politics."
36. Moran and Wood, *States, Regulation, and the Medical Profession*, 132.
37. Royal College of Obstetricians and Gynaecologists, "Legalized Abortion," 852; British Medical Association, "Therapeutic Abortion," 41; British

Medical Association and the Royal College of Obstetricians and Gynaecologists, "Medical Termination of Pregnancy Bill," 1649–50.
38. Royal College of Obstetricians and Gynaecologists, "Legalized Abortion," 852 (emphasis added).
39. David Gullick, Under Secretary, BMA, to Sir John Peel, President, RCOG, "Medical Termination of Pregnancy Bill, Meeting at House of Commons 4th May, 1967," May 4, 1967, Archives of the RCOG A16/4.
40. Houghton, Memorandum to Executive Committee of Abortion Law Reform Association on Amendments to Medical Termination of Pregnancy Bill, 2.
41. David Steel, Member of Parliament, to Sir John Peel, President Royal College of Obstetricians and Gynaecologists, February 8, 1967, Archives of the RCOG A16/2; Sir John Peel, President, Royal College of Obstetricians and Gynaecologists, to David Steel, Member of Parliament, February 10, 1967, Archives of the RCOG A16/2.
42. Hindell and Simms, *Abortion Law Reformed*.
43. Royal College of Obstetricians and Gynaecologists, "Legalized Abortion."
44. British Medical Association and the Royal College of Obstetricians and Gynaecologists, "Medical Termination of Pregnancy Bill," 1649.
45. British Medical Association, "Therapeutic Abortion," 41.
46. British Medical Association and the Royal College of Obstetricians and Gynaecologists, "Medical Termination of Pregnancy Bill," 1649–50.
47. Preventive medicine has historically been the domain of local governments. Local governments retained this responsibility with the creation of the NHS, but now the local health authorities were part of the NHS and had greater resources. This somewhat reduced the traditional separation between the preventive and curative spheres. J. Rogers Hollingsworth, *A Political Economy of Medicine: Great Britain and the United States* (Baltimore: Johns Hopkins University Press, 1986).
48. Tuohy, *Accidental Logics*, 46–47.
49. Sheila Jasanoff, *Designs on Nature: Science and Democracy in Europe and the United States* (Princeton, NJ: Princeton University Press, 2005).
50. The liberal American Public Health Association and the American Medical Women's Association were ahead of the AMA on abortion, calling for the repeal of all restrictions in 1968. Raymond Tatalovich, "After Medicare: Political Determinants of Social Change in the American Medical Association" (PhD, University of Chicago, 1971); C. Gerald Fraser, "Reuther Asks National Health System," *New York Times*, November 15, 1968; *Wall Street Journal*, November 15, 1969, 3. The ACOG was ahead of the AMA on economic hardship grounds, but lagged behind on abortion on request. In 1968, the ACOG endorsed the ALI model, but also added a clause, quoted directly from the British Abortion Act, in which doctors could take account of the "woman's total environment, actual or reasonably foreseeable" while evaluating her physical and mental health. In 1971, the ACOG approved abortion "to safeguard the patient's health or improve her family life

situation" and in 1972, it called for abortion on request. *New York Times*, May 10, 1968; Nanette J. Davis, *From Crime to Choice: The Transformation of Abortion in America* (Westport, CT: Greenwood Press, 1985), 58, 69; Lader, *Abortion II*.

51. Freidson, *Profession of Medicine*; Tatalovich, "After Medicare."
52. Tatalovich, "After Medicare"; Freidson, *Profession of Medicine*.
53. Tuohy, *Accidental Logics*; Julia S. O'Connor, Ann Shola Orloff, and Sheila Shaver, *States, Markets, Families: Gender, Liberalism, and Social Policy in Australia, Canada, Great Britain, and the United States* (Cambridge: Cambridge University Press, 1999).
54. Paul Starr, *The Social Transformation of American Medicine* (New York: Basic Books, 1982); Moran and Wood, *States, Regulation, and the Medical Profession*; Jill S. Quadagno, *One Nation, Uninsured: Why the U.S. Has No National Health Insurance* (Oxford: Oxford University Press, 2005); Jacob S. Hacker, *The Divided Welfare State: The Battle over Public and Private Social Benefits in the United States* (New York: Cambridge University Press, 2002).
55. *Wall Street Journal*, June 22, 1967, 4.
56. Alan F. Guttmacher, "The Genesis of Liberalized Abortion in New York: A Personal Insight," *Case Western Reserve Law Review* 23 (1972): 756–78; Jean Pakter and Frieda Nelson, "Abortion in New York City: The First Nine Months," *Family Planning Perspectives* 3, no. 3 (1971): 5–12; Lader, *Abortion II*; *New York Times*, June 10, 1970, 7; April 11, 1970, 17; June 3, 1970, 44; June 11, 1970, 18; Bernard N. Nathanson, *Aborting America* (Garden City, NY: Doubleday, 1979); "The Widening Horizon of Legal Abortion," *Medical World News*, June 12, 1970; C. Tietze and S. Lewit, "Joint Program for the Study of Abortion (JPSA): Early Medical Complications of Legal Abortion," *Studies in Family Planning* 3, no. 6 (1972): 97–119.
57. *Hearings Before Subcomm. on Health and the Environment of the House Comm. on Energy and Commerce, Part 1, H6*, May 9, 1983 (testimony of Christopher Tietze).
58. Uwe E. Reinhardt, "Resource Allocation in Health Care: The Allocation of Lifestyles to Providers," *Milbank Quarterly* 65, no. 2 (1987): 153–76; Harrison and Schulz, "Clinical Autonomy in the United Kingdom and the United States," 205; Moran and Wood, *States, Regulation, and the Medical Profession*; Rudolf Klein, "Reflections on the American Health Care Condition," *Journal of Health Care, Politics, and Law* 6, no. 2 (1981): 188–204; Tuohy, *Accidental Logics*; Starr and Immergut, "Health Care and the Boundaries of Politics"; Uwe Reinhardt, "Healers and Bureaucrats in the All-American Health Care Fray," in *Technology, Bureaucracy, and Healing in America*, ed. Roger J. Bulger (Iowa City: University of Iowa Press, 1988). For a critique, see Richard A. Culbertson and Philip R. Lee, "Medicare and Physician Autonomy," *Health Care Financing Review* 18, no. 2 (1996): 115–30.
59. Brooks, "Joint Commission on Accreditation of Healthcare Organizations"; Danny Ermann, "Hospital Utilization Review: Past Experience,

Future Directions," *Journal of Health Politics, Policy and Law* 13, no. 4 (1988): 683–704; Fry, *Medicine in Three Societies*.
60. Starr, *Social Transformation of American Medicine*.
61. *New York Times*, June 17, 1960, 38.
62. The committee was chaired by Dr. Raymond T. Holden, a Georgetown University ob/gyn. Holden opposed abortion but supported doctors' right to decide for themselves. Most other members of the committee supported abortion rights, including contraception and pro-choice activists Dr. C. Lee Buxton of Yale University Medical School, who brought the *Griswold* case, and Drs. Mary Calderone and Janet Dingle, both formerly of Planned Parenthood. *Wall Street Journal*, December 1, 1965, 12.
63. Interview with AMA official no. 3, November 2002. All interviews were conducted confidentially, and the names of interviewees are withheld by mutual agreement.
64. All resolutions before the AMA House of Delegates are first sent to a reference committee that hears testimony and makes recommendations.
65. American Medical Association, *House of Delegate Proceedings, Clinical Convention* (Chicago: American Medical Association, 1965), 92.
66. Deborah A. Stone, *The Limits of Professional Power: National Health Care in the Federal Republic of Germany* (Chicago: University of Chicago Press, 1980).
67. *Wall Street Journal*, December 2, 1965, 8; "AMA Defers New Stand on Abortion," *Medical World News*, December 17, 1965; American Medical Association, *House of Delegate Proceedings, Clinical Convention* (1965), 88–93; "House Spurns a Proposal to Loosen Abortion Law," *Medical Tribune*, December 13, 1965; Tatalovich, *Politics of Abortion*.
68. "American Medical Association Policy Statements, 1967 and 1970," in *Before Roe v. Wade: Voices That Shaped the Abortion Debate before the Supreme Court's Ruling*, ed. Linda Greenhouse and Reva Siegel (New York: Kaplan, 2010), 27; American Medical Association, *House of Delegate Proceedings, Annual Convention* (Chicago: American Medical Association, 1967), 40–51, 201–3; *Wall Street Journal*, June 22, 1967, 4.
69. Dick Kirschten, "AMA Relaxes Abortion Stand for First Time since 1871," *Chicago Sun-Times*, June 22, 1967; American Medical Association, *House of Delegate Proceedings, Annual Convention* (1967); *Wall Street Journal*, June 19, 1967, 9; June 22, 1967, 4.
70. American Medical Association, *House of Delegate Proceedings, Clinical Convention* (Chicago: American Medical Association, 1969), 312.
71. Ibid., 241, 312; Lucinda Cisler, "Unfinished Business: Birth Control and Women's Liberation," in *Sisterhood Is Powerful: An Anthology of Writings from the Women's Liberation Movement*, ed. Robin Morgan (New York: Random House, 1970), 245–89.
72. In the end, no national health insurance plan was enacted, but this was

mostly a matter of bad timing. In 1973, the OPEC oil shock, recession, and inflation pushed proposals for national health insurance off the agenda. Starr, *Social Transformation of American Medicine*.

73. Sandra Blakeslee, "Protest Disrupts Meeting of A.M.A.," *New York Times*, July 14, 1969; Jon Nordheimer, "Protestor Likens A.M.A. to Saigon Government," *New York Times*, July 16, 1969; Starr, *Social Transformation of American Medicine*; Frank D. Campion, *The AMA and U.S. Health Policy since 1940* (Chicago: Chicago Review Press, 1984); "Unconventional Convention: American Medical Association," *Nature*, July 11, 1970; "Brush-Off at the Red Lacquer Room," *Medical World News*, July 10, 1970; *New York Times*, July 20, 1969.
74. Interview with AMA official no. 3, November 2002.
75. Interview with AMA official no. 2, November 2002.
76. Ibid.
77. Interview with AMA official no. 4, November 2002.
78. Campion, *AMA and U.S. Health Policy since 1940*; Starr, *Social Transformation of American Medicine*; "AMA," *Medical World News*, June 5, 1970; Walter Bornemeier, "Blueprint for the Future," *JAMA* 217, no. 3 (1971): 321–24; Ernest B. Howard, "Organized Medicine: The AMA," *Scope: A Publication of the Boston University Medical Center*, December 1970.
79. Howard, "Organized Medicine," 10.
80. Patricia G. Steinhoff, *Abortion Politics: The Hawaii Experience* (Honolulu: University Press of Hawaii, 1977); Peter Kihss, "Repeal of Laws on Morals Urged," *New York Times*, February 13, 1969; American Medical Association, *House of Delegate Proceedings, Annual Convention* (Chicago: American Medical Association, 1970); "Abortion Change Proposed," *American Medical News*, May 25, 1970; "AMA Abortion Position Liberalized," *American Medical News*, July 6, 1970.
81. *AMA House of Delegates Proceedings* (Annual 1970), quoted in Tatalovich and Daynes, *Politics of Abortion*, 55.
82. Ibid., 55–56.
83. American Medical Association, *House of Delegate Proceedings, Annual Convention* (1970), 337–39; Tatalovich and Daynes, *Politics of Abortion*; *Wall Street Journal*, June 26, 1970, 5.
84. American Medical Association, *House of Delegate Proceedings, Annual Convention* (1970), 220. At the AMA clinical convention six months later, the New Jersey delegation proposed revoking this resolution. As a compromise, the reference committee proposed combining the 1967 and 1970 resolutions, but the delegates stuck with the 1970 resolution. Said AMA president Dr. Walter Bornemeier, "I think the action of the delegates is quite clear. . . . It is up to each doctor to interpret according to his own conscience what he considers a valid medical reason for performing an abortion." Tatalovich and Daynes, *Politics of Abortion*, 56; *Chicago Tribune*, December 3, 1970, 12.

85. Richard D. Lyons, "Abortion Reform Debated by AMA," *New York Times*, June 23, 1970; Richard D. Lyons, "A.M.A. Eases Abortion Rules," *New York Times*, June 26, 1970; "Abortions: Change of Heart," *Nature*, July 4, 1970.
86. "Abortion Debate: Deep Passion, Little Change," *Medical World News*, July 10, 1970; *Wall Street Journal*, June 26, 1970, 5.
87. *Washington Post*, June 26, 1970, A3.
88. *Wall Street Journal*, June 26, 1970, 5.
89. "Modern Medicine Poll on Socioeconomic Issues: Abortion-Homosexual Practices-Marihuana," *Modern Medicine*, November 3, 1969; "Abortion: The Doctor's Dilemma," *Modern Medicine*, April 24, 1967.
90. Joffe, *Doctors of Conscience*; Philip R. Lee and Lauren B. LeRoy, "Abortion Politics and Public Policy," in *Perspectives on Abortion*, ed. Paul Sachdev (Metuchen, NJ: Scarecrow Press, 1985), 44–58; Jaffe, Lindheim, and Lee, *Abortion Politics*.
91. "Abortion, Training Policies Hold Spotlight at AMA," *Hospital Practice*, August 1970, 19.
92. Robert Hall, *Abortion in a Changing World* (New York: Columbia University Press, 1970), 2:108.
93. Interview with AMA official no. 1, November 2002.
94. Ibid.
95. Starr, *Social Transformation of American Medicine*.
96. Hollingsworth, *Political Economy of Medicine*; Starr, *Social Transformation of American Medicine*.
97. Greenhouse and Siegel, *Before* Roe v. Wade; Linda Greenhouse, *Becoming Justice Blackmun: Harry Blackmun's Supreme Court Journey* (New York: Times Books, 2005); Nan Hunter, "Justice Blackmun, Abortion, and the Myth of Medical Independence," *Brooklyn Law Review* 72 (2006): 147. Hunter contests the notion that Blackmun "wrote *Roe* to center on the best interests of medicine." I do not make such a claim. Instead, I argue that Blackmun had a high regard for medicine and would have been reluctant to expand abortion rights without the acquiescence of the AMA. I agree with Hunter that Blackmun was inclined to write a narrow abortion opinion but was pushed into a broader ruling by other members of the court.
98. Garrow, *Liberty and Sexuality*, 568.
99. Greenhouse and Siegel, *Before* Roe v. Wade.
100. Eva R. Rubin, *Abortion Politics and the Courts* (New York: Greenwood Press, 1987), 38–43; Garrow, *Liberty and Sexuality*.
101. Greenhouse, *Becoming Justice Blackmun*; Garrow, *Liberty and Sexuality*; Del Dickson, *The Supreme Court in Conference, 1940–1985: The Private Discussions behind Nearly 300 Supreme Court Decisions* (Oxford: Oxford University Press, 2001).
102. Greenhouse, *Becoming Justice Blackmun*, 81.
103. Dickson, *Supreme Court in Conference*.

104. Douglas sent a letter of protest to Burger, contesting his right to assign the cases and the assignment of *Doe* to Blackmun. In fact, Douglas had planned to assign *Roe* to Blackmun anyway as an acknowledgment of his break with Burger in conference. But Douglas had not intended to assign *Doe* to Blackmun.
105. Roy Lucas, "New Historical Insights on the Curious Case of *Baird v. Eisenstadt*," *Roger Williams University Law Review* 9 (2003): 9–54.
106. Eisenstadt v. Baird, 405 U.S. 438, 453 (1972).
107. Greenhouse, *Becoming Justice Blackmun*; Garrow, *Liberty and Sexuality*.
108. Garrow, *Liberty and Sexuality*; Greenhouse, *Becoming Justice Blackmun*.
109. Garrow, *Liberty and Sexuality*; Harry A. Blackmun, *Justice Harry A. Blackmun Oral History Project Transcript* (Washington, DC: Library of Congress, 1995); Epstein and Kobylka, *Supreme Court and Legal Change*.
110. Burger eventually joined the majority in both cases. Garrow suggests that he did so to ensure a more unified Court for such an important decision. Garrow, *Liberty and Sexuality*.
111. Ibid.; Hunter, "Justice Blackmun, Abortion, and the Myth of Medical Independence"; Greenhouse, *Becoming Justice Blackmun*. Powell's vote was unexpected. It seemed to contradict his support for judicial restraint. But he was not casting the deciding vote since Blackmun had stuck to his original position. In addition, like many upper-class, educated, mainline Protestants, Powell opposed abortion restrictions on a personal level. Like Blackmun, he had great respect for medical authority (his father-in-law and both brothers-in-law were obstetricians), he had personally intervened with the local prosecutor on behalf of an employee who aided a fatal home abortion, and one of Powell's daughters supported abortion rights. Finally, he felt that common sense rather than the Constitution offered the only answer to the abortion debate. John C. Jeffries, *Justice Lewis F. Powell Jr.* (New York: Charles Scribner's Sons, 1994).
112. Blackmun was not the only justice who viewed abortion mainly as a medical issue. Douglas focused on the protection of doctor-patient privacy in an early *Roe* draft, and Powell insisted that abortion was mainly a medical problem. Hunter, "Justice Blackmun, Abortion, and the Myth of Medical Independence."
113. *Roe v. Wade*, 410 U.S. 113, 152 (1973).
114. Ibid.
115. Ibid., 165–66.
116. "Our cases long have recognized that the Constitution embodies a promise that a certain private sphere of individual liberty will be kept largely beyond the reach of government. That promise extends to women as well as to men. Few decisions are more personal and intimate, more properly private, or more basic to individual dignity and autonomy than a woman's decision—with the guidance of her physician and with the limits specified

in *Roe*—whether to end her pregnancy. A woman's right to make that choice freely is fundamental." *Thornburgh v. American College of Obstetricians & Gynecologists*, 476 U.S. 747, 772 (1986).
117. "No. 70-18—Roe v. Wade, No. 70-40—Doe v. Bolton" in Greenhouse and Siegel, *Before Roe v. Wade*, 251; Garrow, *Liberty and Sexuality*. Greenhouse and Siegel note that Blackmun wrote the hand-down before he saw Burger's concurrence. Once he saw that it disavowed "abortion on demand," he may have believed that the final paragraph of his announcement was redundant. Although the phrase "abortion on demand" was originally coined by pro-choice activists, by the time of the court's decisions, pro-lifers had begun using it as a pejorative term implying abortions without good reasons.
118. *Roe v. Wade*, 410 U.S. at 178.
119. Ibid., 208. In a 1994 oral history interview, Blackmun said he was grateful for Burger's statement: "[The chief justice] said, 'The Court today is not holding for abortion on demand.' I've always been grateful for that. I think the majority opinion said that, certainly implied it, but coming from the chief justice in a separate opinion, I think greatly enforced that posture, that aspect of the case." Blackmun, *Justice Harry A. Blackmun Oral History Project Transcript*, sess. 8, pt. 2.
120. Garrow, *Liberty and Sexuality*; Rubin, *Abortion Politics and the Courts*; Greenhouse, *Becoming Justice Blackmun*.
121. Tuohy, *Accidental Logics*.
122. de Valk, *Morality and Law in Canadian Politics*; Canadian Medical Association, *Transactions of the Ninety-ninth Annual Meeting of the Canadian Medical Association*.
123. Gwendolyn Gray, *Federalism and Health Policy: The Development of Health Systems in Canada and Australia* (Toronto: University of Toronto Press, 1991); Malcolm G. Taylor, *Insuring National Health Care: The Canadian Experience* (Chapel Hill: University of North Carolina Press, 1990).
124. Because health policy was reserved to the provinces, the government could launch a national plan only by attaching conditions to its contributions to provincial medical care programs.
125. Tuohy, *Accidental Logics*.
126. As Dr. D. M. Aitken, assistant secretary of the CMA, put it, "there is a place for a change in the abortion law, even though we are hopeful that this will not be a great number." Canada House of Commons, *Minutes and Proceedings and Evidence of the Standing Committee on Health Welfare and Social Affairs*, 102.
127. Tuohy, *Accidental Logics*, 30.
128. D. Coburn, G. Torrance, and J. Kaufert, "Medical Dominance in Canada in Historical Perspective," *International Journal of Health Services* 13 (1983): 407–32.

129. In Quebec, extra-billing was prohibited and specialists went on strike. However, after the Front de Liberation du Quebec murdered a minister in the provincial government, Prime Minister Trudeau invoked war powers and ordered the specialists back to work. Gray, *Federalism and Health Policy*; Taylor, *Insuring National Health Care*.
130. John Sutton Bennett, *History of the Canadian Medical Association, 1954–94* (Ottawa: Canadian Medical Association, 1996).
131. Jenson, "Getting to Morgentaler"; de Valk, *Morality and Law in Canadian Politics*; *Globe and Mail*, November 3, 1967.
132. Canada House of Commons, *Minutes and Proceedings and Evidence of the Standing Committee on Health Welfare and Social Affairs*, 98.
133. Ibid., 109.
134. Ibid., 101.
135. Carol Sachs Weisman, *Women's Health Care: Activist Traditions and Institutional Change* (Baltimore: Johns Hopkins University Press, 1998); American Medical Association, *House of Delegate Proceedings, Annual Convention* (1970).
136. Blakeslee, "Protest Disrupts Meeting of A.M.A."; Nordheimer, "Protestor Likens A.M.A. to Saigon Government"; "Dispute among the Doctors in A.M.A.'s House," *New York Times*, July 20, 1969; Starr, *Social Transformation of American Medicine*; Campion, *AMA and U.S. Health Policy since 1940*; "Unconventional Convention: American Medical Association"; "Brush-Off at the Red Lacquer Room"; *Wall Street Journal*, June 22, 1970, 8.
137. Lader, *Abortion II*; Garrow, *Liberty and Sexuality*.
138. "Modern Medicine Poll on Socioeconomic Issues"; "Abortion: The Doctor's Dilemma"; Morton A. Silver, "Birth Control and the Private Physician," *Family Planning Perspectives* 4, no. 2 (1972): 42–46; Tatalovich and Daynes, *Politics of Abortion*.

CHAPTER FOUR

1. Robin F. Badgley, Denyse Fortin Caron, and Marion G. Powell, *Report of the Committee on the Operation of the Abortion Law* (Ottawa: Minister of Supply and Services Canada, 1977); Elizabeth Kathleen Lane, *Report of the Committee on the Working of the Abortion Act* (London: Her Majesty's Stationery Office, 1974); Barbara L. Lindheim, "Services, Policies and Costs in U.S. Abortion Facilities," *Family Planning Perspectives* 11, no. 5 (1979): 283–89.
2. About 20 percent of abortion patients were extra-billed, at an average amount of $74. Extra-billing was most common in Alberta (92 percent of patients), Saskatchewan (32 percent), and Nova Scotia, Ontario, and British Columbia (13 to 18 percent).
3. Badgley, Caron, and Powell, *Report of the Committee on the Operation of the Abortion Law*, 402.

NOTES TO PAGES 103–7

4. Gayle Davis, and Roger Davidson, "'A Fifth Freedom' or 'Hideous Atheistic Expediency'? The Medical Community and Abortion Law Reform in Scotland, c. 1960–1975," *Medical History* 50, no. 1 (2006): 29–48.
5. Anne Collins, *The Big Evasion: Abortion: The Issue That Won't Go Away* (Toronto: Lester and Orpen Dennys, 1985).
6. Willard Cates and Christopher Tietze, "Standardized Mortality Rates Associated with Legal Abortion: United States, 1972–1975," *Family Planning Perspectives* 10, no. 2 (1978): 109–12.
7. Badgley, Caron, and Powell, *Report of the Committee on the Operation of the Abortion Law*.
8. Carole Joffe, *Dispatches from the Abortion Wars: The Costs of Fanaticism to Doctors, Patients, and the Rest of Us* (Boston: Beacon Press, 2009).
9. Once small hospitals became dependent on abortion revenue, entrepreneurs used this leverage to obtain reductions on operating room rentals and changes in hospital regulations that hindered economies of scale such as restrictions on frequency of operating room use, anesthesia, the number and qualifications of nurses, and billing and insurance procedures.
10. Michael S. Goldstein, "Creating and Controlling a Medical Market: Abortion in Los Angeles after Liberalization," *Social Problems* 31, no. 5 (1984): 514–29.
11. The actual increase in abortions fell short of these predictions. In the first six months of the new abortion law, New York City provided about 90,000. This was a big increase, but far less than the predicted 500,000. *New York Times*, October 25, 1970, E12; *New York Times*, February 7, 1971. Out-of-state women accounted for 60 percent of the abortions in nonprofit hospitals, 78 percent of those in for-profit hospitals, and 90 percent of those in clinics. *New York Times*, February 7, 1971; *New York Times*, April 11, 1971, SM10.
12. *New York Times*, June 28, 1970, 176.
13. The State Department of Health said that outpatient abortions should be confined to the first twelve weeks of pregnancy and be provided in either hospitals, hospital clinics, or freestanding clinics with a hospital backup, but not in doctor's offices. *New York Times*, May 13, 1970, 37; *New York Times*, June 28, 1970, 176. The State Medical Society took the same position. The New York City Health Services Administration initially ruled that outpatient abortions should be restricted to the first twelve weeks of pregnancy, provided *only in hospitals* and *only to residents*. These guidelines were mandatory for the 18 municipal hospitals but not the other 188 city hospitals. *New York Times*, June 28, 1970, 176. In October 1970, the city incorporated a less restrictive set of regulations into the city health code. These allowed clinic abortions without a residency requirement but required clinics to have an operating room suitable for abdominal surgery and appropriately staffed x-ray, blood bank, and laboratory facilities. The regulations also required clinics to have a backup agreement with a hospi-

tal within ten minutes' driving distance. The regulations prohibited doctors from providing abortions in their offices. Jean Pakter and Frieda Nelson, "Abortion in New York City: The First Nine Months," *Family Planning Perspectives* 3, no. 3 (1971): 5–12; *New York Times*, October 25, 1970, E12.

14. *New York Times*, April 1, 1971, 1. These included the Park East, Park West, Wickersham, and Madison Avenue hospitals.
15. Pakter and Nelson, "Abortion in New York City."
16. *New York Times*, October 20, 1970, 1.
17. Carole E. Joffe, Tracy A. Weitz, and Clare L. Stacey, "Uneasy Allies: Pro-Choice Physicians, Feminist Health Activists, and the Struggle for Abortion Rights," *Sociology of Health and Illness* 26, no. 6 (2004): 775–96; Carole E. Joffe, *The Regulation of Sexuality: Experiences of Family Planning Workers*, Health, Society, and Policy (Philadelphia: Temple University Press, 1986); Joffe, *Dispatches from the Abortion Wars*.
18. Robert E. Hall, "Abortion: Physician and Hospital Attitudes," *American Journal of Public Health* 61, no. 3 (1971): 517.
19. *New York Times*, June 28, 1970, 176.
20. Hall, "Abortion: Physician and Hospital Attitudes," 518–19.
21. *New York Times*, October 25, 1970, E12.
22. Brief of Appellants at 13, 37, 39, 40, *Doe v. Bolton*, 410 U.S. 179 (1973). Hospital requirements were not raised in the appellants' briefs, oral arguments or opinions of *Roe*. But Planned Parenthood's amicus brief noted that the AMA's 1970 resolution allowed abortions in either "hospitals or approved clinics" (which was not actually true) and included a statement by the Joint Program for the Study of Abortion that clinic abortions did not pose a greater risk of complications. The brief also referred to two lower court decisions that had invalidated state hospital requirements. Brief for the Planned Parenthood Federation of America at 9, 16–18, *Roe v. Wade*, 419 U.S. 113 (1973); Gerald N. Rosenberg, *The Hollow Hope: Can Courts Bring About Social Change?* (Chicago: University of Chicago Press, 1991).
23. Brief for the American College of Obstetricians et al. at 5, 85, *Doe v. Bolton*, 410 U.S. 179 (1973).
24. Transcript of Oral Argument at 15, *Doe v. Bolton*, 410 U.S. 179 (1973); Rosenberg, *Hollow Hope*
25. *Doe v. Bolton*, 410 U.S. at 195; C. Tietze and S. Lewit, "Joint Program for the Study of Abortion (JPSA): Early Medical Complications of Legal Abortion," *Studies in Family Planning* 3, no. 6 (1972): 97–119.
26. Lindheim, "Services, Policies, and Costs in U.S. Abortion Facilities"; Stanley K. Henshaw, "Freestanding Abortion Clinics—Services, Structure, Fees," *Family Planning Perspectives* 14, no. 5 (1982): 248–56; Goldstein, "Creating and Controlling a Medical Market"; Michael S. Goldstein, "Abortion as a Medical Career Choice: Entrepreneurs, Community Physicians, and Others," *Journal of Health and Social Behavior* 25, no. 2 (1984): 211–29.

27. Gerald N. Rosenberg, "The Real World of Constitutional Rights: The Supreme Court and the Implementation of the Abortion Decisions," in *Contemplating Courts*, ed. Lee Epstein (Washington, DC: Congressional Quarterly Press, 1995); Edward Weinstock et al., "Legal Abortions in United States since 1973 Supreme Court Decisions," *Family Planning Perspectives* 7, no. 1 (1975): 23–31; Jacqueline Darroch Forrest, Ellen Sullivan, and Christopher Tietze, "Abortion in the United States, 1977–1978," *Family Planning Perspectives* 11, no. 6 (1979): 329; Stanley K. Henshaw and Jennifer Vanvort, "Abortion Services in the United States, 1991 and 1992," *Family Planning Perspectives* 26, no. 3 (1994): 100.
28. Weinstock et al., "Legal Abortions in United States."
29. Ellen Sullivan, Christopher Tietze, and Joy G. Dryfoos, "Legal Abortion in the United States, 1975–1976," *Family Planning Perspectives* 9, no. 3 (1977): 116.
30. Goldstein, "Creating and Controlling a Medical Market," 526.
31. David A. Grimes, "Clinicians Who Provide Abortions: The Thinning Ranks," *Obstetrics and Gynecology* 80, no. 4 (1992): 719–23. Today, the vast majority of ob/gyns still do not provide abortions. Stigma still plays a role, but so does fear of controversy and protest on the part of hospitals and group practices, who often prohibit their doctors from providing abortions. Lori Freedman, *Willing and Unable: Doctors' Constraints in Abortion Care* (Philadelphia: Temple University Press, 2010); Joffe, *Dispatches from the Abortion Wars*.
32. Rosenberg, *Hollow Hope*. Rosenberg identifies four facilitating conditions for the court's limited achievement—existing precedent (*Griswold*), support from professional and political elites, favorable public opinion, and market mechanisms (clinics) for implementing the reform.
33. Neal Devins, "Judicial Matters," *California Law Review* 80 (1992): 1027–69.
34. Willard Cates, "Legal Abortion: The Public Health Record," *Science* 215, no. 4540 (1982): 1586.
35. Mark A. Graber, *Rethinking Abortion: Equal Choice, the Constitution, and Reproductive Politics* (Princeton, NJ: Princeton University Press, 1996); Diana Petitti, *Abortion in California: 1968–1976* (Sacramento: Dept. of Health Services, 1977); *Safe and Legal: 10 Years' Experience with Legal Abortion in New York State* (New York: Alan Guttmacher Institute, 1980). There were also consequences of *Roe* that went beyond the availability and quality of abortion services. It helped reshape the meaning of abortion from health to privacy and body rights. It increased women's control over their reproductive lives. It spurred on the feminist movement. As Rosenberg notes, it also accelerated the pro-life movement—another "significant social change," but he seems to suggest that any court decision would have done so. As I argue in chapter 5, the nature of the decision itself increased controversy. Finally, Rosenberg argues that state-level abortion reforms and repeals would have continued in the absence of *Roe*. In fact, those reforms had come to a halt

by 1970 as antiabortion mobilization gained steam and women's rights and fetal rights meanings of abortion became prominent.

36. Peter Diggory, "Some Experiences of Therapeutic Abortion," *Lancet*, April 26, 1969, 873–75; Keith Hindell and Madeline Simms, *Abortion Law Reformed* (London: Peter Owen, 1971); Elizabeth Kathleen Lane, *Report of the Committee on the Working of the Abortion Act, Statistical Volume* (London: Her Majesty's Stationery Office, 1974), 37; Elizabeth Kathleen Lane, Ann Cartwright, and Susan Lucas, *Report of the Committee on the Working of the Abortion Act, Survey of Abortion Patients* (London: Her Majesty's Stationery Office, 1974), 21. The LPAS initially provided abortions only for resident women but changed this in 1972. Barbara Rose Unterman, "A Study of the Organization of a Non-profit Service Providing Abortions in Great Britain" (master's thesis, Yale University, 1975). BPAS started by referring patients to Calthorpe Clinic in Birmingham or to private consultants in London but later acquired nursing homes in Brighton and Leamington Spa, Warwickshire. Interview with BPAS official, September 2007. LPAS started with a similar setup to BPAS but later acquired Fairfield Nursing Home on the outskirts of London and began employing five full-time gynecologists. Unterman, "A Study of the Organization of a Non-profit Service Providing Abortions in Great Britain." In 1974, LPAS also obtained a number of beds in the Leigham Nursing Home, also in the outskirts of London. Ibid. In the late 1990s, BPAS took over the LPAS after it ran into financial difficulties.
37. John Keown, *Abortion, Doctors, and the Law: Some Aspects of the Legal Regulation of Abortion in England from 1803 to 1982* (Cambridge: Cambridge University Press, 1988); Victoria Greenwood and Jock Young, *Abortion in Demand* (London: Pluto Press, 1976); Hindell and Simms, *Abortion Law Reformed*.
38. John Peel, President, RCOG, to Bernard Braine, Member of Parliament, January 16, 1967, Archives of the RCOG A16/3.
39. *Lancet*, April 19, 1969.
40. Royal College of Obstetricians and Gynaecologists, "Findings of an Inquiry into the First Year's Working of the Act," *British Medical Journal* 2 (1970): 534.
41. Lane, *Report of the Committee on the Working of the Abortion Act*, 2:86–89.
42. Greenwood and Young, *Abortion in Demand*; *Lancet*, February 15, 1969, 355.
43. Hindell and Simms, *Abortion Law Reformed*.
44. Colin Francome, *Abortion Practice in Britain and the United States* (London: Allen and Unwin, 1986).
45. Royal College of Obstetricians and Gynaecologists, "Findings of an Inquiry into the First Year's Working of the Act," 533.
46. Unterman, "Study of the Organization of a Non-profit Service"; F. G. R. Fowkes, J. C. Catford, and R. F. L. Logan, "Abortion and the NHS: The First Decade," *British Medical Journal*, no. 1 (1979): 217–19; E. E. Rawlings and

A. A. Khan, "Effects of the Abortion Law, 1967 on a Gynaecological Unit," *Lancet*, December 4, 1971, 1249–51; *Lancet*, October 2, 1971, 767.
47. *Lancet*, November 13, 1971, 1074.
48. Lane, *Report of the Committee on the Working of the Abortion Act*.
49. Ibid., 125.
50. Lane, *Report of the Committee on the Working of the Abortion Act*, 1:134, 262–63.
51. Ibid., 1:64–65.
52. British Medical Association, "Commentary on the Report of the Lane Committee on the Working of the Abortion Act" (London: Archives of the Royal College of Obstetricians and Gynaecologists, A4/16/18, 1974); British Medical Association, "Commentary on the Abortion (Amendment) Bill" (London: Archives of the Royal College of Obstetricians and Gynaecologists, A4/16/18, 1975); Royal College of Obstetricians and Gynaecologists. "Memorandum to Council on Abortion (Amendment)" (London: Archives of the Royal College of Obstetricians and Gynaecologists, A4/16/18, February 20, 1975).
53. David Steel, "Time to Stop Fiddling About with the Abortion Act," *Times*, February 16, 1976; British Medical Association, "Commentary on the Abortion (Amendment) Bill."
54. ICBH Witness Seminar, "Abortion Act 1967" (paper presented at the Witness Seminar, Institute of Contemporary British History, 2001), 46.
55. About four hundred additional hospitals were devoted to specialty services unrelated to obstetrics and gynecology or general medical care. Tatalovich argues that American and Canadian hospitals were equally resistant to providing abortion services. In 1986, only 35 percent of hospitals in each country provided abortions. Of course, the impact of this was greater for Canadian women since hospital abortions were not supplemented by clinic ones. Raymond Tatalovich, *The Politics of Abortion in the United States and Canada: A Comparative Study* (Armonk, NY: M. E. Sharpe, 1997); Badgley, Caron, and Powell, *Report of the Committee on the Operation of the Abortion Law*.
56. Badgley, Caron, and Powell, *Report of the Committee on the Operation of the Abortion Law*.
57. Ibid., 115–20.
58. Sharon Walls, "Abortion Law and Improved Abortion Services" (discussion paper, National Association of Women and the Law, National Archives of Canada, Ottawa, Record Group 29, 1990-91/248, Box 31, File 0154-A1 vol. 2, 1982).
59. Badgley, Caron, and Powell, *Report of the Committee on the Operation of the Abortion Law*.
60. Walls, "Abortion Law and Improved Abortion Services," 30.
61. Badgley, Caron, and Powell, *Report of the Committee on the Operation of the Abortion Law*, 160.

62. Ibid., 192–200.
63. Britain's Lane Committee noted that "under the present N.H.S. Acts the publicly financed health service could not undertake abortions on the grounds only of the patient's wishes or convenience: an assessment of the patient's health is therefore necessary in each case. Those women who were not in need of abortion on grounds of health would presumably find that, so far as the N.H.S. was concerned, a legal right to abortion on demand or request might be unenforceable." Lane, *Report of the Committee on the Working of the Abortion Act*, 65.
64. Sheila Shaver, "Body Rights, Social Rights, and the Liberal Welfare State," *Critical Social Policy* 13 (1993–94): 66–93; Jane Brodie, "Health vs. Rights: Comparative Perspectives on Abortion Policy in Canada and the United States," in *Power and Decision: The Social Control of Reproduction*, ed. Gita Sen and Rachel C. Snow (Cambridge, MA: Harvard University Press, 1994), 123–46.
65. Rosalind Pollack Petchesky, *Abortion and Woman's Choice: The State, Sexuality, and Reproductive Freedom* (New York: Longman, 1984).
66. The Hyde amendment prohibits federal funding of abortions except in cases of rape, incest, or to save the woman's life, but the following seventeen states use their own money to fund medically necessary abortions: Alaska, Arizona, California, Connecticut, Hawaii, Illinois, Maryland, Massachusetts, Minnesota, Montana, New Jersey, New Mexico, New York, Oregon, Vermont, Washington, and West Virginia. Most of these states provide their funding under court order. Only four states—Hawaii, Massachusetts, New York, and Washington—do so voluntarily. Six additional states use their own funds for a narrower set of circumstances: Indiana (physical health), Iowa (fetal abnormality), Mississippi (fetal abnormality), Utah (physical health and fetal abnormality), Virginia (fetal abnormality), and Wisconsin (physical health). *Abortion Facts: Public Funding for Abortion: Medicaid and the Hyde Amendment* (Washington, DC: National Abortion Federation, 2008), http://www.prochoice.org/about_abortion/facts/public_funding.html; Guttmacher Institute, "State Policies in Brief: An Overview of Abortion Laws," July 1, 2010.
67. *Trends in Abortion in the United States, 1973–2003* (New York: Alan Guttmacher Institute, 2003).
68. Philip J. Cook et al., "The Effects of Short-Term Variation in Abortion Funding on Pregnancy Outcomes," *Journal of Health Economics* 18, no. 2 (1999): 241–57.
69. Heather D. Boonstra, "The Heart of the Matter: Public Funding of Abortion for Poor Women in the United States," *Guttmacher Policy Review* 10, no. 1 (2007): 12–16.
70. Alesha E. Doan, *Opposition and Intimidation: The Abortion Wars and Strategies of Political Harassment* (Ann Arbor: University of Michigan Press, 2007); Carol Mason, *Killing for Life: The Apocalyptic Narrative of Pro-Life Politics*

(Ithaca, NY: Cornell University Press, 2002); Joffe, *Dispatches from the Abortion Wars*.

71. Rachel K. Jones et al., "Abortion in the United States: Incidence and Access to Services, 2005," *Perspectives on Sexual and Reproductive Health* 40, no. 1 (2008): 6–16.
72. Under common law, most medical procedures required parental consent so this was not a change from existing law, but the common law had loose enforcement mechanisms and light penalties which the legally-defined requirements typically strengthened. The key cases were *Planned Parenthood of Central Missouri v. Danforth*, 428 U.S. 52 (1976), *Bellotti v. Baird*, 443 U.S. 622 (1979), and *Planned Parenthood Association of Kansas City, Missouri v. Ashcroft*, 462 U.S. 476 (1983). In the late 1980s and early 1990s, some states loosened consent requirements by allowing grandparents or other family members to provide consent, but in the 2000s, many states tightened them by requiring written or notarized consent from parents, by changing from parental notice to parental consent, or by making it more difficult for minors to obtain a judicial bypass. Jon F. Merz, Catherine A. Jackson, and Jacob A. Klerman, "A Review of Abortion Policy: Legality, Medicaid Funding, and Parental Involvement, 1967–1994," *Women's Rights Law Reporter* 17, no. 1 (1995): 1–61.
73. 492 U.S. 490 (1989).
74. 505 U.S. 833 (1992).
75. Marlene Gerber Fried, "The Economics of Abortion Access in the United States," *Conscience*, Winter 2005–6.
76. Kaiser Family Foundation, "Focus on Health Reform: Access to Abortion Coverage and Health Reform," January 2010; Kaiser Family Foundation, "Summary of New Health Reform Law," June 18, 2010.
77. A Kaiser Family Foundation study found that 46 percent of covered workers had abortion coverage, but 26 percent of the human resources staff interviewed in this study answered "don't know" on this question. Guttmacher Institute, "News in Context: Guttmacher Institute Memo on Insurance Coverage of Abortion," July 22, 2009.
78. Rachel K. Jones, Lawrence B. Finer, and Susheela Singh, "Characteristics of U.S. Abortion Patients, 2008" (New York: Guttmacher Institute, 2010). For an excellent account of the stigma of abortion and the desire of patients for confidentiality, see Joffe, *Dispatches from the Abortion Wars*.
79. Kaiser Family Foundation, "Focus on Health Reform: Access to Abortion Coverage and Health Reform."
80. Sara Rosenbaum, "Abortion Provisions in the Senate Manager's Amendment" (Washington, DC: George Washington University, 2010).
81. The Congressional Budget Office estimates that of the twenty-nine million people in the exchanges by 2019, five million will be covered by small businesses and another five million will be people who previously had nongroup coverage. The remainder will be people who were previously

uninsured. I have halved these estimates to exclude men. Douglas Elmendorf, "Estimate for H.R. 4872, Reconciliation Act of 2010 (Final Health Care Legislation)" (Washington, DC: Congressional Budget Office, 2010).
82. *Sunday Times*, August 24, 1986.
83. Great Britain Office for National Statistics, *Abortion Statistics: Legal Abortions Carried Out under the 1967 Abortion Act in England and Wales*, vol. 28, AB (London: Stationery Office, 2007).
84. *Times*, January 3, 1995.
85. *Guardian*, March 13, 2000; Royal College of Obstetricians and Gynaecologists, "The Care of Women Requesting Induced Abortion, National Evidence-Based Clinical Guidelines No. 7" (London: Royal College of Obstetricians and Gynaecologists, 2000); *Times*, November 5, 2001; Royal College of Obstetricians and Gynaecologists, "The National Audit of Induced Abortion 2000" (London: Royal College of Obstetricians and Gynecologists, 2001). Another factor was the incorporation of the RCOG standards into the Department of Health's 2001 national sexual health strategy and its toolkit for the commissioning of sexual health services by primary care trusts (PCTs). These documents called for a reduction in geographic disparities in NHS abortion funding. Jane Mezzone, *Effective Commissioning of Sexual Health and HIV Services* (London: Department of Health, 2003).
86. *NHS Abortion Services* (London: Voice for Choice, 2004); S. Rowlands, "Caring for Women Seeking Abortion," *Practitioner*, March 2006, 15–16. In 2004, 36 percent of PCTs failed to reach the target of providing 60 percent of funded abortions before ten weeks' gestation.
87. Henry Morgentaler, *Abortion and Contraception* (New York: Beaufort Books, 1982); Frederick Lee Morton, *Pro-Choice vs. Pro-Life: Abortion and the Courts in Canada* (Norman: University of Oklahoma Press, 1993).
88. Abortion Rights Coalition of Canada, *Clinic Funding—Overview of Political Situation* (Vancouver: Abortion Rights Coalition of Canada, 2007).
89. Ibid. The territories do not have large enough populations to support a clinic, but each has a hospital in its largest city providing abortions, and the territorial government provides travel grants so that women can access it. Joyce Arthur, "Abortion in Canada: History, Law and Access," Pro-Choice Action Network, October 1999, http://www.prochoiceactionnetwork-canada.org/articles/canada.shtml.

CHAPTER FIVE

1. Other groups included the Pro-Life Alliance, Christian Voice, UK Life League, Family and Youth Concern, Christian Institute, Christian Affirmation Campaign, Conservative Family Campaign, and the London Institute for Contemporary Christianity. J. Christopher Soper, *Evangelical Christianity in the United States and Great Britain: Religious Beliefs, Political Choices* (New York: New York University Press, 1994).

2. Colin Francome, *Abortion Freedom: A Worldwide Movement* (Winchester, MA: Allen and Unwin, 1984); Keith Hindell and Madeline Simms, *Abortion Law Reformed* (London: Peter Owen, 1971); Joni Lovenduski, "Parliament, Pressure Groups, Networks, and the Women's Movement: The Politics of Abortion Law Reform in Britain (1967–1983)," in *The New Politics of Abortion*, ed. Joni Lovenduski and Joyce Outshoorn (London: Sage, 1986); Melvyn D. Read, "The Pro-Life Movement," *Parliamentary Affairs* 51, no. 3 (1998): 445; Joan Isaac, "The Politics of Morality in the UK," *Parliamentary Affairs* 47, no. 2 (1994): 175; Malcolm Potts, Peter Diggory, and John Peel, *Abortion* (Cambridge: Cambridge University Press, 1977).
3. ALRA and NAC merged in 2003 to form Abortion Rights.
4. Other groups included the Women's Abortion and Contraception Campaign (WACC), British Pregnancy Advisory Service (formerly Birmingham Pregnancy Advisory Service), Marie Stopes International, and Childbirth by Choice Trust. Victoria Greenwood and Jock Young, *Abortion in Demand* (London: Pluto Press, 1976); National Abortion Campaign, *All About NAC* (London: National Abortion Campaign, 1991); National Abortion Campaign, *A Celebration of 25 Years of Safe Legal Abortion, 1967–1992* (London: National Abortion Campaign, 1992); National Abortion Campaign, "A Brief and Partial History of the National Abortion Campaign," in *A Celebration of 25 Years of Safe Legal Abortion*; Lovenduski, "Parliament, Pressure Groups, Networks and the Women's Movement"; Lesley Hoggart, "Feminist Principles Meet Political Reality: The Case of the National Abortion Campaign," 2010, http://www.prochoiceforum.org.uk/al6.php.
5. Other groups included the Coalition for the Protection of Life (formerly Coalition for Life, the political wing of Alliance for Life), Human Life International, Christians Concerned for Life (Calgary), Christian Action Council, Evangelical Fellowship of Canada, Choose Life, Alberta Women of Worth, REAL Women, Women for Life, Faith and Family, Tradition, Family and Property, Alberta Federation of Women United for the Family, and Life Chain.
6. Anne Collins, *The Big Evasion: Abortion: The Issue That Won't Go Away* (Toronto: Lester and Orpen Dennys, 1985); Lorna Kathleen Erwin, "The Politics of Anti-Feminism: The Pro-Family Movement in Canada" (PhD, York University, 1990); Michael W. Cuneo, *Catholics against the Church: Anti-abortion Protest in Toronto, 1969–1985* (Toronto: University of Toronto Press, 1989); Raymond Tatalovich, *The Politics of Abortion in the United States and Canada: A Comparative Study* (Armonk, NY: M. E. Sharpe, 1997); Alphonse de Valk, *Abortion: Lang, Lalonde, Trudeau, Turner* (Toronto: Life Cycle Books, 1975); Catherine Dunphy, *Morgentaler: A Difficult Hero: A Biography* (Toronto: Random House of Canada, 1996).
7. CARAL was later called the Canadian Abortion Rights Action League and is now called Canadians for Choice. Other groups included Association for the Repeal of Canadian Abortion Laws, Vancouver Women's Caucus,

Ontario Coalition for Abortion Clinics (OCAC), Coalition of Reproductive Choice (Winnipeg), Pro-Choice Action Network (PCAN) (formerly BC Coalition for Abortion Clinics), and Abortion Rights Coalition of Canada.

8. Pro-choice unions included the Canadian Labour Congress, the Ontario Federation of Labour, International Ladies' Garment Worker's Union, Steelworkers, United Electrical Workers, and Canadian Auto Workers. Lorna Weir, "Left Popular Politics in Canadian Feminist Abortion Organizing, 1982–1991," *Feminist Studies* 20, no. 2 (1994): 249–74; Memorandum by Freda L. Paltiel, Special Adviser, Welfare and Social Status of Women, National Archives of Canada, Ottawa, December 9, 1974; Frederick Lee Morton, *Pro-Choice vs. Pro-Life: Abortion and the Courts in Canada* (Norman: University of Oklahoma Press, 1993); Jane Jenson, "Getting to Morgentaler: From One Representation to Another," in *The Politics of Abortion*, ed. Janine Brodie, Shelley A. M. Gavigan, and Jane Jenson (Toronto: Oxford University Press, 1992); Larry D. Collins, "The Politics of Abortion: Trends in Canadian Fertility Policy," *Atlantis*, Spring 1982, 2–20; Dunphy, *Morgentaler: A Difficult Hero*; *Toronto Star*, May 15, 2010.

9. Douglas Granberg, "The Abortion Activists," *Family Planning Perspectives* 13, no. 4 (1981): 157.

10. Other groups included Life Amendment PAC, National Pro-Life PAC, March for Life, National Committee for a Human Life Amendment, Americans United for Life, Legal Defense Fund for Unborn Children, American Citizens Concerned for Life, Human Life International, U.S. Coalition for Life, Birthright, Carenet (formerly Christian Action Council), Heartbeat International, Priests for Life, Stand to Reason, Pro-Life Action League, Life Dynamics, Operation Rescue (West), Pro-Life Action Network (Chicago), Missionaries to the Pre-born (Milwaukee), Coalition for Life (College Station, TX), Advocates for Life Ministries (Portland, Oregon), Army of God, and Christian Voice.

11. Crowd estimates are from the *New York Times*, various dates. Where multiple crowd estimates were provided, I list the police estimate. Where a range was provided, I list the lowest one. Some have argued that prevalence of antiabortion violence in the United States stems from an unusually polarized and moralized debate. But Ferree and her coauthors find that German discourse is more moralized and extreme than American discourse, but that Germany has not experienced similar levels of violence. They argue that American antiabortion violence comes mainly from the fringes of the movement. It should also be noted that the United States has higher levels of violence (and political violence) in general than the other countries in this study. Myra Marx Ferree, William A. Gamson, Jurgen Gerhards, and Dieter Rucht, *Shaping Abortion Discourse: Democracy and the Public Sphere in Germany and the United States* (Cambridge: Cambridge University Press, 2002).

12. NARAL is now called NARAL Pro-Choice America. Other groups include National Women's Political Caucus (NWPC), Religious Coalition for

Reproductive Choice (formerly Religious Coalition for Abortion Rights), Zero Population Growth, National Abortion Federation (NAF), Catholics for Free Choice, Republicans for Choice, and Fund for the Feminist Majority.

13. Crowd estimates are from *New York Times*, various dates. Where multiple crowd estimates were provided, I list the police estimate. Where a range was provided, I list the lowest one. N. E. H. Hull and Peter Charles Hoffer, Roe v. Wade: *The Abortion Rights Controversy in American History*, Landmark Law Cases and American Society (Lawrence: University Press of Kansas, 2001); Suzanne Staggenborg, *The Pro-Choice Movement: Organization and Activism in the Abortion Conflict* (New York: Oxford University Press, 1991); Ziad W. Munson, *The Making of Pro-Life Activists: How Social Movement Mobilization Works* (Chicago: University of Chicago Press, 2009); Alesha E. Doan, *Opposition and Intimidation: The Abortion Wars and Strategies of Political Harassment* (Ann Arbor: University of Michigan Press, 2007); Jon A. Shields, *The Democratic Virtues of the Christian Right* (Princeton, NJ: Princeton University Press, 2009); Peter Korn, *Lovejoy: A Year in the Life of an Abortion Clinic* (New York: Atlantic Monthly Press, 1996); Drew Halfmann and Michael P. Young, "War Pictures: The Grotesque as a Mobilizing Tactic," *Mobilization* 15, no. 1 (2010): 1–24; James Risen and Judy L. Thomas, *Wrath of Angels: The American Abortion War* (New York: Basic Books, 1998); National Abortion Federation, "Violence and Disruption Statistics," http://www.prochoice.org/pubs_research/publications/downloads/about_abortion/violence_stats.pdf; Carol Mason, *Killing for Life: The Apocalyptic Narrative of Pro-Life Politics* (Ithaca, NY: Cornell University Press, 2002); Holly Yeager, "Does Emily's List Still Matter?," *American Prospect*, July 7, 2007.

14. Kristin Luker, *Abortion and the Politics of Motherhood* (Berkeley: University of California Press, 1984); Gene Burns, *The Moral Veto: Framing Contraception, Abortion, and Cultural Pluralism in the United States* (Cambridge: Cambridge University Press, 2005).

15. For an argument about the impact of "adversarial policies," see Monica Prasad, *The Politics of Free Markets* (Chicago: University of Chicago Press, 2005).

16. Mark A. Graber, "The Nonmajoritarian Difficulty: Legislative Deference to the Judiciary," *Studies in American Political Development* 7, no. 1 (1993): 35–73; Lovenduski and Outshoorn, "Introduction," in Lovenduski and Outshoorn, *New Politics of Abortion*; Joyce Outshoorn, "The Stability of Compromise: Abortion Politics in Western Europe," in *Abortion Politics: Public Policy in Cross-Cultural Perspective*, ed. Marianne Githens and Dorothy McBride Stetson (New York: Routledge, 1996), 145–64; Alvin Cohan, "Abortion as a Marginal Issue: The Use of Peripheral Mechanisms in Britain and the United States," in Lovenduski and Outshoorn, *New Politics of Abortion*, 27–48; Tatalovich, *Politics of Abortion in the United States and Canada: A Comparative Study*.

17. R. Kent Weaver, "The Politics of Blame Avoidance," *Journal of Public Policy* 6, no. 4 (1986): 371–98. See also Leslie A. Pal and R. Kent Weaver, eds., *The Government Taketh Away: The Politics of Pain in the United States and Canada* (Washington, DC: Georgetown University Press, 2003); Raymond Tatalovich, "Abortion," in Pal and Weaver, *Government Taketh Away*; Tatalovich, *Politics of Abortion in the United States and Canada: A Comparative Study*; Burns, *Moral Veto*.
18. Quoted in Graber, "Nonmajoritarian Difficulty," 58.
19. Ibid. British and Canadian MPs have small, homogenous districts, but they are elected mainly for their affiliation with a national party, and those parties have national constituencies. In both countries, party officials have sometimes discouraged MPs from introducing abortion bills.
20. Barbara Hinkson Craig and David M. O'Brien, *Abortion and American Politics* (Chatham, NJ: Chatham House Publishers, 1993). In 1980, 80 percent of NRLC members said they were single-issue voters while less than half of NARAL members said they were. Granberg, "Abortion Activists."
21. William Saletan, *Bearing Right: How Conservatives Won the Abortion War* (Berkeley: University of California Press, 2004).
22. David S. Meyer and Suzanne Staggenborg, "Countermovement Dynamics in Federal Systems: A Comparison of Abortion Politics in Canada and the United States," *Research in Political Sociology* 8 (1998): 209–40; Soper, *Evangelical Christianity in the United States and Great Britain*; Weaver, "Politics of Blame Avoidance"; Lisa Young, *Feminists and Party Politics* (Vancouver: UBC Press, 2000); Leon D. Epstein, *Political Parties in the American Mold* (Madison: University of Wisconsin Press, 1986); Clive S. Thomas, "The United States: The Paradox of Loose Party-Group Ties in the Context of American Political Development," in *Political Parties and Interest Groups: Shaping Democratic Governance*, ed. Clive S. Thomas (Boulder, CO: Lynne Rienner, 2001); Earl H. Fry, *The Canadian Political System*, ACSUS Papers (Washington, DC: Association for Canadian Studies in the United States, 1996); Frank J. Sorauf, *Money in American Elections* (Glenview, IL: Scott, Foresman, 1988); Duane Murray Oldfield, *The Right and the Righteous: The Christian Right Confronts the Republican Party*, Religious Forces in the Modern Political World (Lanham, MD: Rowman and Littlefield, 1996). The Democratic Party may have been more open to social movements than the Republican Party. Among Democrats, power is based on the group of voters or funders one can claim to represent (e.g., labor, blacks, latinos, Asian Americans, women, gays, or business), and allegiance to one's group often comes before allegiance to the party. The party thinks of itself as a collection of outsiders clamoring to get into the mainstream and is thus particularly open to marginalized groups. Historically, the Republican Party was homogenous, and its members thought of themselves as insider members of the mainstream. There were ethnic, gender, regional, and ideological

groups in the party, but their main allegiance was to the party rather than their group. Those who put their ideological or group interests above the party were not "real" Republicans. The rise of the Christian and New Right altered some of these patterns. Jo Freeman, "The Political Culture of the Democratic and Republican Parties," *Political Science Quarterly* 101, no. 3 (1986): 327–56. See also Todd Gitlin, *The Bulldozer and the Big Tent: Blind Republicans, Lame Democrats, and the Recovery of American Ideals* (New York: Wiley, 2007).

23. It has not always been this way. Prior to 1972, most candidates were chosen through caucuses of state party elites. Hubert Humphrey won the 1968 Democratic nomination without competing in a single primary. But the Democratic Party's 1972 McGovern-Fraser Commission required state parties to either open caucuses to all registered party identifiers or establish primaries. Faced with caucuses that they could no longer control, Democratic state legislatures passed primary legislation that often applied to the Republican Party as well. The number of primaries increased from about fourteen for both the Democrats and Republicans in 1968 to thirty-four for the Democrats and forty-one for the Republicans in 1996. Of the remaining caucuses, national rules ensured that Democratic ones were reasonably open, but Republican caucuses varied widely. The Iowa Republican caucuses are fairly open while the Arizona and Montana caucuses limit participation to elected members of precinct committees. Oldfield, *Right and the Righteous*; Allan J. Cigler, "Political Parties and Interest Groups: Competitors, Collaborators, and Uneasy Allies," in *American Political Parties: A Reader*, ed. Eric M. Uslaner (Itasca, IL: F.E. Peacock, 1993).

24. Epstein, *Political Parties in the American Mold*; Anthony M. Sayers, *Parties, Candidates, and Constituency Campaigns in Canadian Elections* (Vancouver: UBC Press, 1999); Oldfield, *Right and the Righteous*; William J. Crotty, *Party Reform* (New York: Longman, 1983); John C. Green, James L. Guth, and Clyde Wilcox, "Less Than Conquerors: The Christian Right in State Republican Parties," in *Social Movements and American Political Institutions*, ed. Anne N. Costain and Andrew S. McFarland (Lanham, MD: Rowman and Littlefield, 1998); Thomas, "United States: The Paradox of Loose Party-Group Ties"; William P. Cross, *Political Parties* (Vancouver: UBC Press, 2004). Canada's NDP was the exception—party membership did not fluctuate so wildly, and there was a premium on years of service to the party.

25. In 1998, the Progressive Conservatives switched to a vote of the entire party membership, but in 2003, they went back to a delegated convention. In 2004, the Conservative Party (the merger of the PC and Canadian Alliance parties) elected their leader through a vote of the party membership. In 2009, the Liberals decided to do the same for future elections. Paul Pennings and Reuven Y. Hazan, "Democratizing Candidate Selection," *Party Politics* 7, no. 3 (2001): 267–75; Lawrence LeDuc, "Democratizing Party Leadership Selection," *Party Politics* 7, no. 3 (2001): 323.

NOTES TO PAGES 133-34

26. In the United States, the chair of the national party committee is responsible for day-to-day operations, the drafting of the party platform, and electioneering rather than public policy, and the chair is not as powerful as the other members of the party leadership. Other positions within the party hierarchy are also more open to new movements in the United States than in the other countries. The leaders of state and local party organizations are chosen at open, poorly attended meetings that new movements can easily capture. These state and local party organizations have limited power but do determine nomination rules and provide some funds, volunteers, expertise, and networks to candidates, though candidates often obtain the bulk of this support themselves. By contrast, in Britain and Canada, most party positions of importance are at the national level, and the leader of the party appoints them. In Canada, groups can capture local party organizations at election time, but these organizations virtually disappear after the elections so this is not a durable gain. Paul Webb, *The Modern British Party System* (London: Sage, 2000); Cross, *Political Parties*; Sayers, *Parties, Candidates, and Constituency Campaigns*.
27. In the Democratic Party, the nominee chooses the delegates that will represent him or her at the national convention. But in the Republican Party, some delegates are elected in open caucuses or conventions at the precinct, county, district, or state level (or some combination of these). Groups can control these meetings by turning out twenty-five to fifty people for a precinct caucus or about one thousand for a state convention. Though a moderate candidate might win a state's delegates in the primary, conservatives may still dominate the meeting that chooses the delegates that will "represent" the moderate candidate at the convention Douglas Usher, "Strategy, Rules, and Participation: Issue Activists in Republican National Convention Delegations, 1976–1996," *Political Science Quarterly* 53, no. 4 (2000): 887–903.
28. Webb, *Modern British Party System*; Cross, *Political Parties*.
29. Allen D. Hertzke, "Harvest of Discontent: Religion and Populism in the 1988 Presidential Campaign," in *The Bible and the Ballot Box: Religion and Politics in the 1988 Election*, ed. James L. Guth and John C. Green (Boulder, CO: Westview Press, 1991).
30. Turnout in British general elections ranged between 72 and 79 percent between 1970 and 1997 but declined to about 60 percent after that. Jessica Yonwin, "UK Election Statistics, 1918–2004," *House of Commons Library Research Paper* 4, no. 61 (2004). Canadian turnout ranged between 69 and 77 percent between 1972 and 1993, but fell to about 64 percent after that (Elections Canada). U.S. turnout has ranged between 50 and 55 percent for presidential elections since 1972.
31. United States Election Project, http://elections.gmu.edu.
32. Epstein, *Political Parties in the American Mold*; Cigler, "Political Parties and Interest Groups." Prasad makes a similar point, noting that weak parties

tend to have more policy entrepreneurs. Monica Prasad, *The Politics of Free Markets* (Chicago: University of Chicago Press, 2005).

33. Party discipline is especially strong in Canada where there are more confidence votes and dissenting MPs are kicked out of the party caucus and denied renomination for the next election. C. E. S. Franks, "Free Votes in the House of Commons: A Problematic Reform," *Policy Options*, November 1997; D. T. Studlar and K. Christensen, "Is Canada a Westminster or Consensus Democracy? A Brief Analysis," *PS: Political Science and Politics* 39, no. 04 (2006): 837–41.

34. Epstein, *Political Parties in the American Mold*.

35. Cigler, "Political Parties and Interest Groups."

36. Parties with and without long-term members are sometimes referred to as "mass parties" and "cadre parties," respectively, although these ideal types have many other key characteristics as well. Maurice Duverger, *Political Parties, Their Organization, and Activity in the Modern State* (London: Methuen; New York: Wiley, 1955); Epstein, *Political Parties in the American Mold*; Richard S. Katz and Peter Mair, "Changing Models of Party Organization and Party Democracy: The Emergence of the Cartel Party," *Party Politics* 1, no. 1 (1995): 5. American and Canadian parties (with the exception of the NDP) did not have mass memberships, but the British parties did. Young, *Feminists and Party Politics*; Sayers, *Parties, Candidates, and Constituency Campaigns*.

37. Soper, "Political Structures and Interest Group Activism"; Grant Jordan and William A. Maloney, "Britain: Change and Continuity within the New Realities of British Politics," in *Political Parties and Interest Groups: Shaping Democratic Governance*, ed. Clive S. Thomas (Boulder, CO: Lynne Rienner, 2001); Robert Garner and Richard N. Kelly, *British Political Parties Today* (Manchester: Manchester University Press, 1993); William M. Chandler and Alan Siaroff, "Parties and Party Government in Advanced Democracies," in *Canadian Political Parties: Leaders, Candidates, and Organization*, ed. Herman Bakvis (Toronto: Dundurn Press, 1991); Christopher Hamm, *Health Policy in Britain: The Politics and Organization of the National Health Service* (London: MacMillan, 1982); Clive S. Thomas, "Studying the Political Party—Interest Group Relationship," in Thomas, *Political Parties and Interest Groups*.

38. Jill McCalla Vickers and M. Janine Brodie, "Canada," in *Politics of the Second Electorate: Women and Public Participation*, ed. Joni Lovenduski and Jill Hills (London: Routledge and Kegan Paul, 1981); Alan Ware, "Activist-Leader Relations and the Structure of Political Parties: Exchange Models and Vote-Seeking Behaviour in Parties," *British Journal of Political Science* 22 (1991): 71–92; Fry, *Canadian Political System*; R. Kenneth Carty and Lynda Erickson, "Candidate Nomination in Canada's Political Parties," in Bakvis, *Canadian Political Parties*; David Kenney Stewart and Keith Archer, *Quasi-Democracy? Parties and Leadership Selection in Alberta* (Vancouver: UBC Press, 2000); George Perlin, "Attitudes of Liberal Convention Delegates toward

Proposals for Reform of the Process of Leadership Selection," in Bakvis, *Canadian Political Parties*; Rejean Pelletier, Francois Bundock, and Michel Sarra-Bournet, "The Structures of Canadian Political Parties: How They Operate," in Bakvis, *Canadian Political Parties*; R. Kenneth Carty, William Cross, and Lisa Young, "A New Canadian Party System," in *Poltical Parties, Representation, and Electoral Democracy in Canada*, ed. William Cross (Oxford: Oxford University Press, 2002). British and Canadian campaigns are divided into national and constituency levels. At the national level, party leaders campaign through high-visibility media events. At the constituency level, candidates campaign through traditional means such as canvassing, distributing leaflets and posters, and mobilizing supporters on election day. Since the 1950s, conventional wisdom has held that constituency campaigning has little effect on campaign results. More recently, this has been called into question by party dealignment and a decline in class voting. Britain has no restrictions on expenditures for the national campaign but quite strict restrictions on constituency campaigns. Munroe Eagles, "The Effectiveness of Local Campaign Spending in the 1993 and 1997 Federal Elections in Canada," *Canadian Journal of Political Science/Revue canadienne de science politique* 37, no. 01 (2004): 117–36; David Denver and Gordon Hands, *Modern Constituency Electioneering: Local Campaigning in the 1992 General Election* (London: Frank Cass, 1997).

39. Thomas, "United States: The Paradox of Loose Party-Group Ties"; Cigler, "Political Parties and Interest Groups"; Epstein, *Political Parties in the American Mold*. Historically, national parties avoided interfering in the affairs of local parties. In the last two decades, however, coordination between national and state and local parties increased as national parties used state parties as conduits for large sums of money and state parties used those funds to become more professionalized. Joel Paddock, *State and National Parties and American Democracy* (New York: Peter Lang, 2005).

40. Some parties competed only in federal elections (Bloc Quebecois and Canadian Alliance) while others competed only in provincial ones (Parti Quebecois and Saskatchewan Party). In the parties that competed at both levels, the two levels of the party often operated separately and embraced different ideologies. Of the major parties, only the NDP was a true federation. Cross, *Political Parties*.

41. Thomas, "Studying the Political Party"; Graham K. Wilson, "American Interest Groups in Comparative Perspective," in *The Politics of Interests*, ed. Mark P. Petracca (Boulder, CO: Westview Press, 1992), 80–95; Otto Kirchheimer, "The Transformation of the Western European Party Systems," in *Political Parties and Political Development*, ed. Joseph LaPalombara and Myron Weiner (Princeton, NJ: Princeton University Press, 1966), 177–200. In recent years, British parties have become more catch-all. In particular, New Labour has reduced its links to unions—though these remain strong by comparison to the United States. In Canada, from 1969–93, the center-left

Liberals and center-right Tories dominated Canadian politics, with the left-wing NDP a distant third. In 1993, the Liberals trounced the Tories and the NDP while two regional parties, the *independiste* Bloc Quebecois and the western conservative/populist Reform Party, made big gains. In 2000, Reform became the Canadian Alliance as it attempted to broaden beyond the West. In 2003, the Canadian Alliance merged with the remnants of the Progressive Conservative Party to form the Conservative Party. The party won the government in 2006. Lisa Young and William Cross, "The Rise of Plebiscitary Democracy in Canadian Political Parties," *Party Politics* 8, no. 6 (2002): 673–99; Young, *Feminists and Party Politics*; L. Sandy Maisel, *Parties and Elections in America* (Lanham, MD: Rowman and Littlefield, 1999); Oldfield, *Right and the Righteous*.

42. The chief whip sends a weekly letter ("the whip") to MPs each week indicating the votes that they are required to attend. The most important votes are underlined three times. Generally, defiance of a three-line whip results in disciplinary action.

43. David Marsh and Joanna Chambers, *Abortion Politics* (London: Junction Books, 1981).

44. The 1983 manifesto pledged to improve NHS facilities for abortion and remove barriers to implementing the 1967 reform. The 1992 manifesto pledged to reduce abortions through family planning and eliminate regional disparities in abortion services.

45. Marsh and Chambers, *Abortion Politics*; *Times*, September, 15, 1992.

46. *Sunday Times*, February 12, 1995.

47. *Guardian*, March 23, 2005.

48. *Sunday Times*, October 27, 1996; *Times*, December 28, 1996. Around this same time, LIFE founded the Pro-Life Alliance Party and ran fifty candidates in the constituencies of MPs who supported abortion rights and especially members of the Labour leadership. Running so many candidates allowed it to qualify for five minutes of television time in which it planned to show footage of aborted fetuses, but the major television companies rejected the broadcast for "offending good taste or decency." *Times*, December 19, 1996; February 7, 1997; February 10, 1997; April 23, 1997.

49. *Times*, December 28, 1996.

50. *Sunday Telegraph*, October 27, 1996; Ellie Lee, *Abortion, Motherhood, and Mental Health: Medicalizing Reproduction in the United States and Great Britain*, Social Problems and Social Issues (New York: Aldine de Gruyter, 2003). Labour backbencher Ronnie Campbell complained that the party did not actually treat abortion as an issue of conscience: "To say that Labour MPs have had a free-conscience vote is an absolute lie. By God I was put under pressure—by my party and from women's organisations." Campbell said that activists had tried to deselect him for his pro-life views and that he had almost lost his union sponsorship over the issue. The party denied

these allegations. *Sunday Times*, January 5, 1997; *Times*, October 27, 1997; *Economist*, January 4, 1997.
51. *Sunday Times*, March 13, 2005; *Times*, March 14, 2005.
52. Magnus Linklater, *Times*, March 16, 2005. See also the *Independent*, March 16, 2005. The *Guardian*'s Jonathan Freedland argued that "to complain if the subject is raised at election time, when we choose the men and women we send to Parliament and who would cast those crucial votes, is to demand that the people be left out of that decision. It makes no democratic sense." *Guardian*, March 23, 2005.
53. *Guardian*, March 23, 2005; *Times*, March 16, 2005; March 21, 2005; *Guardian*, March 16, 2005; *Daily Mail*, March 15, 2005; *Sunday Telegraph*, March 20, 2005.
54. After the Tories lost the election, the campaign to succeed Howard as party leader briefly involved abortion. Candidate Liam Fox said that he would cut the abortion upper limit to twelve weeks, but other candidates were dismissive. Opponent David Davis said this "is not going to decide whether the party wins or loses. We are not America. This is not a battle between the Religious Right and the rest of the political establishment. Any party leader who tries to tell me what the abortion limit is will get told where to go." *Daily Telegraph*, February 10, 2005.
55. *Daily Telegraph*, April 8, 2010; *Guardian*, April 8, 2010; *Catholic Herald*, June 20, 2008; *Catholic Herald*, April 9, 2010. In 2008, Cameron had supported a reduction in the upper time limit to twenty-two or twenty weeks but opposed a reduction to twelve weeks. But at the same time, he supported allowing abortions with the approval of a single doctor and allowing nurses to provide abortions. Cameron's partner in the new coalition Government, Liberal Democrat Nick Clegg, supported the existing twenty-four-week upper time limit.
56. Philip Cowley, *Conscience and Parliament* (London: Frank Cass, 1998); Philip Cowley, "Party Rules," *Progress*, May 14, 2008, http://www.progressonline.org.uk/articles/article.asp?a=2776.
57. Andre Blais, "Accounting for the Electoral Success of the Liberal Party in Canada Presidential Address to the Canadian Political Science Association London, Ontario June 3, 2005," *Canadian Journal of Political Science/Revue canadienne de science politique* 38, no. 04 (2005): 821–40.
58. Young, *Feminists and Party Politics*, 141
59. Joan Hollobon, "Patient and Doctor Victimized by Abortion Laws, MD Says," *Globe and Mail*, June 28, 1974, 13.
60. *Globe and Mail*, March 15, 1983.
61. *Maclean's*, October 17, 1988, 16.
62. Joyce Arthur, "Abortion in Canada: History, Law and Access," Pro-Choice Action Network, October 1999, http://www.prochoiceactionnetwork-canada.org/articles/canada.shtml.

63. The support of the Ontario NDP Government for abortion rights was in part the result of the high level of intraparty democracy in the NDP. In the early 1980s, the Ontario NDP's Women's Committee and its allies in the Ontario Federation of Labour passed several party resolutions supporting Morgentaler's Toronto clinic over the objections of party leaders. The parliamentary caucus was willing to support the general principle of access to abortion but not Morgentaler's civil disobedience. In the Liberal and Progressive Conservative parties, party leaders could have safely ignored such resolutions, but this was not true in the more democratic NDP. Lorna Weir, "Social Movement Activism in the Formation of Ontario New Democratic Party Policy on Abortion, 1982–1984," *Labour/Le Travail* 35 (1995): 178; Weir, "Left Popular Politics."
64. The Liberals won majority Governments in 1993, 1997, and 2000, and a minority one in 2004. The Conservative Party (a merger of the Canadian Alliance and the Progressive Conservative Party) won a minority Government in 2006.
65. *Toronto Star*, January 23, 1993, A13.
66. *Toronto Star*, January 28, 1993; May 4, 1993.
67. *Toronto Star*, September 9, 1993, A16.
68. *Toronto Star*, May 7, 1997, A10.
69. *Toronto Star*, June 7, 2000.
70. *Toronto Star*, August 19, 2000, NR01; November 8, 2000, A01; November 17, 2000.
71. *Globe and Mail*, June 2, 2004.
72. *Toronto Star*, June 4, 2004. From June 2003 to June 2005 provincial and federal courts ruled that same-sex marriages were protected under the *Charter* in eight of ten provinces. In 2003, the federal Liberal Government announced that it would not appeal these rulings, and in summer 2005, it passed a Government bill allowing same-sex marriages. Cabinet members were required to vote for the bill, but backbenchers had a free vote.
73. *Globe and Mail*, June 2, 2004.
74. *Toronto Star*, June 4, 2004.
75. The clause allows Parliament to designate legislation that is not subject to the *Charter*. *Globe and Mail*, June 7, 2004; Elisabeth Gidengil et al., "Back to the Future? Making Sense of the 2004 Canadian Election Outside Quebec," *Canadian Journal of Political Science/Revue canadienne de science politique* 39, no. 01 (2006): 1–25.
76. *Vancouver Sun*, March 10, 2005.
77. *Globe and Mail*, January 12, 2006.
78. *Globe and Mail*, January 20, 2006; L. Ian MacDonald, "How Harper Forced a Conservative Spring," *Policy Options*, March 2006.
79. *Toronto Star*, February 3, 2010; March 23, 2010; March 24, 2010; CBC News, March 24, 2010; *Globe and Mail*, March 25, 2010; Angelo Persichilli, *Toronto*

Star, March 28, 2010; Andrea Mrozek, "Maternal Madness," *Institute of Marriage and Family Canada, E-Review* 10, no. 5 (2010).
80. *Globe and Mail*, March 31, 2010; April 27, 2010, A1.
81. *Toronto Star*, April 28, 2010, A10. At the G8 Summit in June, the Government announced that it would commit $2.85 billion to the maternal health initiative. The plan would include "sexual and reproductive health care and services, including voluntary family planning," but there was no mention of abortion. Group of Eight, "G8 Muskoka Declaration: Recovery and New Beginnings," June 25–26, 2010.
82. *Toronto Star*, May 15, 2010, A1; May 17, 2010, A6.
83. *Globe and Mail*, May 18, 2010, A4.
84. Jerome L. Himmelstein, *To the Right: The Transformation of American Conservatism* (Berkeley: University of California Press, 1990).
85. I attend to party platforms not as an indicator of eventual policies, but of the campaign positions of candidates and party factions. Most voters do not read the platform, but platform positions are widely disseminated through the media, campaign materials, and candidate speeches. Paddock, *State and National Parties and American Democracy*. The platforms of both parties are drafted by the staff of the winning candidate and then considered and amended by platform committees chosen by the state delegations. This process is more open in the Republican Party. Republican state delegations may choose any two members of their delegation (one man and one woman), but Democratic state delegations must choose from a list of nominees provided by each presidential candidate. Committee members are allocated to each candidate based on his or her delegate count. Jo Freeman, "Change and Continuity for Women at the 1996 Republican and Democratic Conventions," *Off Our Backs*, January 1997, 14–23.
86. Greg D. Adams, "Times of Tumult: Abortion and the Transformation of American Political Parties" (PhD, University of Iowa, 1996); Ted G. Jelen and Clyde Wilcox, "Causes and Consequences of Public Attitudes toward Abortion: A Review and Research Agenda" (paper presented at the Annual Meeting of the Western Political Science Association, 2003, Long Beach, CA); Paul DiMaggio, John Evans, and Bethany Bryson, "Have Americans' Social Attitudes Become More Polarized?," *American Journal of Sociology* 102, no. 3 (1996): 690–755; John H. Evans, "Have Americans' Attitudes Become More Polarized? An Update," *Social Science Quarterly* 84, no. 1 (2003): 72–90; John H. Evans, Bethany Bryson, and Paul DiMaggio, "Opinion Polarization: Important Contributions, Necessary Limitations," *American Journal of Sociology* 106, no. 4 (2001): 944–59; Ted Mouw and Michael E. Sobel, "Culture Wars and Opinion Polarization: The Case of Abortion," *American Journal of Sociology* 106, no. 4 (2001): 913–43; Morris P. Fiorina, Samuel J. Abrams, and Jeremy C. Pope, *Culture War? The Myth of a Polarized America* (New York: Pearson Longman, 2005). This polarization is not the

result of increased polarization in the public. The General Social Survey (GSS) has asked abortion questions for almost forty years (since 1972). The GSS data reveal two things. First, abortion attitudes are clustered into two groups of situations—80 to 90 percent of respondents support legal abortion for situations of rape, birth defects, or a threat to the woman's health, but only 45 to 50 percent of respondents support legal abortion for other situations such as that the woman is poor, she is married and does not want more children, or she is unmarried and does not want to marry the man. Second, abortion attitudes have remained remarkably stable over time. It can be argued that support for abortion in the more controversial situations has declined slightly, but only slightly. A simple additive scale of the six GSS abortion items rounded to a mean of 4 and a median of 3 in most years. Adams, "Times of Tumult"; Jelen and Wilcox, "Causes and Consequences of Public Attitudes." Though the mean and median of abortion attitudes have remained stable, some analysts have argued that their distribution has become more polarized, but this polarization is small and has been questioned by other analysts. DiMaggio, Evans, and Bryson, "Have Americans' Social Attitudes Become More Polarized?"; Evans, "Have Americans' Attitudes Become More Polarized? An Update"; Evans, Bryson, and DiMaggio, "Opinion Polarization"; Mouw and Sobel, "Culture Wars and Opinion Polarization"; Fiorina, Abrams, and Pope, *Culture War?*

87. Nolan McCarty, Keith T. Poole, and Howard Rosenthal, *Polarized America: The Dance of Ideology and Unequal Riches* (Cambridge, MA: MIT Press, 2006); Jacob S. Hacker and Paul Pierson, *Off Center: The Republican Revolution and the Erosion of American Democracy* (New Haven, CT: Yale University Press, 2005); Barbara Sinclair, *Party Wars: Polarization and the Politics of National Policy Making* (Norman: University of Oklahoma Press, 2006).

88. George McKenna, "Democrats, Republicans, and Abortion," *Human Life Review*, Fall 2005; Paige Whaley Eager, *Global Population Policy: From Population Control to Reproductive Rights* (Burlington, VT: Ashgate, 2004).

89. George Gallup, "Abortion Seen Up to Woman, Doctor" in *Before* Roe v. Wade*: Voices That Shaped the Abortion Debate before the Supreme Court's Ruling*, ed. Linda Greenhouse and Reva Siegel (New York: Kaplan, 2010), 207–9.

90. Kevin P. Phillips, *The Emerging Republican Majority* (New York: Anchor Books, 1970); *New York Times*, May 17, 1970.

91. Thomas Byrne Edsall, *Building Red America: The New Conservative Coalition and the Drive for Permanent Power* (New York: Basic Books, 2006); Tanya Melich, *The Republican War against Women: An Insider's Report from Behind the Lines* (New York: Bantam Books, 1996).

92. Lawrence T. King, "Abortion Makes Strange Bedfellows: GOP and GOD," in Greenhouse and Siegel, *Before* Roe v. Wade, 113–15.

93. Linda Greenhouse, *Becoming Justice Blackmun: Harry Blackmun's Supreme Court Journey* (New York: Times Books, 2005), 83.

94. Richard Nixon to Terence Cardinal Cooke, May 16, 1972, in Greenhouse and Siegel, *Before* Roe v. Wade, 158; Donald T. Critchlow, *Intended Consequences: Birth Control, Abortion and Federal Government in Modern America* (New York: Oxford University Press, 1999).
95. "Miscellaneous Issues," *Congressional Quarterly Weekly Report*, September 2, 1972, 2222, quoted in Raymond Tatalovich and Bryon W. Daynes, *The Politics of Abortion: A Study of Community Conflict in Public Policy Making* (New York: Praeger, 1981), 197.
96. *Washington Post*, April 27, 1972, A23. The anonymous source was recently revealed to be Thomas Eagleton (D-MO), McGovern's failed pick for running mate; Robert D. Novak, *The Prince of Darkness* (New York, Crown, 2007).
97. Rick Perlstein, *Nixonland: The Rise of a President and the Fracturing of America* (New York: Scribner, 2008); Greenhouse and Siegel, *Before* Roe v. Wade.
98. Patrick Buchanan, "Assault Book," in Greenhouse and Siegel, *Before* Roe v. Wade, 218.
99. Ibid., 216.
100. *Washington Post*, May 6, 1972, A6.
101. Louis Cassels, "Swing to Right Seen among Catholics, Jews," in Greenhouse and Siegel, *Before* Roe v. Wade, 214.
102. Young, *Feminists and Party Politics*; Christina Wolbrecht, *The Politics of Women's Rights: Parties, Positions, and Change* (Princeton, NJ: Princeton University Press, 2000).
103. Wolbrecht, *Politics of Women's Rights*. McGovern's first and second running mates, Catholics Thomas Eagleton and Sargent Shriver, both opposed abortion rights.
104. Young, *Feminists and Party Politics*; Wolbrecht, *Politics of Women's Rights*.
105. Tanya Melich, *The Republican War against Women: An Insider's Report from Behind the Lines* (New York: Bantam Books, 1996), 29.
106. Ibid.; Wolbrecht, *Politics of Women's Rights*.
107. Young, *Feminists and Party Politics*; Wolbrecht, *Politics of Women's Rights*; *New York Times*, August 6, 1972, 40.
108. Young, *Feminists and Party Politics*; Wolbrecht, *Politics of Women's Rights*; Hull and Hoffer, Roe v. Wade: *The Abortion Rights Controversy in American History*.
109. Laurence H. Tribe, *Abortion: The Clash of Absolutes* (New York: W. W. Norton, 1990); Joseph A. Califano, *Governing America: An Insider's Report from the White House and the Cabinet* (New York: Simon and Schuster, 1981); Andrew R. Flint and Joy Porter, "Jimmy Carter: The Re-emergence of Faith-Based Politics and the Abortion Rights Issue," *Presidential Studies Quarterly* 35, no. 1 (2005): 28–51.
110. Oldfield, *Right and the Righteous*.
111. *New York Times*, November 2, 1975, 82; Melich, *Republican War against Women*; Donald T. Critchlow, *Phyllis Schlafly and Grassroots Conservatism: A*

Woman's Crusade, Politics and Society in Twentieth-Century America (Princeton, NJ: Princeton University Press, 2005); Himmelstein, *To the Right*; Catherine E. Rymph, *Republican Women: Feminism and Conservatism from Suffrage through the Rise of the New Right* (Chapel Hill: University of North Carolina Press, 2006). Schafly's predictions seem to have been borne out as the ACLU has attempted to win Medicaid funding of abortions on equal protection grounds in states that have enacted a state ERA. In 1998, the ACLU won such a battle in New Mexico. Kristen Day, *Democrats for Life: Pro-Life Politics and the Silenced Majority* (Green Forest, AR: New Leaf Press, 2006).

112. Phyllis Schlafly, "Women's Libbers Do NOT Speak for Us," in Greenhouse and Siegel, *Before* Roe v. Wade, 219.
113. *New York Times*, February 4, 1976, 1.
114. Melich, *The Republican War against Women*; Young, *Feminists and Party Politics*; Wolbrecht, *Politics of Women's Rights*. Feminists claimed that Ford's convention chairman, John Rhodes, actually cheated them out of their victory. Rhodes allegedly ignored a request for a roll call vote and then incorrectly awarded the voice vote to the antiabortion forces.
115. Timothy A. Byrnes, "The Politics of the American Catholic Hierarchy," *Political Science Quarterly* 108, no. 3 (1993): 497–514; McKenna, "Democrats, Republicans, and Abortion."
116. Marjorie Randon Hershey, "Citizens' Groups and Political Parties in the United States," *Annals of the American Academy of Political and Social Science* 528 (1993): 142–56; Tatalovich, *Politics of Abortion in the United States and Canada: A Comparative Study*.
117. Wolbrecht, *Politics of Women's Rights*.
118. Cynthia Gorney, *Articles of Faith: A Frontline History of the Abortion Wars* (New York: Simon and Schuster, 1998); David J. Garrow, *Liberty and Sexuality: The Right to Privacy and the Making of* Roe v. Wade (New York: Macmillan, 1994); Oldfield, *Right and the Righteous*.
119. Gorney, *Articles of Faith*; Garrow, *Liberty and Sexuality*; Oldfield, *Right and the Righteous*.
120. Quoted in Lee Epstein and Joseph Kobylka, *The Supreme Court and Legal Change: Abortion and the Death Penalty* (Chapel Hill: University of North Carolina Press, 1992), 232.
121. Oldfield, *Right and the Righteous*; Michelle McKeegan, *Abortion Politics: Mutiny in the Ranks of the Right* (New York: Free Press, 1992); Gorney, *Articles of Faith*; Rymph, *Republican Women*. The movement of the pro-life movement into the Republican Party was reflected at the NRLC, which was led by conservative Republican Mildred Jefferson from 1975 to 1977. James R. Kelly, "Learning and Teaching Consistency: Catholics and the Right-to-Life Movement," in *The Catholic Church and the Politics of Abortion: A View from the States*, ed. Timothy A. Byrnes and Mary C. Segers (Boulder, CO: Westview Press, 1992), 152–68.

122. Jo Freeman, "Feminism vs. Family Values: Women at the 1992 Democratic and Republican Conventions," *PS: Political Science and Politics* 26, no. 1 (1993): 21–28.
123. Wolbrecht, *Politics of Women's Rights*; Freeman, "Feminism vs. Family Values"; Melich, *Republican War against Women*.
124. Saletan, *Bearing Right*.
125. Quoted in Melich, *Republican War against Women*, 289.
126. The Christian Coalition's Ralph Reed claimed that he could mobilize 102 floor whips, 40 runners, and 25 communications hubs for an abortion floor fight. Freeman, "Change and Continuity for Women."
127. Saletan, *Bearing Right*, 251. Bush's primary opponent, Elizabeth Dole, another abortion opponent, also came out against a constitutional amendment. "People want to see us move forward and accomplish some good things, not just kind of endlessly debate something that really is not going anywhere. It's not going to happen." William Murchison, "Abortion Gridlock," *Human Life Review*, Fall 1999.
128. New York *Times*, August 27, 2008.
129. The effect of the parties' abortion positions on voter's choices has been an object of much dispute. Tatalovich, *Politics of Abortion in the United States and Canada: A Comparative Study*; Alan I. Abramowitz, "It's Abortion, Stupid: Policy Voting in the 1992 Presidential Election," *Journal of Politics* 57, no. 1 (1995176-86; Mark J. Wattier, Byron W. Daynes, and Raymond Tatalovich, "Abortion Attitudes, Gender, and Candidate Choice in Presidential Elections: 1972 to 1992," *Women and Politics* 17 (1997): 55–72; Gary Langer and Jon Cohen, "Voters and Values in the 2004 Election," *Public Opinion Quarterly* 69, no. 5 (2005): 744–59; Kenneth Mulligan, "The 'Myth' of Moral Values Voting in the 2004 Presidential Election," *PS: Political Science and Politics* 41, no. 01 (2008): 109–14.
130. William Saletan, "Safe, Legal and Boring," *Slate*, October 16, 2008.
131. Douglas W. Kmiec, "Doug Kmiec Reaffirms Endorsing Sen. Barack Obama," *Catholic Online*, May 3, 2008, http://www.catholic.org/politics/story.php?id=27820; Douglas W. Kmiec, "Barack Obama and Abortion," *America*, September 8, 2008.
132. Prominent examples included Ted Kennedy, Jesse Jackson, Richard Gephardt, Sam Nunn, Al Gore, Paul Simon, Bill Clinton, Bob Kerrey, Tom Harkin, Jerry Brown, George H. W. Bush, Mitt Romney, Rudy Giuliani, and John McCain. Day, *Democrats for Life: Pro-Life Politics and the Silenced Majority*; Melich, *Republican War against Women*. Antiabortion Democratic senators Bill Nelson (D-FL), Dick Durbin (D-IL), and Byron Dorgan (D-ND) became more supportive of abortion rights over time. Day, *Democrats for Life*.
133. In sixteen of these states, the issue was placed on the campaign agenda by the candidates themselves. In four campaigns, it was raised by interest

groups or the media. Thomas M. Carsey, *Campaign Dynamics: The Race for Governor* (Ann Arbor: University of Michigan Press, 2000).
134. The issue was mentioned in 4 percent of all articles in 1988, but 9 percent of all articles in 1990 and 1992.
135. Kim F. Kahn and Patrick J. Kenney, *United States Senate Campaign Strategies and Media Analysis, 1988–1992* [Computer File] (Tempe: Arizona State University [producer], 1995; Ann Arbor, MI: Inter-university Consortium for Political and Social Research [distributor], 2001, 1995).
136. National Abortion Rights Action League, *Who Decides? A State-by-State Review of Abortion and Reproductive Rights* (Washington, DC: National Abortion Rights Action League, 1990).
137. Ibid. The Vermont Republican Party took no position. Democratic parties took no position in Alabama, Georgia, Indiana, Kansas, North Dakota, and South Dakota. The Mississippi Democratic party opposed abortion.
138. Most of these states were in the South, West or Midwest. The Christian Right was most successful in states where nominations for party officials were made through open party caucuses or conventions, in progressive states where party organizations were designed to be weak, and in the South where the history of Democratic dominance left weak Republican organizations. John C. Green, Mark J. Rozell, and Clyde Wilcox, "The Christian Right's Long Political March," in *The Christian Right in American Politics: Marching to the Millennium*, ed. John C. Green, Mark J. Rozell, and Clyde Wilcox (Washington, DC: Georgetown University Press, 2003), 1–20; Green, Guth, and Wilcox, "Less Than Conquerors." A 2000 survey found that the Christian Right had become a substantial presence in eight additional states. John F. Persinos, "Has the Christian Right Taken over the Republican Party?," *Campaigns and Elections*, September 1994; Kimberly H. Conger and John C. Green, "Spreading Out and Digging In: Christian Conservatives and State Republican Parties," *Campaigns and Elections*, February 2002; Green, Guth, and Wilcox, "Less Than Conquerors."
139. Among Republican county chairs, the main recruiting groups were evangelical (25 percent), antiabortion (21 percent), business (16 percent), or farm (10 percent). Among Democratic county chairs, the main recruiting groups were labor (35 percent), teachers (19 percent), or environmental (10 percent). Among Republican state committee members, the main recruiting groups were business (31 percent), antiabortion (18 percent), evangelical (14 percent), conservative (12 percent), or farm (10 percent). Among Democratic state committee members, the main recruiting groups were labor (28 percent), teachers (11 percent), women (10 percent), or civil rights (9 percent). Abortion rights groups recruited only 4 percent. Paddock, *State and National Parties and American Democracy*.
140. The Christian Right was most successful in states where delegates were chosen in open meetings—the smaller the better. In fact, at the 1992 and 1996 conventions, the Christian Right tried unsuccessfully to require that all

delegates be chosen at precinct or county-level meetings. Usher, "Strategy, Rules, and Participation."

141. John C. Green, "The Christian Right and the 1994 Elections: An Overview," in *God at the Grass Roots: The Christian Right in the 1994 Elections*, ed. Mark J. Rozell and Clyde Wilcox (Lanham, MD: Rowman and Littlefield, 1995), 1–16; John C. Green, "The Christian Right and the 1998 Elections: An Overview," in *Prayers in the Precincts: The Christian Right in the 1998 Elections*, ed. John Clifford Green, Mark J. Rozell, and Clyde Wilcox (Washington, DC: Georgetown University Press, 2000), 1–19.

142. Green, "Christian Right and the 1994 Elections"; Mark D. Regnerus, David Sikkink, and Christian Smith, "Voting with the Christian Right: Contextual and Individuals Patterns of Electoral Influence," *Social Forces* 77, no. 4 (1999): 1375–401. The guides were controversial because of charges that they ran afoul of IRS rules requiring nonprofit organizations to be nonpartisan.

143. Oldfield, *Right and the Righteous*; James W. Lamare, Jerry L. Polinard, and Robert D. Wrinkle, "Texas: Religion and Politics in God's Country," in *The Christian Right in American Politics: Marching to the Millennium*, ed. John C. Green, Mark J. Rozell, and Clyde Wilcox (Washington, DC: Georgetown University Press, 2003), 59–78.

144. Ralph Reed, *Active Faith: How Christians Are Changing the Soul of American Politics* (New York: Free Press, 1996), 157. For a discussion of the success of "widespread federated interests" in influencing public policies, see Theda Skocpol, *Protecting Soldiers and Mothers* (Cambridge, MA: Harvard University Press, 1992), 55–57.

145. Some Christian Right leaders criticized Reagan's appointment of Sandra Day O'Connor to the Supreme Court and his lukewarm support of a constitutional amendment banning abortion. Pat Robertson complained that George H. W. Bush appointed too few evangelicals, and Focus on the Family's James Dobson threatened to endorse a third party in 1998. And Christian conservatives were upset about George W. Bush's unsuccessful nomination of the legal lightweight Harriet Miers to the Supreme Court. Oldfield, *Right and the Righteous*; Michael J. Gerson, "A Righteous Indignation," *Newsweek*, May 4, 1998; Hertzke, "Harvest of Discontent."

146. Oldfield, *Right and the Righteous*; Sarah Diamond, *Roads to Dominion: Right-Wing Movements and Political Power in the United States* (New York: Guilford, 1995).

147. Edsall, *Building Red America*; Freeman, "Feminism vs. Family Values."

148. Frank, *What's the Matter with Kansas?*

149. Hull and Hoffer, *Roe v. Wade: The Abortion Rights Controversy in American History*.

150. Fred Block, "Understanding the Diverging Trajectories of the United States and Western Europe: A Neo-Polanyian Analysis," *Politics and Society* 35, no. 1 (2007): 3–33.

151. Paul Weyrich complained that "most leaders of the religious right . . . were so happy, after years of isolation, to get invited to state dinners at the White House that many forgot what moved them to get involved in politics in the first place." Quoted in Oldfield, *Right and the Righteous*, 120.
152. Ibid.
153. Thomas Medvetz, "The Strength of Weekly Ties: Relations of Material and Symbolic Exchange in the Conservative Movement," *Politics and Society* 34, no. 3 (2006): 343–68.
154. Reed, *Active Faith*, 163.
155. Quoted in Oldfield, *Right and the Righteous*, 125.
156. Green, Rozell, and Wilcox, "Christian Right's Long Political March"; Oldfield, *Right and the Righteous*; Diamond, *Roads to Dominion*.
157. *Norfolk Virginian-Pilot*, November 1991.
158. Freeman, "Feminism vs. Family Values"; Paul S. Herrnson, "Do Parties Make a Difference? The Role of Party Organizations in Congressional Elections," *Journal of Politics* 48, no. 3 (1986): 589–615.
159. Edsall, *Building Red America*. In the 2004 elections, concerns about alienating swing voters were less prominent for the GOP, though. After the 2000 elections, Republican pollsters had discovered that few so-called independent voters were truly independent—most typically voted for only one of the parties. With most swing voters unmovable, the GOP focused on mobilizing its base voters through wedge issues such as abortion and same-sex marriage.
160. Diamond, *Roads to Dominion*; Justin Watson, *The Christian Coalition: Dreams of Restoration, Demands for Recognition* (New York: St. Martin's Press, 1997).
161. Verta Taylor, "Social Movement Continuity: The Women's Movement in Abeyance," *American Sociological Review* 54, no. 5 (1989): 761–75.
162. In 1982, 44 percent of Americans claimed to attend church at least once a week compared with 32 percent of Canadians and 14 percent of Britons. European Values Study Group and World Values Survey Association, *European and World Values Surveys Four-Wave Integrated Data File, 1981–2004*, vol. v.20060423 (Madrid, Spain; Tilburg, The Netherlands; Cologne, Germany: Análisis Sociológicos Económicos y Políticos, JD Systems, Zentralarchiv fur Empirische Sozialforschung, 2006). But some scholars argue that American survey respondents overreport their church attendance by as much as 100 percent. Mark Chaves and Laura Stephens, "Church Attendance in the United States," in *Handbook of the Sociology of Religion*, ed. Michelle Dillon (New York: Cambridge University Press, 2003), 85–95. Respondents in other countries probably overreport as well, but we do not know by how much so these numbers are hard to interpret.
163. Minkenberg, "Religion and Public Policy."
164. Chester Gillis, *Roman Catholicism in America* (New York: Columbia University Press, 1999); D. Paul Sullins, "Catholic/Protestant Trends on Abortion:

Convergence and Polarity," *Journal for the Scientific Study of Religion* 38 (1999): 354–69; John C. Green, "The American Religious Landscape and Political Attitudes: A Baseline for 2004" (Washington, DC: Pew Forum on Religion and Public Life, 2004).

165. Meyer and Staggenborg, "Countermovement Dynamics in Federal Systems"; Mildred Schwartz, "Politics and Moral Causes in Canada and the United States," in *Comparative Social Research*, ed. Richard F. Tomasson (Greenwich, CT: JAI Press, 1981); James A. Morone, *Hellfire Nation: The Politics of Sin in American History* (New Haven, CT: Yale University Press, 2003).

166. Mary Ann Glendon, *Abortion and Divorce in Western Law* (Cambridge, MA: Harvard University Press, 1987); Elizabeth Adell Cook, Ted G. Jelen, and Clyde Wilcox, *Between Two Absolutes: Public Opinion and the Politics of Abortion* (Boulder, CO: Westview Press, 1992).

167. Myra Marx Ferree et al., *Shaping Abortion Discourse: Democracy and the Public Sphere in Germany and the United States* (Cambridge: Cambridge University Press, 2002); Michele Dillon, "Cultural Differences in the Abortion Discourse of the Catholic Church: Evidence from Four Countries," *Sociology of Religion* 57, no. 1 (1996): 25–36; Timothy A. Byrnes and Mary C. Segers, *The Catholic Church and the Politics of Abortion: A View from the States* (Boulder, CO: Westview Press, 1992); Greenhouse and Siegel, *Before* Roe v. Wade; David Yamane, *The Catholic Church in State Politics: Negotiating Prophetic Demands and Political Realities* (Lanham, MD: Rowman and Littlefield, 2005).

168. Yamane, *Catholic Church in State Politics*.

169. Catholics preferred Republicans Nixon (1972) and Reagan (1980, 1984) and Democrats Carter (1976), Clinton (1992, 1996), and Obama (2008), but split almost evenly between George H. W. Bush-Dukakis (1988), George W. Bush-Gore (2000), and George W. Bush-Kerry (2004). In terms of party identification, since 2000, slightly more Catholics identify as Democrats than Republicans. The presidential votes are based on an average of Gallup polls, exit polls, and the American National Election Survey. Center for Applied Research in the Apostolate, "Election '08 Forecast: Democrats Have Edge among U.S. Catholics" (Washington, DC: Georgetown University, 2008).

170. Joseph Bernardin, "A Consistent Ethic of Life: An American-Catholic-Dialogue" (Gannon Lecture, Fordham University, New York, NY, December 6, 1983).

171. Joseph Bernardin, "A Consistent Ethic of Life: Continuing the Dialogue" (William Wade Lecture, St. Louis University, St. Louis, MO, March 11, 1984).

172. Byrnes, "Politics of the American Catholic Hierarchy," 508.

173. In 1964, Pope Paul VI announced that a church commission was studying the issue of contraception. In 1965, when the Supreme Court issued its *Griswold* decision striking down restrictions on contraception for married couples, the American Catholic bishops did not protest. They argued that contraception was still immoral but that contraceptive decisions were a

private matter that should not be subject to state regulation. In 1967, the *National Catholic Reporter* obtained leaked copies of both the commission's majority report, recommending that Catholics be permitted to use contraception, and a dissenting minority report. In 1968, the Pope adopted the minority position.

174. Greenhouse and Siegel, *Before* Roe v. Wade; Michael W. Cuneo, *The Smoke of Satan: Conservative and Traditionalist Dissent in Contemporary American Catholicism* (Baltimore: Johns Hopkins University Press, 1999).
175. Gallup, "Abortion Seen Up to Woman, Doctor." See also Gillis, *Roman Catholicism in America*; Sullins, "Catholic/Protestant Trends on Abortion"; Green, "American Religious Landscape and Political Attitudes."
176. Although the conservative groups acknowledge that their tactics may not be particularly persuasive to the secular world, they argue that they are the only way to defeat abortion. Said one activist, "This thing is straight out of hell, and you can't eradicate it without supernatural agency." Chicago activist Julie McCreevy in Cuneo, *Smoke of Satan*, 75–76. Milwaukee pro-life leader Monica Migliorno Miller makes a similar point: "Ultimately abortion is a spiritual war, not a political one. We're fighting an ethic, an entire philosophy of life, which places choice and convenience above the sacredness of created life. Our prayers and our rosaries are repugnant to the news media and repugnant to the secular world in general, but for us they're absolutely central." Ibid., 76.
177. McKenna, "Democrats, Republicans, and Abortion"; Risen and Thomas, *Wrath of Angels*, 154.
178. Risen and Thomas, *Wrath of Angels*, 154.
179. *New York Times*, September 7, 1989; Byrnes, "Politics of the American Catholic Hierarchy."
180. Timothy A. Byrnes, "The Politics of Abortion: Politics and Moral Causes in Canada and the United States," in Byrnes and Segers, *Catholic Church and the Politics of Abortion*.
181. Yamane, *Catholic Church in State Politics*, 151.
182. *New York Times*, May 9, 2009, A17; *America*, May 11, 2009.
183. Cuneo, *Catholics against the Church*.
184. Ibid., 32.
185. *Globe and Mail*, December 12, 1967; Alphonse de Valk, *Morality and Law in Canadian Politics: The Abortion Controversy* (Montreal: Palm, 1974).
186. Cuneo, *Catholics against the Church*, 150.
187. Ibid., 66.
188. Ibid., 79.
189. Tatalovich, *Politics of Abortion in the United States and Canada: A Comparative Study*, 134.
190. At a minimum, evangelicals believe in the literal truth of the Bible, the need to be "born again," and the necessity of witnessing one's faith to others. There are three main groups—fundamentalists, neo-evangelicals, and

Pentecostalists/charismatics. Fundamentalists are doctrinally rigid, avoid associating with people of differing beliefs, and seek to separate themselves from the sinful influences of society. Their most prominent leader was independent Baptist televangelist Jerry Falwell. Neo-evangelicals are more ecumenical and seek to participate in and change society. Their most prominent leader was Billy Graham—though he has also appealed to some fundamentalists. Many fundamentalists and neo-evangelicals are Southern Baptists, the largest denomination in American Protestantism, but they can be found in various other denominations as well. Finally, Pentecostalists believe that the gifts of the Holy Spirit, such as speaking in tongues and faith healing, are not confined to biblical times but are with us today. Fundamentalists, for their part, view this as heresy and are often unwilling to associate with Pentecostalists. Neo-evangelicals, by contrast, have admitted Pentecostal denominations into their main organization, the National Association of evangelicals. The largest Pentecostal denomination is the Assemblies of God and leading Pentecostal figures include Oral Roberts, Jimmy Swaggert, Jim and Tammy Bakker, and Pat Robertson. Finally, a charismatic movement emphasizing the gifts of the Holy Spirit has gained adherents in non-Pentecostal denominations, including Catholicism. Not all white evangelicals support the political positions or the organizations of the Christian Right, and support among conservative Christians for various Christian Right organizations is often limited by theological and denominational concerns. Oldfield, *Right and the Righteous*; Robert D. Woodberry and Christian S. Smith, "Fundamentalism Et Al: Conservative Protestants in America," *Annual Review of Sociology* 24 (1998): 25–56.
191. Risen and Thomas, *Wrath of Angels*.
192. William Martin, *With God on Our Side: The Rise of the Religious Right in America* (New York: Broadway Books, 1996), 194.
193. Ibid.; Harold O. J. Brown, "The Passivity of American Christians," *Christianity Today*, January 16, 1976.
194. Diamond, *Roads to Dominion*; Oldfield, *Right and the Righteous*; Woodberry and Smith, "Fundamentalism Et Al"; Clyde Wilcox and Carin Larson, *Onward Christian Soldiers* (Boulder, CO: Westview Press, 2006); Green, "Christian Right and the 1994 Elections"; Rymph, *Republican Women*.
195. Risen and Thomas, *Wrath of Angels*, 125.
196. Richard Land, "Francis Schaeffer and C. Everett Koop's Invaluable Impact on Pro-Life Evangelicalism," *National Right to Life Committee News*, January 1, 2003; Risen and Thomas, *Wrath of Angels*.
197. Cuneo, *Smoke of Satan*.

CHAPTER SIX

1. Lynn D. Wardle, "The Road to Moderation: The Significance of *Webster* for Legislation Restricting Abortion," *Journal of Law, Medicine, and Ethics* 17,

NOTES TO PAGES 168-71

      no. 4 (1989): 376–83; Raymond Tatalovich, *The Politics of Abortion in the United States and Canada: A Comparative Study* (Armonk, NY: M. E. Sharpe, 1997); Thomas P. Carr, *Issue Brief: Abortion: Legislative Control*, vol. IB88007 (Washington, DC: Congressional Research Service, 1988).
2. I do not include the 2003 ban on so-called partial-birth abortions among the most consequential policy changes since the "intact dilation and extraction" abortion technique is very rare.
3. N. E. H. Hull and Peter Charles Hoffer, Roe v. Wade*: The Abortion Rights Controversy in American History*, Landmark Law Cases and American Society (Lawrence: University Press of Kansas, 2001).
4. Laura Langer and Paul Brace, "The Preemptive Power of State Supreme Courts: Adoption of Abortion and Death Penalty Legislation," *Policy Studies Journal* 33, no. 3 (2005): 317–40.
5. Guttmacher Institute, "State Policies in Brief: An Overview of Abortion Laws," July 1, 2010. In each state, counseling included one or more of the following: discussion of purported links between abortion and breast cancer, discussion of fetal pain, post-abortion syndrome, or the availability of ultrasound.
6. Mifepristone was approved in Britain in 1991 and in the United States in 2000. Canada has not yet approved mifepristone, but a limited number of medication abortions are provided using methotrexate and misoprostol.
7. David Marsh and Melvyn Read, *Private Member's Bills* (Cambridge: Cambridge University Press, 1988).
8. *Times*, September 17, 1987.
9. Thatcher said she was "broadly sympathetic" to Alton's bill, but believed that a time limit of eighteen weeks was going too far. Instead, she supported a twenty-four-week time limit—essentially the status quo. *Sunday Times*, January 17, 1988. In 1985, the RCOG recommended that the legal limit for abortions be reduced from twenty-eight to twenty-four weeks because of changes in fetal viability. The Department of Health persuaded the eight private clinics in England that were authorized to provide late abortions to voluntarily establish twenty-four weeks as their upper time limit. And this was later made a condition of department approval for private clinics. *Times*, July 26, 1985; August, 3, 1985, March 23, 1990; Joan Isaac, "The Politics of Morality in the UK," *Parliamentary Affairs* 47, no. 2 (1994): 175.
10. *Times*, May 13, 1988.
11. *Times*, May 21, 1988.
12. *Guardian*, February 23, 1988; Ann Pettifor, "Abortion Rights: WAC Model Resolution," *Campaign Group News*, 1988.
13. *Times*, March 9, 1989; March 14, 1989; *Sunday Times*, October 22, 1989.
14. *Times*, October, 25, 1989.
15. Sally Sheldon, *Beyond Control: Medical Power and Abortion Law* (London: Pluto Press, 1997); National Abortion Campaign, "A Brief and Partial His-

tory of the National Abortion Campaign," in *A Celebration of 25 Years of Safe Legal Abortion* (London: National Abortion Campaign, 1992), 16–22; Ellie Lee, *Abortion, Motherhood, and Mental Health: Medicalizing Reproduction in the United States and Great Britain*, Social Problems and Social Issues (New York: Aldine de Gruyter, 2003); Susan Millns and Sally Sheldon, "Abortion," in *Conscience and Parliament*, ed. Philip Cowley (London: Frank Cass, 1998); *Times*, April 6, 1990; April 25, 1990; October 24, 1989; Philip Cowley, "What's Two Weeks between Friends?," 2005, http://www.revolts.co.uk.

16. Elizabeth Shepherd, *House of Lords Library Note: Human Fertilisation and Embryology Bill [House of Lords Bill 6, 2007–08]* (London: House of Lords, November 14, 2007).
17. *Times*, May 21, 2008; *Guardian*, October 21–23, 2008; *Daily Telegraph*, July 12, 2008; Sally Sheldon, "A Missed Opportunity to Reform an Outdated Law," *Clinical Ethics* 4, no. 1 (2009): 3; Abortion Rights, "Briefing Paper: Further Abortion Votes This Autumn," 2008; S. Kettell, "Did Secularism Win Out? The Debate over the Human Fertilisation and Embryology Bill," *Political Quarterly* 80, no. 1 (2009): 67–75.
18. Great Britain House of Commons, *The Abortion Act Inquiry: Summary of Conclusions, Some of Its Findings, and List of Recommendations from Report of the Committee on the Working of the Abortion Act* (London: Abortion Law Reform Association, 1974).
19. Victoria Greenwood and Jock Young, *Abortion in Demand* (London: Pluto Press, 1976).
20. Larry D. Collins, "The Politics of Abortion: Trends in Canadian Fertility Policy," *Atlantis*, Spring 1982.
21. Quoted in ibid., 13.
22. *Montreal Gazette*, October 16, 1975.
23. "Ministers and officials, when called upon to explain why the government does not propose any changes in the Abortion law, should stress that there is no consensus for such changes, that the most important causes of the improper operation of the law (which is the concern of most Canadians) are within provincial control, and that the government intends to do everything it can to encourage provincial action to improve the operation of the law." "Record of Cabinet Decision: Strategy for Dealing with the Report of the Committee on the Operation of the Abortion Law" (Ottawa: National Archives of Canada, Record Group 29, Vol. 1629, Box 241, File 4, December 22, 1976).
24. Committee on the Operation of the Abortion Law, *Report of the Committee on the Operation of the Abortion Law* (Ottawa: Department of Supply and Services, 1977), 17.
25. Anne Collins, *The Big Evasion: Abortion: The Issue That Won't Go Away* (Toronto: Lester and Orpen Dennys, 1985).
26. Collins, "Politics of Abortion"; Marc LaLonde, "Statement by the Honourable Marc Lalonde, Minister of National Health and Welfare, March 4"

NOTES TO PAGES 173-77

(Ottawa: National Archives of Canada, Record Group 29 1985-86/235 Box 74, File 6030-C25-1 vol. 1, May 4, 1977).
27. Quoted in Collins, "Politics of Abortion," 15.
28. Ibid.; Brenda Margaret Appelby, "Canada and Birth Control," in *Encyclopedia of Birth Control*, ed. Vern L. Bullough (New York: ABC-Clio, 2001).
29. *Toronto Star*, June 3, 1987.
30. James M. Robertson, *The Evolution of Private Members' Business in the Canadian House of Commons* (Ottawa: Parliamentary Research and Information Service, 2005); Canada House of Commons, *Private Members' Business: Practical Guide* (Ottawa: Canada House of Commons, 2005).
31. *Toronto Star*, April 21, 2008; August 27, 2008.
32. John A. Dickinson and Brian J. Young, *A Short History of Quebec* (Montreal: McGill-Queens University Press, 2003); Graham Fraser, *René Lévesque and the Parti Québécois in Power* (Montreal: McGill-Queens University Press, 2001).
33. Henry Morgentaler, "Report on 5641 Outpatient Abortions by Vacuum Suction Curettage," *Canadian Medical Association Journal* 109, no. 12 (1973): 1202; Catherine Dunphy, *Morgentaler: A Difficult Hero: A Biography* (Toronto: Random House of Canada, 1996).
34. Dunphy, *Morgentaler: A Difficult Hero*.
35. Bédard wrote Federal Justice Minister Ron Basford, "We have tried [to apply the law] with all required energy but it has been shown that this section cannot be enforced as it is worded. . . . The only solution, it appears to me, is to modify the Criminal Code. In the existing constitutional framework, this can only be done by the federal Parliament even when such a process is badly suited to issues such as abortion where profound differences separate Quebec and other provinces." *Montreal Gazette*, December 11, 1976, 1. Morgentaler claimed that the criminal code protected doctors from criminal prosecution when they performed surgery to benefit a patient with reasonable skill and care. *Montreal Gazette*, December 11, 1976, 1.
36. *Montreal Gazette*, December 11, 1976, 1.
37. Fraser, *René Lévesque and the Parti Québécois in Power*. Several days after the Government dropped the charges against Morgentaler, Social Affairs Minister Denis Lazure said that he wanted to see abortion legalized in Quebec, but he noted that this was a personal view. *Montreal Gazette*, December 15, 1976, 3.
38. *Ottawa Citizen*, May 30, 1977, 22; *Montreal Gazette*, June 2, 1977, 9.
39. *Montreal Gazette*, May 8, 3; July 6, 1978, 1.
40. *Montreal Gazette*, April 4, 1977, 4.
41. *Montreal Gazette*, May 8, 1977, 3; July 6, 1978, 1.
42. *Montreal Gazette*, April 18, 1980, 3.
43. *Montreal Gazette*, December 30, 1980, 4.
44. *Montreal Gazette*, December 18, 1980, 28.

45. Stanley K. Henshaw and Elise F. Jones, "The Delivery of Family Planning Services in Ontario and Quebec," *Family Planning Perspectives* 20, no. 2 (1988): 80–87; *Montreal Gazette*, January 6, 1981, 6; March 9, 1982, 3; March 15, 1982, B2.
46. *Montreal Gazette*, March 12, 1982, 1; *Montreal Gazette*, August 10, 1983, 2.
47. Relations between Morgentaler and the feminist abortion rights groups were often strained. The Committee to Establish Abortion Committees (CEAC) and the Ontario Coalition for Abortion Clinics (OCAC) originally made plans with Morgentaler for a women-run clinic employing a doctor that he had recommended. But the clinic's lease fell through, and CEAC was unable to buy a building. Morgentaler swept in and bought and ran a clinic himself. According to CARAL's Norma Scarborough, CEAC had begged Morgentaler not to come to Toronto, but "there was no way Henry could have let that happen. . . . He was too driven to be the center of attention of this cause. He had made this cause his cause. He was not going to sit back and let a clinic open in Ontario or wherever and not be head of that struggle." Quoted in Dunphy, *Morgentaler: A Difficult Hero*, 196. Morgentaler constantly badgered CARAL for money and seemed unappreciative of OCAC and CARAL's role in providing referrals, escorts, safe houses, public education, fund-raising, and lobbying. Said OCAC's spokesperson Judy Rebick, "There were always two opposing factions in the pro-choice movement. There was a wing in the women's movement that wanted nothing to do with Henry" in order to keep the focus on women. "He's not a feminist, but a humanist, which is different. He does understand that the equality of women is one of the central social issues of our society, but he is very much of an individualist. I still don't think he understands the role of the women's movement in it at all." Ibid., 227. Feminist and labor supporters of Morgentaler also disapproved of Morgentaler's lawyer, Morris Manning, who argued several prominent antilabor cases at the time. They urged Morgentaler to fire him. He refused, but did disavow Manning's arguments in the other cases. Ibid.
48. Ibid.
49. Frederick Lee Morton, *Pro-Choice vs. Pro-Life: Abortion and the Courts in Canada* (Norman: University of Oklahoma Press, 1993), 112.
50. The Government also rejected attempts to replace "fundamental principles of justice" with "the principles of due process of law" for fear that such wording might allow the court to rule on not only procedural due process, but substantive due process, as in the United States. This could allow the court to rule on questions such as abortion, contraception, and capital punishment. Ibid.
51. Dunphy, *Morgentaler: A Difficult Hero*.
52. *Rex v. Morgentaler*, (1988) 1 S.C.R. 30, 50. The year after *Morgentaler*, the court handed down two more important abortion decisions. In *Tremblay*

NOTES TO PAGES 178-79

v. *Daigle*, (1989) 2 S.C.R. 530, the court rejected a man's attempt to obtain an injunction preventing his former girlfriend's abortion—ruling that the Quebec Assembly had not intended to confer personhood on fetuses when it enacted the *Quebec Charter*. The court did not rule on the status of fetuses in the *Charter of Rights and Freedoms* since it applies to Government and this was a dispute between individuals. In *Borowski v. Canada*, (1989) 1 S.C.R. 342, antiabortion activist Joe Borowski argued that the *Charter of Rights and Freedoms* applied to the unborn. The court avoided this issue, ruling that Borowski's claim was moot since the court had already struck down the federal abortion statute in *Morgentaler*. Tatalovich, *Politics of Abortion in the United States and Canada: A Comparative Study*.

53. All used a three-stage analysis in which they first determined that the act violated one of the rights enumerated in Section 7, then found that this violation did not conform with "principles of fundamental justice," and finally found that the statute could not be saved under Section 1 of the *Charter*. A statute is valid under Section 1 if it serves important state interests, is applied fairly, is narrowly tailored to its objectives, and appropriately balances state interests and individual rights. Section 1 reads, "The *Canadian Charter of Rights and Freedoms* guarantees the rights and freedoms set out in it subject only to such reasonable limits prescribed by law as can be demonstrably justified in a free and democratic society." Daniel O. Conkle, "Canada's *Roe*: The Canadian Abortion Decision and Its Implications for American Constitutional Law and Theory," *Constitutional Commentary* 6 (1989): 299.
54. Ibid.
55. *Rex v. Morgentaler*, (1988) 1 S.C.R. 30, 90.
56. Ibid., 171.
57. Wilson also found that the statute did not accord with "the fundamental principles of justice" because it violated Section 2's freedom of conscience. She found too that the statute gave disproportionate weight to protecting fetal life because it applied equally to all stages of gestation. Conkle, "Canada's *Roe*."
58. G. P. Crann, "Morgentaler and American Theories of Judicial Review: The *Roe v. Wade* Debate in Canadian Disguise," *University of Toronto Faculty of Law Review* 47 (1989): 499.
59. Conkle, "Canada's *Roe*."
60. On the other hand, the "notwithstanding clause" has never actually been used, and those pondering its use have sometimes been accused of insufficient commitment to the *Charter*, and, by extension, to the rights of Canadians.
61. Glendon, "A Beau Mentir Quie Vient De Loin: The 1988 Canadian Abortion Decision in Comparative Perspective" ; Conkle, "Canada's Roe: The Canadian Abortion Decision and Its Implications for American Constitutional Law and Theory."

62. Daniel O. Conkle, "Canada's Roe: The Canadian Abortion Decision and Its Implications for American Constitutional Law and Theory," *Constitutional Commentary* 6 (1989): 312.
63. Mary Ann Glendon, "A Beau Mentir Quie Vient De Loin: The 1988 Canadian Abortion Decision in Comparative Perspective," *Northwestern University Law Review* 83, no. 3 (1989): 569–91 ; Tatalovich, *Politics of Abortion in the United States and Canada: A Comparative Study*; Conkle, "Canada's Roe."
64. The options included (1) abortion on request, (2) abortion with two doctors' approval for health grounds, and (3) a "compromise" resolution that allowed abortion with a single doctor's approval for broad health grounds in the first trimester, but required two doctors' approval for serious health grounds afterward.
65. Thomas Flanagan argues that Mulroney probably could have enacted an antiabortion bill by imposing the whip but was hesitant to do so because it would have put several women ministers who supported abortion rights in a difficult position. And the Government still would have had difficulty getting the bill through the Senate, which had a Liberal majority and was in open conflict with the Government over a proposed free trade agreement with the United States. Thomas Flanagan, "The Staying Power of the Legislative Status Quo: Collective Choice in Canada's Parliament after Morgentaler," *Canadian Journal of Political Science* 30 (March 1997): 1.
66. Ibid.
67. Dunphy, *Morgentaler: A Difficult Hero*.
68. State courts also played a role. Ten states have explicit privacy guarantees in their constitutions, and several others have implied ones. Seven state courts found that poor women have a right to Medicaid abortions under state constitutions. Neal Devins, "Through the Looking Glass: What Abortion Teaches Us about American Politics," *Columbia Law Review* 94, no. 1 (1994): 293–330. Another key access point, not available in Britain and Canada, was citizen-initiated ballot measures. Between 1973 and 2000, voters considered twenty-two abortion ballot measures, five of which passed. Colorado voters restored public funding, and Arkansas voters restricted it. Washington and Maryland voters codified *Roe*, and Colorado voters required parental notification. Other measures sought to establish waiting periods, restrict partial-birth abortion, and outlaw most abortions. Amy L. Pritchard, "A Brief History of Abortion Related Initiatives and Referendum," in *Initiative and Referendum Almanac*, ed. M. Dane Waters (Durham, NC: Carolina Academic Press, 2003), 731–34.
69. Samuel P. Huntington, *Political Order in Changing Societies* (New Haven, CT: Yale University Press, 1968); Evelyne Huber, Charles Ragin, and John D. Stephens, "Social Democracy, Christian Democracy, Constitutional Structure, and the Welfare State," *American Journal of Sociology* 99 (1993): 711–49.
70. New State Ice Co. v. Liebmann, 285 U.S. 262, 280 (1932) (Brandeis, J.,

NOTES TO PAGES 181-82

dissenting); Jack L. Walker, "The Diffusion of Innovations among the American States," *American Political Science Review* 63 (1969): 880–99; Pierre Trudeau, "The Practice and Theory of Federalism," in *Federalism and the French Canadians*, ed. Pierre Trudeau (Toronto: Macmillan of Canada, 1968); Alan G. Cairns, "The Government and Societies of Canadian Federalism," *Canadian Journal of Political Science* 10, no. 4 (1977): 695–725; Alan G. Cairns, "The Other Crisis in Canadian Federalism," *Canadian Public Administration* 22 (1979): 175–95; Gwendolyn Gray, *Federalism and Health Policy: The Development of Health Systems in Canada and Australia* (Toronto: University of Toronto Press, 1991); David S. Meyer and Suzanne Staggenborg, "Countermovement Dynamics in Federal Systems: A Comparison of Abortion Politics in Canada and the United States," *Research in Political Sociology* 8 (1998): 209–40; Tatalovich, *Politics of Abortion in the United States and Canada: A Comparative Study*. Devins argues against "judicial supremacy" and "majoritarian" views of constitutional interpretation, arguing that "give-and-take between elected governments and the courts permeates all of constitutional decision-making." Neal Devins, *Shaping Constitutional Values: Elected Government, the Supreme Court, and the Abortion Debate*, Interpreting American Politics (Baltimore: Johns Hopkins University Press, 1996), 162.

71. Constitutional amendment requires either that two-thirds of states demand a constitutional convention or that two-thirds of House and Senate members and three-fourths of states approve an amendment. A new constitutional convention has never been called, and the Constitution has been amended only seventeen times since the ratification of the Bill of Rights in 1791. Laurence H. Tribe, *Abortion: The Clash of Absolutes* (New York: W. W. Norton, 1990).

72. Ruth Bader Ginsburg, "Some Thoughts on Autonomy and Equality in Relation to *Roe v. Wade*," *North Carolina Law Review* 63 (1984): 375; Ruth Bader Ginsburg, "Speaking in a Judicial Voice," *New York University Law Review* 67 (1992): 1185; Cass R. Sunstein, "Three Civil Rights Fallacies," *California Law Review* 79 (1991): 751; Mary Ann Glendon, *Abortion and Divorce in Western Law* (Cambridge, MA: Harvard University Press, 1987); Gerald N. Rosenberg, *The Hollow Hope: Can Courts Bring About Social Change?* (Chicago: University of Chicago Press, 1991).

73. Gene Burns, *The Moral Veto: Framing Contraception, Abortion, and Cultural Pluralism in the United States* (Cambridge: Cambridge University Press, 2005); Devins, *Shaping Constitutional Values*; David J. Garrow, "History Lesson for the Judge: What Clinton's Supreme Court Nominee Doesn't Know about *Roe*," *Washington Post*, June 20, 1993; Laurence H. Tribe, *Abortion: The Clash of Absolutes* (New York: W. W. Norton, 1990).

74. In the 1965 *Griswold* decision, the court found that a right of privacy was implied by several enumerated rights and was also guaranteed by the due process clause of the Fourteenth Amendment, which states that no state

shall deprive "any person of life, liberty, or property, without due process of law." Here, the court used "substantive due process," which argues that the government must not only use fair *procedures* but provide adequate *justification* for its actions. Under substantive due process, the court has identified a small number of traditional, natural rights that it deems "fundamental." Statutes restricting such rights are subject to "strict scrutiny"— they must serve a "compelling state interest" and be "narrowly tailored" to that interest. At least four justices relied on substantive due process in *Griswold*. Justice Douglas argued that the right of privacy emanated from the penumbras of other enumerated rights. Critics of substantive due process argue that it allows the court to decide which rights are "fundamental" and thus substitute its own values for those of democratically elected legislatures. Substantive due process is associated with the 1905 *Lochner v. New York* decision in which a conservative court struck down restrictions on the maximum number of hours bakers could work, on the grounds that such restrictions violated the fundamental right of employees to make contracts. "Lochnering" fell into disrepute among the judiciary after struggles over the constitutionality of New Deal programs. But in *Griswold* and *Roe*, it appeared to be back. Jack M. Balkin, "*Roe v. Wade*: An Engine of Controversy," in *What* Roe v. Wade *Should Have Said: The Nation's Top Legal Experts Rewrite America's Most Controversial Decision*, ed. Jack M. Balkin (New York: New York University Press, 2005), 3–27; Edward Keynes, *Liberty, Property, and Privacy: Toward a Jurisprudence of Substantive Due Process* (University Park: Pennsylvania State University Press, 1996). In *Roe*, Blackmun argued that privacy was a fundamental right "broad enough to encompass a woman's decision whether or not to terminate her pregnancy." He provided an extensive history of abortion law to back up his claim that abortion was a traditional, fundamental right. And he wrote that "at common law, at the time of the adoption of our Constitution, and throughout the major portion of the 19th century, abortion was viewed with less disfavor than under most American statutes currently in effect" (410 U.S. at 140).
75. Doe v. Bolton, 410 U.S. 179, 221–22 (1973) (White, J., dissenting).
76. John H. Ely, "The Wages of Crying Wolf: A Comment on *Roe v. Wade*," *Yale Law Journal* 82, no. 5 (1973): 920–49; Keynes, *Liberty, Property, and Privacy*; Jack M. Balkin, ed., *What* Roe v. Wade *Should Have Said: The Nation's Top Legal Experts Rewrite America's Most Controversial Decision* (New York: New York University Press, 2005). For a defense of *Roe*, see Tribe, *Abortion: The Clash of Absolutes*
77. Richard Gregory Morgan, "*Roe v. Wade* and the Lesson of the Pre-*Roe* Case Law," *Michigan Law Review* 77 (1978): 1724.
78. Myra Marx Ferree et al., *Shaping Abortion Discourse: Democracy and the Public Sphere in Germany and the United States* (Cambridge: Cambridge University Press, 2002); Ginsburg, "Speaking in a Judicial Voice"; Balkin, *What* Roe v. Wade *Should Have Said*.

79. Roe v. Wade, 410 U.S. 113, 160 (1973).
80. Mary Ann Glendon, *Rights Talk* (New York: Free Press, 1991).
81. In the Senate, pro-life Republicans Jesse Helms (NC), Orrin Hatch (UT), and Dewey Bartlett (OK) fought it out with pro-choice Republicans Edward Brooke (MA), Robert Packwood (OR), and Lowell Weicker (CT). David Brady and Edward P. Schwartz, "Ideology and Interests in Congressional Voting: The Politics of Abortion in the U.S. Senate," *Public Choice* 84 (1995): 25–48; Raymond Tatalovich and David Schier, "The Persistence of Ideological Cleavage in Voting on Abortion Legislation in the House of Representatives, 1973–1988," in *Understanding the New Politics of Abortion*, ed. Malcolm L. Goggin (Newbury Park, CA: Sage, 1993); Greg D. Adams, "Abortion: Evidence of an Issue Evolution," *American Journal of Political Science* 41, no. 3 (1997): 718–37; Maris A. Vinovskis, "The Politics of Abortion in the House of Representatives in 1976," *Michigan Law Review* 77 (1978): 1790; Barbara Hinkson Craig and David M. O'Brien, *Abortion and American Politics* (Chatham, NJ: Chatham House, 1993).
82. The Democratic leadership in the House during this period included speakers Carl Albert (OK) and Tip O'Neill (MA), majority leader Jim Wright (TX), and whips John McFall (CA) and John Brademas (IN). The Senate leadership included majority leaders Mike Mansfield (MT) and Robert Byrd (WV). O'Neill was personally ambivalent about abortion. Shortly after *Roe*, he supported a constitutional amendment to ban abortion, briefly changed his mind, then changed it back after pressure from his Boston Catholic constituents, but his main priority and that of other party leaders was keeping peace within the party. Said O'Neill, "I've voted both ways on the subject. Sometimes I say to myself I can't vote that way because my religion won't allow me. Next time I say to myself even though I don't believe it, I don't have the right to prevent anyone else. I don't satisfy either group." John A. Farrell, *Tip O'Neill and the Democratic Century* (Boston: Little, Brown, 2001), 524. On the funding ban, House majority leader Jim Wright told his diary, "Tip couldn't take a hand in this one, because of the hard line position of the Catholic bishops in Massachusetts. Brademas can't get out in front because of Notre Dame. That leaves me." Ibid.; Craig and O'Brien, *Abortion and American Politics*; Barbara Sinclair, "The Speaker's Task Force in the Post-Reform House of Representatives," *American Political Science Review* 75, no. 2 (1981): 397–410. In this difficult environment, House speaker Tip O'Neill tried to "keep peace in the family" through the "politics of inclusion"—involving as many members as possible, including junior ones, in the development of coalitions for key bills. Sinclair, "Speaker's Task Force in the Post-Reform House of Representatives"; John A. Farrell, "The O'Neill Speakership," in *The Cannon Centenary Conference: The Changing Nature of the Speakership* (Washington, DC: Government Printing Office, 2003).
83. Authorization bills establish the content of government programs while appropriations bills provide the funding for them.

84. The first funding ban rider was offered in the House in 1974. It was soundly defeated by majorities of both parties, in part because it did not include an exception for life-threatening pregnancies. That same year, the Senate passed a ban that included such an exception with majorities from both parties, but it did not make it out of the House-Senate conference committee. The first funding ban to become law, introduced by Representative Henry Hyde (R-IL), was passed in 1976 with majorities among House Republicans, Senate Republicans and Democrats, and a near majority among House Democrats. The House initially approved a ban with no life exception. In the Senate, majorities of both parties initially voted down the ban, but as elections approached, majorities of both parties accepted a ban with a life exception. In 1977, the ban passed again with even stronger support in the Democratic Party. Fifteen Senate Democrats, among them prominent liberals, changed their positions from the previous year to support the ban. These included Edmund Muskie (D-ME), Edward Kennedy (D-MA), Sam Nunn (D-GA), Hubert Humphrey (D-MN), Patrick Leahy (D-VT), Howard Baker (R-TN), Lawton Chiles (D-FL), and Frank Church (D-ID). Democratic President Carter also expressed support. When asked if the Supreme Court's 1977 rulings approving state and local funding bans were fair, he replied that "there are many things in life that are not fair, that wealthy people can afford and poor people can't. But I don't believe that the federal government should take action to try to make those opportunities exactly equal, particularly when there is a moral factor involved." Frederick S. Jaffe, Barbara L. Lindheim, and Philip R. Lee, *Abortion Politics: Private Morality and Public Policy* (New York: McGraw-Hill, 1981), 132; Craig and O'Brien, *Abortion and American Politics*.
85. House Appropriations Committee chair George Mahon (D-TX) bypassed the head of the House conferees, Edward Flood (D-PA), an adamant abortion opponent, and met secretly with the head of the Senate conferees, Edward Brooke (R-MA). Joseph A. Califano, *Governing America: An Insider's Report from the White House and the Cabinet* (New York: Simon and Schuster, 1981). Speaker Tip O'Neill, with his Boston Catholic constituency, told reporters that he did not participate in the negotiations and did not vote on the amendment (*New York Times*, September 28, 1977; December 7, 1977). Under the compromise, threats to life had to be certified by two doctors, rapes had to be reported promptly to law enforcement or public health officials, and the health exception was limited to "severe and long-lasting physical health damage." Craig and O'Brien, *Abortion and American Politics*.
86. 448 U.S. 297 (1980).
87. Craig and O'Brien, *Abortion and American Politics*.
88. Ibid.
89. B. Norrander and C. Wilcox, "Public Opinion and Policymaking in the States: The Case of Post-*Roe* Abortion Policy," *Policy Studies Journal* 27, no. 4 (1999): 707–22.

90. Most of these targeted abortion exclusively, but some granted minors broad new powers of medical consent while excluding abortion. A separate analysis (available on request) controlled for the number of legislatures held by each party in each period. The number of legislatures held by Republicans increased over time, but this diminished the Republican effect only slightly. Another concern is that states that enact abortion restrictions in early periods are less likely to do so in later periods, but the courts worked against this tendency by frequently resetting the parameters of policy making. After Supreme Court decisions in 1976, 1981, 1983, 1989, and 1992, many states that had previously established policies revised them in the face of new opportunities or constraints.
91. In four states, divided legislatures passed restrictions after 1992. In Iowa and Texas, Democrats fought for looser language that would allow minors to notify relatives or counselors instead of parents. In Oklahoma and South Dakota, the two parties supported similar restrictions. *The Gazette* (Cedar Rapids, IA), March 14, 1996; *San Antonio Express-News*, May 15, 1999; *Daily Breeze* (Torrance, CA), August 2, 1987; *Muskogee Daily Phoenix and Times-Democrat* (OK), April 28, 2005.
92. Steve Alumbaugh and C. K. Rowland, "Links between Platform-Based Appointment Criteria and Trial Judges' Abortion Judgments," *Judicature* 74 (1990): 153.
93. Janet C. Greenburg, *Supreme Conflict: The Inside Story of the Struggle for Control of the United States Supreme Court* (New York: Penguin Press, 2007); Linda Greenhouse, *Becoming Justice Blackmun: Harry Blackmun's Supreme Court Journey* (New York: Times Books, 2005); Michelle McKeegan, *Abortion Politics: Mutiny in the Ranks of the Right* (New York: Free Press, 1992); Lee Epstein and Joseph Kobylka, *The Supreme Court and Legal Change: Abortion and the Death Penalty* (Chapel Hill: University of North Carolina Press, 1992). After the surprises with O'Connor, the Reagan administration took steps to vet future nominees better. It made more extensive background checks, eliminated the independent circuit judge nominating commission, and gave appointment authority to a nine-person committee of top White House and Justice Department appointees. It also favored law professors because they were more likely to have a paper trail on conservative issues. Epstein and Kobylka, *Supreme Court and Legal Change*; McKeegan, *Abortion Politics*. O'Connor was also a strong voice against gender discrimination and may have felt pressured by the feminist movement's renewed embrace of the abortion issue at the time of *Webster*. Finally, her years as a legislator had inclined her to broker compromise on the court. Epstein and Kobylka, *Supreme Court and Legal Change*; Hull and Hoffer, Roe v. Wade: *The Abortion Rights Controversy in American History*. On the day after her nomination, President Reagan wrote in his diary, "Called Judge O'Connor in Arizona and told her she was my nominee for Supreme Court. Already the flak is starting, and from my own supporters. Right-to-life people say she's

pro-abortion. She declares abortion is personally repugnant to her. I think she'll make a good justice" (*New York Times*, January 30, 2008). Epstein and Kobylka argue that pro-choice activists blew a chance to draw O'Connor even closer by inflexibly sticking to the reasoning of *Roe* and ignoring her concerns in their legal briefs. Given her liberal inclinations in gender discrimination cases, they could have used equal protection arguments or realized that the "undue burden" standard suggested by Solicitor General Rex Lee in *Akron* would appeal to her. Instead of ignoring Lee's argument, they could have addressed its weaknesses or, given its vagueness, try to define it in a way that was more favorable to the abortion rights position. Epstein and Kobylka, *Supreme Court and Legal Change*. For a present-day example of such an approach, see L. J. Wharton, S. Frietsche, and K. Kolbert, "Preserving the Core of *Roe*: Reflections on *Planned Parenthood v. Casey*," *Yale Journal of Law and Feminism* 18, no. 2 (2006): 317.

94. Senator Howell Heflin (D-AL) said, "I was troubled by Judge Bork's extremism and admission that he'd been a social democrat, a libertarian, that he'd nearly become a Communist and actually recruited people to attend Communist party meetings and had a strange lifestyle. I was further disturbed by his refusal to discuss his belief in God or the lack thereof." William Saletan, *Bearing Right: How Conservatives Won the Abortion War* (Berkeley: University of California Press, 2004), 52; Greenburg, *Supreme Conflict*; *New York Times*, October 7, 1987, October 23, 1987.
95. Balkin, "*Roe v. Wade*: An Engine of Controversy."
96. Laurence H. Tribe, *Abortion: The Clash of Absolutes* (New York: W. W. Norton, 1990).
97. Ginsburg's nomination was destroyed by allegations that he had smoked marijuana while a law professor. Greenburg, *Supreme Conflict*.
98. *New York Times*, July 24, 1990; P. Reidinger, "Mr. Souter Goes to Washington," *American Bar Association Journal* 76 (1990): 48; Epstein and Kobylka, *Supreme Court and Legal Change*; McKeegan, *Abortion Politics*; Hull and Hoffer, Roe v. Wade: *The Abortion Rights Controversy in American History*.
99. 492 U.S. 490 (1989).
100. 505 U.S. 833 (1992).
101. David J. Garrow, *Liberty and Sexuality: The Right to Privacy and the Making of* Roe v. Wade (New York: Macmillan, 1994); Greenhouse, *Becoming Justice Blackmun*. O'Connor had first applied the "undue burden" standard to abortion in *City of Akron v. Akron Center for Reproductive Health,* 463 U.S. 416 (1983). The standard appeared in U.S. Solicitor General Rex Lee's brief and had also been used in Justice Powell's *Beal* and *Maher* opinions on public funding for the poor. Hull and Hoffer, Roe v. Wade: *The Abortion Rights Controversy in American History*.
102. *Webster*, 492 U.S. at 537.
103. They planned to do so by replacing the "strict scrutiny" standard with a "rationality" standard.

104. For the trio, the "core holding" of *Roe* had three parts: (1) women have the right to have abortions before viability without undue interference by the state, (2) the state can restrict abortions after viability so long as there is an exception for the woman's life or health, and (3) the state has legitimate interests in women's health and potential life from the beginning of pregnancy. This was a plurality opinion: Blackmun and Stevens supported the parts of the opinion supporting *Roe* while White, Rehnquist, Scalia, and Thomas supported the parts modifying it.
105. The trio upheld Pennsylvania's waiting period and parental consent requirements, but overturned its husband notice requirement. They dramatized their support for *Roe* by issuing a joint decision and reading it jointly from the bench. The joint decision imitated the court's 1958 reaffirmation of *Brown v. Board of Education of Topeka* in *Cooper v. Aaron*. Reading decisions from the bench is rare, but this *joint* reading was the only one of the century. Historian David Garrow argues that the ruling "almost certainly guarantees that the central core of [*Roe*] will never again be in any significant danger." David J. Garrow, "A Landmark Decision," *Dissent* 39 (1992): 427. Legal scholar Roy Lucas disagrees. Lucas, "New Historical Insights on the Curious Case of *Baird v. Eisenstadt*," *Roger Williams University Law Review* 9 (2003): 9–54. See also Wharton, Frietsche, and Kolbert, "Preserving the Core of *Roe*," 342; Greenhouse, *Becoming Justice Blackmun*.
106. Garrow, *Liberty and Sexuality*; Chris Whitman, "Looking Back on *Planned Parenthood v. Casey*," *Michigan Law Review* 100, no. 7 (2002): 1980–96; Saletan, *Bearing Right*; *Hearings before Subcomm. on the Constitution of the House Comm. of the Judiciary*, April 22, 1996 (testimony of Douglas W. Kmiec).
107. Quoted in Mark A. Graber, *Rethinking Abortion: Equal Choice, the Constitution, and Reproductive Politics* (Princeton, NJ: Princeton University Press, 1996), 198. See also David J. Garrow, "Abortion before and after *Roe v. Wade*: An Historical Perspective," *Albany Law Review* 62 (1998): 833.
108. Graber, *Rethinking Abortion*.
109. Vanessa Laird, "*Planned Parenthood v. Casey*: The Role of Stare Decisis," *Modern Law Review* 57, no. 3 (1994): 461–67; A. Campbell, "A Divisive Issue and a Divided Court: *Planned Parenthood v. Casey*," *Oxford Journal of Legal Studies* 13, no. 4 (1993): 571–83; Richard H. Fallon, "Legitimacy and the Constitution," *Harvard Law Review* 118, no. 6 (2005): 1787–1844.
110. *Casey*, 505 U.S. at 866–67. The trio articulated a four-prong test for determining whether the court should violate stare decisis—if its central rule is unworkable, if the rule can be removed without social upheaval or unfairness to those who relied on it, if the rule has become a "doctrinal anachronism discounted by society," or if the factual basis of the rule has changed so much as to undermine it (ibid., 835). The trio argued than none of these four conditions had been met in the case of *Roe*. Laird, "*Planned Parenthood v. Casey*"; Campbell, "A Divisive Issue and a Divided Court"; Fallon, "Legitimacy and the Constitution."

111. *Casey*, 505 U.S. at 997–98.
112. *New York Times*, September 12, 2009, 12.
113. Kaiser Family Foundation, "Summary of New Health Reform Law," June 18, 2010; Jonathan Cohn, "How They Did It: The Inside Account of Health Care Reform's Death-Defying Triumph," *New Republic*, June 10, 2010.
114. *Los Angeles Times*, September 4, 2009; U.S. House of Representatives, *Amendment to the Amendment in the Nature of a Substitute to H.R. 3200 Offered by M. Capps* (Washington, DC: 2009).
115. *New York Times*, November 15, 2009, 26; January 7, 2010; Kaiser Family Foundation, "Summary of New Health Reform Law"; Cohn, "How They Did It."
116. Few observers, on either side of the debate, mentioned that the federal government was already subsidizing employer-provided insurance plans, most of which covered abortion, through the income tax exclusion for employer-provided health insurance.
117. The Senate bill had already lost its public plan at the insistence of Senator Joe Lieberman (I-CT), so the issue of abortions in the public plan was now moot.
118. *New York Times*, March 21, 2010, 1; Kaiser Family Foundation, "Summary of New Health Reform Law."
119. William F. Murphy, Daniel DiNardo, and John Wester, "Guest Voices: Health Care for Life and for All," *Washington Post*, March 20, 2010, http://newsweek.washingtonpost.com/onfaith/guestvoices/2010/03/health_care_for_life_and_for_all.html; Secretariat of Pro-Life Activities, "Issues of Life and Conscience in Health Care Reform: An Analysis of the 'Patient Protection and Affordable Care Act' of 2010" (Washington, DC: United States Conference of Catholic Bishops, 2010); United States Conference of Catholic Bishops, "What's Wrong with the Senate Health Care Bill on Abortion? A Response to Professor Jost" (Washington, DC: United States Conference of Catholic Bishops, 2010).
120. Jost responded to the argument that premium credits would pay for *plans* that covered abortion by noting that this was no different from the status quo. Medicaid and Medicare currently provide funds to hospitals that provide abortions. And the exclusion of employer-provided health benefits from income taxation provides a subsidy of $200 billion per year to employer-provided insurance plans, most of which cover abortion. The crucial point in his view was that federal funds themselves did not pay for abortions. *New York Times*, March 20, 2010, 10; Timothy Stoltzfus Jost, "Episcopal Oversight: How the Bishops Conference Gets Health-Care Legislation Wrong," *Commonweal*, May 25, 2010; Timothy Stoltzfus Jost, *The House and Senate Bills on Abortion* (Lexington, VA: Washington and Lee University, 2010); Timothy Stoltzfus Jost, *Response to the United States Conference of Catholic Bishops* (Lexington, VA: Washington and Lee University, 2010).
121. The Democrats lost their sixty-vote Senate majority in January 2010 and

were thus forced to resolve differences between the bills passed by the House and Senate through the budget reconciliation process. By Senate rules, this process could not be used to address abortion funding. As a result, the abortion language in the Senate bill could no longer be amended without killing health reform itself.
122. Representative Christopher Smith (R-NJ) in the *New York Times*, March 20, 2010, 10.
123. Nancy Keenan, "Statement on Health Reform. NARAL Pro-Choice America," March 21, 2010.
124. Sheldon, *Beyond Control*; John Keown, *Abortion, Doctors, and the Law: Some Aspects of the Legal Regulation of Abortion in England from 1803 to 1982* (Cambridge: Cambridge University Press, 1988).
125. Colin Francome, *Abortion Freedom: A Worldwide Movement* (Winchester, MA: Allen and Unwin, 1984); Keown, *Abortion, Doctors, and the Law*; Sheldon, *Beyond Control*.
126. The BMA still did not support abortion on request; delegates rejected a resolution allowing it at the association's 1976 annual meeting. Keown, *Abortion, Doctors, and the Law*; Hindell and Simms, *Abortion Law Reformed*; Sheldon, *Beyond Control*; Francome, *Abortion Freedom*; David Marsh and Joanna Chambers, *Abortion Politics* (London: Junction Books, 1981); *Guardian*, April 4, 1988; April 25, 1988; March 13, 2000; Royal College of Obstetricians and Gynaecologists, "The Care of Women Requesting Induced Abortion, National Evidence-Based Clinical Guidelines No. 7" (London: Royal College of Obstetricians and Gynaecologists, 2000). In 2007, the RCOG supported allowing midwives and nurses to perform first-trimester medication abortions and allowing abortions in GPs offices, but the BMA opposed both of these changes. Both associations supported extending the 1969 Abortion Act to Northern Ireland. *Guardian*, October 11, 2007; British Medical Association, "Wednesday's Updates from the Annual Meeting: Call for End to Two-Signature Rule in Abortions," *BMA News*, June 27, 2007; British Medical Association, "First Trimester Abortion," June 4, 2007; Royal College of Obstetricians and Gynaecologists, "Reasons to Do Away with Two Doctors' Signatures in Approving Abortions—the O&G Perspective," May 2008; Royal College of Obstetricians and Gynaecologists, "Abortion Settings—the O&G Perspective," August 2008.
127. All of the committees approved abortions for grounds of physical or mental health, but not all of them allowed abortions for broader grounds such as fetal abnormality (88 percent of committees allowed it), rape or incest (81 percent), economic hardship (66 percent), extra-marital conception (53 percent), and pregnancies below age eighteen (54 percent). Committees in Ontario and British Columbia were more likely than those in the Maritimes to allow abortions for broad grounds. Robin F. Badgley, Denyse Fortin Caron, and Marion G. Powell, *Report of the Committee on the Operation of the Abortion Law* (Ottawa: Minister of Supply and Services Canada, 1977).

128. Bette Stephenson, "The C.M.A. and Abortion," *Ontario Doctor's Wife*, Spring 1975, 7–8; "Abortion: C.M.A. Prepares M.P.s for Anticipated Commons Debate with Reminder of Current Policy," *Canadian Medical Association Journal* 105 (1971): 522–23; "The C.M.A. Resolutions on Abortion," *Canadian Medical Association Journal* 105 (1971): 441–44.
129. *Globe and Mail*, June 8, 1971, 1.
130. "C.M.A. Resolutions on Abortion," 442.
131. Bette Stephenson, "Abortion: An Open Letter," *Canadian Medical Association Journal* 112 (1975): 494. An official with the National Health and Welfare Department said that "Lang tried to intimidate the hospitals by warning their administrations against too liberal application of the abortion law. The warning went out as a confidential memo, but of course it was leaked." Quoted in Collins, "Politics of Abortion," 12.
132. *Globe and Mail*, March 31, 1975.
133. Stephenson, "Abortion: An Open Letter," 497.
134. Ibid., 494.
135. Joan Hollobon, "Patient and Doctor Victimized by Abortion Laws, MD Says," *Globe and Mail*, June 28, 1974, 13.
136. Douglas A. Geekie, "Abortion: A Review of CMA Policy and Positions," *CMA Journal* 111 (1974): 477.
137. Some doctors complained that the Government had "tried to get something for nothing" by imposing the committees without compensating the doctors who served on them. And many doctors disliked second-guessing colleagues who had submitted abortion applications. Badgley, Caron, and Powell, *Report of the Committee on the Operation of the Abortion Law*, 230.
138. Ibid.
139. Dunphy, *Morgentaler: A Difficult Hero*, 164.
140. *Globe and Mail*, July 1, 1975.
141. *Globe and Mail*, July 28, 1983.
142. *Toronto Star*, January 29, 1988; August 23, 1988; Tatalovich, *Politics of Abortion in the United States and Canada: A Comparative Study*; Canadian Medical Association, "Resolutions Adopted by the General Council of the Canadian Medical Association Pertaining to Abortion, 1970–Present" (Ottawa: Canadian Medical Association, 1981); Canadian Medical Association, "CMA Policy Summary: Induced Abortion," *Canadian Medical Association Journal* 136 (1988): 1176A; Jane Jenson, "Getting to Morgentaler: From One Representation to Another," in *The Politics of Abortion*, ed. Janine Brodie, Shelley A. M. Gavigan, and Jane Jenson (Toronto: Oxford University Press, 1992); Patrick Sullivan, "New Abortion Policy Approved for CMA Despite Some Vocal Opposition," *Canadian Medical Association Journal* 139, no. 6 (1988): 542–44. Dr. Judy Kazimirski, the head of the drafting committee, said, "The association is saying that the woman's physician should prescribe abortion for her if, in the doctor's professional opinion, one is required in the same

way the physician would order any other medical treatment." *Toronto Star*, August 23, 1988.
143. *Toronto Star*, February 6, 1990; February 7, 1990; August 21, 1990.
144. *Toronto Star*, September 10, 1990.
145. *Toronto Star*, October 30, 1990; January 19, 1991.
146. American Medical Association, "House of Delegates Resolution" (1973); American Hospital Association, "House of Delegates Resolution" (1973); Jonathan B. Imber, *Abortion and the Private Practice of Medicine* (New Haven, CT: Yale University Press, 1986); Carole E. Joffe, *Doctors of Conscience: The Struggle to Provide Abortion: Before and after* Roe v. Wade (Boston: Beacon Press, 1995).
147. "Abortion Policy Reaffirmed; Alternatives Stressed," *American Medical News*, July 2/9 1973; Howard Wolinsky and Tom Brune, *The Serpent on the Staff: The Unhealthy Politics of the American Medical Association* (New York: G. P. Putnam's Sons, 1994).
148. The association did respond to a request for information from Senator Edward Brooke. He asked when abortions were medically necessary, and AMA executive vice president James Sammons replied that "the determination of whether or not a proper medical procedure should be performed should not be defined by Congress." Craig and O'Brien, *Abortion and American Politics*.
149. Jaffe, Lindheim, and Lee, *Abortion Politics*.
150. Ibid.
151. Joffe, *Doctors of Conscience*.
152. Quoted in Epstein and Kobylka, *Supreme Court and Legal Change*, 207.
153. Joffe, *Doctors of Conscience*; Imber, *Abortion and the Private Practice of Medicine*.
154. Paul Starr, *The Social Transformation of American Medicine* (New York: Basic Books, 1982); Frederic W. Hafferty and John B. McKinlay, *The Changing Medical Profession* (Oxford: Oxford University Press, 1993); Donald W. Light, "Countervailing Power: The Changing Character of the Medical Profession in the United States," in *The Changing Medical Profession*, ed. Frederic W. Hafferty and John B. McKinlay (Oxford: Oxford University Press, 1993), 69–79.
155. George D. Lundberg and James Stacey, *Severed Trust: Why American Medicine Hasn't Been Fixed* (New York: Basic Books, 2000), 191. The AMA did file amicus briefs in several major abortion rights cases. It supported FDA approval of the abortion pill, and the House of Delegates passed resolutions opposing parental consent and affirming the rights of women to early abortions. But abortion rights activists believed that the AMA's support for abortion rights was lukewarm, especially when it came to lobbying. According to Rachael Pine of the Center for Reproductive Law and Policy, "they have the right views, but politics really intervenes about when and where they'll express them." Wolinsky and Brune, *Serpent on the Staff*, 191.
156. Wolinsky and Brune, *Serpent on the Staff*.

157. *New York Times*, May 29, 1997.
158. Wolinsky and Brune, *Serpent on the Staff*, 194.
159. On the funding ban, the ACOG opposed "the interposition of a third party—the government—without medical expertise between the patient and her attending physician." Jaffe, Lindheim, and Lee, *Abortion Politics*, 48.
160. Carole E. Joffe, *Dispatches from the Abortion Wars: The Costs of Fanaticism to Doctors, Patients, and the Rest of Us* (Boston: Beacon Press, 2009); *New York Times Magazine*, July 12, 2010.
161. Lori Freedman, *Willing and Unable: Doctors' Constraints in Abortion Care* (Philadelphia: Temple University Press, 2010); Joffe, *Dispatches from the Abortion Wars*.

CHAPTER SEVEN

1. Some exceptions are Jonathan B. Imber, *Abortion and the Private Practice of Medicine* (New Haven, CT: Yale University Press, 1986); Frederick S. Jaffe, Barbara L. Lindheim, and Philip R. Lee, *Abortion Politics: Private Morality and Public Policy* (New York: McGraw-Hill, 1981); Carole E. Joffe, *Doctors of Conscience: The Struggle to Provide Abortion: Before and after* Roe v. Wade (Boston: Beacon Press, 1995); Lori Freedman, *Willing and Unable: Doctors' Constraints in Abortion Care* (Philadelphia: Temple University Press, 2010).
2. For example, before she became a Supreme Court justice, Ruth Bader Ginsburg suggested that the court could have ruled more narrowly in *Roe*, striking down the narrow "life" grounds of the Texas abortion statute but upholding the broader "health" grounds of the Georgia statute. Ginsburg, "Some Thoughts on Autonomy and Equality in Relation to Roe v. Wade," *North Carolina Law Review* 63 (1984): 375; Ginsburg, "Speaking in a Judicial Voice," *New York University Law Review* 67 (1992): 1185.
3. Gene Burns, *The Moral Veto: Framing Contraception, Abortion, and Cultural Pluralism in the United States* (Cambridge: Cambridge University Press, 2005).
4. Marie Gottschalk, "The Politics of the Death Penalty," *Perspectives on Politics* 7, no. 4 (2009): 925–28; Joshua Micah Marshall, "Death in Venice," *New Republic*, July 31, 2000.
5. Graber concedes that merely preserving the basic abortion right will not achieve some goals of the pro-choice movement such as public funding or the abolition of parental consent requirements, but he argues that keeping abortions legal (and inexpensive) does more for poor women than public funding could ever do. Mark A. Graber, *Rethinking Abortion: Equal Choice, the Constitution, and Reproductive Politics* (Princeton, NJ: Princeton University Press, 1996)
6. Ibid.; Timothy L. Smith, "Review of *Rethinking Abortion*, by Mark A. Graber," *Law and Politics Book Review* 7, no. 9 (1997): 442–45.

Index

abortion, "elective," 117–18, 206. *See also* abortion gatekeeping; abortion funding

abortion, gestational limits. *See* abortion, late-term

abortion, husband's consent, 11, 102, 104–5, 167–68, 247n38

abortion, illegal, 43, 51, 55, 79, 87, 175

abortion, late-term: Britain, 3, 29, 138–39, 169–72, 217, 322n9; Canada, 104–5, 180, 196, 198; OECD, 245n30; United States, 42, 90, 190, 200, 334n104, 269n36; United States, "partial birth" (dilation and extraction) 150–51, 186–87

abortion, parental consent: OECD, 11, 247n38; United States, 120, 150, 166–68, 186, 298n72, 332n90, 332n91; United States, Britain, and Canada, 104–5

abortion, "partial-birth" (dilation and extraction). *See under* abortion, late-term

abortion, public opinion: OECD, 15; and religiosity, 158; United States, 56, 63–64, 182; United States, Britain, and Canada, 44–45, 158, 164, 206–8, 231, 234–36

abortion clinics. *See* abortion facilities, clinics

abortion committees. *See* abortion gatekeeping, committees

abortion counseling: Britain, 113, 170–71; OECD, 10, 12–13, 245n33; pro-choice, United States, 53, 107; pro-life, United States, 102, 118, 124, 166–68, 322n5

abortion facilities, clinics: 12–13, 35–43, 118–23, 206; Britain, 110–15, 195, Canada, 115–17, 127, 141, 174–80, 195–98, 218; United States, 56, 80–81, 106–10, 199, 203, 292n9. *See also* abortion services

abortion facilities, hospital requirement: 35–36, 68–70; Canada, 36, 39; United States, 43, 107–9, 293n22. *See also* abortion gatekeeping

abortion facilities, hospitals, 12–13, 118–24, 206; Britain, 101–6, 110–15; Canada, 101–6, 115–17, 174–80, 195–98, 279n8, 296n55; and medical gatekeeping, 35–36, 68–70; United States, 39–43, 80–81, 101–10, 146, 199–200, 203–4

abortion facilities, nursing homes (Britain), 69–70, 111

abortion funding: Canada, 143–44, 174, 176, 180, 218; Canada, and extra billing, 93–94, 102, 291n129, 291n2; OECD, 12–13, 247nn43–46; United States, 148–50, 183–86, 198–200, 297n66, 331nn84–85; United States, Britain, and Canada, 12–13,

341

INDEX

abortion funding (*cont.*)
101–6, 117–24, 166–68, 232–33; United States, health reform, 191–93, 298n81, 335n116, 335n120, 335n121. *See also* abortion services

abortion gatekeeping: Britain, 102, 110–14, 167–68, 170, 195; Britain, "statistical argument," 112, 114, 122, 265n11; Canada, 115–17, 141, 167–68, 174, 195–99; and issue meaning, 23, 130; OECD, 2, 10–14; types, 10–14; United States, Britain, and Canada, 35–43, 66–97, 104–6, 209–11; and waiting periods, 104. *See also* abortion, husband's consent; abortion, parental consent; abortion counseling; abortion facilities, clinics; abortion facilities, hospitals; abortion facilities, nursing homes (Britain); "abortion on demand"; abortion waiting periods; *and specific medical associations*

abortion gatekeeping, committees: Canada, 101–6, 115–17, 174–80, 195–98, 336n127; and medical profession, 35, 68–70; OECD, 10; United States, 39–43

abortion grounds. *See* abortion gatekeeping

abortion issue: agenda-setting, 40–41, 47; avoidance, 137, 176; and Catholics, 159–63; controversy of, 130–31; and courts, 26, 63, 178–82, 189, 209–11; and evangelical Christians, 163–65; and federalism, 55–57, 180–82, 209–11; future of, 216–18; judicial review, 180–82; meaning of, 1–2, 7, 23–24, 55–58, 130, 180–82; medical meaning of, 66–67, 117–18, 210; OECD, 214; and parties, 125–53, 209–11; and parties, Britain, 137–40; and parties, Canada, 140–44, 172–80; and parties, United States, 182–86, 144–53; politicization of, 125–53, 157–65, 180–82; and religiosity, 157–64, 208–9; as social policy, 6; types of politics, 15–16. *See also* issues of conscience

Abortion Law Reform Association. *See* ALRA (Abortion Law Reform Association)

abortion medications, 36, 39, 168, 322n6

abortion movements, 2–3, 18–23, 46–49, 126–30; and abortion services, 107; and AMA, 95–96; Britain, 49–50, 126–27, 299n1, 300n4; Canada, 50, 127, 173, 178, 300n5, 300n7, 301n8; and Catholics, 158–63; and evangelical Christians, 163–65; OECD, 13–16; and political parties, 132–53; United States, 50–58, 127–31, 181, 189, 191, 193–94, 301n10, 301n12, 273n91. *See also* Christian Right (United States); feminism; New Right; *and specific movement organizations*

abortion pill. *See* abortion medications

abortion policy: Britain, 3–4, 10–13, 36–38, 169–71; Canada, 4, 10–13, 38–39, 172–80; future of, 216–18; nineteenth-century, 2, 5, 36, 42, 54, 62, 74, 88, 266n19, 265n6; OECD, 1–2, 9–13, 239n10; types of, 9–11, 244n29; United States, 3, 10–13, 39–43, 182–93, 264n1. *See also* abortion gatekeeping; abortion services

abortion politics: Britain, 43–65, 125–40, 157–59, 166–72; Canada, 43–65, 125–37, 140–44, 157–59, 162–63, 166–68, 172–80; future of, 216–28; and medical profession, 66–97; OECD, 1–2, 13–16; and political institutions, 16–29; types of, 13–16; United States, 43–65, 125–37, 144–57, 157–68, 180–94; United States, reform vs. repeal, 47–53, 272n66

abortion rates, 105, 244n29

abortion referral services: Britain, 114, 170, 172; Canada, 104; United States, 53, 58, 107, 109

abortion services: Britain, private sector, 12, 103, 110–15, 117, 122; OECD, 10–12; outpatient, 105, 113; Quebec, 175–77; stigma of providing, 108–9; United States, Canada, and Britain, 12–13, 35–43, 101–24, 165–68, 206–8, 232–33. *See also* abortion facilities, clinics; abortion facilities, hospitals; abortion facilities, nursing homes (Britain); abortion funding

abortion waiting periods: OECD, 10–11, 245n33; United States, Britain, and Canada; 12–13, 120, 166–68, 170–71. *See also* abortion gatekeeping

abortion "on demand": Britain, 112–13, 122, 126, 139; Canada, 176–77, 195–98; United States, 53, 55, 82, 91–92, 146, 279n7. *See also* abortion gatekeeping

abortion, on request. *See* abortion gatekeeping

Abzug, Bella, 41

access points, 24, 135–36, 166, 180–81, 194
Accreditation Council for Graduate Medical Education (ACGME), 200
ACLU (American Civil Liberties Union), 40, 53–55, 129, 199
ACOG (American College of Obstetricians and Gynecologists), and abortion reform, 57, 108, 282n26, 284n50; and post-reform abortion politics, 199–200, 339n159
adoption, 60, 151–52
agenda control, 24, 27, 169–74, 182–86
Aitken, D. M., 94–95, 290n126
Ajello, Carl R., 55
Alan Guttmacher Institute, 193
Alaska, 41–42, 48, 74
Alberta, 102, 123, 197
Alberta Medical Association, 196
ALI (American Law Institute), 40–44, 47–48, 50, 88, 267n23, 267n25
Alito, Samuel, 188
ALRA (Abortion Law Reform Association): agenda-setting, 47; demands of, 49; impact on abortion reform, 37, 70, 95, 111, 126
Alton, David, 3, 169–71, 322n9
AMA (American Medical Association): and abortion reform, 56–57, 66–74, 79–87, 95–97; 203–4, 282n26, 286n62; and feminist protests, 52–53; and issue definition, 23; in nineteenth century, 39; and post-reform abortion politics, 198–200, 338n148, 338n155; and Supreme Court, 3, 87–92
AMCAL (Association for the Modernization of Canadian Abortion Laws), 50, 93
Amenta, Edwin: and institutionalism, 7; and political mediation theory, 22, 46, 57, 255nn69–70, 255n72
American Bar Association (ABA), 56–57, 64
American Civil Liberties Union. *See* ACLU (American Civil Liberties Union)
American College of Obstetricians and Gynecologists (ACOG). *See* ACOG (American College of Obstetricians and Gynecologists)
American Creed, 44–46
American Hospital Association, 198
American Jewish Congress, 57
American Journal of Public Health, 64
American Law Institute. *See* ALI (American Law Institute)
American Life League, 127–28, 161
American Medical Association. *See* AMA (American Medical Association)
American Psychiatric Association, 57
American Public Health Association, 57, 64, 200, 284n50
Americans for Tax Reform, 156
amicus briefs (United States), 54, 71, 108–9, 198–99
AMPAC (American Medical Political Action Committee), 83
Amulree, Lord, 47
Andrews, Kenneth, 22
Anglican church, 73, 159
antifeminism, 141, 148
antistatism, 30, 44–46
antiwar movement, 52, 146
Arizona, 49, 53, 187
ASA (Association for the Study of Abortion) (United States) 51, 53, 55, 86, 106, 272n64, 273n77
Atlanta Journal-Constitution, 64
Australia, 11, 14
Austria, 10–11, 14, 251n49, 252n55

backbench MPs, 27, 59–60, 141, 169, 180
Badgley, Robin (Badgley Committee), 115–16, 140, 172–73, 197
Baird, Dugald, 37, 73, 280n14
ballot initiatives (United States), 327n68
Basford, Ron, 173, 175
Bédard, Marc-André, 175, 324n35
Beetz, Jean, 178
Begin, Monique, 173
Belgium, 11, 14, 252n50
Belous, Leon, 54, 56, 273n82, 273n91
Benham, Flip, 163
Bernardin, Joseph, 160
Birmingham, 112
Blackmun, Harry: and hospital requirement, 109; and medical profession, 87–92, 288n97; and *Roe*, 63–64, 87–92, 182, 290n117, 290n119, 289n104; and *Roe* progeny, 3, 187–88
Blair, Tony, 138–39
blame avoidance: and abortion, 59–65, 137–44; OECD, 214; and political institutions, 27–29, 205–6; and political mediation

343

INDEX

blame avoidance (*cont.*)
    theory, 22; and secular majoritarian politics, 15
Blassingame, F. J. L., 83
Bloc Québécois, 144
BMA (British Medical Association): and abortion reform, 37, 66–79, 204, 282n27; compared to AMA and CMA, 82, 92, 94–95; and post-reform abortion politics, 111–15, 194–96, 336n126
Bork, Robert, 187, 189, 333n94
Borowski v. Canada, 325n52
Boston Women's Health Collective, 53
Bourne, Aleck, 37
BPAS (British Pregnancy Advisory Service, formerly Birmingham Pregnancy Advisory Service), 32, 111, 114, 122 295n36
Braine, Bernard, 169
Brennan, William, 88–90, 187–88, 190
British Columbia, 116, 123
British Columbia Medical Association, 73
British Medical Association. *See* BMA (British Medical Association)
British Survey of Attitudes, 158
Brown v. Board of Education, 63
Brown, Gordon, 171
Brown, Jerry, 146
Brown, O. J., 163
Browne, Stella, 37, 49
Bryce, Edward, 161
Buchanan, Patrick (Pat), 146–47, 150, 155, 157
buck passing, 24, 26–27, 131, 138
Buffett, Warren, 54
Burger, Warren, 88–91, 188–89, 289n104, 289n110, 290n117, 290n119
Burns, Gene, 23, 57, 61, 130, 211
Bush, George H. W., 150–51, 154–55, 157, 187, 189–90, 317n145
Bush, George W., 143–44, 150–51, 187, 200, 317n145
Byrnes, Timothy, 162

California: and abortion clinics, 106–8, 110; and abortion reform, 41–42, 47–50, 53–54, 56, 146, 272nn66–67, 273n82; and medical profession, 74, 80, 82, 84
California Medical Association, 281n21
California Supreme Court, 42, 54
Cameron, David, 139, 309n55

Campaign Life, 127, 162–63, 180
campaigns. *See* elections
Campbell, Kim, 142, 198
Canadian Abortion Rights Action League (CARAL), previously Canadian Association for the Repeal of Abortion Laws (CARAL), 127, 129, 325n47
Canadian Alliance, 142
Canadian Bar Association (CBA), 60, 71, 93, 275n104
Canadian Catholic Conference (CCC), 162
Canadian Medical Association. *See* CMA (Canadian Medical Association)
Canadian Psychiatric Association, 196
Carter, Emmett, 162
Carter, Jimmy: abortion policy, 182–83, 185; abortion position, 132, 148–49, 151; Catholic support for, 160; evangelical Christian support for, 164; and judicial appointments, 187
cases, small number of, 30–31
Casey, Robert P., Jr. (Bob), 152
Casey, Robert P., Sr. (Bob), 150
Cassels, Louis, 147
Castles, Francis, 30
Catholic Herald, 139
Catholics (Catholic Church); and abortion, Britain, 43, 138–39, 158; and abortion, Canada, 43, 123, 162–63, 176; and abortion, OECD, 15–16; and abortion, United States: 43, 55, 61, 158–62, 192, 319n169; and contraception, 63, 319n173; and medical profession, 84, 86
Catholic Women's League (Canada), 162
CBA (Canadian Bar Association), 60, 71, 93, 275n104
CCTA (California Committee on Therapeutic Abortion), 54, 272n66, 273n91
Center for Bio-ethical Reform, 127
Center for Constitutional Rights, 55
Centre local de services communautaires (CLSC), 177
Charter of Rights and Freedoms (Canada), 143, 162, 173–75, 177–79, 325n50
Chatelaine (Canada), 47
Chicago, 52
Chicago's Women's Liberation Abortion Counseling Service (JANE), 53
Chicago Women's Liberation Union, 52
Chretien, Jean, 141–42, 177
Christian Action Council, 128, 163

344

Christian Action Research and Education (CARE), 126, 128
Christian Coalition (United States), 127–28, 150, 153–57, 315n127. *See also* Christian Right (United States); evangelical Christians
Christian democratic parties, 13–15, 17–18, 158, 205, 213
Christianity Today (United States), 163
Christian Right (United States): and abortion issue, 163–65; and future of abortion politics, 215–17; and Republican Party, 145–46, 148–59, 316n138, 316n140, 318n151. *See also* Christian Coalition (United States); evangelical Christians
civil disobedience, 58, 161, 164
civil liberties organizations, 23, 27, 56, 65, 204, 209
civil rights (United States), 25, 52, 62, 145–46, 189
Clark, Joe, 142
Clark, Tom, 89
classical liberalism, 30, 44, 208, 269nn43–44. *See also* American Creed
Clinton, Bill, 150–51, 155, 168, 187, 190
Clinton, Hillary, 144
CMA (Canadian Medical Association): and abortion reform, 47, 66–74, 92–96, 204, 290n126, 281n18; and hospital requirement, 279n8; and post-reform politics, 140, 172, 195–98, 337n137, 337n142
Colorado, 41, 48–49, 51, 54, 82, 273n89
Columbia University, 40, 51
Commonweal, 193
comparative historical analysis, 30
comparative sociology, 5
Congress, U.S.: and abortion funding, 118, 183–85; and abortion reform, 41; and health reform, 191–94; and issue avoidance, 61; and judicial appointments, 189–91; and party organizations, 132–33, 136; and post-reform abortion politics, 150, 152, 168, 182–86, 198–200; and private member's bills, 29; and women's rights, 147, 149
Conkle, Daniel, 179
Connecticut, 48–49, 54–55, 118, 182
conscience protections for health workers, 193, 200
Conservative Party (Britain), 3, 133–34, 137–39, 170–71, 217, 309n54

Conservative Party (Canada), 142–44, 174, 304n25, 310n64. *See also* Canadian Alliance; Progressive Conservative Party (Canada)
conservatives (United States). *See* Christian Right (United States); New Right
consistent ethic of life (United States). *See* seamless garment (United States)
Constitution, Canada, 92, 175. See also *Charter of Rights and Freedoms* (Canada)
Constitution, U.S., proposals to amend, 148–51, 168, 185, 328n71
consultant requirement (Britain), 73, 79, 111, 170
consultants (Britain), 70, 73, 75–76, 111–12, 122
consumers' movement (United States), 83
contraception: abortion as, 196; Britain, 28, 59; Canada, 39, 60, 162, 173; and Catholics, 40, 161, 319n173; clinics, 122, 170–71, 176–77; and medical profession, 213; as moral regulation, 215; and National Right to Life Committee, 161; and Republican Party, 145
Cooke, Terence, 146
Co-ordinating Committee in Defence of the 1967 Act, 127
Corrie, John, 170
Cosmopolitan (Britain), 139
courts: Canada, 3–4, 118, 178–80; and democratic usurpation, 179, 194; Germany, 158; in OECD, 14–15, 214, 252n53; as policy venue, 9, 24–26, 205–6, 212, 258n82; and social movements, 258n82; United States, abortion clinics, 108–10; United States, abortion reform; 42, 44, 46–48, 53–58, 62–64; United States, appointments to, 149, 187, 190; United States, medical profession, 87–92; United States, post-reform abortion politics, 3–4, 120, 168, 180–82, 187–91
Cress, Daniel, 23
crisis pregnancy centers, 126–27, 164
Crossman, Richard, 59
Czech Republic, 11

Daily Mail (Britain), 139
de Gaulle, Charles, 174
de Tocqueville, Alexis, 5, 25
Delaware, 41, 48–49, 74
democratic accountability, 28, 63, 215

345

democratic legitimacy, 131, 214
Democratic Party (United States): and abortion reform, 61–62; and Catholic Church, 160–62, 319n169; conservatives in, 152, 192; and grassroots mobilization, 156; and post-reform abortion politics, 131–32, 144–53, 183–93, 207, 216–17, 221–27, 330n82; rules and institutions in, 304n23; 311n85, 305n27; and social movements, 129, 303n22
Democratic Unionist Party (Northern Ireland), 172
democratic usurpation. *See under* courts
Denmark, 11, 14
Department of Health (Britain), 115, 122
Department of Health, Education, and Welfare, U.S., 83, 118
Department of Justice, U.S., 187
Detroit, 52–53
Dickson, Brian, 178–79
diffusion, crossnational, 43, 3269n41
Diggory, Peter, 72
distress model, 10–11. *See also* abortion gatekeeping
District of Columbia: and abortion clinics, 106, 108; and abortion reform, 42, 48, 53–54, 56, 80, 268n33
divorce: and Canadian abortion reform, 39; and Canadian bishops, 162; as conscience issue, 28; and Roy Jenkins, 59; as moral regulation, 215; and practices of American Catholics, 161
Doe v. Bolton, 42, 87–91, 108–9, 118. See also *Roe v. Wade*
Dolan, Terry, 155
Douglas, William O., 88–90, 188, 289n104, 289n112
Dworkin, Ronald, 17, 190

East Anglia, 112
Edelin, Kenneth, 200
EFC (Evangelical Fellowship Council), 128
Eisenhower, Dwight, 3, 188
Eisenstadt v. Baird, 88–89
elections: and abortion, Britain, 137–40; and abortion, Canada, 140–44; and abortion, United States, 144–53, 216; candidate-centered, 20, 132, 207, 212; and Catholics, 159–60; and Christian Right, 153–57; finance, 132–37, 306n38, 306n38; rules and procedures, 9, 20–21, 132–37, 207; party-centered, 28, 213–14; turnout, 9, 134–35, 154, 163, 212, 305n30
embryology bills (Britain), 29, 170–71, 195, 217
Emily's List PAC (United States), 129
English-speaking countries, 14, 20, 30, 214. *See also specific countries*
Equal Rights Amendment (ERA), 145, 147–49, 163
Erlich, Paul, 53
Estey, Willard, 178
eugenics movement, 37
Europe, 13–14, 20, 44, 115, 195, 215. *See also specific countries*
Evangelical Alliance, 159
evangelical Christians: United States, 126–29, 153–59, 163–64, 208–9, 216–17, 190n320; Canada, 127–28, 142, 157–59. *See also* Christian Coalition (United States); Christian Right (United States)
Evangelical Fellowship of Canada, 127–28
extra billing (Canada). *See under* abortion funding

Falwell, Jerry, 149, 164
Family Planning Division (FPD) (Canada), 172–73
federal courts, U.S., 41–42, 54, 62, 118, 161, 187. *See also* Supreme Court, U.S.
federalism: as policy venue, 26–27, 212; United States, 30, 46–58, 154, 180–82, 276n115; Canada, 30, 174–80, 271n56. *See also* provinces (Canada); states (United States)
feminism: and abortion clinics, 109; and Britain, abortion reform, 37, 49–50; and Canada, abortion reform, 50; and meaning of abortion issue, 7, 22–23, 43, 204, 209, 211; and political parties, 13, 15, 131, 213, 137, 145–52; 176–77; and reproductive freedom, 1, 9; and United States, abortion reform, 50–57, 82, 90–92, 95–96; and social movements, 126–30
Ferree, Myra Marx, 159
Finkbine, Sherri, 41, 43
Finland, 11, 14
Florida, 41, 48–49, 54
FLQ (Front de libération du Québec), 174
Focus on the Family Canada, 128

focusing events, 24
Ford, Gerald, 132, 145, 148–49, 151, 160, 182–83
Foucault, Michel, 5
framing. *See* issue definition
France, 11, 14, 252n50
free voting. *See* nonpartisan policy making processes, free voting
Friedan, Betty, 52
Freidson, Eliot, 67
Front de libération du Québec (FLQ), 174

Gallup polls, 45, 64, 145, 158, 231, 235
Gampell, Ralph, 40
Gamson, William, 257n75
Garrow, David J., 63, 273n91
Geekie, Douglas, 197
general practitioners (GPs). *See* PCPs (primary care practitioners)
General Social Survey (GSS), 158, 235, 311n86
Georgia: and abortion reform, 41–43, 48–49, 54, 64, 88–92, 108; and medical profession, 74, 96
Germany, 11, 14, 158–59, 214, 245n32, 252n50, 253n55
Gingrich, Newt, 150
Ginsburg, Douglas, 333n97, 189
Ginsburg, Ruth Bader, 181, 188, 339n2
Glendon, Mary Ann, 44, 181, 269n43
Globe and Mail (Canada), 47, 197
goals of collective actors, 16–17; symbolic vs. material, 215
Goldwater, Barry, 146
GOP (Grand Old Party). *See* Republican Party (United States)
GPs (general practitioners). *See* PCPs (primary care practitioners)
Graber, Mark, 216, 339n5
Greece, 11, 14
Greenhouse, Linda, 64
Griswold v. Connecticut, 53–54, 56, 63, 88–89, 182
Group of Eight (G8), 143
Gullick, David, 72
Guttmacher, Alan, 40, 51, 53, 86

Hall, Robert, 51, 53, 86, 106–8
Hall, Wesley, 85
Hames, Margie, 109
Hardin, Garrett, 50
Harper, Stephen, 142–44, 174

Hatch, Orrin, 185
Hawaii, 41–42, 48–49, 80, 84
health-care systems: and abortion services and funding, 101–24, 206, 218; and insurance reform, United States, 191–94, 298n81, 335n116, 335n120, 335n121; and medical profession, Britain, 75–79, 283n33; 284n47; and medical profession, Canada, 92–95; and medical profession, United States, 79–87, 199–200; as policy legacies, 74–75, 203–04
Helms, Jesse, 185
Herridge, H. W., 48
Hippocratic oath, 36–37, 87–88
historical contingency, 8
historical institutionalism. *See* institutionalism
historical sociology, 5
Hodgson, Jane, 54
homosexuality, 28, 39, 59–61, 275n100
hospitals. *See* abortion facilities, hospitals
Houghton, Douglas, 49, 59
Houghton, Vera, 49–50, 59, 77
House of Commons (Britain): and abortion reform 49, 59–60, 206; and medical profession, 70–73, 77–78, 194–95, 204; and nonpartisan policy making processes, 28–29; and post-reform abortion politics, 3, 113–14, 137–38, 169–72, 207, 217
House of Commons (Canada): and abortion reform, 60–61, 204, 206; and nonpartisan policy making processes, 28–29; and post-reform policy, 141, 172–75, 178–79, 196–98, 207
House of Lords (Britain), 38, 47, 59, 112, 171
House of Representatives, U.S., 132, 152, 183–85, 192–93. *See also* Congress, U.S.
Howard, Ernest B., 83
Howard, Michael, 84, 139
Human Life International, 161
Humanae Vitae, 161
Humanist Fellowship of Canada, 50, 93
Hume, Basil, 138
Hungary, 11
Hyde amendment, 118, 121, 191–92

identities of collective actors, 7–8, 16, 30, 211
Ignatieff, Michael, 143–44
Illinois, 49
Illinois Citizens for the Medical Control of Abortion (ICMCA), 50–51

INDEX

Indiana, 49, 149
individualism, 30, 44–46
Infant Life Preservation Act, 37
institutionalism: historical, 7–8; new, 8; political, 7–9, 16, 211, 215; sociological, 7–8
institutions: defined, 241n12. *See also* political institutions
interest construction, 16–18, 211–12; and abortion reform, United States, 46–58; and Catholics, 159–63; and evangelical Christians, 163–64; and medical profession, 66–97, 194–200, 203–4; and political parties, 125–53, 155, 213–14
interest group theories of policy making, 16–18, 67–68, 203
Iowa, 48–49, 54
Ireland, 11, 14, 158, 170
irregular physicians, 36–37, 39
Irvine, Bryant Godman, 170
issue avoidance, 27–29, 131–32. *See also* abortion issue: avoidance
issue definition, 21–23
issue settlement, 26–27; United States, 181, 194, 212, 216
issues of conscience: Britain, 137–40, 169–72; Canada, 140–44; and issue avoidance, 131; and nonpartisan policy making processes, 28–29
Italy, 11, 14, 252n55

James Madison Constitutional Law Institute, 55
Japan, 11, 14
Jasper, James, 16, 256n73
Jenkins, Alice, 37
Jenkins, Roy, 59–60
Johns Hopkins University, 81
Johnson, Lyndon, 80
Joint Commission on Accreditation of Hospitals, 81
Jost, Timothy Stoltzfus, 193
judicial review, 24–26, 213, 215; Britain, 259n84; Canada, 175, 179; United States, 180–81, 190
Justice for All, 127

Kagan, Elena, 188, 217
Kansas, 41–42, 48–49
Kennedy, Anthony, 187–90
Kennedy, Edward, 149, 187–90

Kenyon, Dorothy, 40
Kerry, John, 151, 162
Kissinger, Henry, 145
Kmiec, Douglas, 152
Knickerbocker Hospital, 50
Knights of Columbus (Canada), 162
Koop, C. Everett, 163–64
Korea, 11, 14

La Forest, Gérard Vincent, 179
Labour Abortion Rights Campaign (LARC) (Britain), 137
Labour Party (Britain): and abortion reform, 36–38, 58–60, 70, 78; and post-reform abortion politics, 3, 137–39, 169–72, 217; and private provision, 111, 113; and social movements, 133–37
Labour Women's Action Committee (Britain), 171
Lader, Lawrence, 51, 53, 57
Lalonde, Marc, 173
Lamer, Joseph, 179
Land, Richard, 164
Lane, Elizabeth Kathleen (Lane Committee), 113–14, 138, 172, 195, 297n63
Lang, Otto, 196–97
Lassoe, John, 51
Law, Bernard, 160
Lazure, Denis, 176–77, 324n37
Leavy, Zad, 54
Leeds, 112
left-wing parties: Canada, 141, 176; OECD, 13–16, 20, 213–14; United States, Britain, and Canada, 58, 131. *See also* Labour Party (Britain); NDP (New Democratic Party, Canada); Parti Québécois (PQ, Canada)
Lévesque, René, 174–6
Liberal Democrats (Britain), 37, 137. *See also* Liberal Party (Britain)
liberal gatekeeping model, 10–11. *See also* abortion gatekeeping
liberal parties, 13
Liberal Party (Britain), 37, 137
Liberal Party (Canada): and abortion reform, 60–61; and medical profession, 92; and post-reform abortion politics, 140–44, 172–80, 218; and social movements, 132–37, 304n25, 310n64
Liberals for Life (Canada), 141
Lieberman, Joseph, 152

LIFE (Britain), 126
London, 3, 112
Long 1960s, 237n4
longitudinal analysis, 31–32
Louisiana, 49
LPAS (London Pregnancy Advisory Service), 111, 114, 295n36
Lucas, Roy, 53–54, 56, 58, 88
Luker, Kristin, 23, 130, 273n91

MacEachen, Alan, 61
MacLennan, Hector, 72
Maginnis, Pat, 50
Maine, 49
majoritarian party systems, 30
Manitoba, 123, 141, 177, 197
Manning, Preston, 142
Marbury v. Madison, 25
March for Life (United States, Canada), 126, 144
Marshall, Thurgood, 88–90, 188
Martin, Keith, 142
Martin, Paul, 143
Marx, Karl, 5, 211
Maryland, 41, 48–49, 74
Massachusetts, 49
Mayo Clinic, 87
McCain, John, 150–52
McGovern, George, 146–47, 151
McLaren, Hugh, 112
McLaughlin, Audrey, 141
Mears, Judith, 199
Medicaid (United States). *See* abortion funding; health-care systems
medical profession, 66–97. *See also* ACOG (American College of Obstetricians and Gynecologists); AMA (American Medical Association); BMA (British Medical Association); CMA (Canadian Medical Association); RCOG (Royal College of Obstetricians and Gynaecologists)
Medicare (Canada). *See* abortion funding; health-care systems
Melich, Tanya, 148
menstrual blockage, 264n4
Mexico, 11, 54, 84
Michigan, 48–49
midwives, 35, 170–71
mifepristone. *See* abortion medications
Minnesota, 49, 54
Mississippi, 41–42, 48–49

Missouri, 3, 49, 190
Modern Medicine, 96
Montreal, 127, 174, 175, 177
Moral Majority (United States), 127, 149
Moran, Michael, 76
Morgentaler, Henry: and abortion clinics, 163; and abortion reform, 93; and medical profession, 196–97; and political parties, 140–41; and post-reform abortion politics, 174–80; and social movements, 127, 325n47
"most similar systems" research design, 30, 32
Mulroney, Brian, 141–42, 179–80, 196, 198, 327nn64–65
Munday, Diane, 49
Munger, Charles, 54
Murphy-O'Connor, Cormac, 139
Myers, Lonny, 50–51

NAC (National Abortion Campaign) (Britain), 126, 129
NARAL (National Abortion Rights Action League, previously National Association for the Repeal of Abortion Laws), 51–52, 55, 107, 129, 193, 199
Nathanson, Bernard, 107
National Abortion Federation (NAF) (United States and Canada), 119, 186, 199–200
National Action Committee on the Status of Women (Canada), 127, 129, 178
National Conference of Catholic Bishops (NCCB), 127. *See also* U.S. Conference of Catholic Bishops (USCCB)
National Council of Women (Canada), 50, 93
National Federation of Catholic Physicians' Guilds (United States), 84
National Governor's Association (United States), 83
National Health Service (Britain). *See* NHS (National Health Service)
National Institutes of Health, U.S., 83
National Network of Abortion Funds (United States), 119–20
National Opinion Research Center (NORC) (United States), 45, 64, 231
National Organization for Women (United States), 52, 129, 272n71
National Right to Life Committee (United States). *See* NRLC (National Right to Life Committee, United States)
national values theory, 5–6, 44–45, 208

National Women's Political Caucus (NWPC) (United States), 129, 147, 149
NDP (New Democratic Party, Canada), 136, 141, 144, 180, 310n63
negotiated type of abortion politics, 13–16
Nelson, Ben, 192
Netherlands, 11, 14, 251n49–50, 252n55
Nevada, 49
New Brunswick, 116, 119, 123, 180, 197
new democracy type of abortion politics, 13–15
New Democratic Party (NDP, Canada). *See* NDP (New Democratic Party, Canada)
New Hampshire, 48–49, 268n26
New Jersey, 49, 54, 84, 184
New Left, 52
New Mexico, 41, 48–49
New Right, 145, 148–49, 164–65, 207
New York: and abortion clinics, 107, 110, 292n11, 292n13; and abortion reform, 51, 53, 275n108
New York Radical Women, 52
New York Times, 40–41, 51
New Zealand, 11, 14
Newcastle, 112
Newfoundland, 123
NHS (National Health Service): and abortion services, 12, 101–6, 110–18, 122, 167, 206, 299n85; consultants, 69–70; and medical profession, 75–79, 195
Nixon, Richard, 61, 83, 88, 90, 145–48, 151
nonpartisan policy making processes, 27–29, 208, 212
nonpartisan policy making processes, free voting: Britain, 138–40, 171–72, 217, 261n100, 262n104; Canada, 39, 60–61, 140–44, 179–80; OECD, 13, 214–15. *See also* issues of conscience
nonpartisan policy making processes, private member's bills, 27–29, 208, 260nn95–96, 262n101; and abortion politics, OECD, 214–15; and abortion reform, Britain, 37–38, 47, 59–60, 274n99; and abortion reform, Canada, 266n14, 47; and post-reform abortion politics, Britain, 111, 137–39, 169, 217; and post-reform abortion politics, Canada, 143, 172–74. *See also* issues of conscience
Nordic countries, 9–13, 20, 58. *See also specific countries*
Norquist, Grover, 156

North Carolina, 41, 48–49, 51, 54, 82
North Dakota, 48–49
Northern Ireland, 38, 171–72
Norway, 11, 14, 251n49
Notre Dame, University of, 162
notwithstanding clause (Canada), 143, 179, 326n60
Nova Scotia, 102, 116, 123, 180
NRLC (National Right to Life Committee, United States), 55, 127–28, 161, 314n121
nursing homes. *See* abortion facilities, nursing homes (Britain)
NWPC (National Women's Political Caucus, United States), 129, 147, 149

Obama, Barack, 144, 151–52, 162, 192, 216–17
Ober, William, 50
obstetrician-gynecologists (ob-gyns): Britain, 111–12, 114–15; Canada, 197; United States, 40, 80–81, 107, 294n31. *See also* ACOG (American College of Obstetricians and Gynecologists); RCOG (Royal College of Obstetricians and Gynaecologists)
O'Connor, John, 160
O'Connor, Sandra Day, 187–90, 332n93
Ohio, 49
Ontario, 141, 177–78, 197
Ontario Medical Association (OMA), 73, 266n17
Operation Rescue, 127, 163–64
Oregon, 41–42, 48, 54, 74, 84, 268n30
Organisation for Economic Co-operation and Development (OECD): abortion policy in, 9–13, 245n30–247n39; abortion politics in, 1–2, 13–16, 210, 213–14; and religiosity, 157. *See also specific countries*
Orloff, Ann, 9
own reasons model, 10–11. *See also* abortion gatekeeping

Packer, Herbert, 40
Packwood, Robert (Bob), 41, 61, 185
Paintin, David, 115
Palin, Sarah, 152
Parliament. *See* House of Commons (Britain); House of Commons (Canada); House of Lords (Britain); Senate, Canada

Parliament Hill (Canada), 127, 144
Parliamentary Labour Party (PLP, Britain), 49, 59, 134
parliamentary systems, 27, 29
Parti Québécois (PQ, Canada), 140, 174–77, 324n37
partisanship theories of policy making, 20, 58, 162, 205, 213–14
PCPs (primary care practitioners), 74–76, 79–80, 92, 96, 113, 197
Pearson, Lester, 60–61
Peel, John, 78
Pennsylvania, 49, 118, 150, 190
Petchesky, Rosalind, 273n91
Phelan, Lana, 50
Phillips, Kevin, 146–47
Pilpel, Harriet, 53, 58, 63
Planned Parenthood Federation of America. *See* PPFA (Planned Parenthood Federation of America)
Planned Parenthood of Southeastern Pennsylvania v. Casey, 120, 167–68, 188–90, 199, 217, 334nn104–5, 334n110
PLP (Parliamentary Labour Party) (Britain), 49, 59, 134
Poland, 11, 14
policy learning, 17, 23, 27, 56–58
policy legacies. *See under* political institutions
policy venues, 21–29, 40, 46, 58, 62–64, 130. *See also* courts; nonpartisan policy making processes; provinces (Canada); states (United States)
political culture. *See* national values theory
political institutions, 202–9; and abortion politics in OECD, 213–15; and abortion reform, 35–65, 241n11; and abortion services, 101–25; change in, 167, 174; courts as, 24–26; defined, 5; free voting as, 27–29; and future of abortion politics, 216–18; and interest construction, 16–18; and issue meaning, 23; and medical profession, 16–18, 66–97; nonpartisan policy-making processes as, 27–29; policy legacies as, 9, 66–97, 277n2; policy venues as, 24–29; and political parties, 18–21; and politicization of abortion; 125–65; and post-reform abortion politics, 166–201; private member's bills as, 27–29; and social movements, 18–23; subnational policy making as, 26–27; and theories of politics and policy, 6–7; 211–12. *See also* courts; elections; federalism; institutionalism; nonpartisan policy making processes; political parties
political opportunity theory, 129, 212
political parties: and abortion politics, 13–16, 137–65, 248n47; centralization of, 136, 307n40; as coalitions, 21, 132, 136, 207, 212, 307n41; democracy within, 132–36; discipline, 29, 31, 60, 135, 183, 306n33; as organizations, 132–36; polarization of, 14, 145, 216, 252n52, 311n86; as political institutions, 18–21; and social movements, 18–21, 132–36, 315n132; in two-party systems, 30, 214, 252n51. *See also specific parties*
population control, 7, 50, 53, 56, 65, 145–46. *See also* Zero Population Growth (ZPG)
Portugal, 11, 14
Potts, Malcolm, 72
Powell, Lewis, 63–64, 88–90, 188–89, 277n122, 289nn111–12
PPFA (Planned Parenthood Federation of America): and abortion clinics, 107–8; and abortion reform, 40, 51, 57, 63; and pro-choice movement, 129
PQ (Parti Québécois), 140, 174–77, 324n37
preferences. *See* interest construction
primary care practitioners. *See* PCPs (primary care practitioners)
Prince Edward Island, 116, 123, 180
priorities. *See* interest construction
private member's bills. *See* nonpartisan policy making processes
process tracing, 31, 263n115
pro-family movement, 130, 142, 148
professional dominance perspective, 67, 70, 73
professional elites, 43, 51, 55, 57, 62, 215
Progressive Conservative Party (Canada), 304n25; and abortion reform, 61; and goal-setting, 134; and post-reform abortion politics, 4, 140–42, 177–80
Pro-Life Action League (United States), 161
protest: Britain, 4, 126; Canada, 4, 127, 163, 175; and issue avoidance, 131; United States, 3, 52–58, 96, 127–29, 161, 164; as tactic, 21; violent, 120, 127, 129, 301n11
Protestants, 30, 39, 43, 145, 161

provinces (Canada): and abortion services, 39, 102–4, 116, 119, 122–23, 180; and buck passing, 27, 131; and health-care system, 92–93; and issue avoidance, 15; medical associations in, 73; as policy venues, 26–27, 56, 204, 212–13; and post-reform abortion politics, 173–77. *See also* federalism; *specific provinces*
psychiatrists, 75–76, 96
public opinion: and courts, 24–25, 212; and democratic accountability, 215; and national values theories of policy making, 44–45; *See also* abortion, public opinion

Quebec: abortion policy in, 140, 168, 174–77, 197; abortion services in, 115–16, 122–23; and federal abortion reform, 61. *See also* Morgentaler, Henry; Parti Québécois (PQ, Canada)
Quiet Revolution (Quebec), 174

rational choice theory, 212
RCOG (Royal College of Obstetricians and Gynaecologists): and abortion reform, 69–73, 75–79, 204; and post-reform abortion politics, 111–13, 122, 195, 322n9, 336n126
Reader's Digest, 40
Reagan, Ronald: and Catholic Church, 159–60; and judicial appointments, 187–90, 332n93; and Republican party position on abortion, 148–51, 183, 185; and social conservatives, 145, 317n145
REAL Women, 128–29
Red toryism, 79
Redbook, 40
Reed, Ralph, 154, 156, 315n127
Reeves, Joseph, 47
Reform Party (Canada), 142
Rehnquist, William, 88–90, 188–90
Reid, Harry, 192
religion, 157–65, 318n162. *See also* Catholics (Catholic Church); evangelical Christians
Religious Rights Watch, 149
Renaissance Canada, 128
Republican Party (United States): and abortion reform, 58, 61–62; and Catholic Church, 159–62, 319n169; and future of abortion politics, 216–17; and goal setting, 133; and judicial appointments, 187–91; and post-reform abortion politics, 145–57, 183–94, 207, 221–27, 330n81; and social movements, 127, 132–37, 303n22, 304n23, 305n27, 311n85, 316n139, 318n159
Rescue UK, 126
resource mobilization theory, 46, 130
Rex v. Bourne, 37–38, 70, 73
Rex v. Morgentaler, 178–80, 196, 198, 325n53, 325n57
Rhode Island, 49, 54
rich democracies. *See* Organisation for Economic Co-operation and Development (OECD)
rights, 23, 25–27, 46, 55–57, 61, 66–67, 130
Robertson, Pat, 155–56, 317n145
Robinson, Kenneth, 47, 59, 113
Rockefeller, Nelson, 41
Rockefeller Commission, 146
Roe v. Wade, 42–43; and abortion clinics, 108–10; attempts to overturn, 3, 151, 167–68, 180–82, 187–91; compared to *Morgentaler* decision, 178–79; critiques of, 181–82, 339n2, 328n74; decision making, 61–64, 87–92, 288n97; and national values theories of policy making, 44, 208; and policy learning, 56; and political parties, 150–52, 217; reactions to, 63, 130, 132, 148, 198; trimester framework, 42, 109, 167, 179, 190, 195, 269n36; and social movements, 273n91. See also *Doe v. Bolton*
Rosenberg, Gerald, 25, 110, 294n32, 294n35, n259n87
Royal College of Obstetricians and Gynaecologists. *See* RCOG (Royal College of Obstetricians and Gynaecologists)
rubella, 41
Rudman, Warren, 189

Saletan, William, 23, 150
same-sex marriage, 142–43, 217, 310n72
Sammons, James, 199
Saturday Evening Post, 50
Scalia, Antonin, 187–91
Schaeffer, Francis, 164
Schiavo, Terri, 155
Schlafly, Phyllis, 148, 155, 164

school prayer, 156
scope conditions, 211–16
Scopes Trial (United States), 163
Scotland, 37, 102–3, 110, 112, 159, 280n14
Scott, Hugh, 147
Scott, Wendell G., 85
seamless garment (United States), 160–62
secular majoritarian type of abortion politics, 13–16
Select Committee on the Abortion Act, House of Commons (Britain), 172
Senate, Canada, 4, 180, 198
Senate, U.S., 153, 183–85, 187, 189, 192–93. *See also* Congress, U.S.
Sheffield, 112
Short, Renee, 47
Siegel, Reva, 64
Silkin, John, 59
Silkin, Lewis (Lord), 37, 47–48, 59, 70, 265n9
Simms, Madeleine, 49
single-issue politics, 139, 149
Slovakia, 11
Snow, David, 23
social classes, 6–7
Social Credit Party (Canada), 61
social democratic parties. *See* left-wing parties
social democratic type of abortion politics, 13–16
social grounds. *See* abortion gatekeeping
social issues, 59, 83, 214, 217
social learning, 56, 62, 65
social movements: and courts, 24–26, 273n77; and issue definition, 21–23, 256n73; new, 20–21, 132–40, 213, 215, 254n62; and policy impacts, 7, 20–22, 204; political mediation theory of, 17, 22, 46, 255nn69–70, 255n72; and political parties, 18–21, 132–40, 207; and public opinion, 270n45; theories of, 21–22, 46, 204, 212; and venue change, 22
social policy, 6–7, 16–18, 30–31, 44, 58, 248n47
Socialist Worker's Party (United States), 53
Society for Humane Abortion (SHA), 50, 53, 272n61
Society for the Protection of Unborn Children (SPUC), 126, 128
Sotomayor, Sonia, 188, 217
Souter, David, 187–90

South Carolina, 41, 84, 95
South Dakota, 49
sovereignty-association (Quebec), 176
Spain, 11, 14, 16, 159
St. John Stevas, Norman, 170
state hospital associations, 199
states (United States): and abortion clinics, 106–10; and abortion funding, 118; and abortion reform, 41–44, 47–48, 50–58, 61–63; Christian Right in, 154; courts, 62, 118, 189–91, 327n68; federal usurpation of, 149–50, 181–82; and health reform, 191–94; and medical profession, 79–87; as policy venues, 26–27, 56, 204, 212–13; political parties and elections in, 132–37, 207; and post-reform abortion politics, 120–21, 132, 167–68, 186; southern, 26, 48, 61. *See also* federalism; issue settlement; *specific states*
statistical argument (Britain). *See under* abortion gatekeeping
Stearns, Nancy, 55
Steel, David: and abortion reform, 37, 47, 59; and Alton bill, 169; and medical profession, 70–73, 77–79, 95, 111
Stephenson, Bette, 140, 197
Stevens, John Paul, 187–88
Stewart, Potter, 88–90, 188
strategic learning, 56, 62, 65
strict gatekeeping model, 10–11. *See also* abortion gatekeeping
Stupak, Bart, 192
subnational policy making. *See* federalism; provinces (Canada); states (United States)
suddenly imposed grievances, 24
Sunday commerce laws, 28, 140
Sununu, John, 189
Supreme Court, Canada, 4, 25, 123, 143, 175, 178. See also *Charter of Rights and Freedoms* (Canada); *Rex v. Morgentaler*
Supreme Court, U.S.: and abortion funding, 118, 185; and abortion reform, 42–44, 56, 61–64, 108–10, 211, 217; appointments to, 150–51, 187–89; and meaning of abortion issue, 23, 130; and medical profession, 87–91; and institutional legitimacy, 63, 191, 194; as policy venue, 26–26, 180–82, 194, 207; and post-reform abortion politics, 120, 167–68,

Supreme Court, U.S. (*cont.*)
  180–82, 190–91, 217, 228–30; and procedures, 54, 276n116; and public opinion, 65; and state usurpation, 149–50, 181–82, 257n78, 277n128
Susan B. Anthony List, 127
Sweden, 11, 14
Switzerland, 11, 14, 252n50

Taverne, Dick, 59
territories of Canada, 299n89
Texas, 42, 48–49, 54, 62, 154
thalidomide, 41, 43, 49
Thatcher, Margaret, 169, 322n9
Thomas, Clarence, 187–88, 190
Thornburgh v. American College of Obstetricians and Gynecologists, 91, 289n116
Tiller, George, 129
Time magazine, 51
Times (London), 139
Todd, James S., 200
Toronto, 52, 127, 162, 177–78
Toronto Women's Liberation Group, 50, 93
Tory. *See* Conservative Party (Britain); Progressive Conservative Party (Canada)
Tremblay v. Daigle, 325n52
Tribe, Laurence, 189, 269n43
Trudeau, Pierre, 60–61, 128, 174–75, 197
Tuohy, Carolyn, 93
Turkey, 11
Turner, John, 39, 60, 141

undue burden (United States), 120, 167, 190, 333n101
University of California, San Francisco (UCSF), 81, 200
University of Toronto Medical Journal, 73
U.S. Conference of Catholic Bishops (USCCB), 160. *See also* National Conference of Catholic Bishops (NCCB)
Utah, 49

Vancouver, 127
Vermont, 49, 55
veto points, 26, 181, 215

Viguerie, Richard, 155
violence. *See under* protest
Virginia, 41, 48–49, 51

Wahn, Ian, 47
Wakeham, John, 169
Wallace, George, 146
Washington (state), 41–42, 48–49, 54, 275n108
Washington, DC. *See* District of Columbia
Washington Post, 64, 85, 146
Weaver, R. Kent, 131
Weber, Max, 5
Webster v. Reproductive Health Services, 120, 149, 167–68, 189–90, 238n5
Weddington, Sarah, 88
Weld, William, 150
Weyrich, Paul, 155
What Ever Happened to the Human Race?, 164
Wheaton College, 163
whipped voting, 27–29; Britain, 137, 308n42; OECD, 251n49; Canada, 143–44, 179–80. *See also* political parties: discipline
White, Byron, 89, 182
White, James, 115, 170
Widdecombe, Ann, 171
Williams, Glanville, 40, 50
Wilson, Bertha, 178
Wilson, Harold, 59
winner-take-all issues, 24, 131, 181, 212, 215
Winning, Thomas, 138
Winnipeg, 127, 177
Winstanley, Michael, 77
Wisconsin, 49, 54
within-case analysis, 31
Women's Equity Action League (United States), 52
Women's National Abortion Action Coalition (WONAAC) (United States), 53
Wood, Bruce, 76
World Values Survey, 158, 234, 236

Zero Population Growth (ZPG), 53, 55, 147
Zussman, Leon, 108